Army Surveillance in America, 1775–1980

JOAN M. JENSEN

Army Surveillance in America, 1775–1980

Yale University Press

New Haven and London

Designed by James J. Johnson and
set in Times Roman type by
Brevis Press, Bethany, Connecticut.

Printed in the United States of America by
BookCrafters, Inc., Chelsea, Michigan.

The paper in this book meets the guidelines
for permanence and durability of the Committee on Production Guidelines for Book
Longevity of the Council on Library
Resources.

10 9 8 7 6 5 4 3 2 1

*Library of Congress Cataloging-in-
Publication Data*

Jensen, Joan M.
    Army surveillance in America, 1775–
1980 / Joan M. Jensen.
    p. cm.
    Includes bibliographical references and
index.
    ISBN 0-300-04668-5
    1. United States. Army—History.
    2. Internal security—United States.
    I. Title.
UA25.J53 1991
355.3'43'0973—dc20   91-4669
                                        CIP

There is no end now in sight to our living as a people in arms; we must plan to go for generations with a resoluteness we had thought to have left off. And during this uneasy time of war and half-war, we shall always be faced with choices affecting our liberties, made on guesses as to the future, choices we cannot avoid, because even inaction requires a choice.

ARTHUR E. SUTHERLAND, JR.
"Freedom and Internal Security"

Contents

Part IV   Paths to the Present

Acknowledgments

The research for this book has now extended over so many years that it is impossible to thank all of the many scholars, archivists, and interested friends who have contributed to its progress. It was financed in part by grants from New Mexico State University and from Project '87, which is sponsored by the American Historical Association and the American Political Association to encourage discussion of the Constitution. J. E. Taylor and later Timothy Nenninger of the National Archives helped me through the labyrinth there, each providing necessary introductions to a mass of documents that seemed overwhelming.

In some ways, my father must take the first credit for interesting me in the military through his years as an army officer and my upbringing on the margins of the military. During World War II, he trained Chiang Kai-shek's troops in the art of anti-aircraft defense; my brothers were both in military school; and I had just joined the Girl Scouts. He wrote from China how proud he was to have us all in uniform. My involvement with the Girl Scouts was short and, I am afraid, not too successful. However, my interest in the military continued, and, I suppose, had the 1950s been a time when women were welcomed as officers, I might have ended up within the military.

Instead, I have wondered how the lives of civilians have interacted, as mine did, with the military. That interest in civilians and the military was first encouraged by Harold Hyman, who as my dissertation adviser suggested the subject of internal security in the late 1950s. He remains the person to whom I owe the greatest debt. Other scholars have also given their support in various ways to this project, some for periods of time that seem appallingly long in retrospect. Now, at last, the book is done.

Introduction

American internal security policy evolved over two centuries to become one that maintained restraint, sometimes precariously, in using the army to defend the government from the domestic population. This book attempts to place the evolution of that policy in its historical context and to explain why, despite constitutional restraints buttressed by strong ideological beliefs that opposed army intervention in domestic disputes, the executive frequently used the army to maintain internal security. It also explains how Americans used their Constitution and their political process to maintain the United States as a nation where the military exercised a minimum of influence domestically. It is the story of how Americans have battled for over two hundred years to give form to that policy.

Before the 1920s, no systematic plan existed to guide the army's response in case of a domestic rebellion. Nevertheless, the executive used the army to intervene domestically on numerous occasions. The use of the army in civil disturbances provoked emotionally charged debates over civil liberties and the limits of government power. Such interventions and reactions to them gradually led to formal internal security policies. War Plans White—contingency plans for a war against American civilians—were drawn up between 1920 and 1922 by the United States Army War College. The plans were revised in the 1930s, again after World War II, and presumably exist in some form today.

For many years, no formal policy defined the limits of the army in internal security. Policy was implicit in practices, attitudes, and circumstances. Never clearly articulated but always a field of contention within the executive, policies gradually emerged, shaped in response to public opinion as well as to attitudes and activities within various segments of the executive branch of the federal government. Although remaining mostly invisible, usually uncoordinated, and often incoherent, internal security policies changed as the military role in internal security swelled and subsided with each domestic crisis. American political ideology, supported by the Constitution, dictated a minimal internal security apparatus; an expanding government seemed to dictate an expansive one. The interplay of those two conflicting traditions is the focus of this book.

When I first began research in the 1950s on what was then only vaguely known as internal security policy, I spent considerable time in the library at the University of California at Los Angeles, diligently searching for a definition of internal security. Internal security was then a topic of hot debate in southern California as elsewhere in the country because of a domestic cold war that had set Americans quarreling over the question of loyalty. The few sources I found provided a framework for the studies I have had under way since. The term "internal security" had just then been coined to describe policies still not entirely visible, coordinated, or coherent. They remain so today.

Perhaps the simplest definition I found was that of John Caughey, a professor of history discharged from UCLA for refusing to take a loyalty oath and reinstated only after a seven-year legal battle. He defined internal security as a program to protect a nation against activities from within—such as espionage, sabotage, or treason—that could contribute to the success of an attack from abroad, and to guard against an attack from within—a revolution or rebellion.

In a more elaborate discussion, a New York Bar Association report defined internal security as one element of national security. They ranked internal security as fourth in importance, after positive security (being economic and political strength), military security, and international security (strengthening the nations of the free world). The report went on to divide internal security measures into three types: criminal laws, such as those relating to treason, espionage, sabotage, and the overthrow of the government by force and violence; preventive or counterespionage measures designed to discover and bar unreliable persons from critical areas; and personnel security, to remove or block persons dangerous to national security in government or certain types of private employment because of disloyalty or for other reasons. The report noted that the history of internal security measures began in the early days of the Republic, but the authors spent little time on history. Instead, as lawyers, they focused on the laws and measures passed after World War I.

A third, more expansive definition was one I found in a 1955 *Internal Security Manual*. It included all laws designed to protect the security of the armed forces, the executive branch of government, international agencies, the civilian population, ports and borders against illegal immigration, and atomic energy installations and defense factories. In fact, the manual maintained that internal security included all those laws that might be encountered by federal security experts.

I have used each of these three definitions—all creations of the mid-twentieth century concern with internal security—in attempting to examine the past policies and activities of the American army. This book is not meant to offer a complete analysis of the role of the army in internal security (although such a study needs to be done). I have examined overall military policy and the elements that made up that policy, but my primary concern is to examine that part of military policy that directly involved the civilian population between 1775 and 1980 and the constitutional issues involved.

Part I traces the origin of internal security policies in the army until 1898. Part II focuses on the Spanish-American War and then the Philippine-American War. These wars provided an entirely new experience for dealing with large populations opposed to government and army control. The resultant policies, especially those developed in the Philippines, directly affected subsequent policies within the United States.

Part III concentrates on the period between 1914 and 1924, a period that saw the rapid expansion of the army to include internal security and its containment because of public opposition. Part IV then traces the expansion of the army again during World War II, as a growing activity in the 1950s, and a flourishing one during the Vietnam war before it was once again curtailed by public outcry. The surveillance of foreign civilians during the temporary occupation of countries following World War II is excluded here because this experience is far removed from military policy and law as they applied to citizens. The surveillance of American civilians overseas after World War II is not included although constitutional issues were involved.

One major theme that emerges from this study is the dynamic balance between expansion and constraint of the army in internal security. At various times, necessity, bureaucratic competitiveness, a willingness to ignore legal restrictions, and ideological persuasion combined to promote expansion. At other times, ideological, bureaucratic, legal, and political conditions all promoted constraint. Pressures from outside the government fed each tendency in turn.

Expansion did not win completely. By the end of the first two centuries of the American government, bureaucratic structures for the widespread military surveillance of civilians were in place, and the constitutional issues surrounding that surveillance had been raised but not settled. Justice William Douglas, in his dissent in *Laird v. Tatum* (1972), called military surveillance a violation of First Amendment rights and a cancer on the body politic. The majority of the Court did not agree. It held that military surveillance did not, in fact, chill First Amendment rights as the petitioners had claimed. The Court upheld the constitutional right of the Defense Department to conduct such surveillance. The dialectic of constraint subsequently reemerged, and two years later, in a series of federal court cases resulting from the occupation by Indians of the village of Wounded Knee, South Dakota, to demand reform in Indian tribal government, judges declared military participation in law enforcement in the absence of a presidential proclamation to be a violation of the 1878 Posse Comitatus Act. Congress subsequently amended the act to allow limited military participation in certain law enforcement cases, but generally restraint—though entrusted to the executive—remained a powerful tradition.

I hope this book will encourage other historians to venture more deeply into this area of public policy studies, for no area has so consistently raised issues involving human rights. Citizens define their rights, to a great extent, by testing, responding to, and questioning the control government has on their lives. In this country that process has been going on for over two hundred years. Yet the question of how people participate in public policy making and whether clandestine government inhibits them in this activity remains unanswered. How can constitutional policy balance the needs of government against the basic need of people to know their government and to evaluate continually their own needs, particularly in times of social and economic change? The policy issues explored here are not ones that can be resolved either with anecdotal stories of spies and counterspies or with a denunciation of individual injustices. There are crucial issues that need thoughtful and probing analysis. My hope is that such an analysis not only will define the specific constitutional issues raised by past policy but also will help illuminate larger issues of human and political rights involved in making any government internally secure.

PART I

The Legacy at Home, 1775–1898

CHAPTER ONE

The New Nation

In 1775, the American colonies went to war against the empire that had created them, opening the debate on the role of the army in internal security. Americans soon voiced their concerns over what the policy of the new government would be toward civilians who for some reason did not comply with the orders of civilian or military authorities. What should the proper response of the military be to a civilian whose actions appear to be disloyal and possibly treasonous?

The year was 1780, the lowest point in the morale of the new American army and its commanding general, George Washington. In September, one of his trusted officers, Gen. Benedict Arnold, betrayed West Point. A British officer, Maj. John André, crossed American lines and then received Arnold's written plans of West Point. One of the local gentry, Josiah Hett Smith, whom Washington had invited to dine a few days before, was implicated in the plot.

Arnold defected before he could be arrested, but the Americans captured André and Smith. An American militia patrol discovered Major André in disguise with the incriminating plans and brought him to Washington. Militia, under the command of a French officer, captured Smith at his home and marched him the twelve miles to Washington's headquarters. Smith later wrote of the anger of Washington and his troops that September in 1780. As Smith passed through the huts of the soldiers in

7

the camp, he heard nothing but talk of execution. Washington had threatened Smith with execution as a traitor unless he divulged the names of his accomplices. Smith retorted that as a citizen he did not consider himself amenable to military jurisdiction. Furious, Washington warned that both Smith and André would hang before sundown.[1]

Washington probably would have included Arnold in his threats had he found him in September 1780. Benedict Arnold was "notorious" and the commanding general had the authority to execute his subordinate. Congress in 1775 had ruled mutiny, sedition, and aiding the enemy to be offenses for the army, punishable by court-martial. Washington had court-martialed, convicted, and hanged his first officer in June 1776 as an example to deter others who had conspired against his command. Congress subsequently required oaths of all commissioned officers and adopted the Articles of War to cover army discipline. Arnold had taken an oath of loyalty as an officer; his violation of that oath would have made him legally a traitor, subject to court-martial and execution if found guilty.[2]

The commanding general's attitude toward traitorous officers had generally been moderate. He ordered that executions be used sparingly, mainly as a deterrent and "not with too much vigor." He once wrote to Brig. Gen. George Clinton that only the most notorious should be executed, for "by making executions too common, they lose their intended force and rather bear the Appearance of cruelty than Justice." Washington had been known to pardon convicted officers. He insisted on approving all army courts-martial involving capital offenses, and had approved the acquittal of a number of officers whose activities he considered treasonable. On 4 July 1779, he pardoned all prisoners who were under sentence of death.[3]

Arnold's actions would have been difficult to excuse, and once the army acted, Congress would not have intervened. Civilian authorities during the eighteenth century believed they should not intervene in matters of military discipline. Even near the end of the nineteenth century, when the courts were claiming greater involvement in executive policy, the doctrine of judicial restraint still kept them from interfering with the administration of the army; if the army had legal jurisdiction, they refused to investigate. It seems unlikely that Arnold would have been spared.[4]

Smith and André did not hang before sundown. Instead, Washington took them to West Point where he handled the two cases differently. In the case of André, Washington adhered closely to the rules of war. Under the common law of war accepted in the eighteenth century, spies were defined as persons who secretly, in disguise or under false pretenses, sought information with the intention of communicating it to the enemy. André had crossed American lines in disguise and obtained secret information from Arnold. Even had André not succeeded in obtaining information, his actions were punishable with death by hanging. The spy provision in the Articles of War applied to anyone found lurking near posts or military installations. Washington had already approved the court-martial convictions of ten accused spies between 1776 and the time André was captured. He made no exception for André. Washington did assemble a "Board of General Officers," composed of fourteen high-ranking officers who agreed that "agreeable to the Law and usage of nations," André should be hanged. Washington approved the verdict and hanged André within a few days of the board's decision.[5]

Smith was neither a spy nor a traitorous officer. He was a civilian who, for reasons never totally clear, became involved in Arnold's plot. Washington could threaten Smith that he too would hang before sundown, but Washington could not carry out that threat without repercussions. He had to conduct military operations within a civilian environment that provided an ever-present reality and boundary for internal security policies. Civilians jealously competed for jurisdiction. Delegates to Congress, as well as state officials, watched and discussed Washington's conduct. This scrutiny provided an incentive for Washington to cultivate civilian-military relations carefully as part of his overall military strategy.[6]

Washington's letters clearly reflect his concern over military arrests and trials of civilians. As early as the fall of 1775, Washington had arrested civilians and tried them by court-martial under the Articles of War, but he was very uneasy about the trials. He turned one prisoner over to civil authorities, then queried Congress about how to handle inhabitants of New York because their treatment was "so extremely critical and delicate, and which in the consideration of it involves many important consequences." In April 1777, he asked Gov. William Livingston about jurisdiction, writing that if Livingston thought the civilian suspect fell within civil jurisdiction, "I will most cheerfully give him up to you." In August of that year Washington reprimanded one general for executing a Tory illegally because the execution had "a tendency to excite discontent, jealousy and murmurs among the people." He closed by saying, "The temper of the Americans and the principles on which the present contest turns, will not countenance proceedings of this nature."[7]

At first, Washington used loyalty oaths to coerce civilians. When his subordinates started loyalty testing in Rhode Island early in 1776, congressional delegates immediately complained, and Congress passed a resolution outlawing the oaths in the military. Early in 1777, as the war shifted to the mid-Atlantic region—where civil authority was weak and disloyalty a real threat to unity—Washington established his own loyalty oath program. Again delegates complained. This time a congressional committee that had investigated the practice reported that the proclamation did not interfere with civil laws. In practice, Washington advised his officers not to apply the policy rigidly; in cases where suspects exhibited friendly conduct, to let it "slip over as a matter unnoticed." As the states soon demanded their own loyalty acts, military loyalty oaths— never uniform in any case—became a minor issue. Loyalty oaths functioned mainly as a part of military strategy in the mid-Atlantic, and Washington used them sparingly and only for a limited time.[8]

The experience with Congress on loyalty oaths left Washington unsure about the extent of his power to execute men who had gone to the enemy and returned within American lines. In reply to Washington's query, Congress gave him extensive powers in its 8 October 1777 resolve, authorizing him to try by court-martial and to execute as "traitor, assassin, and spy" any citizen found aiding the enemy within thirty miles of his headquarters. Such powers could have been used extensively, but Washington later wrote to Livingston: "I imagine this Resolve was passed with an intent to operate principally in Pennsylvania, where as you know, the Civil Authority is extremely weak." Soon after passing the Resolve, Congress also gave Washington the power to arrest and confine civilians. The line between civil and military authority on arrests did not trouble Washington as much as did military trials. Nowhere in his correspondence did he mention any concern over the army's right to arrest civilians, but he was uncertain just what to do with civilians after he had arrested them. In one New Jersey case, the general held an accused citizen prisoner for a time, then turned him over to the civil authorities. In at least three later cases, Washington ordered that even armed inhabitants be turned over to the civil power so that they could be punished under civil law. His criterion seemed to be that if they were inhabitants of a state where civil authority operated, then the civil authorities had jurisdiction.[9]

Washington established no formal mechanism for collecting intelligence. He hired civilian spies and accepted information from volunteers. Smith, the civilian charged with treason, had in fact earlier collected intelligence for Washington, and in at least one case, Washington had asked a governor to watch a suspect. Most surveillance seems to have been conducted by civilian authorities. Washington wanted information on the enemy army and on armed citizens loyal to the British. His understanding of the attitudes of civilians came not from reports on specific civilians but from general information gathered informally as he moved his head-quarters from farmhouse to farmhouse. Overt activities, not beliefs, counted most during the Revolution, and Washington's firm restraint of the Continental army contrasted markedly with the vacillating policies of the British.[10]

Smith, the civilian arrested with André in 1780, was one of the ben-eficiaries of the bold defense of civil rights made by various states. Cer-tainly belief in the power of civilian authorities enabled Smith as a civilian during a revolution to make his elaborate defense of the right to be free from military trials. Smith argued that a New York treason law super-seded the 1776 congressional resolve that would have allowed him to be executed by the army. He also argued that no resolve could abrogate a fundamental article of any civil constitution, for that would make the civil authority subordinate to the military and establish a dangerous precedent to the liberties of a subject. Finally, he warned, his execution would cause indignation among his fellow citizens since one of the reasons for sepa-ration had been the use of military power by the British.[11]

Despite Smith's arguments, Washington did convene a court-martial. The court, however, decided that Smith could not be convicted of any charge. Washington turned Smith over to the sheriff to be tried for treason in the New York courts. A grand jury subsequently refused to indict him. He lived to relate his experiences from the safety of British soil.[12]

Smith's experience is important in two respects. Although he probably collaborated with André, he was not executed as might have been ex-pected during twentieth-century revolutions. His experience, though har-rowing, was symbolic of the relative restraint with which the army treated civilians, perhaps a half a million of whom dissented from the war. Re-straint within the military both reflected and influenced a general un-willingness to use violence against the enemies of the new states. While the Continental army watched suspected civilians, arrested hundreds of them, removed many behind enemy lines, and confined some to their farms or jail, it executed relatively few, either for espionage or subversion. In other words, officers of the new American army were successful in restricting their troops primarily to violence against opposing armies. The British, although less successful in incorporating military restraint toward civilians into military strategy, did not encourage civilians to engage in guerrilla warfare except in the South, and there only briefly. As a con-sequence, military violence against civilians did not become a heritage of the American Revolution.[13]

The Declaration of Independence stated as one of its grievances that the king had kept standing armies without the consent of the colonists' legislatures and "affected to render the Military independent of and superior to the Civil Power." American colonists nourished a strong opposition to the maintenance of standing armies in peacetime. Even during the Revolution, after an initial upsurge of militarism, Americans tended to lose interest in their own army and criticize it. During peace, the colonists expected militias or civilians, called together as a posse comitatus, to maintain internal security. Colonial governors usually organized expeditionary forces against Indians and then dispersed the men. For colonists, the British regulars constituted a standing army, outside their control. Colonial debates revolved around two questions: who would control the standing army during wartime when one was necessary, and what would replace it during peacetime when it was not. If a regular army was needed for an exceptional reason, the question again was who would control it. Almost all colonists who joined in war against the British feared the use of the regular military or standing army in peacetime, but there was even a fear of the regular army during the revolutionary war. Washington commented ironically on this fear of standing armies: "It is our policy to be prejudiced against them in time of *war*."[14]

The fear that Americans had of military power greatly influenced the response of the military. Even during 1780—the low point in the Revolution—when some high-ranking officers talked of dictatorship, the highest military officers remained committed to civilian rule. While using the Continental army as a vehicle for enforcing the Declaration of Independence, the rebels were able to formulate policies that did not subvert those principles in practice.

The principle of limiting military jurisdiction emerged from the war strengthened rather than weakened. The colonists' fear of a standing army and its potential for abuse in internal security did not subside when they became republicans. Instead, it led to widespread postwar opposition to a regular peacetime army. Federalists as well as anti-Federalists disclaimed any desire for a standing army, although former officers, such as Washington and Alexander Hamilton, felt the country needed a small peacetime military establishment. During the first five years of the new government, Congress jealously held the line against the expansion of the army in internal security. It continued to use a small regular army on the frontier and allowed volunteers to be enrolled, but in 1782 it provided that federal marshals could use the militia only to enforce federal laws and that a federal judge had to certify that the judicial process had collapsed before the executive could call up troops. In 1784, Congress reduced the army to a handful of officers and eighty soldiers and refused to discuss the broader questions of national security.[15]

Fear of army involvement in internal security led the Framers of the Constitution of 1787 to restrict federal military power. The Constitution allowed Congress to raise and support armies and provided for calling forth the militia to execute federal law, suppress insurrections, and repel invasions, dividing responsibility for the militia between federal and state governments. Although not mentioned specifically in the Constitution, enemy spies still remained subject to the common law of war and could be tried by the military under the Articles of War. On the other hand, the Constitution explicitly defined treason by citizens as levying war against the United States or adhering to the enemy or giving them aid and comfort, a crime punishable only after being convicted by the testimony of two witnesses in open court to the same overt act. Troops could not be quartered in civilian's homes in peacetime, and citizens could retain arms. Trial by jury and the Bill of Rights provided additional safeguards for suspected traitors. The role of the federal army in law enforcement or internal security was not explicitly mentioned because Congress expected to control the army in both war and peace. The Uniform Militia Act of 1792 gave the president power only to ask state governments for the use of their militia after a supreme court justice had certified that local civil authorities were unable to maintain order.[16]

Thus hedged by restrictions, the former military commander, now civilian commander-in-chief, faced his first internal security crisis when western Pennsylvanians rebelled at paying the federal whiskey tax in 1794. After being notified by Supreme Court Justice James Wilson that Pennsylvania authorities could not maintain order, Washington carefully followed constitutional and congressional guidelines and called out state militias to enforce the federal excise law. He issued proclamations ordering the rebels to disperse but warned his commanding general, Gov. Henry Lee of Virginia, to maintain a scrupulous regard for the rights of persons and property; to confine the militia to attacking and subduing armed opponents of the laws, and to aiding civil officers in the execution of their functions. Washington even sent a federal judge and the United States attorney for the district to accompany the militia to ensure that the prisoners were turned over immediately to civil magistrates for trial.

Even with Washington's careful policy in the 1794 Whiskey Rebellion, militia actions engendered resentment and criticism. Some citizens in Maryland and Virginia refused to heed the call to arms and rioted. In

Pennsylvania, opposition was so strong that the governor had to appeal to feelings of vengeance to get his troops to march. The fifteen thousand militiamen arrived late and unruly. Resistance had disappeared before the militia arrived, but troops rounded up suspects, threw them in jails and barns, and tied them in cellars. Army officials released all but twenty men whom they sent to Philadelphia to await civilian trials. Some of these suspects remained in prison for months before civilian courts cleared them and convicted only two of treason.[17]

To avoid similar conditions of reluctant and undisciplined militia being used to enforce federal law among civilians, Congress expanded the role of the regular army. The regular army now added internal security to its frontier duties of fighting Indians. Although the act of 1794 allowed deployment of regulars in civil commotions, it restricted their use to clearly defined cases, by power of the president alone, and only after a proclamation to disperse had been made.

Within a few years, political leaders came close to using the army to suppress political opposition. After 1794, the conflict in Europe over the French Revolution began to be reflected in American politics. The party of Washington, Alexander Hamilton, and John Adams—the Federalists, as they called themselves—began to fear that the French might extend their revolution to the New World. Between 1796 and 1798, spurred by alarms over French military activities and their support of an Irish rebellion, a Federalist-dominated Congress quadrupled the regular army and passed the Sedition Act. The original 1794 Federalist proposals for an increase in the army did not envision its use in internal security. By 1797, however, Hamilton and other Federalists feared an internal revolt. In 1798, the secretary of war argued that a provisional army of twenty thousand was needed to suppress domestic insurrection. A year later, Congress authorized an army of up to forty-one thousand men. There is no doubt that extreme Federalists expected to use the army to intimidate political opponents and to suppress dissent.[18]

Army involvement in such political activity could have led to serious conflict. President John Adams moved slowly in using the power given him by extreme Federalists. Adams did use regulars to back up the state militias in enforcing federal taxes in eastern Pennsylvania during the 1799 Fries Rebellion, but he depended primarily upon state militia. During the height of the war scare with France, he consciously chose to use the civilian branch of the government rather than the army to enforce internal security laws. Secretary of State Timothy Pickering and United States attorneys enforced the Sedition Act with the aid of paid private informers.

In 1800, when extreme Federalists in his cabinet questioned his policy of restraint, Adams got rid of them. Then he pardoned the Fries rebels and announced he would dismantle the army if Congress gave him authority.[19]

Despite Adams's restrained response to the demands of his own party for ruthless measures against the Republicans, his political opponents capitalized on fears within the citizenry over the potential coercive strength of the central government. Politicians found the public easily roused to oppose the demands of extreme Federalists to use both military force and more repressive civilian force against political opponents.

The increasingly repressive response of Europeans to the French Revolution also alarmed some Americans. Like the Federalist government, the English government used civilian measures to quell dissent, but Parliament regulated public meetings so strictly that magistrates could adjourn meetings at which citizens made "exceptional" statements. Legislation also allowed the systematic listing of arriving aliens and required them to carry identification papers at all times. To help enforce these acts, the British government encouraged the formation of private associations under the heading "Society for the Protection of Liberty and Property against Republicans and Levellers," to help suppress political discussion and to report seditious utterances. These regulations had much to do with breaking the thrust toward a republican government in England in the late eighteenth century.[20]

In Europe, revolutionists were turning against each other as well as becoming increasingly vindictive against the nobility. The principles of the French revolutionary government of 1793 drew a distinction between constitutional and revolutionary regimes: The former should protect individuals from the abuse of public power; the latter must defend itself against all factions. By 1796, France had a death penalty for those who spoke or wrote in defense of a government other than that established by the constitution. Under Napoleon there was no freedom of political expression, the press had become a state institution devoted to strengthening the position of the emperor, and a bureau of secret police conducted domestic espionage. Political repression in Europe culminated under the Russian tsar Nicholas I with the establishment of the Third Department, charged with the surveillance of youth infected with dangerous revolutionary ideas and of public morale. Eventually military police meddled in family life, business deals, and personal quarrels, and extended its surveillance to Polish émigrés in France, England, and Belgium, as well as to foreigners in Russia.[21]

The American government and its army avoided such extremes by replacing the men who governed. Republicans replaced Federalists. Although the American Republicans had based their opposition to Federalists on federal military and civilian interference in internal security, they too occasionally used the regular army as well as the militia to enforce federal laws. President Thomas Jefferson ordered his newly reformed and "republicanized" army to arrest Aaron Burr for treason before turning him over to civilian courts for trial. Jefferson also used regular troops to enforce embargo laws on the northeastern border from the summer of 1808 to March 1809 and increased the army to ten thousand. Soldiers arrested numerous civilians during the War of 1812. But Jefferson and the Republicans always used federal troops with great caution and always as a matter of expediency rather than policy. Courts followed a cautious policy as well, distinguishing between citizens, who could not be tried by court-martial but who could be tried for treason, and aliens, who were subject to international law. The tension of rival claims among politically equal men, combined with a willingness of men in power to reconcile these claims within the democratic process, greatly extended individual freedom for Euro-Americans during this early national era. Euro-Americans escaped the terror and the secret surveillance of Europe through executive restraint and the courts' principle that citizens could not be court-martialed. While the army could arrest civilians in emergencies, courts insisted that it was civilians who had final jurisdiction over those arrested.[22]

As the new United States reached mid-nineteenth century, the issue of the army in internal security hardly concerned most Euro-Americans. There was no widespread support for an expanded army and no need for one in the flood of nationalism that followed the War of 1812. President Jackson used the army once in a labor dispute in 1834, and soldiers again arrested civilians in the Dorr Rebellion in Rhode Island in 1849. The responsibility for internal security, however—whether trials for treason or military arrest—remained primarily a state matter during the early nineteenth century. In the United States political conflicts were solved not by reliance on military force or secret surveillance but by open (if sometimes ruthlessly partisan) politics. Despite the extension of the vote to poorer Euro-American males, changes in parties left the government controlled by different men from a similarly wealthy class, all committed to civilian restraint in the use of the army in internal security. Military officers developed a conception of the army as an apolitical instrument of public policy. European governments used their armies to put down the revolutions of 1848 by force, but Euro-Americans had little to fear from their central government.[23]

If Euro-Americans remained singularly free from military interference in their daily lives, ethnic Americans outside the political process were highly vulnerable to military force. Most American Indians remained aliens, subject to the laws of their own nations unless endowed with citizenship rights by Congress. Indians were therefore aliens who could not commit treason against the United States but who were subject to international law. Beginning in the late 1820s the federal government used the regular army to force Indian civilians to move westward. The Seminole conflict started with such deportations in 1835 and ended in war when the Seminoles resisted the army. After six years of war, the army abandoned conventional warfare of pitched battles against warriors for a policy of crop-and-dwelling destruction. In the guerrilla warfare that followed the Mexican War, state militias often tried rebel Indians by military courts and pressured army officers into military trials and executions, despite the fact that many federal army officers felt that Indians captured in military engagements should either be considered prisoners of war or be tried by civilian courts for murder. The result, in any event, placed the small regular army uncomfortably between the militias and courts of the Euro-Americans in individual states, and the Indians who contested that power. Most Euro-Americans supported the use of federal military force against native Americans, considering them outside the body politic. Few Euro-Americans questioned the role of the regular army in the lives of American Indians, either warrior or noncombatant, during the early nineteenth century.[24]

Nor did most Euro-Americans at first question the system that kept African Americans enslaved. The federal Fugitive Slave Act of 1793 established the principle that the American government would support slave owners in their efforts to maintain slavery. The army did not have to protect slavery in the South, however, for blacks in North America did not resort to widespread organized revolt as they did in other parts of the New World. Most black people used other forms of resistance, including escaping individually or in small groups, despite increasingly harsh security measures imposed by white Southerners. To perpetuate the slavery of African Americans, white slave owners elaborated an ideology of white supremacy and backed it with an internal security system composed of sheriffs and armed posses, called "patrollers," and well-organized state militias.

Although slave owners seldom relied on the regular army to maintain the institution of slavery in the South, the force of the army was always available and could be used if state militias proved inadequate. In 1816, President James Madison sent Andrew Jackson to destroy a fort being maintained by escaped slaves in an area of Florida still belonging to Spain and to return the blacks to their owners. In the destruction of the fort that followed, most of the three hundred men, women, and children died. Fifteen years later, President Jackson mobilized regulars in Virginia and Louisiana when Nat Turner organized a slave insurrection. The militia put down the revolt before the federal troops could arrive.

In spite of internal security precautions, blacks continued to escape and to seek support from both black and white allies in the North. These Northern allies also sought to extend American concepts of civil rights to include all people regardless of their race. During the 1840s, some Northern courts began to expand the rights of blacks, if not to full rights, at least to include liberty of person, property, conscience, and access to courts. Northern courts also began to hold that states could not enact laws to assist in the return of slaves. These cases virtually nullified the original 1793 Fugitive Slave Act and led to the new Fugitive Slave Law of 1850.[25]

Congress passed the new law in 1850 to solve the problems of federal law enforcement. Federal judges had been charged with the enforcement of the old law; the new law gave United States Commissioners concurrent jurisdiction over fugitive slave cases and charged marshals with the responsibility for arrests. These changes did little to solve the problem of enforcement: within a month, two federal judges in Pennsylvania had asked President Millard Fillmore to use troops to enforce the law. The president and cabinet agreed that if federal judges certified that troops were necessary, they could be used.

The first violent episode following passage of the 1850 law occurred in Christiana, Pennsylvania. The incident at Christiana is important because it symbolized the growing resistance of blacks to efforts to reenslave them once they had reached states where slavery no longer existed. Pennsylvania was a slave-free state by 1850. Christiana lay twenty miles southeast of Lancaster and fifteen miles north of the Maryland border. On the other side of that border, the Mason-Dixon line, blacks could be legally held in bondage. Twenty-five miles to the east was the town of West Chester and a rural countryside known for its Quaker opponents to slavery. Practicing civil disobedience and violating the Fugitive Slave Act, these Quakers regularly helped escaped black families on their way North.

Quakers took in refugees, fed and reclothed them in Northern garb, and helped them reach Philadelphia where black resisters arranged for passage to Canada. Large numbers of free blacks lived in the townships along the Maryland border. In some, twenty percent of the population was black by 1850. Black households sheltered refugees before sending them on to Quaker farm families. A number of blacks, both free and refugee, were living on a small tenant farm near Christiana growing corn and wheat when in 1851, a slave owner appeared demanding the return of a former slave. The blacks resisted, killing the Southern slave owner and wounding his son.[26]

The response of the federal government was immediate. The United States marshals organized fifty railroad workmen as a posse comitatus. Some forty-five United States marines soon arrived in Christiana. The marines searched households, roughly handled whites as well as blacks, and arrested civilians at bayonet point. Following the arrests, a federal court indicted thirty-eight people for treason for armed and organized resistance to the execution of laws of Congress. In spite of the violence of the blacks' response, sympathy for the defendants was widespread. Quakers helped a number of the black resisters escape to Canada, and abolitionists provided clothing for the black defendants. The Quaker preacher Lucretia Mott sat knitting at the trial, and other Quaker women crowded in to hear the federal judge instruct the jury that there was not enough evidence of premeditation to warrant a conviction for treason. All were acquitted.[27]

The question of the use of military force in law enforcement had become a national issue. In 1854, the attorney general affirmed that United States marshals had the same powers as state sheriffs, that is, the power to call for the aid of all able-bodied men—both citizens in general and armed forces—as a posse comitatus of the United States. That year Congress passed a third Fugitive Slave Law allowing the president to call on the army to assist in returning fugitives to their former masters. The army was now at the disposal of the president to force Northern citizens to assist in returning black refugees to Southern slavery. In one particularly unpopular use of the army, the federal marshal called out two battalions of regular infantry and the adjutant general himself supervised the return of a fugitive from Boston amid widespread public protest.[28]

The army was becoming embroiled in enforcing unpopular laws. As opposition to expansion of slavery began to polarize American society, the army occupied a larger and more uncomfortable position between contending political forces. The national army could be used as a posse comitatus against a growing number of white citizens who opposed the laws of the land.

Kansas became the focal point of the conflict. Proslavery and antislavery settlers poured into Kansas territory in 1856, each hoping to influence the decision as to whether Kansas would join the union as a slave or free state. Guerrilla warfare broke out as the two groups contended for control of the new state government. Unable to restore order, the governor asked President Franklin Pierce for federal troops to assist the sheriff of Douglas County to enforce law and protect the peace. Soldiers swept into Lawrence looking for fugitive Free-Soilers. Free-Soil party members, in turn, refused to recognize the proslavery government and set up their own legislature. The governor again had to appeal to President Pierce for federal troops, and on 4 July, a cavalry colonel led two hundred soldiers to the house where the Free-Soil delegates had assembled in convention, went into the hall, and ordered the men to disperse.

Word of the colonel's action traveled east with great swiftness. Four days after the army had dispersed the legislature, the Northern majority in the House of Representatives held up an army appropriations bill, demanding a proviso that the regular army should not be used in putting down Free-Soil men in the territory of Kansas. The House adjourned in deadlock. Secretary of War Jefferson Davis then criticized the colonel for using military force to disperse the meeting "in anticipation of serious difficulties" and removed him from command. Northern members of Congress, mollified by this action, supported the army appropriations bill when Pierce called them back into special session late in August. Other Northerners, however, used the incident to point out the danger of using the central government to enforce the institution of slavery. In 1856 William Phillips brought his book *Conquest of Kansas* to a ringing close with the warning: "It is a grave fact that must never be forgotten by the American people, military power is and must ever be inimical to popular institutions." Such rhetoric helped the growth of the new Republican party, which came into being in part because of the growing opposition in the North to the use of federal troops to enforce slavery in the territories.[29]

As Northerners became more belligerent in their opposition to protecting slavery in the territories, Southerners became more determined to control the executive to exercise federal power in the defense of slavery. In 1859, Congress officially sanctioned the use of the army to enforce the Fugitive Slave Act without a presidential proclamation and began what seemed to many Northerners to be a dangerous executive use of military force. In 1859, President James Buchanan ordered federal troops to pursue abolitionist John Brown and a group of fugitive slaves until they made their escape from Kansas to Canada. He later called out troops when Brown returned with armed men to raid Harpers Ferry and help liberate enslaved blacks.

The raid at Harpers Ferry brought the question of use of the military east once more. Harpers Ferry was federal property, but the issue was not the destruction of federal property; it was slavery. At Harpers Ferry, the commander of the regular army, Robert E. Lee, offered the local militia commander the honor of leading the first assault against Brown and his few black allies. The commander declined because, he said, the army was composed of mercenaries paid to risk their lives, while the militia was composed of men with wives and children who had been called away from their regular jobs. One can only speculate on what might have happened had the South been able to maintain control of the executive and the army, despite growing opposition from the North to the use of federal forces in questions involving slavery. That they could not maintain that control led to the first breakdown in the consensus by which a relatively small group of Euro-Americans had controlled the federal government since the Revolution. The new Republican party was determined to prevent rebel military control of federal property in the South once the confederated southern states had organized their Army of the South. That Republican determination brought the Army of the North to a central place in internal security for the first time in American history.[30]

Internal security was the crucial element in national security during the secession crisis in the winter of 1860. The United States had no internal security mechanism—either civilian or military—and federal officials simply turned over federal property to seceding state governments. Officers resigned their commissions in the United States army to travel south and offer their services to state governments. No federal spies— civilian or military—investigated violations of federal law or kept watch on Southerners as they seceded from the young nation.

Later, army officers would argue that there *should* have been such agents. But the government had no precedent and President Buchanan saw no reason to send such agents. Buchanan had no investigative force trained in intelligence or surveillance. Postal agents investigated fraud and mail robberies. In 1859, when the president wanted to investigate possible violations of a federal law that prohibited the importation of slaves, the newly formed Interior Department sent an agent disguised as a slave buyer to Mississippi. Such investigations were ad hoc, the agents temporary.[31]

Military and civilian officials shared a widely held belief that officers should not spy, even in wartime. Spying was an opportunity for civilians, not army officers, to prove their patriotism. While there was no clear, popular distinction between intelligence gathering and espionage at the time, the common concept of espionage was that it was something done by civilians in the pay of governments. A good spy, for most Americans, was a civilian who volunteered for the dangerous assignment of espionage. Army officers agreed.

Popular literature preserved the tradition of the civilian spy in an era when most civilians had little interest in the intelligence-gathering methods of governments. The ideology of the civilian spy was most easily available in the large, nineteenth-century canon of spy fiction and pseudo-autobiographical memoirs. Most famous was James Fenimore Cooper's novel *The Spy* (1821), which contained the classic statement of the ideal American spy. He was a civilian, operated in wartime, and against a hostile enemy army. Cooper's protagonist was Harvey Birch, a person of ungentlemanly origin elevated in status by his patriotic motive in becoming a spy. *The Spy* became a best-seller, launching Cooper as the first American novelist. The fictional Birch became the first good spy.[32]

The celebrity of Cooper's good civilian spy was nowhere matched in popular literature by a good American officer spy. There was one renowned officer spy of the nineteenth century, but he was not American. The British officer Major John André, whom Washington had executed for his role in obtaining information on West Point from Benedict Arnold in 1780, achieved surprising popularity as a tragic character in American patriotic literature and art. Nineteenth-century playwrights and artists alike portrayed André as gallant and dignified, a true gentleman officer, while condemning his actions as a spy. With the approval of American officials, André's bones were even dug up in 1821 and sent back to England to be buried in Westminster Abbey. Thereafter André's dignified though barefooted figure circulated in thousands of engraved copies of A. B. Durand's oil painting entitled "The Capture of Major André."[33]

No American officer spy achieved a comparable reputation. Americans knew much more about the tragic fate of André than they did of Nathan Hale, the young school-teacher-turned-militia-officer who volunteered for a revolutionary spy mission, was discovered, captured, and hanged in 1776. Later, Hale received grateful recognition as a hero by both the CIA and the FBI when statues were erected in his honor, but such fame is of relatively recent origin. During the revolutionary period and the early nineteenth century, the image of Hale as an American "martyr-spy" was not a common one, and Hale remained a local hero. Cooper mentioned Hale once in his 1821 novel, explaining in a footnote for readers obviously not familiar with his exploits that Hale compared favorably to André, who was much better known. Hale achieved his first recognition as a national hero only during the 1880s when at least some Americans appeared ready to accept the officer as a good spy.[34]

While Hale remained only a local hero, popular writers had begun to flood the market with simple stories that catered to the demand for civilian spy heroes. The spy hero, according to some literary critics, grew out of the picaresque adventure story where the hero, immersed in a world different from his own, was always in peril. Since the early nineteenth century, this literary spy hero has consistently fed a deep American need for vicarious danger and secrecy. Cooper's Harvey Birch followed this older hero tradition rather closely. Although there have been other outstanding novelists who have used the spy hero—Joseph Conrad is the best example—authors have tended to produce spy stories with simple, stock characters. Often they wrote a series of stories, changing only the locale of the adventures of the archetype hero to attract the male reader, much as the Gothic novel of danger and escape has attracted the female reader. The British author Ian Fleming created the James Bond series using precise details and a convincing social framework to convey a simplified cold-war ideology that was extremely popular in America in the 1960s. Bond attracted the attention of literary scholars because he was so clearly an archetypal hero who defeated the forces of evil, who suffered in order to save the reader from disaster.

This genre had only begun to find a large audience when Americans found themselves at war with one another. The tradition of civilian spies and the attempts of officials to control that tradition dominated the internal security policies of the next four years of conflict. Once Americans had reunited the nation, it would flourish through the late nineteenth century.

CHAPTER TWO

Domestic Law Enforcement

On 4 March 1861, Abraham Lincoln became the president of a divided United States. President Buchanan had ordered tight security for the inauguration. As an additional security precaution, Lincoln traveled to Washington almost in secret. From the beginning of his presidency, internal security was an issue, and private detectives were central to the army's internal security mechanism.

During the spring of 1861, when Southern states began to secede from the United States, a private detective named Allan Pinkerton offered his services to the beleaguered Republican administration. An ardent abolitionist and friend of John Brown, Pinkerton volunteered to establish a centralized secret service department for the government.[1]

Pinkerton, the son of a Glasgow policeman, had begun his career by helping a local sheriff chase counterfeiters after he arrived in the United States in 1842. In 1848 he moved to Chicago and soon became the first detective on the Chicago police force. When Pinkerton became Chicago's only detective, police departments, as well as professional detectives, were relatively new in the major cities of the world. Harried by growing urban populations, city governments hired whomever they could find to watch suspected criminals. Sometimes men accused or convicted of crimes escaped punishment by offering to catch others. The model inspector was Eugène François Vidocq, the notorious underworld figure who created for Parisian officials a ruthless force of detective criminals. Before he retired in 1827, Vidocq had roamed the streets of Paris in a series of disguises. His reputation lived on in literature and later was parodied in the film adventures of Inspector Jacques Clouseau. By the 1840s, detectives had become a part of the police forces of all major cities. They sometimes described their work as involving "deception reduced to a science or profession." They were not well liked, however, and it is not surprising that Pinkerton left the Chicago police force in 1850. He formed a private detective agency to provide security for the growing network of Northern railroads that were easy prey for thieves. For three dollars a day, Pinkerton provided an operative; for eight dollars a day, a supervisor; and for twelve, he would take over the job himself.[2]

Lincoln's cabinet, however, wanted nothing to do with the enterprising immigrant businessman. Pinkerton next sought Gen. George Brinton McClellan, a West Point officer who had returned to active duty at the beginning of the war after being a railroad official for several years. McClellan, who had hired Pinkerton to perform detective work for his Chicago-based railway, agreed that someone should be watching disloyal Americans. By the end of April 1861, McClellan had asked Pinkerton to form a secret service for his Ohio volunteers' department. McClellan kept Pinkerton with him as he successively became commander of the regular army's Department of the Ohio, commander of the troops defending Washington, and then commanding general of the army in November 1861. Pinkerton then organized a force for the entire army.[3]

He began to tap the desire of civilians to do something for the Union. His corps of detectives—white and black, male and female—were soon infiltrating "traitorous organizations" and roaming the South in disguise. He organized escaped slaves into a Loyal League to furnish information to Union commanders on the movements of Southern armies. He sent white agents into dissident groups, such as the Knights of Liberty, to report on disloyal Democrats.[4]

As one commentator noted, McClellan had a "voracious appetite for intelligence reports." Information soon became a substitute for action. The more McClellan read, the more he believed that the Confederates had unbeatable forces. Finally, in May 1862, after seven months, Lincoln removed him from command and Pinkerton resigned.[5]

Pinkerton's forces were only one part of the sprawling internal security apparatus that bloomed during the first months of the war. Secretary of State William H. Seward had control—though "control" is too strong a word—over another group of civilians who wanted to spy for the government. Lafayette Baker headed Seward's civilian volunteers. Baker had been an adventurer and a member of the San Francisco Vigilantes before heading east for Philadelphia just as the Southern states began to secede. The Vigilantes were notorious for night raids, brutal inquisitions, spies, and informers. Baker also recruited private detectives to infiltrate suspicious political organizations and to make loyalty investigations.

On the reports of these enthusiastic civilians, the Union army was soon arresting hundreds of civilian suspects. Because Lincoln had suspended the writ of habeas corpus, the army was holding people for long periods of time and, in some cases, trying them by military courts. The lack of military restraint in dealing with civilians grew during the first year of the war. Victims of this confused system of internal security appealed to anyone who would listen, whether disgruntled opponents of Lincoln or principled officials. The Supreme Court, then Congress, and finally Lincoln responded to the demands for restraint.[6]

During the first year of the war, Maryland was the center of many of the disputes over how much control the military should exercise over civilians. It was also a slave state with strong secessionist sentiment. Lincoln was determined to hold Maryland in the Union because its loss would have left the capital surrounded by the enemy and virtually captured. Repression began in May 1861 when Brig. Gen. Benjamin F. Butler occupied Baltimore and arrested a member of the Maryland legislature on a charge of treason. Lincoln immediately ordered the official released on parole and relieved Butler of his command, but the army gave Butler's replacement written authority to arrest civilians "under certain circumstances." Later the War Department ordered the commander to arrest a police chief and the board of police commissioners and allowed military dragnets to round up secessionist members of the state legislature. It was almost inevitable that a strong judicial challenge would come from Maryland. John Merryman, one of the civilians arrested by the military, obtained a writ of habeas corpus. The general in charge argued that Lincoln had authorized him to suspend the writ, and Merryman took his case to the federal circuit judge in Baltimore for a decision.[7]

In the Merryman case, Chief Justice Roger Taney upheld the right of officers to arrest civilians but not to hold or try them. Moreover, he argued that only Congress, and not the executive, had the power to suspend a writ of habeas corpus. This was the view of a chief justice already discredited in the North for his Dred Scott decision, a decision in which he argued that blacks could never be citizens. But defenders of civil rights saw also the need for restraint. Congress generally supported Lincoln's right to call out the regular army when it was impractical to enforce the law by ordinary means, but Seward's use of the army to try civilian political prisoners in military courts drew heavy criticism.

In response to congressional critics, Lincoln reorganized and centralized his internal security system in the War Department early in 1862. The new secretary of war, Edwin Stanton, used loyalty oaths as a way to release most civilians if they promised not to give "aid and comfort" to the enemy or to sue the army for false arrest. Stanton then created a corps of civilian provost marshals who could make arrests on the authority of the governor, a general commanding a military district, or the judge advocate general of the army. Eventually, Congress gave approval to the president to appoint a military provost marshal general to control conscription and security within the military and to replace civilian with military provost marshals. In addition, Congress allotted funds for special counsel to defend officers sued for false arrest and for the removal of contested cases to federal courts.

By 1863 the primary internal security issue was not secession, as it had been in Maryland, but disaffection with the war. Democrats responded to this war weariness in the Midwest, using it as an occasion to criticize Lincoln's war policies and to call for peace and compromise. Republicans called such critics Copperheads, and Secretary of War Stanton used the army to arrest thousands of midwestern Democrats on charges of disloyalty.

Ohio Democrat Clement Vallandigham became the best known of these arrested Copperheads. Every step in Vallandigham's case was accompanied by wide publicity, from his public denunciation of the Ohio general's orders to arrest anyone "declaring sympathy for the enemy," to his arrest by a company of soldiers at his Dayton home in the early hours of 5 May 1863, to military trial, conviction, and appeal to the Supreme Court the following January. Vallandigham argued that army officers had no right to try citizens not connected with the armed forces. The Supreme Court responded that it could not review the proceedings of a military commission. Lincoln, meanwhile, argued that such arrests were "preventative," not "vindictive," and ordered Vallandigham banished to Confederate lines rather than imprisoned. Lincoln won support at the November 1864 polls despite his sometimes harsh internal security measures.[8]

Ultimately, Lincoln and Stanton put their trust in generals less concerned with watching civilians than with defeating the enemy army. Gen. Ulysses Grant exercised the same restraint that Washington had exercised almost a century before. Exposing the conspiracies would not, in his view, solve the military's problems; he understood the political nature of the war. He later said that "in a popular war, we ha[ve] to consider political exigencies." It was precisely that attitude that held civilian support for the military in both the Revolution and the Civil War. The government's policy did not eliminate the harassment of civilians by the military, but it did minimize it and subject it to larger policies that did not envision civilians collectively as an enemy to be watched but rather saw them as partners in carrying out a policy.[9]

In the North, civilian detectives furnished much of the information upon which the military based its arrests. Stanton used civilian detectives to conduct interrogations, collect photographs, compile dossiers on suspects, and conduct surveillance. At the state level, volunteer groups like the Loyal League of America—formed first in Illinois in 1862 and which then spread throughout the North—kept civilians under surveillance. With the end of the war, however, officials quickly dismantled this surveillance machinery in the North. The process may have been accelerated by the hundreds of Northern civilians that were suing provost marshals for damages, claiming they had arrested innocent persons, employed perjured witnesses and agents provocateurs, and used arrests to extort money from victims. Perhaps because of these complaints, the war left no permanent detective bureau in the War Department. Pinkerton had already gone home to Chicago. Baker disbanded his "National Detective Force." The Treasury Department established a small "secret service" charged with the duty of tracking down counterfeiters of the new federal "greenbacks."

Soon after the war ended, the Supreme Court reiterated its opposition to military arrests in the *Ex parte* Milligan case of December 1866. Like Vallandigham, Lambdin Milligan was a midwestern Copperhead. Arrested, tried, and sentenced to hang by a military commission in Indiana, Milligan argued that because civil courts were open, he had a right to a civil trial. Lincoln's assassins had been arrested, tried, and executed by the army, but that had involved Southerners from states where the Union did not recognize the courts. The Johnson administration argued that Indiana was also a war zone and that the president's war powers applied. This time the court reaffirmed its traditional stand that martial law could not exist where, as in Indiana, the courts were open, but must be confined to the actual war. A civilian could not be tried legally by army commissions in states loyal to civilian authority.[10]

In the South, the internal security apparatus remained in place while

Congress debated how to restore loyal civilian governments in the states. There military commissions and provost-courts tried civilians until Congress readmitted the reconstructed state governments into the Union. After Grant became president and William Tecumseh Sherman became commander of the army, the role of the army in the South gradually decreased. Grant's Attorney General Amos Akerman even suggested that Congress create a full-time civil rights office to watch for infringements of the newly won rights of blacks. When Congress passed the Ku Klux Klan Act in April 1871, its enforcement rested with the military, but as the army withdrew from the South, blacks had to depend on protection from local civilian governments.[11]

The role of the military in Southern reconstruction was always an ambiguous one. Sheriffs and marshals throughout the South called on troops to assist in law enforcement, a practice that resulted in hostility, law suits, and confusion on the part of officers over the extent of their powers. After military reconstruction ended in most states, orders from Washington about the proper role of the army in law enforcement remained vague and contradictory. The secretary of war simply asked generals to use their discretion. As Southern states enfranchised black men, President Grant withdrew the regular army from the South. By 1876, detachments remained in only three Southern states.[12]

Thus, as the new nation celebrated its first centennial, there appeared to be little need for the government to use the army in internal security or law enforcement. Northern reformers who had been willing to use the army as an instrument of reform in the South returned to their old conviction that the military force of the central government could not be expanded without peril to civil liberties. They imagined that African American men, like Euro-American men, could defend their rights with the ballot.

White Southerners, feeling harassed by the federal defense of the civil rights of blacks, wholeheartedly approved of such restraint. Although the use of military force in the South had involved very little terrorism and little physical punishment of white civilians, Southerners had learned a lesson. Political cunning and coalitions might have given them what their own military had not—home rule. At a time when the French government was ruthlessly suppressing workers who had established a Paris commune, most Americans congratulated themselves that they had been able to end the controversy over slavery—at a terrible cost in men's lives to be sure—without leaving a powerful central government or a heritage of military control of civilians.

In the centennial celebrations of 1876, Americans proudly pronounced the republic sound, united, and firmly controlled by civilians.
While Union veterans paraded as visible symbols of national power,
Americans seldom saw soldiers in their midst except occasionally in minor
domestic disturbances. Congress reduced its wartime army of over 1 million to just over twenty-seven thousand in twelve years. The executive
sent the remaining troops west to end the last of the Indian wars in the
western territories. The role of the army in internal security would then
be at an end.

As the army withdrew from the South in the 1870s, professional officers began to contemplate their future. Even before the Civil War, a few
officers had warned that the Indian wars must some day end and that the
army would need a more permanent function or it would have no reason
to exist. Career officers of the 1870s watched the most intelligent and
aggressive young men seek their fortunes in medicine or law, fields accepted as valuable to a society becoming more professionalized and
developing national organizations. Compared to the modernization oc-
curring in other institutions, the army seemed hopelessly old-fashioned.
It had been engaged in almost continuous war since its creation a century
before with little change in structure. Structural change normally followed political necessity, as perceived by civilians, with little influence
from career officers. Yet with the country reunited and the Indian wars
near an end, civilians seemed to be losing interest in the army.

The United States army seemed particularly outdated compared with
European armies. It was now what it had been before the Civil War: a
frontier army fighting irregulars in isolated and inglorious campaigns.
Even Indian campaigns soured in the summer of 1876 when Sioux warriors soundly defeated the American army at the battle of the Little Big
Horn. Although the army had immediately planned a counteroffensive
and the civilian secretary of the interior had given the military more control over civilian Indians who were resupplying the warriors in what had
become a guerrilla war, the wars against the Sioux nation dragged on.

American officers looked at European armies in envy. There the armies had been able to reform their structures from within, professionalize
them and gain considerable status in society. The Prussian army most
impressed American officers. In Prussia, theory and practice had con-
verged in the development of peacetime military preparedness. After the
Napoleonic Wars, Prussia could not maintain a large standing army like
other European countries because it lacked the resources to do so. Instead, the government developed a cheap mass army based on militia or-

ganizations called the *Landwehr.* Usually prominent local bourgeois and liberals whom the king feared, Landwehr officers could be called up only for wars of national defense and became trained active reservists after three years of duty. The king's officer corps had control over the leadership of the Landwehr. The Prussian state was thus able to have a large, well-trained army at little cost and seemingly little danger to domestic political institutions. The pivot of this new army was a permanent general staff system that collected information about the organization, tactics, and armament of foreign armies and operated directly under the king, independent of all civilian control. The general staff prepared plans for future wars, including the mobilization and education of officers. It sent attachés to foreign countries to collect information for the benefit of the army. It created an "intelligence bureau" that arranged and kept in readiness the most recent information on foreign armies and probable theaters of war.[13]

This modern Prussian army achieved a stunning victory over France in 1870. The Prussian victory seemed to be the result of an unbeatable combination of peacetime preparation and widespread espionage. The Prussians had a complete collection of maps of France and, according to the French, an awesome *espionage militaire.* The unpreparedness of France—it was rumored that Napoleon III had to use enemy maps of France for his own troops—gave birth to the myth that Prussia had covered France with over thirty thousand spies. In fact, Prussia had few spies. Its troops were armed with better weapons, and its general staff coordinated preparations.

European industrialization also made big navies possible. American officers believed that eventually European powers could bring mass armies to the New World. Some American officers were already beginning to argue this when the War Department sent Maj. Emory Upton abroad to study Asian and European armies in 1876.

Upton was most impressed with the staff system of the new German empire, its mass army, its military information collection and reporting, and its freedom from civilian control. He proposed that in the future the United States armed forces be led and controlled by the regular army rather than by civilians in arms. He recommended that the army be reformed to enable rapid expansion in time of war; that it be organized around a general staff to administer and collect information on foreign armies, analyze past American wars, and compile dossiers on each officer so that the army could use their abilities efficiently. He urged the collection of information on Canada, Mexico, and Cuba.[14]

Upton had difficulty in justifying the reforms he wished so ardently. He could offer no real reason to civilians for why they needed a reformed and expanded army. European peoples had been led by their governments to regard the army as "the only true field for the exercise of courage and patriotism," as Upton noted in a report. Although large segments of the European population opposed the governmental systems under which they lived, armies no longer existed in Europe primarily for internal security. Civilian police forces generally had the duty of suppressing domestic uprisings. In Europe, military theorists assumed that mass armies of young men would be created to contend for new territory and increased power, an aspiration that Europeans shared with their respective governments. Most Americans did not share a lust for overseas territory. The United States had few territorial interests beyond the western part of the continent. Thus there was little prospect for a new army role beyond its constabulary duties on the frontier. Two alternatives, both unpleasant, faced the younger officer corps, the ambitious men who still hoped to find a career in the postwar army. The first was to face the stagnation of inactivity that brought restricted budgets, slow promotion, and low morale. The second alternative was even more distasteful to many officers: remaining involved in duties that were essentially law enforcement tasks in the South.

By 1876 President Grant had withdrawn the army from most areas of the South. He had kept troops only in South Carolina and Louisiana where the Republican-controlled governments were still being challenged by local and, he felt, potentially disloyal political factions. In these areas, the army was still being used as a backup for civilian law enforcement officials. General Sherman, Grant's successor as commander of the army in 1869, like his officers, was concerned about the future role of the professional soldier. He was convinced that acting as bailiffs and constables was beneath a soldier's vocation.

The contested election of 1876–77 reinforced Sherman's conviction that continued involvement in domestic politics would lower the prestige of the army still further. When no clear presidential victor emerged from the November election and the House of Representatives assumed its constitutional duty of choosing a successor to President Grant, there were rumors of renewed war if politicians could not reach a compromise. The inability to compromise just sixteen years before had driven the country into its most bloody and costly war. Now Grant ordered General Sherman to reinforce the Washington garrison and to protect the last Republican-controlled governments in South Carolina and Louisiana. When the third session of the 44th Congress met in the spring of 1877, the use of the army in law enforcement was a major concern. The debates that followed revolved around the role of the president in controlling the army in peacetime. Democrats urged Congress to pass legislation to prohibit the use of the army in support of state governments. Democrat David Field of New York argued that it was "a monstrous doctrine" that the president could use the army as he pleased, particularly when the people "hold the purse-strings." Republicans, in turn, supported the power of the president to keep peace and cautioned against new laws.[15]

Members of Congress from the newly reconstructed Southern states were not the only ones edgy about the president's use of troops domestically. On all sides there seemed to be a desire to decrease that power and visibility of the army, which had played such a crucial role in the history of the country during the previous fifteen years. Debate over the limitation of the number of soldiers and the amount of money to be expended for their care, what supplemental equipment they needed, and how they would be organized bogged down repeatedly as the discussion continually moved into broader issues of the constitutional role of the army. In March, House Democrats introduced a rider to the army appropriations bill that prohibited any part of the army from being used to enforce federal law in Louisiana, where an election was about to be held. The bill provoked partisan comments: the Republicans opposing it, the Democrats speaking in its defense. Appealing to the long, historical memory of Congress, Southerners reminded Northerners of their pre–Civil War hostility to the military, especially to the use of the army in the Kansas abolitionist controversy of 1856. These reminders opened up the first full congressional debate on the role of the army in internal security since 1856. Too few members of Congress supported the proposed law for its passage. In fact, there was enough disagreement to block passage of the army appropriations bill. At an impasse, the 44th Congress adjourned without appropriating any funds for the army.[16]

The electoral commission had, meanwhile, awarded the contested election to the Republican candidate. Democrats made the withdrawal of federal troops from the South the primary condition of their acceptance of the agreement. In April newly elected President Rutherford Hayes withdrew half of the remaining troops from the South and confined the rest to military posts. Hayes did not call Congress back into special session until November, probably because he wanted time to remove the troops from the South before asking Congress for army appropriations. Meanwhile, Hayes also had to decide whether to use the army in the strikes of the summer of 1877.

In July 1877, a wildcat strike by firemen and brakemen touched off a spontaneous strike of railway workers in thirty-eight cities. Beginning in West Virginia, the strike spread to every major railroad center in the East and Midwest where workers in a variety of industries and jobs—including waitresses in railroad hotels in one instance—struck for higher wages. After hurried cabinet discussions, President Hayes called out federal troops against the strikers. For the first time since President Jackson had used regular troops in the 1834 strike, soldiers confronted workers. Gen. Philip H. Sheridan entered Chicago with orders to open communications with Pittsburgh while other regulars moved into Pennsylvania and New York. In a number of cases the militia refused to fire on strikers and would fight only when reinforced by the regular army. Forty-five thousand militia and two thousand regular army troops confronted angry workers during the brief but widespread strike. By August, resistance was crushed; workers returned to their jobs.

The army now faced the possibility of continued involvement in domestic disputes. During the strike of 1877 the executive had not intended to use the army to buttress capitalist forces in this new industrial warfare. The intent was to restore law and order. Given the growing class stratification of the period, that restoration inevitably damaged the chances of the workers to wrest from management greater control over working conditions. At no point, however, did the workers mount any widespread resistance to the army or engage in what might be termed insurrection against the federal government. The restraint of the workers was matched by the restraint of the government. Violent confrontations between the regular army and workers almost never occurred. Workers continued to believe that the government represented their interests and that the national government would respond to their concerns by staying out of domestic battles.[17]

When the strike ended, public debate revived over the proper role of the army in domestic disputes. President Hayes owed his presidency, at least in part, to his commitment to reduce the army in the South. He had shown considerable concern over the issue of constitutionality in this unprecedented situation. He delayed the original movement of federal troops into West Virginia until he had issued a proclamation to disperse. He followed all the constitutional formalities in three of the six states to which he sent troops, responding to a call from the governor and issuing a proclamation to disperse. In three other states, he sent troops to protect government property and to aid United States marshals in enforcing court orders.

Despite this restraint, critics charged that the president had mishandled the whole affair. Because Hayes had no internal security policy, he yielded to the pressure of the governors to intervene before the states had exhausted their ability to deal with the conflict and gave the governors tactical control of the army. The governors, in turn, allowed commanders to respond whenever railroad officials asked for assistance. Some commanders, such as one in St. Louis, kept his troops under tight control. Others simply provided company management with protection against belligerent workers when intervention by federal troops was clearly unnecessary.[18]

The role of the army in this first nationwide strike gave professional soldiers a glimpse of a possible place for the army in American life. Because of the 1877 strike, Major Upton recommended in his report that the United States government should strengthen its regular army to defend itself from radicals, emphasizing the savings in blood and property to be gained from such a service. In spite of press denunciation of the role of communists and anarchists in the strike, there was little public support for Upton's advice to expand the regular army. Even Upton admitted privately to a friend that he did not consider organized labor a threat to American institutions.

When Congress reassembled in October 1877, many congressmen advocated further restrictions on the regular army. Most agreed that the army was necessary to take care of forts on the ocean front, to protect the border settlements from Indians, and to repel cattle thieves on the lower Rio Grande. The troops that had so angered Southern Democrats had already been removed. Still hostility to the army lingered, and the appropriations bill rekindled the earlier debate on constitutional issues, now expanded to consider the role of the army in strikes as well as in Southern politics. Complaints of "standing armies," of insulting American soldiers by making them policemen, and praise of "men who have seen fit to strike against the oppression of monopolies," threaded through the debate. Congress did not pass the needed appropriations bill until late November.

During this fall session, the first debates began on the use of the army in law enforcement. The most important bill was one that prohibited the use of federal funds to suppress insurrection, maintain order, or support any state government unless state legislatures applied for them. While still aimed at the use of the army to supervise elections in the South, this new provision was also calculated to gain the support of disgruntled Northerners. It is clear from the *Congressional Record* that this broader bill and the debate on the use of the army in strikes gained the support of some Republicans. When the Senate voted to set the limit for the regular army at twenty-five thousand instead of the twenty thousand as advocated by the House, the House approved the higher limit by only five votes.[19]

By the time the House debated the next army appropriations bill in May 1878, this five-vote margin had slipped away. Members of Congress now introduced reports indicating that generals had used the army to suppress strikes, execute local laws, collect revenue, and arrest offenders at the request of both federal and state officials. In some cases no proclamations for crowds to disperse had been made, and in a few cases no applications for troops had even been made to the president. These reports drew Congress back into a review of the constitutionality of such actions, and Representative William Kimmel of Maryland introduced a new bill that, when revised, read: "Whoever, except in cases and under circumstances expressly authorized by the Constitution or Act of Congress, willfully uses any part of the Army as a posse comitatus or otherwise to execute the laws shall be fined not more than $10,000 or imprisoned not more than two years, or both."

From the reports and comments surrounding the debate over this last bill, it is evident that several factions combined to support the restriction on using the army as a posse comitatus. The Posse Comitatus Act was not a Reconstruction law. Democrats were still concerned about a Republican president using the army in the South, but with troops already withdrawn from the South, it is unlikely that Southern Democrats would have been able to get support for the bill had Northern members of Congress not responded to the rhetoric expressing opposition to a standing army. By resurrecting the old Republican fears of 1856, raising the specter of the army being used against laboring men, and examining the difference between suppressing domestic violence and the execution of the law, proponents were able to convince many members that the act merely declared a truth about the limits of the military in American society. Although one Republican protested against enacting legislation that embodied a "truth," a vote to strike the bill failed. In little more than a year, a congressional majority had moved from opposing the limitation of the role of the army in any way, to a broad restriction on the domestic use of the army. Even the Senate supported the Posse Comitatus Act, keeping it in the appropriations bill by a vote of twenty-nine to twenty-one.[20]

The act did not completely prohibit the use of the army domestically. The Ku Klux Klan Act gave the president explicit authority to use troops to enforce the civil rights of individuals, and the Civil Rights Act allowed him to use troops to enforce those civil rights deprived by the states. Constitutional provisions still allowed the president to use troops to assist governors or to protect federal property. The act did seem to preclude any further use by state, local, and federal officials of army troops in law enforcement and implied that troops could be used only by the president as commander-in-chief upon issuing a proclamation ordering the people to disperse or be considered part of an insurrection against the federal government.

Members of Congress were aware of the uniqueness of their hostility to large, standing armies in the context of European politics of the time. During the House debates of May 1878, Congressman Herman Humphrey of Wisconsin reminded his colleagues that England had an army of 300,000, Italy of 500,000, Austria of 800,000, Russia and Prussia of about 1 million each, and France an army of over 1 million, while the United States had only 40,000 troops. Congress did not mention the ruthless suppression of workers who had established the Paris commune in 1871 by French army troops, but most Americans were concerned about such military-civilian confrontations. The sentiment against standing armies masked the intent of some white Southerners to regain control of their state governments and to nullify the civil rights defenses of black Americans established by the regular army under the authority of Congress. Such attitudes reflected the intent of other members of Congress to keep the use of federal troops in labor disputes to a minimum. The law was not the final triumph of the Southern faction in Congress in ending Reconstruction. Rather, it was the first example of post-Reconstruction political coalitions. The law enabled Southern Congress members to buttress their political success in ending military occupation of the South with a law backed by members of Congress in other parts of the country who were concerned about the use of the army in disputes between labor and management.

Subsequent court decisions in the 1880s upheld the Posse Comitatus Act, and executive policy appears to have conformed generally to the act after its passage. Attorneys general rendered opinions confirming that presidents could not use troops as a posse comitatus to enforce revenue laws or even to enforce laws in the territories where no other law enforcement bodies existed. Presidents often turned down requests for federal troops, and when authorizing their use, such as in the New Mexico territory in 1878–80, the president carefully issued a proclamation. To solve the problems of continued violence in New Mexico, the president appointed a former army colonel as territorial governor. The new governor organized a territory-wide military force to deal with border ruffians.[21]

The army itself endorsed the Posse Comitatus Act. Officers argued that since passage of the act, a new chain of command existed—from the commander-in-chief down through the army—that excluded any control by governors or other state and federal officials. This new control was implied in general orders of the 1880s and was explicitly stated in General Orders 15 and 26 in 1894. The military power of the United States was to act under the president and not other civil officers, and the army was not to make arrests. The army's function was to suppress lawless resistance only.[22]

Issuance of general orders of this sort usually meant that a practice was not firmly in place and that commanders had not yet accepted the policy of the high command or its control. Yet the orders also reflected a change in attitude on the part of officers between 1880 and 1894. John M. Schofield's action in civil disturbances may be taken as an example of the gradual conversion of officers to a restricted view of the army's role in civil disturbances. As a major in command of the Military Division of Missouri with headquarters in Chicago, Schofield worked out contingency plans for moving federal troops into Chicago in case of riot, working with railroad officials to identify strategic points and with industrialists to establish a new fort just north of Chicago. In 1892, when Schofield moved troops into Coeur d'Alene in Idaho, he allowed state officials to use federal troops to remove pro-miner county officials, to assist in arresting about three hundred union members, and in guarding strikebreakers. Regular officers, such as Schofield, made no attempt to exert independent action. Once in Washington as commanding general, however, Schofield became concerned about the lax adherence to the Posse Comitatus Act. He began a campaign to educate officers about the constitutional and military limits on their acts and in 1894 instructed them on these limitations.[23]

The change in attitude may have been brought about in part by the controversy over the army arrest of the Ponca Indians in the 1890s. In 1894, a district judge in Nebraska heard Standing Bear's argument that the army had no right to arrest Poncas, that in peacetime civilians must govern by regular constitutional procedures, and that the army could execute laws only on reservations. The court, in affirming that American Indians off the reservation and not at war could not be controlled by the military, restated the concept of a limited role for the military and expanded it to a new group of Americans. Off the reservation, the court ruled, the army had to turn Indians over to civilian authorities immediately for legal action. In war, the executive could arrest and hold the enemy; in peace, the army had limited powers.[24]

Although never appealed to the Supreme Court by the government, the Ponca case attracted considerable attention among reformers in the northeast who were beginning to argue that Indians be granted Fourteenth Amendment rights. It also attracted considerable attention among generals, many of whom accepted the court's distinction between war and peace. Some officers had, in fact, helped to bring the court case to trial. Schofield and other army generals were thus important in restricting the role of the army in civilian affairs during the 1890s. Still the army was not centralized enough to enforce the policies of the army high command on its commanders in the field. There were also exceptions to the policy during times of crisis, even in the absence of war. During the Pullman strike of 1894, for example, Schofield violated the policy for six of eight department commanders, giving them authority to respond to requests from the Justice Department for assistance in enforcing federal injunctions.[25]

A uniform policy of riot duty might have eliminated these exceptions, but the lack of planning for riot duty in the 1880s and 1890s may have had the effect of keeping the army out of greater involvement with local and private officials. Although informal ties existed—especially through social activities involving officers and the industrial elite—there was little formal contingency planning beyond that done by Schofield in Chicago and by Maj. Gen. Oliver Howard in the northeast region. The lack of centralized planning did result in confusion—including the sending of troops to Nebraska when there was no need in 1882 and to various states in the West during attacks by American workers on Chinese workers in 1885–86. But lack of planning also conformed to congressional desires to minimize the army's involvement in growing labor turbulence during the last two decades of the century.

Major Upton had raised the spectre of "homegrown communism." In a work left unfinished by his suicide in 1881, he warned that the primary danger to the United States would come from "civil commotion." General Sherman, commander of the army from 1869 to 1884, echoed Upton's concern after he retired: "The better classes are tired of the insane howlings of the lower strata, and they mean to stop them." Nevertheless, during the 1880s, most professional officers continued to regard the army primarily as an instrument of national security and not internal security, even though foreign policy at the time required no armed enforcement.[26]

Most states relied on their newly formed national guards rather than on the federal army to control industrial conflict. State national guards had intervened in at least 150 labor disputes in the last thirty years of the nineteenth century. The restraint on repression by various state national guards varied depending on the politics of the governor and the state legislatures. Some states allowed management to use private armies in strike conflicts.[27]

Allan Pinkerton provided most of these private armies. Between 1865, when he resigned from the federal government, and his death in 1884, Pinkerton built a detective empire. During these almost twenty years he neatly filled the gap left by the military, providing not only detectives but also whole armies to industrialists who feared the growing conflict with labor. Pinkerton soon turned over his detective empire to his two sons, Robert and William, and concentrated his energies on feeding the growing public appetite for spy literature. He published at least seventeen anecdotal spy adventure books in the 1870s. Along with the taste for "ragged Dick" stories, whose young hero inevitably became an economic success, were Pinkerton's detective Dick stories, where the hero always solved the crime. Pinkerton both fed and profited from the growing belief in these new heroes.

The Pinkerton Agency flourished in the first fifteen years after the railroad strike of 1877. With the regular army restricted and governors sometimes responsive to the workers at the ballot box, corporations began to hire armed guards to protect private property from angry strikers. The Pinkertons provided security forces in at least seventy strikes between 1877 and 1892 and developed a force of over thirty thousand regulars and reserves. During this time, federal marshals as well as sheriffs began to deputize Pinkerton "regulars" to act as posses in place of regular army forces. Workers despised Pinkerton "regulars," who they claimed were petty criminals blackmailed by Pinkerton detectives into their jobs for self-protection. They supported legislation to keep companies from importing armed guards from other states to guard property. By early 1892, state legislatures in Massachusetts, New Jersey, and New York had passed anti-Pinkerton laws, which prohibited the hiring of people from out of state and made corporations liable for any ensuing injury by nonresidents.[28]

Although less visible than Pinkerton regulars, Pinkerton detectives also made themselves feared and hated among workers during the 1870s and 1880s. In 1873, the Pinkerton Agency began the first of a long line of investigations of workers when an operative infiltrated the Molly Maguires, a secret workers' organization functioning among Pennsylvania miners. Four years later, ten Mollies were executed on evidence that Pinkerton claimed had come from his detective. By the 1880s, municipal law enforcement agencies had already eliminated much of the Pinkertons' work as city detectives. The Pinkerton Agency then relied more on big corporate clients who offered them large yearly retainers for their detective services.

Soon even the government wanted to hire Pinkerton detectives. Congress had established the Justice Department under the attorney general in 1872 but gave him no authority to make regular investigations. The small group of Secret Service agents in the Treasury Department concentrated on investigating counterfeiting and land fraud. Because Congress remained reluctant to expand appropriations for investigations, the attorney general, secretary of the treasury, and the postmaster general all developed the practice of hiring private detectives by the day to investigate violations of federal law. Often these detectives were Pinkertons. Such work of the Pinkerton detectives might have continued quietly if Pinkerton regulars had not become involved in the Homestead strike of 1892.

Union workers had traditionally controlled much of the production of the Carnegie Steel Company in Homestead. As long as they did so, there were few disputes with management. As competition among steel companies increased in the late 1880s, however, Carnegie determined to break the power of the workers. In 1889, the company tried to reduce wages and end collective bargaining. The workers struck in retaliation and prohibited the local sheriff and a posse from entering the plant. Carnegie gave in and signed a three-year contract. In early 1892, the company proposed another wage reduction and stepped up production. The workers seemed prepared for another strike. Chairman Henry Frick then ordered three hundred Pinkerton regulars and laid off the entire work force. In July, the three hundred Pinkertons assembled from different parts of the country and on 5 July, armed with Winchester rifles, they boarded barges at Pittsburgh and headed down river to the Homestead plant. Workers, meanwhile, organized their own army and when the Pinkertons attempted to land, opened fire. The Pinkertons returned fire. When the battle ended, seven workers and five Pinkertons lay dead. The Pennsylvania governor ordered the militia in to protect the plant while the company brought in strikebreakers.

In Washington, meanwhile, Populists had already demanded action by the federal government to control the use of Pinkertons. Tom Watson of Georgia described Pinkertons as "a menace to the civil institutions of the country" and demanded that Congress should control this private armed force that acted as a militia in worker disputes with employers. Four months of congressional maneuvering followed, with considerable support for a broad inquiry into Pinkerton activities. Republicans in control of the Committee of the Judiciary finally whittled the inquiry down to an investigation of possible obstruction of interstate commerce or mails.[29]

In the Senate, Populists also demanded an investigation of these "private armies of irresponsible men." Senators argued that the government had an obligation to protect the American citizen and not just legislate protection for corporations. Opponents attempted to counter Populist demands with threats to investigate the lynching of blacks in the South and the refusal to admit blacks into hotels in the North. William Jennings Bryan rose to argue that governments were organized to protect life and property and should not transfer this duty to private individuals. The Senate passed a resolution calling for an investigation. Then came news of the massacre at Homestead.[30]

The news roused Populists to demand control of the Pinkertons once more. The head of the Senate select committee reported that the existence and employment of Pinkertons was "contrary to the genius of American institutions and subversive to liberty." One resolution termed the employment by Carnegie of Pinkertons as "levying war on the United States" and ordered the attorney general to try the Pinkertons for an attack on the people of the United States. In the House, hearings expanded to include the employment of Pinkertons by the post office as well as in the Homestead riot. Petitions from workers condemned the Pinkertons and called for an investigation of their activities. Reports also indicated that Pinkertons had been used to oversee elections. When these reports became known, some Republicans joined Populists in condemning Pinkertons. Republican Sen. John Sherman called them powerful, unscrupulous, secret, serviceable to those who hired them, a semipolitical organization capable of immense mischief, and dangerous. Sentiment among members of Congress was so strong by early August that they passed a rider on the general appropriations act stating that "no employee of the Pinkerton Detective Agency or similar agency, shall be employed in any Government service or by any officer of the District of Columbia."

Not since debate on the Posse Comitatus Act fifteen years earlier had Congress dealt with an issue of internal security at this level.[31]

Populists, anxious to make political capital among urban workers, denounced the Pinkertons. The 1892 Populist national convention condemned the "hireling standing army" of the corporations established to shoot down urban workers; called for abolition of the use of Pinkertons against striking workers; and enlisted orator Mary Elizabeth Lease to take up the Pinkerton issue: "Today the world stands aghast at the attempt of a Scotch baron entrenched and fortified by Republican legislation, to perpetuate a system of social cannibalism, and force by the aid of Pinkerton cutthroats, the American laborers to accept starvation wages," she thundered at Populist meetings in Kansas.[32]

Such political rhetoric proved strong enough to sweep Populists into office in Kansas and to help Democrats capture the presidency in 1894, but it did not destroy the Pinkertons. After the election, a Republican-controlled Senate committee that held hearings in Chicago, Pittsburgh, and New York reported against further federal anti-Pinkerton legislation. The majority report of the House committee also affirmed that Pinkertons were legal and that Carnegie had a right to protect his property because the civil authorities had provided insufficient protection, and concluded that workers too could employ Pinkertons. The minority report argued that the execution of laws should not be farmed out to individuals in the employ of private persons or corporations and condemned the Pinkertons as a "foreign force" likely to impress both the peaceful citizen and the excited worker that his home, his rights, and his liberties were being invaded. Although not strong enough to force legislation, public indignation did have an effect on the Pinkerton Agency. Fearing a loss of business, the agency announced that it would not furnish watchmen in labor disputes. In 1893 Congress passed another appropriations bill forbidding federal agencies' use of Pinkertons and took steps to curtail the use of Secret Service agents, reducing appropriations and forbidding them from investigating land frauds.

During the late 1890s, the Pinkerton company did not go out of business. It flourished with branch offices that were opened to avoid those state laws that prohibited bringing forces from out of state. Surveillance work for management increased, as did work for state governments and European governments, among them the Spanish government after the outbreak of the Spanish-Cuban war in April 1895. Pinkertons provided a convenient reserve force for government at all levels even though that use remained limited.

The new limitations on the federal government in hiring Pinkertons were not tested during the next internal security crisis. In the spring of 1894, armies of unemployed men marched on Washington under the leadership of Jacob Coxey. When word began to trickle into Washington that "Coxey's army" was coming, government officials ordered Secret Service agents to infiltrate and report on Coxey's plans. The administration feared all types of destruction: the city might be looted, leaders threatened, or the treasury sacked. Military and naval officers conferred over the defense of Washington and readied regular troops, the National Guard, and two hundred special policemen for action. Because of Justice Department pressure, some violations of the Posse Comitatus Act occurred. Still, General Schofield exercised a strong moderating role by insisting that the army adhere to the law, and because the march was peaceful, there was little need to use Pinkertons.[33]

The 1894 Pullman strike occurred immediately after the Coxey march crisis, and this time the army did use private detectives. Like the Carnegie strike two years before, the Pullman strike began with wage controversies but escalated to larger questions of worker control. Under the influence of Eugene V. Debs, Pullman workers had united in a militant American Railway Union. The arrogance of Pullman in return, and the men's sense of need to unite against corporate power, swept the union into a boycott against Pullman. On 26 June 1894, switchmen on roads out of Chicago refused to switch Pullman cars. With virtually all the twenty-six lines out of Chicago and almost all transcontinental lines stopped, an estimated five hundred thousand were out of work. By 3 July the *Chicago Tribune* was calling the strike an "insurrection."[34]

Would the army be drawn into this nationwide strike again as it had in 1877 before the passage of the Posse Comitatus Act? The governor of Illinois said army troops were not necessary. President Grover Cleveland had clear power to intervene even though the governor did not ask for troops, but past presidents had been reluctant to intervene. Now, however, one industrial center could affect the whole country. The attorney general told reporters: "We have been brought to the ragged edge of anarchy." Debs announced: "The first shot fired by the regular soldiers at the mob here will be the signal for a civil war." The president ordered Gen. Nelson Miles to take ten thousand troops into Chicago.

Miles was convinced that he faced an insurgency to overthrow the government rather than merely a strike. Miles had come up through the ranks of the old Indian-fighting army during the last battles with the Plains Indians. There he had developed the practice of recruiting informants among friendly Indians to infiltrate enemy encampments and bring back word of their plans. Miles had also witnessed the public's perception of Indian warriors change from seeing them as soldiers of enemy nations to seeing them as insurgents, a problem of internal rather than national security. Now, as crowds appeared on railroad property, throwing switches, toppling boxcars, burning yards, firing railroad property, Miles saw the workers as insurgents rather as Indian warriors were perceived as insurgents. He ordered soldiers to run the railroads; the confrontations in the next few days resulted in thirteen deaths and over fifty injuries. President Cleveland put Chicago virtually under martial law and gave Miles control.[35]

Once in control, Miles allowed his troops to act as a posse comitatus for United States marshals. He worked closely with railroad managers and used railway company spies to conduct a surveillance of workers; sent out at least one soldier to make investigations; and established a thousand-dollar espionage fund. Later, Miles would write that the crisis in Chicago involved "red-hot anarchy, insurrectionary and revolutionary!" Miles used such claims as justification for refusing to withdraw troops after the emergency had passed. There is no doubt that Miles had violated both the Posse Comitatus Act and the restriction on the use of Pinkertons.[36]

There is little evidence that commanders elsewhere tapped the growing surveillance networks established by management or engaged in widespread violations of these acts. Generals did work with railroad officials in a way that exceeded necessity and sometimes guarded railroad property, but outside of Chicago there was little worker opposition to the activities of federal troops. President Cleveland sent an estimated total of sixteen thousand troops to Colorado, Illinois, Kansas, Oregon, and Texas in 1894, but not because of insurrection. Even in Chicago, the mobs dispersed after a few days. Moreover, neither the executive nor Congress moved to a more institutionalized response to labor conflict during the next few years. Congress refused to increase army strength to thirty thousand, and it made no move to expand its internal defenses against labor or political radicals.[37]

In the last thirty years of the nineteenth century, the regular army intervened only in the major strikes of 1877 and 1894 and in a handful of isolated incidents. Through the Posse Comitatus Act, Congress restricted the executive from using federal forces extensively, probably saving the federal government from becoming embroiled in the industrial wars of the period and allowing it to emerge with its power intact and unchallenged domestically.[38]

The industrial conflict of the late nineteenth century did not lead the government into institutionalized domestic spying. Military and civilian officials, as well as the public, opposed such a practice. The expansion of the American empire would change these attitudes. One way to look at these changes is by examining the career of Lt. Andrew Rowan, the first officer spy.

PART II

The Legacy of Colonial Wars

CHAPTER THREE

Andrew Rowan: An Officer and a Spy

I n 1922, the War Department nominated retired army officer Andrew Rowan to receive the Distinguished Service Cross for heroism in Cuba by "securing secret information relative to existing conditions." Rowan received this medal—one of the first awards for men who had not performed gallantry in action—for an exploit popularly known as carrying "the message for García." Rowan's popularity symbolized a new attitude among Americans and army officials that it was acceptable for officers to be spies.

After Major Upton returned from his study of the armies of Asia and Europe in 1876, he suggested that the army engage in espionage. Convinced that a general staff should be established on the Prussian model, Upton proposed that an American staff collect information on all foreign armies, analyze past American wars, and compile dossiers on each American officer to catalog his abilities. Looking back at the Civil War, Upton concluded that the North should have had spies to infiltrate the South before the war and bring back word of secession plans. An immediate invasion by the North could then have ended the war cheaply and quickly, in accord with the professional officers' new model of the Franco-Prussian War of 1870.[1]

Within two years of Upton's recommendation, the army began its first peacetime ventures in information gathering. The change can be charted in the different responses to the Canadian crises of 1870 and 1878. In the

1870 dispute, when the United States and Canada quarreled over fisheries, the military made no war preparations. In the 1878 dispute over United States–Canadian boundary lines, the adjutant general's office gathered information and formulated invasion plans. In 1880, Gen. William T. Sherman, commander of the army, ordered all army officers who traveled to foreign countries to collect "information of value to the military service" and to report it in writing to the adjutant general. During the next few years, the army gave officers leave for hunting and fishing in Canada to conduct military reconnaissance. By fall 1885, when Adj. Gen. R. C. Drum established the first regular "military information" unit, officers had already been collecting information on Canada for at least seven years. That year the United States was involved in a diplomatic crisis with Great Britain over the Canadian seizure of American fishing boats and, according to official army accounts, Secretary of War W. C. Endicott asked Adjutant General Drum about the military strength of "some nation." It was undoubtedly Canada.[2]

Endicott's request—whether it was verbal or written is unclear since no documents exist from that time—resulted in the first public notice that the War Department intended to engage in peacetime intelligence gathering. In response to the request, Drum asked the Civil Service Commission to certify two clerks to form the nucleus of an intelligence bureau similar to one already established in the Navy Department, and the commission announced in the newspapers that it would be examining applicants for the new intelligence bureau. Drum, obviously embarrassed by the publicity, quickly said that no organizing would be done immediately, that he had applied for the clerks merely to have them available when a suitable time came for the formation of the new army intelligence bureau.[3]

Regardless of what he told the public, Drum was developing a new intelligence bureau in Washington, and from its beginning the name of Lt. Andrew Rowan would be associated with it. Born in Monroe County, Virginia, in 1857, Rowan moved to West Virginia sometime during his childhood. Rowan never wrote about his early life, and early military records are sketchy. His father, a state legislator, had enough political influence to get him a cadetship at West Point in 1877, the year that Congress was heatedly debating the role of the army in law enforcement. Rowan graduated in 1881, forty-second in a class of fifty-three. He then served a number of short tours of duty in the West and in Colorado, New Mexico, South Dakota, and Texas. In 1887, the War Department ordered him to make a mapping tour of Canada.[4]

Rowan arrived in Washington in 1889 to become part of this early intelligence gathering venture. In 1890, he returned to Canada to chart railroad routes, defenses, and waterways—especially the St. Lawrence. Back in Washington, the army put him in charge of indexing and carding reports on special reconnaissance missions to the Esquimalt and Halifax fortifications and the Welland Canal, and made him responsible for the mapping of Ontario. The reports that Rowan and other officers collected became the basis for the first United States war plans. Had conflict with Canada continued, Rowan might have gone back to Canada as part of an invading army acting on those plans.

The invasion of Canada did not occur, but intelligence gathering continued. In 1888, Congress appropriated a salary for a clerk to organize information collected by army officers in other countries. This inch given by Congress allowed the War Department to take its new mission seriously. Always in the wake of the navy, which had already established an intelligence bureau and had found a forceful proponent of naval preparedness in Alfred T. Mahan, the army now established a regular system of military attachés similar to those of major European countries. The influx of information, sent directly to the War Department, led to the establishment, "confidentially," of a Military Information Division (MID) in the office of the adjutant general. In addition to being in charge of collecting and arranging information on the geography, economic resources, and armed forces of foreign countries and the United States, the secretary of war charged this new MID with publishing and distributing books and maps on military subjects to the army, maintaining contact with state militias, and most importantly, preparing and keeping track of mobilization plans. The functions of MID now paralleled those of foreign general staffs. Rowan was reassigned to the MID in 1893.[5]

During the next few years, as the northern border conflict subsided, MID gradually turned its focus from Canada to the Caribbean and to areas that might prove suitable to the coaling needs of the expanding navy. By the early 1890s, the secretary of war was acknowledging publicly in his *Annual Report* that MID existed and that it was collecting information on America's neighbors to the north and south. He noted in 1893 that information was necessary because warfare was becoming "an art dependent on the exact sciences quite as much as on personal bravery." The following year he reminded the president that the information collected by MID would be useful to all branches of the government, not just the military. Such brief notices and timid justifications mirrored the insecure toehold that peacetime espionage still held in the army bureaucracy in Washington.[6] Then, in April 1895, the Cubans revolted against Spanish rule. The United States became involved in this war not only because Cuba lay ninety miles off its southern coast, but also because Cuban revolutionaries turned to Americans for support in their efforts to free Cuba from Spanish control.

The outbreak of Spanish-Cuban conflict and the efforts by Cubans to involve Americans on their behalf opened opportunities for the expansion of American control in the Caribbean. American officials had coveted Cuba at various times for almost a century. Because of this, it is tempting to see the response of the American government, as one historian has said, as "a climax to a hundred years of policy" and as "shrewd, purposeful, and calculated." Such an interpretation, however, grants too much unity and calculation to the long-term policies of the American government. Still, the three years between the beginning of the war in April 1895 and the entry of the United States into that war in 1898 revealed a growing interest by army officers and by the executive in the internal conditions of the island. That interest would culminate in bringing Lieutenant Rowan and Gen. Calexto García together in a brief but memorable meeting at Bayamo in Cuba.[7]

Two months after the Spanish-Cuban conflict began, on 12 June 1895, President Cleveland proclaimed neutrality, warned Americans to obey neutrality laws, and called on federal employees to be vigilant. Just who was to be responsible for investigating suspected violators of the neutrality laws was not clear. The first arrest of Cuban *expedicionarios* occurred in August, four months after the revolt began. A United States marshal in Wilmington, Delaware, accompanied by a posse of Wilmington policemen and two private detectives, arrested thirty Cubans suspected of launching a filibuster expedition in violation of the law. The detectives, probably in the employ of Spanish diplomats, had arrived in the city the day before with the information that the Cubans were sailing from Wilmington on a steamer bound for Cuba. The marshal charged the thirty suspects with violation of the neutrality law that prohibited the outfitting of a military expedition against a country with which the United States was at peace. The defendants argued that the government must prove that the military expedition was not only prepared in the United States to fight Spain, but also that it was officered and equipped for immediate hostile operations when it landed in Cuba. The men testified that they were doctors, editors, engineers, lawyers, and merchants, and that while they had arms and ammunition on board, they were not equipped for immediate hostile operations. The jury acquitted all thirty amid the cheers of their compatriots. Other Cubans succeeded in leaving port with little interference from the government.[8]

On the morning of 18 November 1895, General García, the man whose name was later to be linked to Rowan's, arrived in New York from France on *La Champagne*. That afternoon Cuban patriots from the New York City area flocked to see the tall, white-haired Cuban Creole in his late fifties who looked robust and energetic. García reviewed his revolutionary past for reporters: how he had fought for Cuba from 1868 to 1875, how he had put a bullet through his own chin to escape surrender, and how the bullet came out between his eyebrows, leaving an unhealed wound that he kept stuffed with a small wad of cotton. García had spent four years in a dungeon in Madrid before being liberated, again taking up arms against the Spanish and again being taken to Madrid. After fifteen years of parole in Spain, he fled to Paris vowing to return to Cuba to renew the Cuban war for independence: "I am under the Provisional Government and my sword is in its service," García announced with a flourish. "It has arms and ammunition stored in many places in this country, Canada, and the South American countries, and means are now being devised to get the most important part of this ammunition—cartridges—to the island." García promised he would take what was needed with him.[9]

This was not the first time that General García had rallied his fellow citizens in New York. Almost sixteen years earlier he had organized a Cuban revolutionary committee there and prepared an expeditionary force to attempt to free Cuba from Spain's control. That attempt, "La Guerra Chiquita" of 1879–80, was as unsuccessful as "La Guerra Grande," which lasted from 1868 to 1878. Now García was back for yet another try, urging Cuban immigrants to support a free Cuba again. This attempt would be different, however, for this time the Spanish government was determined that García would not launch his expedition so easily. García's 1895 visit is worth following more closely because of what it reveals about the attempts of the Spanish and American governments to control Cuban revolutionary activity.[10]

Cubans had already formed a Department of Expeditions to smuggle arms and ammunition south. In January 1896, they arranged for García and more than one hundred Cubans to board the *J. W. Hawkins* secretly, load it with ammunition, and sail for Cuba. Off the south shore, the wooden ship foundered—the work of Spanish spies, according to the Cubans. While the ship apparently went down of its own accord, the Spanish minister immediately ordered a surveillance of the survivors by private detectives. By Sunday morning, 24 February, detectives believed that another smuggling attempt would be made by García and the Cubans aboard the *Bermuda*. They notified the Spanish consul in New York who cabled the information to Secretary of State Richard Olney, who contacted Attorney General Justin Harmon.

The attorney general turned to his marshals. He sent Marshal John McCarty of New York a telegram to warn of the attempted filibuster but also ordered McCarty not to make arrests without positive proof that the ship was starting a filibustering expedition. On Monday detectives arrived at McCarty's office with what they considered conclusive evidence of such an expedition. McCarty deputized a dozen detectives who had been following the Cubans and rounded up another eight deputy marshals. All armed themselves and boarded the Treasury Department cutter *Hudson*. At 11 P.M. Monday evening off Liberty Island, the *Hudson* pulled along side the *Bermuda,* and the marshals and detectives—with drawn revolvers—swarmed aboard. The marshals confiscated the ship and its cargo, arrested everyone, and charged them with the violation of neutrality laws. McCarty told reporters that he regarded the capture as "successful and satisfactory in every way."

Not everyone thought so. Cubans filed scores of complaints about detectives who, they charged, had rifled their belongings and threatened those who asked for search warrants with violence. After holding the men for a day, the government released all but García and a few other leaders, hinting it had insufficient evidence to convict. A prominent New York lawyer announced that the arrests were illegal and offered his services to the Cubans. The Cuban junta, as the Cuban government in exile was called, sent a representative to Washington to negotiate. He emerged from a conference with the attorney general to tell reporters: "The government had no case, no law, no facts." The attorney general ordered the discharge of the *Bermuda* and all her cargo except some crates of unmarked explosives that by law should have been marked. The government seemed to have no case but was protecting itself from suits for false arrest by patching up a case against García and the other leaders. The government indicted García and his associates and then released them on bail.

The *Bermuda* cleared New York for a second time on 15 March, without government interference and with no Cubans on board. When reporters rushed over to García's home, his wife assured them he would be back for dinner. García did not return for dinner; instead he boarded a steamer for Tuckahoe, New Jersey, where the *Bermuda* met him the next day. García and over sixty compatriots and volunteers boarded the ship.

The Spanish spies followed the ship down the Delaware, then lost it in a heavy fog. Ten days later, the *New York Times* announced that the *Bermuda* had reached Cuba safely, and on 10 April a jury acquitted the men left behind to stand trial. The *Bermuda* case symbolized the situation exactly. The Spanish and their growing force of private detectives were providing the surveillance of Cubans for the United States government, and the Justice Department was willingly arresting Cuban suspects, but juries would not convict. The *Bermuda* was one of the best-known ships; others left United States ports with the growing assistance of Americans.

The Cuban immigrant community in the United States was not large in 1895 and would not have seemed to pose a problem for the government. When the Cuban rebellion began in April 1895, there were approximately forty thousand Cubans in the United States, many of them poor migrants who had come seeking higher wages. The main Cuban colonies were in Tampa where thousands worked making cigars, and in New York where Cubans worked at a variety of occupations. Americans subjected dark-skinned, Spanish-speaking Cuban Catholics to various levels of discrimination, but these same Americans were captivated by the ardent nationalism and the rhetoric of freedom of the wealthy and politically articulate Creole revolutionaries.

These wealthy Cubans had fled the countryside to foreign capitals as the Spanish laid waste to the interior of the island. They set up revolutionary juntas to help with the final overthrow of their colonial masters. Cubans had juntas in other Caribbean countries and Latin America, as well as in the United States, but in the United States they had access to far more resources. The United States junta raised money to buy and ship arms and ammunition, encouraged assistance from American adventurers and filibusters, negotiated recognition by the United States government, and promoted popular support for Cuban independence.

The success of the Cuban rebels in maintaining the rebellion made it impossible for the American government to ignore the conflict at their doorstep. Although American officials beginning with Thomas Jefferson had sought Cuba as an American colony, Americans were not eager for involvement during the rebellion from 1868 to 1878. By the rebellion of 1895, there was much more interest. The government followed an official policy of neutrality, but the continued turmoil and the enthusiastic participation of Americans inevitably involved the administration. The longer the insurgents maintained their determination to be free, the better able they were to buttress their determination with ideological, political, and financial structures. As the Spanish were learning, the longer an in-surgery could survive against traditional diplomatic and military weapons, the less likely those weapons were to triumph ultimately. The Cuban provisional government appointed Tomás Estrada Palma and Gonzalo de Quesada, both naturalized American citizens, to act as its representatives in Washington to work for recognition, first of belligerency and then of independence.

The task of the Spanish government and its diplomats, of course, was to thwart the Cubans. The Spanish hoped for strict enforcement of the neutrality laws, noninvolvement by the Americans, and no recognition of belligerent status for the Cubans. Spain believed it could crush the insurgents again only if Americans could be kept from assisting them. Within a week after the Cubans revolted, the Spanish minister in Washington complained of Cuban violations of United States neutrality acts that prohibited the outfitting of military expeditions against nations with which the United States was at peace. When the United States government ignored his complaints, the minister hired detectives to patrol the shoreline, to watch ammunition purchases, and to trail Cuban revolutionaries.[11]

In his report for 1895, the secretary of the treasury promised that his revenue cutters were "a cordon of vigilant sentinels" around the peninsula of Florida, but arrests were infrequent and convictions almost impossible to obtain in the first flush of American enthusiasm for the rebels. Although the secretary of the treasury volunteered his services if Congress would appropriate funds, Congress remained unenthusiastic. Reports confirmed the Cuban desire for independence, but still Cleveland hesitated to recognize a state of belligerency. Faced with growing public demands that the government recognize belligerency, the Cleveland administration clung to neutrality and demanded a nonpartisan foreign policy. The secretary of state, meanwhile, urged Spain to grant autonomy to Cubans as a device to prevent the Cubans from obtaining independence.[12]

Spanish ministers in the United States kept the Cleveland administration supplied with information on the activities of the Cubans in the United States and on the situation in Cuba. They constantly overemphasized the activity of the Cubans in the United States and disparaged the accomplishments of the Cuban Liberating Army. The Americans in Cuba who owned land tended to confirm the negative information about the Cubans. Planter informant Edwin Atkins, for example, wrote confidential reports to Secretary of State Olney frequently, arguing that the Cubans had no government and no organized army. He opposed recognition of belligerency because he believed the Spanish would then withdraw their protection of American property. Atkins also sought to discredit the Cuban junta leaders by arguing that Palma, a naturalized American citizen, was advocating the destruction of American property to advance the cause of the rebels. The Cubans, meanwhile, continued to forward papers to the State Department that showed that the Cuban army had the support of the people. With all these conflicting reports streaming into Washington, it is not surprising that Cleveland put off action. Cuban conditions seemed just too complicated. As Cubans continued their activities in the United States, it became increasingly difficult for the administration to ignore them but just as difficult to stop them. The *Bermuda* episode exemplified their continuing success.[13]

By the spring of 1896, the Cubans were winning the war for American support. On 6 April the House and Senate passed a concurrent resolution declaring that a public war existed in Cuba and granting belligerent status to the Cuban rebels. Anti-American riots followed in Spain, led by students who sought to bolster the sagging Spanish war spirit with their enthusiastic support.[14]

In response to the congressional resolution, Cleveland began to take more control over foreign affairs. He replaced the United States consul in Havana, Ramón Williams, who the Spanish had complained was pro-insurgent. Williams had been consul for over twenty years, spoke Spanish fluently, and was known for his defense of the American expedicionarios captured and court-martialed for working with the Cubans. Cleveland replaced Williams with Fitzhugh Lee, the ebullient nephew of Robert E. Lee and an ex-governor of Virginia. Lee had knowledge neither of Spanish nor of diplomatic matters, facts that reporters took as evidence that Cleveland was interested in a report on the military strength of the insurrection to guide the State Department. Lee told Cleveland that the United States should purchase Cuba.[15]

In addition to Lee's reports, the State Department continued to depend on information from all sides in the conflict: Cubans, Spaniards, and Americans in Cuba. Reports varied depending on the source. American planters continued to oppose the rebels, appealing to racism by emphasizing the black Cuban support for independence and claiming support for autonomy among other Cubans. The Cuban junta emphasized that Cubans would not accept autonomy, only independence. American reporters tended to support the Cubans, confirming that a good majority of the Cuban population did likewise.[16]

Spanish officials again warned Cleveland to enforce neutrality legislation, suppress the Cuban junta, and convince Americans they should not aid the Cubans. Cleveland did tighten the enforcement of neutrality laws. The State Department issued a proclamation from the president that warned citizens against furnishing or aiding transportation for a "military expedition." The proclamation even threatened to apply the conspiracy statute to neutrality laws, that if two or more persons conspired to commit an offense, the act of one conspirator made all liable to fine and imprisonment. Cleveland invoked the aid of "all good citizens" to enforce the law and to join in the detection and apprehension of offenders. At the same time, Cleveland announced that sending arms and ammunition to Cuba was not illegal and warned Spain that it should crush the rebellion. He also told Congress that the recognition of belligerency was an executive prerogative and that he would not recognize Cuban independence even if Congress passed another resolution as it had in April. Cleveland successfully kept Cuba from becoming an issue in the election of 1896. After the election, he exhibited a less sympathetic attitude toward Spain, an attitude also reflected by McKinley when he took office as president in April 1897.[17]

During the next year, Lieutenant Rowan and two other officers assigned to MID became increasingly interested in Cuba. Between April 1897 and the end of July 1897, MID added six officers trained in topography and in the Spanish language to its staff. Rowan had already begun work on a large map of the island and had contributed an account to *The Island of Cuba* published in 1896. The army had sent several officers to Cuba to gather information openly. The Military Information Division now occupied three rooms on the main floor of the old State, War, and Navy Building. To assist the nine officers in processing information on Cuba and other Spanish possessions, a corps of civilian clerks, stenographers, and drafters were at work. It was obvious in those rooms that the McKinley administration was preparing for a possible war with Spain and that MID was increasingly respected for its ability to provide knowledge about the troubled affairs of Cuba.[18]

None of these MID officers yet functioned as a real spy, that is, none traveled in disguise to a country with which the United States was engaged in hostilities or with which the United States expected hostilities. The navy during this time was much less restricted in its activities. Not only did it plan a strategy for a war with Spain that would eventually include a strike at the Spanish fleet in the Philippines, but it also sent the first United States spy to Cuba. In disguise and under an assumed name, this agent made an exhaustive survey of fortifications and topography in July 1897. The head of MID, Maj. Arthur L. Wagner, asked at the same time

to send an army spy as well. The new adjutant general refused to send an
army spy to Cuba because, he said, it would be unethical. "Official" espionage, done openly by army officers in uniform as military attachés or
on leave, was acceptable. Having officers collect information in disguise
and under assumed names was not.[19]

The Military Information Division had not yet overcome the popular,
widely held attitude that officers should not spy in peacetime. Nor had it
supplanted the idea that civilians, not army officers, should be responsible
for clandestine spying. While there was no clear, popular distinction between intelligence gathering and espionage at this time, the popular concept of espionage was that it was still something done by civilians in the
pay of governments. A good spy, for most Americans, was a civilian who
volunteered for this dangerous assignment. In the decades after 1877,
anecdotal spy literature had flooded the United States. Pinkerton's spy
books and Lafayette Baker's Civil War memoirs were reprinted in official
and pirated versions many times during the 1880s. Historians have wisely
warned that this literature is not a reliable guide to intelligence practices
during the Civil War. It is, however, a barometer of the popular thirst for
civilian spy stories.[20]

By the time the United States declared war on Spain in 1898, the good
spy was widely established as an American archetypal hero. Not until the
popular press discovered Lieutenant Rowan, MID's first publicly acknowledged spy, did the older image of a civilian spy hero become fused to the
newer idea of an officer spy hero and thereby legitimize espionage as an
activity becoming an officer and a gentleman.

After being turned down in July 1897 in his request to send an army
spy to Cuba, Major Wagner composed a formal argument as to why the
United States should, in fact, send a spy. His argument is important, for
it shows both the lack of precedent for such a step and that a plan for
espionage had been formulated within MID by December 1897. In his
memorandum, Wagner argued that reports from Consul Fitzhugh Lee
were inadequate because they were limited to Havana and Spanish
sources and that reports from newspapers were colored to reflect their
own policies, not real conditions. The need to send an officer to Cuba
seemed real to Wagner, yet precedent was poor for sending a spy into a
country with whom the United States was at peace. Wagner pointed to
the Civil War visits of foreign officers to the Confederacy and the Union.
Although these foreign officers had obtained the consent of the armies
that they visited, Wagner brushed such consent aside as unnecessary in
the case of Spain and recommended that two officers be sent to Cuba to

conduct espionage. The officers were to volunteer for the duty and to receive a leave of absence to visit the insurgents, but the government was to pay their expenses. The official status of the officers would begin only with the outbreak of war with Spain. Wagner also forwarded to Secretary of War Russell Alger a list of the officers in MID who might be sent on such a special mission to Cuba. Rowan's name headed the list.[21]

In form, this reconnaissance was little different from that still being conducted in Canada. The context made it far different, however, for the rebellion against Spain under way in Cuba involved large armies in the field. By 1898, the Cubans had the tenacious Máximo Gómez as commanding general and the brilliant and popular García as second-in-command. Both generals were scrupulously loyal to the civilian leaders who were attempting to establish the government, obtain its recognition by foreign powers, and bring the United States into the war as an ally. The Cubans saw the United States much as Americans had viewed the French in the American Revolution, as noble allies who would turn the tide for the rebels, then graciously withdraw leaving the Cubans in control of their own country, with perhaps some sort of trade treaty to cement the friendship of the two nations.

The administration refused to send officers south as Wagner wished. It did, however, make one last attempt to mediate between the Spanish and the Cuban commanding general Gómez through an American war correspondent and the United States consul at Sancti Spíritus. In December, the Spanish allowed the two men to cross their lines with a message for General Gómez to try to influence the insurgents to make peace. Gómez indicated his pleasure with the special envoy but firmly refused to reply. He said he was not allowed to correspond directly with foreign powers and would reply only through the Cuban government in exile at Washington.[22]

The Cuban junta had engineered a number of activities to bring the United States into the war as an ally. Their most successful action was the theft of a letter from the Spanish minister Enrique Dupuy de Lôme from a Spanish official in Havana, its publication in New York, and then its delivery to Secretary of State John Sherman. Publication of the letter in which de Lôme referred to McKinley as a foolish politician and admitted that Spain was only trying to gain time through negotiations—followed soon after by the sinking of the American battleship *Maine* in Cuban waters—brought overwhelming support for preparedness in Congress. On 9 March, without a dissenting vote, Congress voted $50,000 for the War Department. By this time MID had twelve officers, ten clerks, and two messengers in Washington, forty officers on duty with national guard and militia units, and sixteen military attachés.[23]

Late in March 1898, army and navy officers met to plan coastal defenses and to organize a joint assault on Cuba. Major Wagner was now able to compare plans with navy representatives on how best to assist the Cubans in driving out the Spanish army and establish an independent nation. By 2 April, Wagner and the navy were considering the most desirable point to be used as a central embarkation point for troops, but the army apparently still considered its job to be one of sending a small force to aid the insurgents with weapons, supplies, and technical advisers; taking over Puerto Rico; and perhaps holding a coaling base in Cuba. Sometime soon after, someone in the administration leaked word to the newspapers that McKinley would ask for intervention without recognition of the Cuban government. A Cuban leader who had been called upon to testify before the House Committee on Foreign Affairs warned that if independence were not recognized, it would be considered as a declaration of war against the Cuban insurgents. The next day the president and secretary of war agreed that Wagner could send two spies south immediately. The first was forty-one-year-old Rowan. The second was Lt. Henry Whitney, a thirty-two-year-old West Point graduate from Pennsylvania who began working with Rowan in 1897.[24]

Wagner appointed Rowan and Whitney as military attachés to Buenos Aires, Argentina, and Santiago, Chile, to cover their activities. Both were to go to Cuba. Rowan left Washington on 7 April, four days before McKinley asked Congress for permission to intervene in the Spanish-Cuban war as an impartial neutral. Whitney left on 12 April, the day after McKinley's message to Congress seeking to intervene but twelve days before Congress formally declared war on Spain. Thus, technically, the United States and Spain were still at peace when the two officer spies left for Cuba.[25]

After the two men left Washington, the record is rather murky. Wagner gave the men their instructions orally, making it impossible to know exactly what orders they received. Both Whitney and Rowan later gave reporters public versions of their orders, each containing gaps and inconsistencies. Rowan apparently received orders to proceed south but was not told whether he would ultimately go to Cuba or to Puerto Rico, which the United States at that time planned to occupy. Rowan said later that he was given general orders to find out how many Spanish troops there were, how they were equipped, what their morale was, how the sanitary conditions were, and to bring information back on the Cuban army. He was to carry no papers other than those to identify him to the American consul general at Kingston, Jamaica, and the Cuban junta there. The map Rowan had prepared of Cuba was a large-scale map printed on cloth to be used in the field rather than a topographical map, so he had to use Spanish maps. He disguised himself as an English hunter. In Jamaica, Rowan had to wait while the Cubans extracted a promise in writing from the War Department to pay for Rowan's expenses. Then, on 21 April a cipher telegram arrived saying, "Join García as soon as possible." Two days later, the Cubans escorted Rowan to the southern coast of eastern Cuba and into García's camp at Bayamo. Significantly, Rowan did not see a Spanish soldier during this entire time.[26]

Like Gómez in 1897, García was circumspect in dealing directly with the War Department. He refused to allow Rowan to remain in Cuba to collect information. Instead he wrote a message to the secretary of war outlining his need for military supplies, especially ammunition, and sent two officers, Gen. Ernesto Collazo and Col. Carlos Hernández, back to Washington with Rowan. Both Collazo and Hernández had been in the United States previously to organize expeditions, and Hernández, who had been educated in Massachusetts, spoke English well. García instructed the officers to report first to the Cuban junta in Washington, then to outline García's plan in detail to the secretary of war and to the commander of the army, General Miles. Eight days later the three men arrived at Nassau in the Bahamas. From there they proceeded to Key West and then on to Tampa. From the record, it would appear that Rowan had no specific message for García, beyond the news that the United States would intervene. Certainly he had no written message, and he did not perform any espionage activities in Cuba. García considered the Cuban junta in Washington as his civilian command in the matter of negotiations with the American government.[27]

Later, Cuban historians would argue that there was a sinister reason for the administration to send a message to García. It planned to divide the rebels and cause dissension; Rowan's requests embarrassed García because he felt the first message should have gone to Gómez as head of the Cuban Liberating Army. It might seem, in retrospect, as though the administration had this in mind, as there is evidence that it later sought this result. The administration was probably not this calculating in the confused days of late April and early May. McKinley was moving toward outright intervention without recognition of Cuba, and the Cubans certainly distrusted the Americans, as both the caution of the junta in Jamaica and General García had showed. But the administration simply did not have that much control over the situation or over its potential spies at the time.[28]

Furthermore, the War Department did order Whitney to contact Gómez on 5 May. According to Whitney's 1898 account, which is substantiated by War Department documents, he joined the American fleet off Cuba, communicated with General Gómez from the north coast, and proceeded with the fleet toward San Juan, arriving at St. Thomas in the Danish West Indies on a press boat. Whitney did collect intelligence information off the coast of Puerto Rico and narrowly escaped capture by the Spanish while disguised as an English sailor there. He functioned much more in the role of a spy than Rowan. The American government also contacted Gómez through the corps of reporters that roamed the Caribbean looking for news and jobs as civilian spies.[29]

As historians have shifted their attention from the causes of what was once known as "a splendid little war" to its consequences for America's place as a world power, their interest in yellow journalism as a cause of the war has faded. In more recent interpretations, journalists have been supplanted by officials and businessmen as those most influential in foreign policy. Yet if the wielders of direct economic and political power were ultimately responsible for intervention, it is still true that intervention in support of the Cubans was popular and that war correspondents played an important role in the Spanish-Cuban and later in the Spanish-American War. During the Spanish-Cuban war, reporters had generally supported the Cuban liberation movement, the Cuban junta, and the Cuban Liberating Army. Once the United States decided to intervene, the War Department attempted to control news, first by accrediting correspondents; then on 25 April, by taking over cable and telegraph lines to prevent information on the projected movements of troops and naval vessels from reaching the press; and finally by asking the press to voluntarily censor news that would "embarrass" the administration or be detrimental to the success of military operations. During the first few weeks of April, the war correspondents played an important role in collecting information for the navy and in disseminating information on military activities to the public, including information on the efforts of Rowan and Whitney to reach Gómez and García.[30]

While the navy was the first to send a spy to Cuba, it nevertheless relied primarily on civilian spies for its intelligence during the early days of the war. When Whitney joined the American fleet in April, Adm. William T. Sampson was trying to find the Spanish fleet and to gather information for an expected landing at Havana. Sampson had already begun to use accredited war correspondents as a volunteer intelligence group. He sent a photographer from *Collier's* to photograph coastal fortifications and allowed Ralph D. Paine of the *World* to land reporters on the Cuban coast from his newspaper launch in order to discover the location and power of Spanish fortifications, to find out how Cuban troops could be supplied, and what joint operations could be arranged with the Cuban Liberating Army. On 26 April, two days after Congress declared war, just as Rowan was leaving Jamaica for Cuba, Sampson allowed Sylvester Scoval to plan an expedition to reach Gómez to inform him of the declaration of war by the United States and to get ideas for cooperation. When Scoval's three correspondents reached Gómez, a reporter from the New York *Herald* was already there. It may have been these reporters who actually carried a message from Whitney to Gómez as it is not clear that Whitney's "contact" with Gómez involved actually landing in Cuba. Whitney may, of course, have been disguised as one of the reporters who landed.[31]

Rowan, meanwhile, had met Elmer R. Roberts of the Associated Press in Jamaica and agreed to allow him to accompany him to Cuba. Roberts intimated that he knew of the proposed expedition, asked to go along to deliver letters from the New York Cuban junta for García, and promised to maintain absolute secrecy. Rowan wrote to Wagner of his plans to have Roberts accompany him to Cuba. When the State Department received word of this plan, it immediately sent a cable to the American consul ordering Rowan not to let Roberts go to Cuba. As soon as Rowan had left Jamaica on 23 April, however, a newspaper reporter— probably Roberts—cabled the news to New York that Rowan was going to arrange for the cooperation of insurgents in the invasion of eastern Cuba. Newspapers also announced that a messenger had been dispatched to Gómez to inform him of the contemplated movements by the United States forces and that an officer had been sent to the Cuban government. On 5 May the *New York Times* announced that Gómez had thanked the people of the United States for aid, accepted the alliance, and was waiting for an officer to discuss plans of the campaign. When Rowan arrived in Key West, he also told reporters that García had expressed joy at the intervention and had asked how the insurgents could help.

It is almost an axiom of history that the most crucial decisions are often the least well documented. The decision of President McKinley to invade Cuba immediately was one such decision, made in the last week of April. That decision reflected the inability of peacetime planning by MID to affect military decisions and probably resulted in the elevation of Rowan to his status as the first hero of the Spanish-American War and the first officer spy hero in American history.

Once Rowan and Whitney had been dispatched south, Major Wagner turned the attention of his MID staff to consider when the troops should invade Cuba. Reports hastily assembled by MID indicated that because of unhealthy tropical health conditions (malaria, yellow fever, and typhoid), the army should not be sent to Cuba in the summer. The Military Information Division also wanted more time to plan the invasion carefully. On 18 April the surgeon general advised against putting troops in Cuba during the "sickly season," and at a meeting shortly after, the president agreed with Wagner that the main invasion should be scheduled for the fall, with only a small expeditionary force earlier to help the Cubans. But then Consul Lee warned from Havana that the climate was even worse in September, October, and November. If delayed until December, the invasion would be greatly improved by careful MID planning, but the political problems would also be greatly increased. Congress would be back in Washington demanding a share in the war and peacemaking; volunteers for the army would be swarming to the Capitol asking their representatives for preferment; and—most importantly—if the American government furnished the assistance it had promised to the Cubans, the Cuban Liberating Army might defeat the Spanish and the Cuban junta might declare independence. On 1 May, McKinley authorized a full-scale invasion with fifty thousand troops. The political needs of the moment thus overrode the needs of the army. Reporters quoted McKinley as saying that "God made the climate." He ordered the army south regardless of health hazards.[32]

There was nothing for Major Wagner to do now but close the MID office and follow the army into the field. He returned most of the MID officers to their regular regiments to train in Florida or detailed them to other crucial duties. He himself left for Tampa to establish a bureau of information composed of spies and scouts to gather intelligence, leaving a lone lieutenant in Washington to guard MID files.

The political needs of the civilians left the army in chaos. Not only was the army unprepared to invade and occupy a tropical country, its generals were unwilling to command it. Secretary of War Alger asked Gen. Wesley Merritt to head the Cuban expedition, but he declined because he thought it too unimportant. Alger then ordered Cmdg. Gen. Nelson A. Miles to take personal command and invade Cuba at once. Miles refused and got McKinley to cancel the order. The secretary of war finally assigned the aged and ailing Civil War veteran Gen. William R.

Shafter to head an expedition of twelve thousand men because his was the only group partially ready for combat. Finally, on 7 June, McKinley ordered Shafter to leave for Cuba at once.

Rowan, meanwhile, had returned to Tampa the second week in May to report to Major Wagner. There, amid disorder and frustration, the regular officers were attempting to coordinate the departure of eighteen thousand men on thirty troop ships. Rowan was the first American officer to return from Cuba and, given the rising tide of criticism the army was encountering from its own men as well as from the volunteers, it is not surprising that Wagner made the most of it, calling Rowan's trip one of the most gallant and brilliant exploits in military history. Rowan told reporters that García had eight thousand men under arms and could raise twenty thousand more if supplied with arms and ammunition. "One Cuban in the bush is equal to two Spaniards," he quipped to reporters. As for himself, he would only say modestly: "I was ordered to go and I went."[33]

When Rowan arrived in Washington, Adj. Gen. Henry Corbin was waiting for him. Corbin threatened to court-martial Rowan for revealing his activities to reporters, and one of the first things the new hero had to do was to make a sworn statement concerning his relation with Roberts and the reporters in Jamaica. Rowan recounted his meetings with Roberts but swore that he was not responsible for the notices that had gone out to the English and American newspapers and that he had not talked to any other newspaper correspondents in Jamaica. The statement apparently convinced the adjutant general and General Miles, for after a copy of Rowan's sworn deposition had gone to Secretary of War Alger, General Miles announced that he was recommending Rowan for a promotion for performing "a perilous undertaking" with "heroism and cool daring." Miles also recommended Rowan for a promotion to lieutenant colonel in the Immunes, a special force of men believed to be immune to yellow fever, organized into four black and six white regiments, all with white officers. Then Miles, who had decided that the safest place for his troops to attack was Puerto Rico, took Rowan along to conduct intelligence during the invasion there. When Rowan returned in July, he posed for Frances Johnston, the well-known Washington photographer, in a trim, dark suit with a rose in the lapel, and in August *McClure's Magazine* published his account.[34]

Rowan identified his guides only as "unknown friends" in his article. "My companions," he said, "were filibusters and I was a spy." Despite Rowan's attempts to deemphasize the role of the Cubans in the article, his own adventures seemed so remote from the war that the editor felt constrained to remind readers of the dangers of a "dispatch carrier" in enemy territory. Late in October, Rowan again posed for a photograph, this time attired in a crisp linen uniform with a dapper straw hat. He told reporters that he thought the Cubans would want to become part of the United States and wanted only to be free to try their hand at self-government for a limited period from a mere "sentimental" standpoint. The war had produced few heroes. It appeared to be anything but the developer of courage that Stephen Crane had portrayed in *The Red Badge of Courage* just three years before. Thousands of soldiers were returning to the United States with yellow fever and malaria and dying in camps of typhoid. The elevation of the officer spy who had glided so effortlessly through Cuba was understandable.[35]

Early in 1899, Rowan received his final canonization when Elbert Hubbard published "A Message for García." Hubbard, a retired business executive who had made a comfortable fortune as a soap company executive before turning to the writing and publishing of popular history, presented the public with a story sufficiently vague and rhetorical to elevate the officer spy to a new status in popular literature. While attempting at Harvard to finish an education delayed by business activities, Hubbard had conceived of a type of social history of the United States that would emphasize the role of common people rather than fighters, warriors, and politicians in changing history. Rowan fit nicely into this new concept of history for he had not been a general or even a fighting man but someone who the public believed had performed an essential and normally unpraised act of heroism. In March 1899, Hubbard published a glib account of how Lieutenant Rowan had strapped a dispatch case across his breast, landed in Cuba in an open boat, disappeared into the jungle, and three weeks later emerged on the other side of the island to deliver a message to General García. Hubbard praised Rowan for following orders without questioning them. Fourteen years later, Hubbard attributed the idea for the essay to his sixteen-year-old son who, he said, had commented one evening at dinner that Rowan was the real hero of the Cuban war because he had gone alone and "done the thing"—carried the message to García. Hubbard claimed that 40 million copies of his essay had been published by that time. Allowing for some exaggeration, it is probable that he published over one hundred thousand copies. Ironically, Rowan's growing fame rested on the desire of many businesspeople to increase worker loyalty, initiative, and thoroughness, for Hubbard had emphasized submission to authority in his essay. Businesses reprinted and distributed copies of Hubbard's essay free or for a nominal price. The New York Central Railroad alone printed and distributed at least four hundred thousand.[36]

Thus the old picaresque hero of adventure was transformed into an archetypal officer spy operating in response to absolute authority. The officer spy image, of course, contradicted both the older image of the civilian spy and the military hero who achieved greatness in battle. It is not surprising that Stephen Crane was one of the first to recognize the significance of the new officer spy image that Hubbard had created. Hubbard had previously published several of Crane's stories, and when Crane read "A Message for García," he wrote to Hubbard in disgust that Rowan had not done anything worthy at all, yet had received praise for a feat that "about forty newspaper correspondents had already performed at the usual price of fifty dollars a week and expenses." Crane said he had met Rowan in Cuba, going about Havana in a yachting cap, and that he was "personally a chump." He warned Hubbard not to "monkey" with national heroes.[37]

Despite the popularity of the new officer spy, the War Department was reluctant to claim Rowan as their own hero after the end of the war. When Wagner published his revised edition of *The Service of Security and Information* in 1903, the official handbook for army officers, he did not use Rowan as an example of the modern use of army officers as spies. Instead he mentioned Whitney. Wagner did, however, denounce the use of civilian spies and assert that "other things being equal the commander will be victorious who has the best secret service." A major corner in the ideology of intelligence had thus been turned. The Military Information Division could now say publicly and with confidence that their own professionally trained secret agents were superior to civilians. And MID could say it, apparently, without the old fear than an officer engaged in espionage would be defined as ungentlemanly.[38]

Wagner's comments appeared to apply only to wartime. Questions lingered within the army about the ethics of peacetime espionage. In 1902, the army awarded a silver medal to a young officer named T. Bentley Mott for his defense of peacetime intelligence gathering. Mott was the first officer to present a systematic defense of peacetime espionage and to propose a permanent peacetime establishment based on the European model. Mott argued that the modest information establishment that had been recognized by Congress in 1902 with an appropriation of less than $7,000 be expanded to equal those of European countries. Assuming that the question of officers conducting espionage in wartime had been settled, he went on to argue that the spy and the employer of spies should be honored in time of peace as well as in time of war. Responsible men of honor had to do things as individuals that they would find abominable in time of peace because the safety of the nation and war preparedness was such a grave trust. Mott proceeded from a rather simple metaphor about the need to fight the devil with his own weapons to the rather surprising conclusion that officers could be used as espionage agents in peacetime without congressional approval. "The nation seemed to have a natural repugnance for spies," Mott admitted, therefore Congress was not likely to appropriate money without regular methods of auditing. To borrow Secret Service agents would require the cooperation of other members of the cabinet. Therefore, the War Department should use officers as agents or spies without the approval of Congress. Twenty agents would make the United States the equal of France, Germany, and Russia, he advised. Consuls and military attachés were inadequate; surplus officers and former officers must be sent abroad on special missions to collect the latest foreign ideas for dissemination to the army.[39]

The new secretary of war, Elihu Root, did not follow Mott's suggestions immediately, but he did place MID under the War College Division when he reorganized the army in 1903, bringing it more in line with advanced European general staff organizations. Congress's reluctance to appropriate money for espionage did not change—it gave MID only $10,000 in 1903 and refused to increase its official duties. Although Root did send officers to foreign countries as observers, he did not send spies, nor did any other secretary of war do so before 1914.

The War Department did not even seem anxious to exploit the popular support for Rowan or to provide any further publicity for him once the war with Spain was over. When someone wrote to the War Department in January 1905 to ask about the record of Rowan's message to García, a note penciled on the letter for reply said that the message was probably a confidential transaction, if it had occurred at all. Another penciled note added that Rowan had arranged with García for the cooperation of the Cuban forces with the American army, but that there was no documentation. In 1911, when Sen. Clarence Weyland Watson of West Virginia introduced a bill in the Senate to erect a statue at the War College to commemorate Rowan, Secretary of War Henry Stimson curtly replied that such a thing was not possible—statues were reserved only for great and dead generals, foreign or domestic. The War Department showed no interest in 1915 when D. W. Griffith filmed a five-reel feature film based on the article "A Message for García."[40]

The reluctance of the War Department to add to Rowan's fame may have been due, in part, to Rowan's undistinguished military career after the war. Rowan apparently was a good officer under fire, for he was awarded a medal for an engagement in Cebu in the Philippines in February 1900, but he found it increasingly difficult to get along with his fellow officers. Rowan had been a competent, dutiful, and subordinate information officer between 1893 and 1898, much as Hubbard had portrayed him. Soon after arriving for duty in the Philippines, however, Rowan became involved in a violent altercation with a fellow officer, called him a "son of a bitch" and a "liar," and refused to apologize until threatened with court-martial proceedings for conduct unbecoming an officer. After ten months of angry controversy, Rowan finally apologized and the matter was closed.[41]

Within two months, a private lodged new complaints charging that, among other things, Rowan had struck him and ordered the shooting of a pregnant Filipino woman. This time Rowan's commanding officer supported Rowan and assured the War Department that complaints arose only because Rowan was a stern taskmaster. Rowan's trouble with the private was soon forgotten, and he was assigned to become professor of military science and tactics at Kansas State Agricultural College, then one of the main university centers for military training.

In Kansas, Rowan's two conflicts in the Philippines began to assume part of a larger pattern that pointed to a problem of alcoholism. Rowan had married a Kansas woman in 1877 and had at least one daughter when he left for Cuba. Whether his wife died or left him is not clear, but Kansas apparently put an additional personal strain on Rowan. In August 1903, the president of the college wrote to the adjutant general that Rowan had become the center of controversy. Kansas was one of the areas swept by the fires of the great crusade against alcohol in the late nineteenth century, and the Woman's Christian Temperance Union detected Rowan as a drinker rather early in his career in Kansas. In May he was showing up on campus drunk and going on four- and five-day binges. The Woman's Christian Temperance Union asked President Theodore Roosevelt to investigate. Following the investigation, Rowan was relieved of duty and sent to Vancouver Barracks, Washington. Rowan's problems did not disappear after he arrived at Vancouver Barracks. The next year a report indicated that he still had "intemperate habits," that he was not performing his job, and that he was taking extended leaves. In 1904, Rowan married again and in 1905, now a major, he returned to the Philippines for two years. The army, in reviewing Rowan when he came up for promotion, gave him every benefit of doubt, encouraged and counseled reform, and finally gave him a chance to end his career with dignity. Rowan retired in 1909 as a major.

That was all forgotten in the aftermath of World War I when the army very much wanted to confirm the importance of officer spies. The way was now clear for the final flourishing of the officer spy ideology. In 1923, the year after the aging Rowan received the Distinguished Service Cross, he published the pamphlet, "How I Carried the Message to García." He claimed a circulation of 100 million copies.

Thus Rowan became the outward public symbol of an internal structural change. During the years from 1877 to 1923, the army committed itself to peacetime espionage and to the use of regular army officers to gather intelligence in peace as well as war. But that commitment came slowly and was based on the army's experiences in a series of colonial wars, first in Cuba and then in the Philippines.

CHAPTER FOUR

Spanish Spies and Cuban Insurgents

he ambivalence of the War Department about its first officer spy hero before World War I reflected the ambivalence of the American government and people. Over a century of debate about the role of the army in the re-public had left an ambiguous heritage. Should America join European nations in the development of large standing modern armies? Should the government develop the capacity to spy on foreign countries and to defend itself against foreign espionage? Should the American government spy on its own citizens? If so, should that be only in wartime and only in zones of military action? If the government did spy, should the army be re-sponsible rather than civilians? All these questions would be asked during the war that the United States entered with Spain in 1898. The presence of Cuban insurgents and Spanish spies in the United States had forced the American government to deal with these abstract questions of policy in a specific context.

In spite of the fanfare surrounding Rowan's mission to Cuba, the ad-ministration had confused and changing goals regarding Cuba. Early newspaper reports emphasized cooperation between the Cubans and Americans. The War Department used Rowan and Whitney in a way that indicated officers also regarded the Cubans as allies. On 2 June General Miles sent a message to García, probably a written one this time, asking him to maintain a force near Santiago and to signal the army and navy on their arrival. He asked the Cubans to harass Spanish troops to prevent reinforcement of the garrison. Major Wagner, meanwhile, joined General Shafter in Tampa, and then left on the first ship for Cuba. After waiting offshore for a week for word of the Spanish fleet and hearing that it was safely bottled up in the Santiago harbor, the expedition finally headed for Santiago. To many Americans, it certainly seemed that the United States was entering the Spanish-Cuban war to help liberate the island.

It also appeared that way to many Cubans. García hoped to receive arms and ammunition from the Americans, to obtain a military victory, and then go west to join Gómez. The American army, for the most part, accepted García's plan of disembarkation, but as soon as the Americans were safely on the beach, they began to quarrel with the Cubans. In less than a month the Spaniards had surrendered Santiago to the Americans who then shouldered aside the Cuban Liberating Army (CLA). García was not allowed to enter Santiago. Shafter, on orders from McKinley, refused any control to Cubans, censored Cuban newspapers that advocated self-government, allowed the Spanish officials to remain in place where possible, and had the mayor of Santiago resume control. Even with these precautions, by the time Spain and the United States signed an armistice on 12 August, Cubans controlled much of the island.[1]

Congress, meanwhile, had adjourned, and Washington was quiet. Any support that might have come for Cubans from Congress had disappeared. The War Department sent a trusted Nebraskan, Charles E. Magoon, to New York to negotiate with the Cuban junta. Quesada, one of the leaders of the junta, had asked the War Department to order the customhouse at Key West to clear two schooners to take provisions to Gómez. It seems probable that the War Department halted these supplies as soon as the armistice was signed, since the Cuban leader Palma asked Magoon for ships to communicate with the Cuban forces and for assistance in sending food and supplies. After several telephone conversations with the White House, Magoon reluctantly agreed to allow Palma to accept the armistice in his official capacity as Cuban minister to the United States on condition that Palma ask the CLA to suspend hostilities. Just what arrangements for food and supplies were made is not clear from the documents, but Palma signed a public statement that he had confidence in the good intentions of the government and "in the satisfactory outcome of the struggle for the independence of Cuba which is now assured."[2]

The lack of planning for occupation was also reflected in the War Department's minimal foreign intelligence effort. In part, the effort remained small because of the assumption at the beginning of the war that the Cubans were allies who would provide the principal information needed for the army.

Symbolic of that cooperation was the distribution by MID of three new cipher machines the War Department had ordered that spring. These ciphographs, part of the first U.S. intelligence technology, were attachments for typewriters that transformed messages into incomprehensible cipher. Army experts had opposed the new technology—perhaps because it would put skillful experts out of work—but the civilian secretary of war was delighted with their convenience. The Military Information Division kept one machine in Tampa at MID headquarters, sent the second to the Cubans, and the third to Major Wagner in Santiago. Wagner returned to the United States almost immediately because of illness, leaving the army to function without any coordinated intelligence in the field. It arranged with each separate column to employ its own secret service men and assigned MID officers to other duties. The Signal Corps, whose task was to investigate the fraud and theft of government property, acted as the main link between the field operations and Washington. On 10 July the Tampa MID office gave its remaining funds to the Signal Corps censor in Tampa. The activities of MID headquarters indicate an expectation that the Cubans would be central to intelligence work in Cuba. Capt. W. S. Scott, who took charge of MID in Tampa, spent most of his meager allotment to hire a ship that sailed under the joint command of an army lieutenant and a Cuban to take supplies to General Gómez. These supplies included everything from Springfield rifles to shells, corn meal, mules, blankets, and bugles. Then Scott hired a civilian named Somerford for one hundred dollars to go to Cuba to ascertain conditions and to communicate with Gómez. Somerford returned with a letter from Gómez for the secretary of war, then sailed again for Cuba with a second joint force of Cubans and American regulars with arms, ammunition, and food for the insurgents.[3]

In Puerto Rico, where the United States planned permanent occupation, the army also used civilian spies. The Secret Service sent one man to Puerto Rico to investigate counterfeiting and to establish a permanent agency there. A record of five civilians hired in Puerto Rico also remains. The first entry of this quaint document reads: "Services as Spy, Visiting Various Small Towns and San Juan Puerto Rico, July 31 to August 5, Nepomaceno Cordoba, $25.00." Two other men with Spanish surnames performed similar "spy" work, and one German was employed as a "detective." Scott neatly tallied $127.00 spent on these missions.[4]

Although American foreign espionage remained almost nonexistent in the Spanish-American War, domestic counterespionage was more popular and more visible. Public discussion of and enthusiasm for counterespionage grew during the 1890s. Most European countries accepted military attachés as "official spies," but the secret espionage networks that foreign officers might develop seemed to constitute a growing concern of governments and of the press. The Dreyfus affair in France created international interest in espionage when the French government arrested and court-martialed Capt. Alfred Dreyfus, a French general staff officer, for passing official secrets to the Germans. Public pressure forced the government to reopen the Dreyfus case in 1898, and Dreyfus was proved to be the innocent scapegoat for a group of highly placed German spies. Such peacetime espionage activities inevitably led to heightened fears of spies when two countries went to war.

Popular interest in America over French and German espionage slowly extended to concern over Spanish spies. The Spanish apparently were not interested in American military secrets but rather in keeping Cuban revolutionaries under surveillance. Newspaper accounts of the time often mentioned the activities of Pinkerton detectives in connection with the attempts of Spanish officials to stop filibustering expeditions, and the Pinkerton superintendent in Philadelphia offered to turn over the Spanish cipher code to the War Department after war was declared. The only internal security measure taken by the army seems to have been a caution from Secretary of War Alger to commandants at various forts throughout the country to keep watch for Spanish spies. Newspapers promised that in case of war, any spies caught would be executed.[5]

Once the United States declared war in April 1898, the familiar "rage militaire"—the reaction that later intelligence experts would identify as the "surge"—began. This reaction was a mounting tide of accusations by Americans against other residents, both citizen and alien, of being spies for the newly declared enemy. These agents of an evil enemy government, "bad spies," would penetrate the internal defenses of the country, thus attacking it from within, and bring about military defeat by sending information to the enemy. Following this first "surge," government agencies and citizens alike competed in their efforts to find spies. Inevitably they found them, then publicly claimed the nation's gratitude for saving the body politic from disaster. This internal security ritual occurred again in both world wars and formed the context within which much wartime internal security policy was formulated by the executive and Congress.

In the war with Spain, Congress declared war, approved a large national defense appropriation for McKinley, and then adjourned. Thus the

executive had complete freedom to establish its own internal security policies. McKinley did not invoke the 1798 Alien Enemies Act to arrest any
Spaniards among the approximately twenty thousand living in the United
States, nor did he issue a proclamation on the status of Spaniards. According to a 1795 treaty with Spain, Spanish subjects had one year to
remove their goods and depart, but they had implied permission to remain
during that time without restrictions if they were not chargeable with actual hostility or crimes against public safety.[6]

Considering the insignificant role of army intelligence on the war
front, it is surprising how concerned the administration was over Spanish
spies on the home front and the considerable internal security activity that
occurred. The surge against Spanish spies began early in April as the
government engaged in active war preparations. It surfaced around the
Spanish communities of Florida, Louisiana, New York, and the south-
western states of Arizona and Colorado. A dark complexion or Spanish
speech could trigger complaints to federal officials about suspected spies
but so too could Catholics who might be "Spanish sympathizers." One
Nebraskan accused Catholics of donating cash to the Spanish war efforts.
An Iowan reported that many local citizens were in sympathy with Spain
and that a law was needed "to take care of such curs." From Denver came
complaints about Mexicans, Spaniards, and "half-breeds" suspected of
sympathy with Spain; from New Orleans, that Spanish cigar-makers were
collecting money; from Phoenix came denunciations of "hot head Mexicans! Spanish sympathizers and the renegades who are ever alert to ran-
sack and plunder." Other concerned citizens reported waiters, students,
and Pinkertons as being in the pay of the Spanish. One reported a suspicious carrier pigeon.[7]

Newspapers began to report spy suspects in late April. A doctor in
Atlanta said that two Spanish spies were using Negroes as fronts to blow
up bridges and troop trains in the South; a New Orleans man was arrested
as a spy for having films and maps of the government works at Port Eads.
The post office encouraged the scare by announcing it had intercepted a
letter from Santa Clara, California, with information on western coastal
defenses. These reports came from the *New York Times*; each local newspaper carried its own versions of spy activities. The *New York Times* continued to report the activities of spies in May. One had felled a sentinel
in Atlanta; another had been lynched at Fort Smith, Arkansas; and three
Spanish spies had attempted to blow up a fortification in Key West.[8]

Americans organized against the threat of spies. In New Orleans the
engineer corps formed a defense committee to defend approaches to the

city and port. Arizona towns and mining camps organized committees of safety. The deputy collector from Phoenix reported that two troops of soldiers were patrolling borders west from Nogales. A Chicago citizen asked that detectives be appointed at power mills and the mail service and in all ranks of the military and that all be educated, staunch Protestants. Another warned that the country was infested with Spanish spies and that the government should simply offer a five-hundred-dollar reward for their detection, capture, and conviction. Later in May newspapers warned that a Secret Service agent had stolen a list of Spanish spies from the Spanish minister in Montreal and that the New York–based Cuban junta had information about a Spanish spy system being directed from Canada.[9]

The government official responsible for these sensational spy charges was the chief of the Secret Service of the Treasury Department, John E. Wilkie. The Treasury Department had been only peripherally involved in the prewar search for violations of neutrality laws. Once war was declared, however, the administration ordered all federal officials to turn over their spy accusation letters to Wilkie. A former city editor of the *Chicago Tribune,* Wilkie had joined the Treasury Department in 1897 on the recommendation of Assistant Secretary of the Treasury Frank A. Vanderlip, who had worked under Wilkie before his own political ascent within the McKinley administration. Wilkie entered the new post with the announced enthusiasm of a reformer, moving into the Secret Service offices on the top floor of the Treasury building with a pledge to eradicate the use of "police methods" among Secret Service agents—use of the third degree, stool-pigeons, informants, and arrests with insufficient evidence. He installed a telegraph in his second floor study at home and began to cram the study with criminal relics: counterfeiting paraphernalia, bogus money, derringers, muzzle-loading flintlocks, and "sinister" knives.[10]

Wilkie took up chasing suspected Spanish spies with considerable enthusiasm and with little regard for the legal standards he had enunciated. His first concern was the Spanish Naval Attaché Ramón Carranza, who went to Canada upon declaration of war to recruit men from neutral countries to collect military information. Using some of his modest five-thousand-dollar prewar appropriation illegally, Wilkie hired agents to follow Carranza to Canada. There agents kept Carranza under surveillance, posing as gas inspectors, insurance agents, and job hunters to gain entrance to his offices and intercept United States mail. Wilkie capped off rumors in June by publishing a letter purportedly stolen from Carranza.

The letter, translated from Spanish by Secret Service agents, disclosed an elaborate spy ring from which two spies had already been arrested. Then, Wilkie engineered the arrest of George Downing.

At midnight on 7 May, an army officer under orders from Assistant Secretary of War George Meiklejohn arrested Downing, a thirty-three-year-old British-American. The War Department charged that Downing, formerly a yeoman on the cruiser *Brooklyn,* had sent naval information to the Spanish consulate in Montreal. The army held Downing in the Washington, D.C., arsenal under heavy guard, then, using evidence turned over to the War Department by Wilkie, the judge advocate prepared court-martial charges against Downing under the forty-sixth article of war. According to this article, being a spy and giving intelligence to the enemy, and "lurking or acting as a spy" on or about "posts, fortifications, quarters, or encampments" was an offense triable by court-martial. If convicted, the penalty was death. The attorney general immediately protested to the secretary of war that Downing was clearly not within military jurisdiction and therefore must be tried by a civilian court. While the two cabinet members debated this "puzzling point of law," Downing hanged himself.[11]

The Downing episode forced McKinley to take his first step in shaping an internal security policy. Three days after Downing's arrest, McKinley ordered Assistant Secretary of War Meiklejohn to take charge of all military "secret service" work during the war and put Wilkie and his entire corps of agents under his control. Apparently, McKinley was following Civil War precedent in charging the War Department with all wartime internal security responsibilities. He was also, no doubt, ensuring that Wilkie and the Secret Service would be under the control of his trusted friend, Meiklejohn.

Meiklejohn had not been McKinley's first choice for assistant secretary of war. McKinley wanted a soldier as assistant secretary, but the first two military men he asked had refused. Meiklejohn was a Wisconsin farm son and Iowa school teacher who had obtained a law degree at the University of Michigan and practiced law in Lincoln, Nebraska. Then he served as congressman from Nebraska without achieving national fame. He had pleased his Midwestern constituents by introducing a bill to prohibit the sale of intoxicants to Indians and by supporting the restriction of immigration. Meiklejohn had a way with patronage. Loyal friends in Nebraska, among them young John Pershing, assured McKinley that as a civilian Meiklejohn would be a good balance to military men in the department. Pershing had already picked out his favorite positions in the

War Department and sent Meiklejohn a list of them in precise order of preference. Meiklejohn had an enormous capacity for paperwork and often remained at his office from 9 A.M. to midnight supervising the quartermaster, commissary, and ordnance bureaus, as well as internal security matters, and maintained a huge correspondence on business and patronage matters. Meiklejohn claimed he had no jobs to dispense, but he often lent a sympathetic ear to complaining Nebraskans and kept his political fences well mended through key supporters in Lincoln. He also kept watch for McKinley on fellow Nebraskan William Jennings Bryan.[12]

Once Meiklejohn had taken over internal security matters for McKinley, the War Department publicly announced that it would investigate all letters received about suspected spies and keep strict surveillance over every person suspected of being connected with the Spanish government or furnishing it with material detrimental to the United States. McKinley allotted fifty thousand dollars from national defense funds to the investigation of persons suspected of extending aid to Spain.[13]

While the responsibility for internal security policies rested officially with the War Department, the Secret Service conducted the investigations because the army had no trained investigators. Meiklejohn refused to commission any officers as special investigators, merely ordering commanders to take measures to determine the loyalty of their men and to eliminate Spanish "emissaries or sympathizers" from their ranks. The records show that army surveillance in Tampa was conducted by two private detectives who received forty-five dollars for several days' work. Since Meiklejohn had previously made inquiries to the Pinkertons to hire two "first-class" detectives, they may have been from that company. It is possible that these two men were hired as independent investigators, thus circumventing the Pinkerton law of 1894.[14]

Newspapers reported that Meiklejohn turned down offers of assistance from the Pinkerton brothers. William Pinkerton, nevertheless, appeared in Washington where he told reporters that he was on good terms with Chief Wilkie. Soon after Pinkerton's appearance in Washington, Wilkie developed an "auxiliary" force of Spanish-speaking agents, whom he paid four dollars a day plus traveling and living expenses. Pinkerton at that time charged six dollars a day for his detectives, but he may have given the government special rates. Wilkie spent more than seven thousand dollars in the first six weeks of his spy-catching activities. In his top floor offices, Wilkie set up a large map of the United States posted with numbered flags attached to steel pins for operatives in the field who reported daily in letters addressed to "John Ehlen." Suspects included both officers and civilians, and agents had a free rein in devising their tactics. One used his wife to entrap suspects. Wilkie's son later estimated at least six hundred persons were put under surveillance during the war. There is no discussion in extant Secret Service documents of the Pinkerton law, and the records show no direct evidence of its violation. As with the War Department, however, agents may simply have been hired as individuals, thus circumventing the law.[15]

The new policy settled control of the Secret Service but not the limits on War Department powers. The Downing case occurred before Meiklejohn officially took charge of internal security, but the Montesi case, which followed his assumption of responsibility, indicated that the War Department considered it had special war powers to arrest suspected spies even if they were not near a military reservation. The arrest of Edward Montesi led to an explicit statement by Meiklejohn about his power in internal security.

Edward Montesi, an Italian immigrant, was reported to postal inspectors to be taking letters to Spain. Wilkie received the complaint, sent an agent to the United States attorney in New York to check the postal law, then dutifully requested an army officer make the arrest. After Meiklejohn wired his approval, the Secret Service agent, a postal inspector, and three army men went out to the steamer that Montesi had already boarded to search his luggage. The search turned up two letters to Spain with nothing suspicious in them. Undeterred, the officer arrested Montesi and held him without charges under military guard on Governor's Island. Meiklejohn ordered his release two days later. When queried by the general at Governor's Island about a permanent policy on similar arrests, Meiklejohn replied there was no permanent policy but that his orders were sufficient authority for arrest and detention of civilians without warrant or other process of law. Meiklejohn ordered the arrest of at least one more suspected spy later in June.[16]

The army confined an additional eight men arrested in Florida by civilian authorities on espionage charges during the summer of 1898. Of the eight men, two were English, one Canadian, one a former Spanish naval officer, and three were poor Spanish fishermen. One Englishman died in prison of typhoid; the second was released because the commanding general believed him to be insane; the Spanish naval officer was held as a prisoner of war. Wilkie had suggested the Canadian might be induced to confess if subjected to "a good hard sweating," but MID officer Captain Scott believed him to be innocent, and there is no evidence that Wilkie's advice was taken. Two of the Spanish fishermen were arrested by the chief of police of Tybee Island for reasons unclear from the records. The third, who had agreed to act as an interpreter was, according to his later deposition, arrested when he said he did not believe the men to be spies. The adjutant general released the seven men at the end of the war.[17]

The emergency force of the Secret Service continued until the signing of the peace protocol in early 1899, then the special employees were released as rapidly as possible. The total amount charged to the national defense during the fiscal year 1898–99 was, as Chief Wilkie reported to the president, precisely $18,890.28. The War Department used very little of the fifty thousand dollars but kept the rest for future peacetime needs. It made no public report on surveillance activities.[18]

After the war, intelligence gathering continued decentralized and uncoordinated. During September, the administration sent a number of civilian agents to Cuba to determine the sentiments of the Cubans. The secretary of war asked William Davis, an interpreter and translator with the military commission at Havana, for a report on the sentiments and aspirations of different groups in Cuba. President McKinley sent the English-born journalist Robert P. Porter to make a study of currency and tariffs. The War Department also sent Lieutenant Rowan back to Cuba to make an inspection to ascertain which portions of the island were the most important for military purposes.

None of the reports was reassuring. Davis found that the Cuban rebels were claiming a victory that entitled them to control the destinies of the island. They resented any act of the United States to curtail this authority. Two other groups, said Davis, the Spaniards and those he termed the "order-loving Cubans" who represented the propertied class, accepted the situation, were obedient to the United States, and felt that if the rebels took over the government, it would mean the inevitable ruin and destruction of the island's material interests. Davis considered the masses either skillfully ambitious, dishonest, indolent, ignorant, or corrupt. He recommended a good strong government and effective reconciliation between the Spanish and Cubans. He asked that persons without partiality toward either group be appointed. Porter made a number of reports to McKinley that winter and later published a book called *Industrial Cuba,* in which he argued that it should be united with the United States. Rowan confirmed in a public interview later in October that the Cubans were still in arms.[19]

On the basis of these reports, the administration began negotiations to disband the CLA. The Cuban provisional government had already been replaced by the Cuban Assembly, which now represented the CLA. The revolutionary party, dominated by the generals and the Cuban junta, still functioned. Thus, the CLA was a potent and organized political power. In fall 1898, a Cuban delegation traveled to Washington to discuss the still uncertain future of Cuba with McKinley and with junta leaders. The administration received the delegation but would not recognize it, agreeing only to discuss disbanding the Cuban army. McKinley emphasized in his message to Congress in early December that there was no time limit on United States occupation and that the United States would withdraw only after "complete tranquility" and a "stable government" had been restored. On 10 December the United States formally signed a peace treaty with Spain. In spite of strong statements about Cuban independence, General Gómez soon counseled Cubans to accept an offer of $3 million from unspent defense appropriations to pay Cuban soldiers.[20]

The army set about its task of governing Cuba. Revolutionary patriotic committees in Havana planned in February to celebrate the removal of Spanish troops, but the new military governor Gen. John R. Brooke ordered that no Cuban soldiers enter Havana. The day the Treaty of Paris was ratified making Cuba a protectorate of the United States, 6 February 1899, passed quietly. By March the administration had increased its army of occupation from twenty-four thousand to forty-five thousand troops while continuing to pressure General Gómez to muster out the Cuban army. The Cuban Assembly finally fired Gómez, and soon after dissolved itself. By the end of summer most of the CLA had been mustered out, and pacification of the civilian population began. In Santiago, Gen. Leonard Wood suppressed critical editorials, established a "rural guard" to put down agitators who opposed the presence of the American army, broke up strikes, and intimidated workers. Wood, who favored permanent occupation, minimized the opposition to U.S. occupation in his reports, while Brooke wrote privately to McKinley that the Cubans could not establish a stable government. The American army stayed on. The only protest movement of any importance came in November 1899, following rumors of the establishment of a civil government, which Cubans interpreted to mean permanent occupation. At first, the army established no regular military secret service apparatus in Cuba. The War Department continued to gather most of its intelligence from civilians or from military commanders. After 1898, there was almost no open opposition to American military occupation, and thus the army had no need to develop an extensive internal security mechanism.

The main concern of the administration in these first years of occupation seemed to be to guard against fraud in the Havana customhouse. When the young officer assigned as collector of customs for Cuba uncovered fraud, anti-imperialists were quick to use the fraud to launch an assault on army occupation. The customs officer replaced the guilty men, asked for special agents to investigate, and the War Department assigned an auditor to guard against future financial scandals. The army arrested only one private in Santiago on counterfeiting charges. A second soldier arrested on espionage charges was never court-martialed. The quick excision of the guilty men undercut opposition to the occupation. Counterinsurgency and counterespionage never had to be developed in Cuba during this first occupation.[21]

The administration was thus able to continue military rule unhampered. Although the second military administration, established by General Wood on 20 December 1899, must have drawn some opposition, Wood assured Washington that there was no serious disturbance. A greatly restricted franchise enabled the establishment of a pro-American government that agreed to give up independence and to give important concessions to the United States, including the right to intervene to maintain law and order. By 20 March 1902, Wood had decreed tranquility of the island restored; on 20 May military rule ended. This was not the republic Cubans had fought for, nor the absolute independence many Cubans had dreamed of, but there it was. The American army was at last gone, and Cubans could attempt to rebuild their divided and ravaged country.

Four years passed after the Americans withdrew from Cuba before the first revolt against the pro–United States government broke out. Almost immediately President Theodore Roosevelt approved the purchase of ammunition and asked his new chief of staff, Gen. J. Franklin Bell, a veteran of both the Indian and Philippine campaigns, for an estimate on the availability of troops. Within five days, Bell made his recommendation, warning Secretary of War William Howard Taft that the army was likely to run into a contest not to be settled by military strength and fighting quality alone. It was heart breaking, he wrote, to fight guerrilla wars. The army went forth with military ardor, "with all the pomp and panoply of war, to enthusiastically meet and conquer the enemy, only to discover it could find nothing to fight." General Bell suggested that Taft send officers to Cuba at once to collect information on the insurgents, on their homes, arms, suppliers, residence, and occupation if the United States intended to support the present Cuban government. To break the rebellion, he recommended a network of spies to get the names of "every individual secretly connected with their supply, information, and communication service." Bell thought that guerrilla warfare would call for a larger commitment than five thousand troops, perhaps even fifteen thousand. The report so alarmed Roosevelt that he approved the dispatch of two army officers to report on conditions in Cuba. Two veterans of Wood's military government left immediately.[22]

Notwithstanding the concern of both Roosevelt and Taft that they might have another war in Cuba, they agreed to dispatch warships to the islands when Cuban president Palma requested them. The State Department warned the American consul general in Havana, Frank Steinhart, that "immediate intervention" was out of the question. The ships and marines were there only to protect American lives and property. Nevertheless, news that the vessels were on their way stiffened President Palma's resolve. He extended martial law and refused all compromise. The American commander, ordered by the secretary of the navy to use his own discretion on landing sailors, promptly landed them. Roosevelt sent a tardy cable the next day ordering that sailors not be landed without his approval. The commander tried to round up the sailors, but his captain convinced him that he should leave the troops in the city overnight. While American troops occupied the city, the Cuban government regrouped its troops, distributed more arms, and continued to fortify the city. The next morning, the sailors marched back to their ship. By this time, both sides were asking for United States intervention.[23]

President Roosevelt dispatched three battleships, a cruiser, and a transport with a marine battalion. By 17 September two more marine battalions had been sent and plans for an eighteen-thousand-troop intervention were being finalized. Marines had already landed in Cuba when a peace mission under Secretary of War Taft and Assistant Secretary of State Robert Bacon arrived there. Taft and Bacon had been briefed by secret service operatives who had worked for Wood during the first intervention and by an aide to Wood before they left for Cuba. Military information officers reported that public opinion was against the Cuban government, especially in rural areas.[24]

By that time, the marines were already taking over the railroads, and Taft decided to keep Palma in power. Military agents investigated sources of funds of opposition to the government to find out if American business interests had financed the revolt. Although they found no evidence of American financial support, Taft wanted immediate intervention. Roosevelt, on the other hand, stalled because he wanted the American people to be convinced of the absolute necessity for intervention. On 29 September, Palma resigned, and the United States assumed political control with Taft as governor and Chief of Staff General Bell in command.[25]

With General Bell in charge, organization went forward quickly. Bell had information officers in Cuba compile roles of all the insurgents to include their names, homes, physical descriptions, and types and number of arms. Then he dispatched two officers from MID in Washington to Havana to set up an MID branch for the Army of Cuban Pacification (ACP) to be financed with twenty thousand dollars from the War Department's emergency fund that had been created in 1899. The MID organized twenty-six intelligence districts, one at each garrison outside Havana, with an information officer to collect and forward information. Officers supervised mapping, collected photographs and personality sketches, and wrote descriptions of towns and community systems. The MID provided an analysis of political conditions throughout Cuba for Provisional Governor Charles Magoon, who took over from Taft in October 1906. While this work went on undercover, Bell had Cuba mapped and this work publicized as a deterrent to rebels. The MID employed Cuban agents as well and was soon spending one thousand dollars a month.[26]

Civilians usually worked in harmony with the generals during this Cuban intervention. The administration played down the army's role, and generals worried about their status and authority, but once occupation had been achieved peacefully, officers talked of staying. Intelligence officers reported political unrest as the army extended what one historian has called its "benign paternalism." The reports of MID indicated that the army officers were horrified by the prospect of anarchy and violence from a revolt that never came.[27]

The administration attempted to disentangle itself from Cuba as soon as possible. During late 1906 and 1907, the movement for the annexation of Cuba grew among planters and businesspeople in Cuba who felt that the longer the army stayed, the better the chance for a protectorate. One way to get the army to stay was to encourage insecurity with small revolts. By February 1907 MID reports on revolts had helped heighten that sense of insecurity. Rumors kept MID officers running. Special investigations of arms usually turned out to have been started by planters and merchants who wanted annexation, but the fact that Cubans had not turned in their arms kept the possibility of armed resistance open. Seven dollars for each gun turned in was offered by MID and its staff posed as revolutionaries buying guns. As the sugar cane harvest began, MID concerns decreased. Still speculators often used rumors of revolt to cash in on scares, renting armed gangs to protect the fields from disgruntled workers.[28]

The MID continued to collect copies of political manifestos and to receive alarming reports from the secret police. Paramilitary organizations formed in the spring of 1907; a black movement began to call for broad-based social reform, complete reorganization of the economy, elimination of discrimination in the courts, and full political participation. Reports of revolt came from all areas of Cuba. The MID told the governor that plans for revolt had been set, arms cached, and a revolt scheduled. The day before the expected revolt, the government arrested seven men and charged them with conspiracy to revolt. The movement, whatever it was, collapsed. The next election, watched closely by MID, transferred power to men who supported the United States. The election satisfied President Roosevelt of the prospects for stability, and he announced the withdrawal of U.S. troops.

There remained the problem of exercising power after the United States withdrew the military. A first plan was to leave American advisers to the armed forces and to the government behind. Instead, General Bell ordered a study of the character of Cuba's political leaders and a report on who the best or the most suited men were to be "used by the Americans." The report of 16 November 1908 emphasized that a "good" public figure would be honest and resemble Porfirio Díaz, the dictator in Mexico. The list of potential collaborators had varied political pasts, but they all had in common that they could be counted on for support should the United States go back into Cuba.[29]

This 1908 report also contained the first detailed argument in support of the military surveillance of civilians. Capt. J. W. Furlong, the military information officer in Cuba, made the argument in "Notes on Field Service in Cuba," a survey of counterinsurgency tactics to be undertaken by the army. Furlong concluded that the success of Cuban rebels was based on their ability to organize juntas in towns, villages, and settlements, and to maintain communication links with insurgents through washerwomen. The insurgent army cut off supplies from the countryside to the villages; forced city people out into the country to join insurgents in order to live; established military farms; and helped peasants to cultivate the farms when not at war. The effectiveness of this organization led Furlong to conclude that revolutions grew because they were not quickly suppressed and that a revolution must be quickly and ruthlessly suppressed when small. Wars must be short, sharp, and decisive. He recommended a combination of relentless pursuit of rebels and, since there was no way to garrison the numerous villages, a reconcentration of villagers. The food supply in the country could then be diminished by confiscating or destroying it, and towns sealed against communication by watching the washer-women who went to the rivers and used the occasion to communicate with insurgents.[30]

According to Furlong, the job of the intelligence officer was crucial. Not only should he collect traditional military information, such as the location and movement of insurgent bands, but also the officer should identify those junta members who supported rebels and furnished them with information and supplies. These rebels could then be located, arrested, and pressured into forcing local bands to surrender. Officers should have a large secret service fund with which to buy information, send in all papers found on prisoners, question all prisoners ruthlessly, and use police methods with them, not allowing them to sleep until they had confessed. Then officers were to obtain the official roles of the rebels, the names of their officers, how many rebels there were, and the quantities of arms and ammunition. Intelligence officers also were to investigate the morale and conditions of insurgent bands. A single intelligence officer should collect information; administer the post office and secret service; collect reconnaissance information and forward maps and sketches; and serve as provost marshal and judge advocate.

This statement about the role of military intelligence officers in insurgency created a rationale for civilian surveillance. Furlong assumed that the Cubans were children politically, that they were dependent on a strong central government, and that the only way they knew how to resist was to organize an armed revolution. Furlong did not seem to realize that insurgency was the result of a deeply held political commitment to independence and that the solution must ultimately be a political one. Instead, it was to be an internal security solution executed by the military.

How could the army establish such a sophisticated internal security plan for Cuba in such a few short years? The major precedent came not from Cuba itself, for there had been no surveillance in the original occupation. Nor did it come from the United States where a relatively small internal security mechanism existed during the war. Instead it came from the experience of the army and MID in the Philippines. It was there that the army developed its first widespread internal security structures and its theories about surveillance.

CHAPTER FIVE

Filipino Revolutionaries

The surveillance of Filipinos—military and civilian—allowed the United States to maintain control of the Philippines with a small military force. Filipino opposition to American control drove the American government to adopt an internal security policy that kept civilians and their political activities permanently under surveillance by the military. For the Filipino, military surveillance helped spell defeat. For the American government, it signaled the beginning of a real fear of both foreign and domestic espionage.

In 1907, three years after America had officially ended the Philippine War and proclaimed its dominance over the Philippines, a wave of nationalism swept over the islands. Katipunan groups, which had organized much of the original opposition to Spanish rule among the Filipino peasants, began to spring up around Manila and to display their flags prominently. At one demonstration, a large Katipunan flag was carried at the head of the group, and a small American flag relegated to the rear. Outraged, the American colony in Manila met and demanded action. The Philippine government outlawed the use of the Katipunan flag and ordered its constabulary to suppress Katipunan societies. When Filipino dissidents turned to labor unions to vocalize their dissent, the government arrested leaders who demanded independence. In summing up the summer of unrest, Harry Bandholtz, the American army officer who headed the constabulary wrote: "At heart, all the Filipinos desire their independence."[1]

More than any other American official in the Philippines, Bandholtz was in a position to know. As chief of the constabulary, Bandholtz also controlled the main American internal security intelligence files, which gave him as much access to the Filipino "heart" as Americans would probably ever get. Bandholtz, who was born in Michigan and graduated from West Point in 1890, arrived in the Philippines in 1900 just as the Filipinos began to fight their new colonial masters. He served as governor of Tayabas when Filipinos abandoned open warfare for guerrilla wars to defend their newly formed republic. He became assistant chief of the constabulary after the rebels had acknowledged their defeat by the Americans and chief in 1907. He stayed as chief until 1913, one of the few American officers to remain for such a long tour of duty. That was fifteen years after the United States had gone to war against Spain and the Philippines.[2]

The Spanish, in the sixteenth century, took possession of the seven thousand islands that made up this Southeast Asian nation. They conquered the diverse peoples of the archipelago, Hispanized and Christianized them, and put down uprisings. Gradually, the Spanish developed Manila as a leading trade center of the Far East, sending "Manila galleons" out to become the prey of the English pirates. In the seventeenth century, northern Mexico and the Philippines were parallel frontiers of Spain, both unprofitable for the crown. In northern Mexico, the colonials were able to struggle to independence before being conquered by the Americans in 1845. The Spanish held on to their Asian frontier for another fifty years, against recurring uprisings and growing discontent.[3]

During the early nineteenth century, trade linked Asia and the United States; San Francisco imported much of its food from Hawaii. By the late nineteenth century there was much less contact and few Filipino immigrants came to the United States. Chinese, Japanese, and Asian Indians received an increasingly hostile reception from laborers along the West Coast. Western nativism and anti-Asian sentiment would have made Filipino immigrants unwelcome had they come to the Pacific shores. That they did not meant that there were no immigrants to provide information on the Philippines, and when Filipinos rebelled against Spain, they did not appeal to Americans for help.[4]

The growing Filipino opposition to Spanish rule in the last quarter of the nineteenth century was complex. Had late-nineteenth-century Americans been concerned—and few were before 1898—the politics of the Philippines would have seemed incomprehensible.

The Spanish imposed their control on groups of relatively autonomous kin-based cultures. Using kinship units as the basis for local government, the Spanish gradually consolidated their control at the top, allowing local elites to control the labor of the people at the bottom. Spaniards and Spanish control remained concentrated in Manila and a few provinces, while small detachments of Spanish troops with a Filipino militia commanded by Filipino officers put down local uprisings. Most of the Filipino troops were Pampangans, who remained loyal to the Spanish.[5]

The main cause of Filipino discontent stemmed from the economic development of the islands during the last two decades of the nineteenth century. The Philippines were primarily agricultural, based on rice-centered subsistence farming. With this economy, a second commercial export economy bloomed in the 1880s as ambitious entrepreneurs tapped the international market for sugar, hemp, tobacco, and coconuts. The commercial development forced subsistence farmers in some areas into unstable marginal positions as sharecroppers and wage laborers. Similar dislocations took place around the world as international agricultural trade began to feed the industrialization and urbanization of Western Europe and the United States. These economic changes produced severe social and political tensions in traditional subsistence-based cultures. In the Philippines, the areas around Manila were affected first and most. There, Catholic friars rented their large estates to agents who subleased them to peasants. Southern Luzon, just north of Manila and the heartland of the Tagalog people, became the birthplace of the insurrection.[6]

The first groups of Filipinos to respond to the changes were at the top rather than the bottom of the social scale. During the 1880s and early 1890s, a wealthy group gradually consolidated power on the islands. Called the *ilustrados,* this elite based its power on education, personal influence, and wealth. Within the ilustrados two groups supported reforms that would lead to home rule and considered themselves Filipinos. A less wealthy group, composed of urban clerks and provincial elite, was willing to lead an active revolt. They believed that the Spanish empire must be maintained but reformed if prosperity was to continue. A liberal, modern, free, and well-governed Filipino nation, preferably still tied to Spain but leaving the Filipinos in control, was their goal. Gradually, however, they came to believe the Spanish liberals to be incapable of reforming the empire and moved to support independence. In August 1896, the ilustrados led an armed revolt.[7]

The rebellion was fueled and organized from the bottom by the Katipunan societies. The *Katipuneros* were fired by the demands for reform by both the ilustrados from above and the peasants below. Katipunan men were middle-class rather than working class, many in the lower levels of commerce, who belonged to the masons and who were Hispanized. A few among them were the sons of the *principales,* rural landowners at the top of the old social and political order, who were losing their place. The Katipunan society spread quickly through the Manila hinterland. From an estimated three hundred at the beginning of 1896, it grew to thirty thousand within the next eight months. The Katipunan society supported the ilustrado ideology but combined it with a powerful grass-roots network. The Katipuneros preached spiritual equality but accepted unequal wealth. In August 1896, the Spanish authorities learned of the secret Katipuneros and their plans for rebellion. They swiftly arrested three hundred leaders and declared war in eight provinces. Within a month the Spanish had quelled the rebellion. Emilio Aguinaldo, the son of a lawyer and landowner and a local officeholder who had considerable local power, emerged as leader of this first rebellion. Aguinaldo agreed to go into voluntary exile in Hong Kong in return for money and reforms.[8]

Spain never completely paid the money and no reforms followed. The Filipinos formed a government in exile with Aguinaldo at its head, and in February 1898, he led another revolt. Meanwhile, he sought the United States as an ally. By this time, however, the events in Cuba and the United States had moved the United States toward war. When Thomas E. Dewey left Hong Kong in April 1898, Filipino officers went with him. Aguinaldo arrived soon after on an American naval ship under Dewey's command to take charge of Filipinos already in arms against Spain. At that time, Dewey was saying that the Filipinos were capable of self-government. President McKinley decided to occupy Manila after Dewey defeated the Spanish fleet on 1 May, but not until 26 May did the secretary of the navy warn Dewey not to make a "political alliance" with the Filipino revolutionaries. By that time Aguinaldo had assumed control of the revolution and believed the United States would recognize Philippine independence. On 12 June the Filipinos declared their independence from Spain.[9]

Just how much Gen. Wesley Merritt, the man McKinley chose to command the American forces in the Philippines, knew of this complex history is difficult to determine. By the end of May, Merritt had convinced

McKinley that he needed twenty thousand troops for his army of occupation and dispatched the first contingent of twenty-five hundred men. Merritt did not leave San Francisco until late June and arrived off the coast of Luzon on 25 July.[10]

The Military Information Division was totally unprepared for a war against Spain in the Philippines. Officers and volunteers knew a considerable amount about Cuba and the Cubans; they knew almost nothing about the Philippines and the Filipinos who rose up in revolt against colonial domination. There is no evidence in MID files that the army prepared in any way for a war in the Pacific. Although the navy planned a strike at the Philippine islands as early as 1897, the army had no war plans for the Philippines and MID had no maps. There were no secret missions to contact rebels or to scout the Spanish forces. Merritt expected little fighting. McKinley ordered Merritt to overcome those Spanish who remained, maintain order, protect the lives and property of foreigners, assert the authority of the United States, and establish a provisional military government.[11]

Only after mobilization plans had been formulated did Merritt begin to collect intelligence on the islands and plan the invasion. Officers based invasion plans primarily on consular reports and information from Admiral Dewey on Manila's garrison and terrain. The War Department had done so little advance preparation that it reportedly studied the invasion of California in 1845 as a guide. The MID hastily copied excerpts from the *Encyclopaedia Britannica* and classified them as confidential; gathered some information on flora, fauna, and trade statistics; and compiled a small, crude map. This was the total intelligence information given to Thomas Mott, Merritt's aide-de-camp, before he left for the West Coast with Merritt. General Merritt appointed Maj. J. Franklin Bell, a fifty-four-year-old veteran of the Indian wars in the West, to head his army's division of military information. Bell scoured bookstores purchasing maps and books.[12]

During the two months it took Merritt to reach the Philippines, momentous changes had taken place. Aguinaldo, with a Filipino army of thousands—some with arms supplied by Admiral Dewey—was leading the rebellion and had virtually surrounded Manila, where most of the Spanish had taken refuge. Ten thousand Filipino militiamen had deserted to the rebels, and they had captured or cut off most of the Spanish forts. By the end of June, Filipino troops held central Luzon, and the uprising had spread to the southern islands. Aguinaldo had established a civil government for the Philippine Republic at Malolos. Elections followed the liberation of the provinces. Merritt thus faced not one army but two when he arrived. Refusing to meet with Aguinaldo, Merritt maneuvered eighty-five hundred men into position around Manila. On the morning of 13 August, Merritt ordered his troops to attack and sent Aguinaldo an ultimatum not to try to move his troops into Manila. Major Bell, still with little more information than he had on leaving the United States, observed the battle from atop the walls of an old monastery.[13]

There was not much to see. The American army began a brief skirmish to the accompaniment of the Colorado divisional band playing "There'll Be a Hot Time in the Old town Tonight." The Spanish killed seventeen American enlisted men and ten officers before surrendering, but the Americans occupied Manila with only a feigned resistance from the Spanish. Two weeks later Merritt turned his command over to Gen. Elwell Otis and steamed out of Manila for San Francisco. Bell stayed in Manila, for the first time learning the full extent of the control of the new Malolos Republic and its army. By mid-September, republican forces held all of Luzon except Manila, Cavite, and a small portion of the province of Albay. In the suburbs of Manila, where rebels and American soldiers held nearby positions, tensions were growing.[14]

Even though the army of the Malolos Republic held most of the Philippines, in Washington President McKinley was planning to extend the control of Manila to occupation of the entire island of Luzon. McKinley did not discuss the policy publicly, but the postmaster general informed reporters that generals had told McKinley that they could not hold Manila without occupying the rest of Luzon. The first general to arrive had warned the War Department that the Filipinos were fierce fighters and that establishing an American government would probably bring conflict. Merritt, who was in the Philippines for less than a month, seems to have reassured Washington officials that there would be no effective resistance if the United States annexed the entire group of islands. By the time the United States had signed the Treaty of Paris in late October, the Malolos Republic had reorganized most of the provisional governments, selecting officials from within the old local elite. The problem, as with all new revolutionary governments, was to secure the continuing allegiance of those civilians who had supported it, to control the army, and to withstand any counterattack from the outside. A few days before Christmas 1898, McKinley ordered his secretary of war to extend the military government to all the islands. Otis thought the Malolos Republic would dissolve from internal weakness. McKinley thought that tact and kindness would convince the Filipinos to accept American sovereignty.[15]

If McKinley seems to have known relatively little about the Philippines, the American people knew less. The president imposed rigid censorship on news from the islands. The War Department regularly denied there were any problems in the islands, even after open warfare had begun. General Otis allowed only optimistic news to reach the public. The news blackout finally provoked a protest by correspondents, but McKinley continued to support rigid censorship. Even after the new secretary of war, Elihu Root, recalled Otis in April 1900, he continued to maintain that conditions were satisfactory in the Philippines. Reporters scurried for news from European capitals. Aguinaldo's agent in London angrily denounced General Merritt for calling Filipinos "children" who would loot and plunder if allowed to control the islands. "Filipinos will never again submit to the yoke of colonial government," he vowed; they would fight to the bitter end in defense of their freedom to choose a government.[16]

In the Philippines, Aguinaldo was conciliatory to General Otis at first. For example, when Otis ordered the occupation of Pandacan, a suburb of Manila, Aguinaldo ordered his troops to withdraw. Aguinaldo also entered into negotiations with Otis over the release of those Spanish clergy taken prisoners. Late in January, however, the administration ordered Otis to end all negotiations with Aguinaldo. On the evening of 4 February, a United States sentry killed a Filipino soldier, skirmishing followed, and Otis put his contingency plan for attack into operation. That day the Senate had ratified the Treaty of Paris, and the Philippines were transferred from Spain to the United States. The Philippine War had begun.[17]

American authorities attempted to give the American public the impression that the fighting was against irregular forces who had attacked American troops; "armed dogs," Dewey called them. McKinley officials emphasized that Otis was only "maintaining order." Some Americans were beginning to distrust their government. A letter to the War Department scoffed at the claim that the United States was only maintaining law and order. Our boys, wrote one mother, were being compelled to die in an unrighteous cause "slaughtering those whom we went to defend." "Maintaining order" was becoming increasingly difficult for the twenty thousand American troops in the Philippines.[18]

This was the context of the first attempts by Otis to establish an intelligence office in the islands in 1899. Soon after conflict began with the Filipinos, soldiers captured Filipino documents and sent them to Otis's headquarters. To translate the documents and track the enemy, Otis established a Bureau of Military Insurgent Records at the Spanish ordnance headquarters in Manila. From these documents, Otis selected evidence to send to the War Department of plots and uprisings and to defend the army against accusations by Filipinos that it was slaughtering women and children. The captured Filipino military documents purportedly ordered the extermination of all but Filipino families. The search for documents, from the beginning, had both a strategic and a political aim. The War Department released the documents to the press but continued to deny that it was having any trouble with Otis, with control of American troops, or that it had an organized rebellion on its hands.[19]

Behind the facade of order and optimism being maintained by the War Department was a growing realization that it did not know what was happening in the islands. The administration sent a commission to the Philippines in early 1899. When it arrived in March, a month after hostilities had begun, it set up its own spy system under a medical doctor, Frank S. Bourne, who had served on the staff of one of the generals. But the administration did not consider this spy system to be trustworthy, because neither Bourne nor civilians in Washington or the Philippines trusted the military command to provide accurate information. They were impatient at the slowness of Otis in defeating the Filipinos. They were worried about the next American election and how Americans would respond if the Filipinos continued to resist. In June, Assistant Secretary of War Meiklejohn asked a civilian agent, James West, to go to the islands and make a confidential investigation of conditions.[20]

The West report is important because it provided civilians with independent information on conditions in the islands. West reported to Meiklejohn that people in military circles were privately expressing grave doubts of a favorable outcome to the war against the Filipinos. Filipinos held territory only two and one-half to three miles outside of Manila. Towns would be taken, the rebels driven away, United States forces would vacate, and the rebels would then return. In some places, Filipinos held ground between American forces and railroads, supplies, mail lines, and reinforcements. These areas could be crossed only with armed escorts of several hundred men. At San Fernando, forty-two miles from Manila, Gen. Arthur MacArthur was surrounded except on the railroad line. West believed that the rebels had twelve to fifteen thousand men and were receiving daily reinforcements. Few officers were in the field, said West, more were safely in Manila where Otis was holding dancing parties and receptions regularly. Although Otis needed 30 to 50 doctors and 120 experienced nurses, he would not permit the medical staff to request them for fear of alarming the country. One battery at the front had 90 percent of the men on sick call, 7,000 soldiers were in hospitals, and the death rate was 4 a day. Volunteers were promising to denounce Otis when they returned to the States, and a Populist had already arrived in Manila to collect first-hand information on conditions. West urged that Otis, who was not in good health, be replaced before stronger opposition developed.[21]

Meiklejohn also had a less formal report from W. S. Jenkins, a civilian who had gone to the islands as a military administrator. Jenkins, a naturalized citizen from Glasgow, Scotland, and a friend of Meiklejohn's, complained of his dull, slow, routine office job, of the curfew that forbade visiting after 8:30 P.M., and of officers who treated civilian officials like enlisted men. Life under military law was anything but pleasant, and everyone would be thankful when it ended, Jenkins wrote Meiklejohn.[22]

Notwithstanding the pessimistic reports about American military rule, Filipinos too were encountering real difficulties by the fall of 1899. As it became evident that the Americans were not to be allies of the new Malolos Republic but intent on crushing its army, the Filipinos began to encounter problems from within. When Spanish colonial rule crumbled, many of the old elite—the ilustrados—supported the republic because they had no alternative. Now some who wanted reform rather than independence began to seek American protection. Others acted as informants for General Otis. Farther down the social ladder, Filipinos worried that the new republic was not controlling its army. Civilians protested against the army's interference in political affairs. As Americans occupied towns, the Filipinos took refuge in the countryside, and, finally, in November 1899, Aguinaldo no longer had enough troops or arms to sustain open war. He turned to guerrilla warfare. Like the Republican administration, Filipinos awaited the American elections.[23]

The hopes and fears of the opposing sides pivoted on how Americans would respond to the administration's Philippine policy. An anti-imperialist coalition that opposed the treaty with Spain crumbled when Congress ratified it, and many former opponents of occupation now considered the main question to be how the new territories should be ruled. Still, the inability of the military to control the islands totally soon gave rise to old arguments against standing armies. A new anti-administration movement formed around the question of military control of the Philippines. To undercut growing criticism, McKinley emphasized his commitment to early civilian control for the islands. He appointed a second civilian commission headed by William Howard Taft to negotiate with the Filipinos and to report on conditions in the islands. Military rule, the administration announced in February 1900, would be replaced with a civil government that would move toward civil rule everywhere as soon as the Filipinos "demonstrate their worthiness." Secretary of War Root announced in April that Otis would be replaced by General MacArthur. By that time, sixty thousand American troops were in the islands.[24]

Despite the administration's concern, Taft did not move quickly. He had planned to arrive on 2 May 1900, the same day that General MacArthur was to replace Otis as commanding general, but he did not leave San Francisco until April and then lingered in Tokyo where the Philippine commission was entertained by the emperor. It was 21 May before the *Hancock* stopped to coal at Nagasaki and Sunday, 3 June, before the ship dropped anchor in Manila Bay.[25]

Taft's first concern was to transfer control from the military to civilians. Taft wrote on 12 June to his brother: "I am very anxious that civil government shall be established." He concluded that the rebellion would soon be broken and that the Filipinos were anxious to be rid of "policing by shoulder straps." He predicted the civilians would be in control in sixty to ninety days. Taft also worried that the military might convince Root "of some fancied danger of an uprising which is always held up by military men as a bogey." He wrote on 15 July 1900 to Secretary of War Root that they would have to wink at the blackmailing by police because they were valuable in unearthing insurrectionary conspirators and in securing the capture of *insurrectos*.[26]

The Philippine commission ignored the Bureau of Military Insurgent Records and used its own "secret service" funds to hire informants. The military felt that the Filipinos were constantly plotting against it. Taft, however, was convinced that Manila was not full of plots and conspiracies, that the "unruly spirits" who circulated rumors of uprisings had been captured and were in prison. He recommended that civilian government be established in Manila immediately. "I fear a good soldier does not always make a safe politician," Taft warned Root.[27]

General MacArthur attempted in the summer of 1900 to use amnesty to end resistance. He negotiated with Gen. José Alejandrino of the Philippine Revolutionary Army to arrange a conference with Aguinaldo. MacArthur offered no political concessions, only the establishment of a government guaranteeing to Filipinos the same personal liberties and rights Americans enjoyed. Alejandrino told MacArthur that the Filipinos were tired of promises and preferred to die rather than surrender unconditionally. A colonial form of government gave the executive too much latitude, and rights could later be revoked. MacArthur argued that there was no hope of success, that to adopt guerrilla warfare was to be guilty of the murder of all men who fell. Instead, Filipinos should throw themselves upon the generosity of the United States. Four hundred years of deceit, retorted Alejandrino, had made Filipinos skeptical regarding promises, and the Americans had already broken promises to make the islands independent. Alejandrino admitted that as a property owner and career officer he desired peace, but he would not surrender without a command from Aguinaldo. MacArthur wrote after the conference: "The war must continue with uninterrupted violence until the Filipino people, and especially the leaders in arms, realize that it is a matter of self-interest for themselves and the good of the Filipino people to accept the amnesty offered, and which for a time will be extended by the United States." In fact, MacArthur's amnesty program showed meager results. During September guerrillas besieged isolated American garrisons and scored a number of small victories.[28]

Conflict between Taft and Col. William P. Duvall in the Benguet district, about 150 miles from Manila, illustrated the growing tensions between civilians and military. About fifteen thousand Igorots lived in mountainous Benguet. Most had been loyal to the Spanish. The question remained whether they would also be loyal to the Americans.

The military commander of the area ordered municipal governments to be set up in Benguet in early 1900. Officers soon became convinced that the revolutionaries had organized resistance throughout the area. When a leader of the Guardia de Honor, a religious sect that had supported the Spanish, offered to identify guerrillas, officers accepted his assistance. Further investigation convinced the officers, and MacArthur, that the guerrillas had an elaborate structure established throughout the towns of the area. Colonel Duvall, then in charge of one area, developed elaborate counterinsurgency methods using the Guardia as a vigilante force. With hundreds of volunteers, the Guardia ranged through Benguet hunting down guerrillas. Duvall used the Guardia reports as a basis for a series of military trials of civilians.[29]

Taft believed that the province of Benguet was among the first to accept control by the military and one of the quietest. Duvall and the military in Benguet became an example of the harm the military had done to the American cause by instituting a "system of terrorism by using a secret society opposed to the insurrection." Such uncontrolled power of military commanders, Taft reported to Root on 10 October 1900, necessitated civilian control. Taft instituted civilian control in Benguet soon after.[30]

The American civilian-military conflict in the Philippines reflected the immediate political problem at home. The Democrats nominated William Jennings Bryan again in 1900, and he promised in his acceptance speech to call a special session of Congress if elected to consider granting immediate independence to the Philippines. The Democratic platform echoed Bryan's promise, one that might stiffen the hopes of the insurrectos and result in the maintenance of the status quo until after the November election.

Meiklejohn was already holding the lid on one scandal in the customhouses of the islands that had perhaps resulted in one hundred thousand dollars being taken. By the end of June, Jenkins, Meiklejohn's friend, was asking that competent "Secret Service" men be employed to check the customhouses. Surely something was wrong, he warned Meiklejohn, when employees drawing twelve hundred to eighteen hundred dollars a year sported race horses and diamonds. Jenkins especially suspected one deputy collector, a colonel, who was very popular with the merchants. Jenkins conveyed such suspicions in closely guarded "confidential" letters.[31]

Anti-Filipino rhetoric in the United States escalated in the fall of 1900 as fighting continued in the Philippines. Vice-presidential candidate Theodore Roosevelt, campaigning in the West for McKinley, used the rhetoric of white supremacy to convince westerners that driving the Spaniards out had been "a great anti-imperialist strike" and that the presence of American troops in the Philippines was akin to having troops stationed in the Midwest to put down the uprisings of the Sioux. To offer self-government to Aguinaldo was like granting self-government to an Apache reservation under some local chief, Roosevelt argued. The reservation would simply be put at the mercy of a "syndicate of Chinese half-breeds," a derogatory reference to the fact that Aguinaldo was part Chinese. Roosevelt compared the rebels to the Boxers whom he called "a mob of unspeakably cruel barbarians" and used the Boxer Rebellion of June to justify the acquisition of the Philippines. He repeated variations on this theme as he visited the western states.[32]

Other Republicans defended their Philippine policy with less inflammatory and racist rhetoric. Supporters of Assistant Secretary of War Meiklejohn took to the stump in Nebraska to argue that Democrats themselves had voted to increase the army to one hundred thousand during the war with Spain and that the bill would expire on 30 June 1901, thus returning the army to its prewar level. Meiklejohn even had army officers prepare a report showing that in proportion to the population, the standing army under McKinley was half as many as it was under Washington almost one hundred years earlier, one-half a man per one thousand population compared with one man per one thousand. In September Taft and the civilian commission were to assume all the legislative functions in the islands, leaving MacArthur and the military only executive functions. Taft was doing his best to convince the War Department that the army was the main cause of unrest. As the deadline neared without civilian control, the War Department released documents from the Bureau of Military Insurgent Records detailing alleged plots against the military in Manila and calls by Filipinos to fight the oppressor and spare neither men, women, children, nor old people.[33]

Foreign wars, even their own, failed to interest American voters in November 1900. Managed news combined with the political mistakes of the Democrats contributed to a mood that allowed the Republicans to maintain control of the executive and, hence, of the colonial policy in the Philippines. By joining forces with the Democrats, anti-imperialists did give impetus to civilian control, but they failed to stop the war and to end the political control of the people in the Philippines.[34]

After the election, restraint by the administration ceased. The day following the election, the administration ordered MacArthur to eliminate Filipino opposition to American control. Taft supported elimination by the military of the remaining dissent. He suggested that MacArthur suppress all newspapers that advocated continuance of war and imprison their editors; that a large contingency fund be given MacArthur to "buy information"; and that a bureau of information be set up to handle reporting on subversives. Civilian agents should then be sent to Hong Kong to negotiate a surrender. The revolution, according to this plan, could be ended by a combination of bribery, antisubversive investigations, and suppression. One of MacArthur's aides told Taft that MacArthur needed a bureau of information but that it was difficult to secure the right men.[35]

Finally, during the last weeks of November, the counterinsurgency campaign began in earnest. Brigadier General Bell and his agents collected documents and arrested Filipinos in Manila. Late in December, MacArthur declared all the islands to be under martial law. He established the Military Information Division to function as a part of the army adjutant general's office. The army made wholesale arrests, suppressed newspapers, deported suspects, and court-martialed civilians.

Taft was not pleased. He complained to Root that MacArthur lacked "discretion" in arresting suspects, lacked "political sagacity and experience," and had no flexibility. Most of all Taft wanted civilians to be above the military, not under it. He wrote to Root in January 1901 that he felt the military arm was entrenched and did not intend to retreat before the civil government except under distinct orders. "If we could only have a civil government supreme here with an efficient police force," Taft wrote to his brother, "the situation of the islands would change marvelously."[36]

During February 1901, the army established its first systematic surveillance of Filipinos. The War Department transferred one of its MID officers to Manila to reorganize the army's collection of maps and records. He moved the records to the ground floor of the Estado Mayor, on the left bank of the Pasig River, where MacArthur had his headquarters. Within a few months, the officer had hired a number of Filipinos and one American to work undercover among the civilian population. He ordered that information officers be appointed by the commanders of each of the 450 post commands. Each officer was to submit a sketch map of the territory around the post for ten miles, to report its topography, and to take a census of important Filipinos. Officers were to collect information about Filipino opponents of American rule and about efforts to obtain assistance from other countries in throwing out the American invaders.[37]

The final blow to the Malolos Republic was the capture of Aguinaldo in March 1901. Three weeks later, Aguinaldo had quietly taken an oath of allegiance to the United States. With its leader arrested and promising loyalty, the republic seemed doomed. Still Filipinos resisted. When the administration relieved MacArthur on 4 July 1901 and established an American civil government in the Philippines with Taft as the first civilian governor, fifty-five of the seventy-five provinces were still under military rule.

Civilian control did not end opposition to American rule. In October 1901, fifty American soldiers were massacred at Samar. Soon after, MID claimed to have uncovered a plot for an attack on Manila and the proposed assassination of all the important military officers in the city. News of the plot, combined with the massacre, completely unsettled the officers. Mounted patrols roamed the streets of Manila, generals insisted to Taft that they were standing on a volcano, and rumors of insurrection became the chief topic of conversation at the Army and Navy Club. To his dismay, Taft found that Gen. Adna R. Chaffee, who had replaced MacArthur as military commander, shared MacArthur's views about military supremacy. Chaffee insisted that there was still military danger, and commanders echoed his conviction that the military should be supreme. Information from MID buttressed their claims for control[38]

To counter continued opposition, the army expanded its counterinsurgency tactics. Taft still put his faith in the police department and surveillance by a regular detective bureau. When the proposed chief was discovered to be maltreating witnesses and beating them with a black snake while investigating a Katipunan "conspiracy," Taft wrote to Root that the civil government could not condone such treatment, even though many officers approved of such beatings as legitimate counterinsurgency war tactics. The detective was convicted for the beatings and served a sentence but then was allowed to rejoin the force and work his way up the ranks again. Political surveillance, whatever its faults, was Taft's method of dealing with opposition to American occupation and became a permanent part of American colonial civilian government.[39]

Bell moved to a central place in the counterinsurgency effort. MacArthur named Bell as commander of the troubled First District to replace Duvall in late February 1901, and in November he took over south Luzon. Bell insisted that the army needed to continue its use of groups such as the Guardia in the provinces and continued to arrest civilians, threatening them with execution. In his most controversial policy, he herded the population of contested areas into "protected zones." These concentration camps decimated the refugees because of overcrowding, unsanitary conditions, and malnutrition. Bell and his provost martials purged the towns of all civilian sympathizers.[40]

Filipinos told Taft that military control was the cause of the trouble. The chief of police in Manila argued that there was no evidence of an uprising but insisted that if Americans continued to denounce Filipinos it might lead to trouble, for the people feared military government and the possibility of military tribunals. Under Spanish control, the chief told Taft, it had been common both in military and civil courts for perjured statements and forged letters to be used to convict political enemies. Although Filipinos did not trust the civilian courts entirely, they felt it was more difficult to convict on false evidence there than in military courts. On the basis of the police chief's information, Taft wrote to Root that there was "not the slightest danger of insurrection in Manila." To quiet the hysteria and bolster the power of the civilian government, Taft endorsed a sedition and libel law. This done, he left for the United States to review Philippine matters with the secretary of war and to have minor surgery.[41]

The Military Information Division continued to investigate political and revolutionary tendencies among the Filipino population. It forwarded newspaper articles and reports on individuals' activities to the War Department. One article from the *Renacimiento* referred to the black "wings of militarism" that it hoped would soon be removed. Bell, who was becoming increasingly disillusioned with the policy of the concentration of inhabitants, also forwarded telegrams to the War Department reporting on the activities of the military. Later destroyed because of fear the public would learn of the harsh measures and consider them unnecessary, inhuman, or cruel, these telegrams apparently reported not only the widespread military surveillance of civilians but also the abuse of prisoners. It was hard on Bell's "sympathetic nature," General Chaffee explained, to be forced to bring a large proportion of the inhabitants under surveillance, and he hoped Bell would be allowed to reestablish them in their homes. Chaffee even discussed the trials of army officers who had allowed information to be forced from prisoners but recommended that twenty-five thousand troops be left to garrison the islands.[42]

When Taft returned to the United States, he recommended that the regular army be reduced to fifteen thousand and that the Filipino constabulary, which Congress had authorized in February 1901, become the main internal security force. Because the government was concerned that this native force might transfer allegiance to agitators and provide arms for another rebellion, the War Department increased and centralized surveillance. On 18 June 1902, MID in Manila was annexed to MID in Washington to render the operations "broader and more effective." Originals or certified copies of all material in the files and everything obtained in the future that was of a general character, interest, or value to the War Department was to be forwarded to MID in Washington along with all reports from field information officers and a monthly summary of their work. Commanders were to be bypassed, and reports were to go directly to the adjutant general in Washington. The adjutant general was then to furnish information he felt necessary to the subordinate generals. The War Department now had its first MID field office. On 4 July 1902, Roosevelt declared the war to be at an end.[43]

A dual system of the surveillance of Filipinos existed from that time on—one by civilians and one by the military. Taft continued to buttress civilian control by the surveillance of Filipino dissidents. During outbreaks of resistance in 1902, Taft used the census to locate suspected rebels and instituted a system of registration cards. Taft was busy suppressing what he called "seditious plays," revolutionary societies, and *ladrones* (bandits).

Congress never made a complete investigation into the activities of the army in the Philippines. There was a congressional investigation into atrocities, and Roosevelt reluctantly supported court-martials for offending soldiers, but the administration never admitted the costs of imposing American rule on the Philippines. At the peak of the war in late 1900, seventy thousand American troops were in the Philippines. About four thousand Americans died in the Philippine War before it officially ended. Historians are still attempting to estimate Filipino deaths from the war, reconcentrations, and subsequent epidemics that ravaged the war-torn nation. It reached hundreds of thousands.[44]

The Philippine war officially ended in 1902, as did organized opposition by the leaders of the Malolos Republic. The disruptions of the war, however, contributed to unsettled conditions that led to continued opposition to American control. Young Douglas MacArthur, assigned as an engineer to the Department of the Visayas in 1904, found American troops in combat there. He also witnessed the public hanging of a Filipino insurrecto. Hostile Moros fired on General Bliss in 1907 on Mindanao. In the province of Negros, a guerrilla leader named Isio fought for ten years, finally being captured in 1908.[45]

After 1902, the Philippine constabulary received increasing responsibility for maintaining the internal security of the islands and for collecting intelligence. Established in the summer of 1901 to serve under the new governor general, the constabulary functioned somewhere between a National Guard and a state police force. It was composed primarily of regular American and a few Filipino officers who commanded Filipino troops from various cultures. The khaki-clad Filipino troops with their red sleeve chevrons and the officers with red shoulder straps were visible in battles against whoever disturbed the peace and order of the new regime. The constabulary engaged in hundreds of small, isolated skirmishes during its first ten years, losing 50 officers and over 1,000 men while claiming almost 5,000 enemies killed and almost 12,000 captured. Companies of 45 to 60 men, stationed in each province, eventually included both Muslim Moros, who wore a red fez, and Igorots who wore a G-string. Officers faced bolos and spears, as well as bullets, arrows, and barongs. Among the causes of death in the early years were crocodiles, drowning, dysentery, malaria, poisoning, tuberculosis, and typhoid. During its first years under Maj. Henry T. Allen and his assistant Bandholtz, the constabulary numbered over seven thousand. The constabulary also established its own Military Information Division.[46]

Although constabulary officers were technically civilians under the legislative department of the Philippines, a statute passed in January 1903 authorized Bandholtz and other officers of the army to hold office in the constabulary and in the regular U.S. army concurrently. The constabulary was to maintain civil order in the islands and, in case of serious disturbance, to call on the United States army. The army also called on the constabulary. It marched with the army in Mindanao, Jolo, Samar, and Leyte, in campaigns during 1905 and 1906.

Much as it had in the American West, the army used scouts from among the indigenous peoples. In the Philippines, the army first recruited scouts from among Macabebes who had fought with the Spanish. The Scouts were organized in 1899, given official status in 1901, and by October 1902 numbered five thousand. Between 1903 and 1908 as many as thirty-one Scout companies served under the command of constabulary officers, most in campaigns from 1905 to 1907 when the governor requested that three-fifths of the companies be placed on duty with the Philippine government. They wore khaki pants, blue cotton shirts, and—at least originally—straw hats and no shoes. After a series of Scout disasters, the army gradually discontinued their use. Between 1907 and 1911, as the major campaigns had ended, the Scouts were withdrawn from work with the constabulary. The Scouts then became a garrison force with little to do.[47]

Even though the hostilities had ended, Bandholtz continued to worry about the internal security of the islands during the years from 1907 to 1911. In correspondence with officers who had returned to Washington from the Philippines, he constantly voiced his concern that Filipino opposition to American rule would make Americans willing to pull out of the Philippines. Bandholtz had no doubt that Filipinos were still organizing against American control. To eliminate even the appearance of political opposition, Bandholtz used information gathered through surveillance and his wide personal networks to help the American government manipulate Filipino leaders and kept moderate politicians in control of the Assembly. He boasted to the chief of the Bureau of Insular Affairs that Americans kept the Assembly "confined to fairly reasonable channels."[48]

While there certainly was little organized opposition to American rule by 1907, a series of war scares with Japan kept American administrators in the Philippines constantly concerned over internal security in the Philippines. Bandholtz opposed any reduction in American troops in 1911. He felt the thirteen thousand members of the regular army were central to American control. The Scouts now stood at 5,600 and were garrisoned throughout the islands. According to Bandholtz, Scouts were overdrilled, overfed, overequipped, and underworked. In contrast to the Scouts, the constabulary was under the control of the governor general. Troops lived in various towns and took part in the local affairs of the community. Band-holtz did not trust any of the Filipino forces in the event of a foreign war or a general insurrection and used them only to maintain law and order and suppress local uprisings. "They are Orientals," Bandholtz wrote, and because he himself was highly conscious of race, he believed that race would be the basis for any uprising.[49]

With the continued operation of the internal security apparatus most subversion could be halted. The power of the constabulary rested on the elaborate network of surveillance in place. Bandholtz exercised control at the highest level of Filipino politics. He once wrote to Manuel Quezon, the man who was leader of the majority party in the Philippine Assembly, "As you know I am in a position to make it pretty warm for some As-semblymen, and for the entire Nationalista party in case of necessity." He wrote to an officer friend in October 1911, "these poor devils are entirely in our hands and can make no moves without our knowledge."[50]

The persistent desire for independence by Filipinos made military of-ficials continually fearful of civilians and subject to scores of insurrection scares. It also made some officers concerned that in their desire to be free, the Filipinos might look for allies. The only country capable and possibly willing to promote that fear was Japan. Out of these fears came major war scares in 1901, 1902, 1907, 1910, and 1911.[51]

Recent studies of Japanese intelligence during these years have con-cluded that the Japanese were not preparing for war with the United States. Japanese generals had gathered operational intelligence for pos-sible use in wartime, but Japanese officials overall saw no immediate pos-sibility of war. Japanese army intelligence officers focused on Russia and China. When their interest did turn to the Philippines in the late 1930s, they were able to depend primarily on reconnaissance flights for intelli-gence information about American forces there. In fact, neither Japanese nor American intelligence officers saw the Philippines before World War II in a context of the larger policy of collecting information on Asia.[52]

That was the conclusion of Taft and his civilian advisers as well. Dur-ing early war scares, Taft consistently urged diplomacy to maintain peace with Japan. While acting as adviser to Theodore Roosevelt, Taft sup-ported American civilian and local Filipino control as the course most likely to reconcile Filipinos to American rule. Taft convinced Roosevelt that the Japanese were not likely to attack and that the Filipinos preferred American to Japanese control. Taft endorsed a tacit approval of the Jap-anese occupation of Korea in return for Japanese acceptance of American occupation of the Philippines.[53]

Taft believed, as did many of his military advisers, that Japan was too busy paying war debts and providing capital to develop Korea to contemplate war. In March 1908 he wrote to President Roosevelt dismissing stories about Japanese espionage in the Philippines: "I am sure the people don't want the Japs at all. It is only a few disgruntled persons who think it would increase their importance that are other than disturbed by talk of the Japanese coming."[54.]

As president, Taft continued his policy of consolidating civilian control. He appointed as secretary of war Jacob M. Dickinson, a southern Democrat and a railway attorney, to emphasize his desire for civilian rule in the Philippines. As governor general of the Philippines, Taft chose W. Cameron Forbes, who was committed to economic development. Like Taft, Forbes attached little importance to reports of Japanese espionage and hoped to end the last military control in Moro province.[55]

During the 1910 Japanese war scare in the Philippines, the Taft administration responded coolly. Assistant Secretary of War Robert Shaw Oliver checked with the Insular Bureau and the State Department, then informed the secretary of war that an attack on the islands was highly improbable. Forbes added his reassurance that although the Japanese were collecting information, there was a decreasing amount of such activity. Taft replied to the War Department's report about Japanese information gathering: "I don't regard the matter as of any particular significance." Bandholtz also assured Taft's private secretary that foreign security was not a problem. Taft decided to send his secretary of war to the Philippines in July 1910 but also saw no cause for alarm about the Japanese. "I am on excellent terms with all the Japanese authorities," Taft wrote to a friend on 24 November 1910, and "my closeness to the leading men has been a comfort to me in all these sensational attempts to create difficulties between the countries." A new treaty of commerce and navigation with Japan affirmed the status quo in the Pacific—the Japanese controlled Korea; the United States the Philippines.[56]

Taft handled the 1911 scare over revolutionary propaganda with the same calm response. He advised Secretary of War Dickinson to forget the matter. Dickinson agreed that attention to opposition would just magnify the importance of the insurgents with no real results. "People in Manila seem to get brain-storms," Dickinson responded to Taft, "It is a narrow treadmill, infested with gossip." Alarms from the Philippines could no longer evoke any reaction but understanding in Washington.[57]

Despite promises of future independence for the Filipinos, the internal security structure remained in place. World War I provided only a temporary change in the Philippines. The War Department withdrew the regular army, merged the constabulary and the Scouts to form a National Guard, and put Filipinos in command. As soon as the war ended, the War Department reconstituted the Scouts and reestablished American control. During the early 1920s, the War Department formulated "War Plans Brown," the color code for a Philippine rebellion, to deal with Filipino insurrection but directed officers to conduct no intelligence gathering in the Philippines among the civilian population. Field officers disobeyed these orders because officers were convinced that all Filipinos still desired independence and therefore could not be trusted. As one officer concluded, "The white Americans constitute the only group whose loyalty can be relied upon in all situations." Or as another described the situation: "With a small white force of unquestioned loyalty we hold under our control a numerous subject, alien and colored people whose leaders seek help where it may be found without reckoning future consequences." Believing that the Filipinos "always present elements which may be classed as potential enemies of the United States," these officers violated their orders and continued surveillance of the civilian population. Brief mutinies by Scouts in 1924 and in the 1930s brought concern in the War Department that War Plans Brown might have to be used. The mutinies turned out to be minor ones, but the plan remained in force.[58]

The establishment of civilian surveillance in the Philippines kept it firmly under American control. However, American administrators learned from the continued Filipino resistance to American control. Their experience in the Philippines led to a decision not to remain in Cuba in 1906 and not to invade Mexico in 1910. The establishment of the first systematic army surveillance system in the Philippines did spread, however, first to the Mexican border in 1914 and then throughout the country in 1917.

PART III

The Legacy of World War I

CHAPTER SIX

The Mexican Border: Bringing Intelligence Home

The Mexican revolution that began in 1910 raised all the potential problems of internal security again: fear of espionage; counterespionage prosecution; jurisdictional squabbles between civilians and military about who should enforce laws; and the question of how intelligence would be gathered. In the crucible of revolution along its southern border, the War Department finally institutionalized the army's role in internal security within the United States. The War Department moved into internal security reluctantly. Top army officers, raised in an atmosphere of civilian criticism of military expansion, fought the efforts of young officers dedicated to developing an institutionalized capacity to spy. Led by young intelligence officer Ralph Van Deman, these officers persisted until, in the first flush of World War I, they finally obtained what they wanted—an espionage structure that would spy on foreign agents and dissident Americans as well.

During the Mexican revolution a quieter revolution was taking place in the War Department over the question of intelligence. This revolution brought the Philippine internal security system to the Mexican border. The battle lines formed around the question of whether or not the War Department should develop a separate intelligence agency for the entire army similar to the one developed in the Philippines. The major proponent of the plan was Van Deman.

Sometimes called the "father of intelligence" by later admirers, Van Deman deserves careful attention not just because of his ultimate success, but also because his attitudes made a deep and lasting impression on the agency he created. Born in Delaware, Ohio, at the end of the Civil War, Van Deman received his first military training as a cadet at Ohio Wesleyan University in 1883. He served as a member of the Ohio National Guard in bitter labor disputes in the Hocking Valley during 1884 and 1885, finished his bachelor's degree at Harvard in 1888, and received his medical degree from Miami Medical School in Cincinnati five years later. Van Deman received his first commission as a second lieutenant in 1891. Although his father was a lawyer, he knew surprisingly little about the legal structure of the United States. In a test on constitutional law in 1891, he confused the judge advocate general with the attorney general as the adviser on laws. Over six feet tall, slender, and spectacled, Van Deman seemed best fitted for staff work. By 1897, he had joined Wagner's fledgling MID.[1]

Van Deman stayed in Washington until after the Spanish-American War had ended, then went briefly to Cuba and Puerto Rico before being assigned to the Philippines. For two years he mapped terrain, then was ordered to Manila in February 1901 to reorganize the Bureau of Military Insurgent Records into the Military Information Division of the Philippines. Following orders, Van Deman set up a military information unit with a map section, clerks, and undercover agents. To Van Deman must go the credit for expanding MID to cover each of the 450 separate posts that existed in the Philippines at the time. There was no connection between the Philippines MID and MID in Washington: Van Deman worked directly for General MacArthur. In a later account of his Philippine work, Van Deman emphasized that Japanese officers were in Manila as early as 1902 attempting to gather information, and that a few years later he had clashed with General Bell over the question of returning papers relating to Japanese activities to a man who had voluntarily submitted them to the army to prove his loyalty to the new government. In an army where personal loyalty still mattered more than agency loyalty, this was to become crucial for Van Deman's ambitions for intelligence. As Van Deman later recalled, "from that time on he was never favorably inclined to the Military Information Division." Van Deman surely overemphasized the response of Bell. Nevertheless, the interest shown by the Japanese in the Philippines, combined with Bell's refusal to take Van Deman's alarms seriously, made an indelible mark on the young officer. Henceforth, he saw both Bell and the Japanese as enemies with whom he would have to contend.[2]

During the war scares of 1907 and 1910, Van Deman was not in the Philippines. In June 1906, the general staff assigned him to a secret China mission to prepare a topographical map of the area from Peking and Tunken to the sea and to report on railways and roads. The ostensible purpose was to have this information should American troops garrisoned in China after the Boxer Rebellion need to protect American nationals. Van Deman returned to Washington from his mapping of China convinced that the Japanese had an elaborate espionage network there. One of his first projects was to ask for additional internal security legislation.[3]

Van Deman made his first analysis of the role of espionage in an argument for expanded espionage legislation in the fall of 1907. The War Department decided not to follow Van Deman's recommendations at the time, but his argument, like that made previously by Furlong for peacetime espionage and counterinsurgency, marks a new way of thinking about the role of the army in internal security. It was also an argument that, three years later during the 1910 war scare, provided the basis for new espionage legislation.

Before 1907 there was no peacetime internal security legislation. The Secret Service, which had so publicly pursued Spanish spies during 1898, did not have legal authority to guard the president, although the chief had assigned agents to that job. There was much criticism of the Secret Service after the assassination of President McKinley in September 1901. Robert Pinkerton called for a special organization to handle anarchists in the same way that Pinkertons had handled the Molly Maguires—through infiltration. Pinkerton argued that the infiltration of organizations could have put Emma Goldman and other anarchists in the hands of the law and would allow authorities to know their private utterances. Once located and arrested, anarchists should be sent to an island, perhaps the Philippines, Pinkerton suggested. Under a proper system of espionage, he felt, the government could arrest the leaders, the brains behind the "loudmouthed tribe." There was discussion in the media and Congress about punishing domestic anarchists, and in his annual message to Congress, Roosevelt called for a war against those who actively or passively sympathized with anarchism. His recommendations fell considerably short of total war, for he asked that laws be passed to exclude anarchists from immigration and provide for higher economic and educational requirements for all immigrants admitted to the United States. Congress refused to pass bills aimed at the punishment of domestic anarchists, which would have led to their surveillance. Congress did exclude the immigration of anarchists in 1903, but it gave the responsibility for enforcement of the new regulations to the secretary of commerce and labor rather than to the Secret Service.[4]

Most Americans still considered domestic surveillance a wartime activity necessitated by foreign spies and not a proper peacetime governmental practice, whether civilian or military. The Department of Labor was using increasingly ruthless and illegal methods in its effort to enforce the exclusion of Chinese from the United States, but few white Americans found this troubling. Racism had become a national ideology at the turn of the century; nativism had not. The fear of anarchism did not triumph over the acceptance of white immigrants: attempts to deport immigrants suspected of anarchism generally failed. Although many white native-born Americans shared a suspicion that some European immigrants might not be as patriotic as themselves, this sentiment had not yet been transferred into a national ideology or policy. General MacArthur learned this when he returned to the United States in 1903 to take up his peacetime duties. In December, when MacArthur predicted war with Germany in the near future and questioned the patriotism of German-Americans, Roosevelt privately called MacArthur "unfit to hold a commission in the National Guard" and sent a sharp rebuke to San Francisco. The rebuke silenced MacArthur, and he thereafter confined his public activities to entertaining Californians and campaigning against the grog shops and brothels outside the gates of the San Francisco Presidio.[5]

Thus the 1907 discussion of anti-espionage legislation marked an important point in the development of internal security policies. Drawing on his own memory, refreshed by old files from the islands that had been returned to the Bureau of Insular Affairs in Washington, Van Deman concluded that the United States needed internal security legislation. According to Van Deman, Japanese officers in disguise had been obtaining information in the Philippines, United States, and Cuba; and German officers had also been in the United States and Cuba.

Van Deman was quite aware of public sentiment against additional internal security legislation when he drafted his 1907 bill. In his argument for this peacetime espionage law, Van Deman carefully distinguished between three aspects of espionage: during war, during peace when war threatened or was contemplated, and in time of profound peace. Espionage in time of war was as old as recorded history, wrote Van Deman, citing Caesar, Hannibal, and Napoleon as having conducted espionage to secure information immediately before war. Van Deman dated the origin of peacetime intelligence gathering from the Prussian army of 1821. He then went on to argue that peacetime espionage was now frequent but was known as "procuring military information." This practice accepted, Van Deman then proceeded to explain that internal defense was necessary against others collecting information on the United States, citing a list of British, French, German, and Italian arrests for espionage between 1893 and 1905.[6]

Van Deman's bill prohibited "aliens" from obtaining military information under a penalty of eighteen months in prison and a maximum one-thousand dollar fine. Albert Todd, the general staff officer who endorsed Van Deman's bill, called it an ineffective piece of legislation, because it included no enforcement provision, but felt it would have a valuable moral effect. Todd also made a significant change in the bill. He substituted "any person" for "alien," arguing that the bill would be discriminatory if it applied only to aliens. Congress remained opposed to such legislation in 1907, thus the main significance of Van Deman's work was the formal justification it gave to peacetime espionage and internal security legislation.

The following year, Van Deman became involved in squabbles to determine the fate of the records accumulating in MID over the previous twenty years. Bell became chief of staff in 1906, and in an effort to make his office more efficient, he established two separate sections. Bell kept the administrative section in the old building west of the White House where it continued to advise the secretary of war. He moved the Army War College (AWC) across town to a new building on Greenleaf Point (now Fort McNair) and put it in charge of planning, intelligence, and education. In 1903, when the new general staff system was organized by Root, Bell transferred MID from the Adjutant General's Office to the general staff Bell kept MID, and Van Deman, in downtown Washington. The Army War College asked that MID records go with it across town. Van Deman successfully blocked this first attempt to transfer the records, but within a few months the AWC renewed its demand. It had only one automobile at the time, a White Steamer, and no way to obtain information quickly. In May 1908 AWC again appealed to Chief of Staff Bell to move MID. This time Van Deman lost. Bell ordered the transfer. In late May, Van Deman moved MID records to the new Army War College building. There were, according to Van Deman's calculations, 141 double wagon loads, weighing 609,000 pounds, of records, publications, maps, and military attaché reports. The Military Information Division had, again according to Van

Deman's meticulous records, answered 2,376 calls for information during the year in addition to overseeing fourteen military attachés and branch offices in Manila and Havana.[7]

Soon after Van Deman moved the records, the War College Division (WCD) asked Bell to place MID entirely under its jurisdiction. Such a merger was logical from the standpoint of bureaucratic oversight but being attached to WCD removed MID from its previous central position in the general staff where its reports could directly influence War Department policy decisions. Van Deman felt that Bell still distrusted him for his zealousness in Manila. Probably the use of intelligence records did disturb Bell, and placing MID under WCD may have been a way to control Van Deman.

Van Deman was relieved of his general staff duties in January 1910 and stayed in Washington only a few months longer to complete the work of carding maps on file in the map section and in the library. Van Deman, who had finished his work and was convinced that the man who worked steadily and did his best would go to the top, was ready to leave Washington. He was pleased that General Wood, whom he liked and considered an able officer, would succeed Bell as chief of staff. He still believed Bell disliked him personally and had blocked the independence of MID while under his control. Van Deman wrote to a friend before leaving Washington that he was hopeful that Congress would appropriate funds for the Philippines but that he was worried that the "peace at any price" people in Boston would be successful in their campaign against armament. Perhaps, he wrote, the labor riots in Philadelphia would make the disarmament proponents glad they had not yet disarmed.[8]

Van Deman's replacement, D. A. Frederick, took up the crusade. On 15 September 1910 Frederick made another attempt to create an independent MID. In a memorandum for the new chief of staff, Frederick argued that his office must have complete control over its agents, meaning military attachés. The information necessary for war had to be collected in time of peace, but, he lamented, unfortunately in time of peace attention was diverted, and when war came the sources of information were cut off. One office should have control. Not only did the new chief of staff veto the plan, but also, less than two weeks later, he ordered that the Military Information Committee, charged with collecting and classifying military information, be stripped of that function. Only military attachés or military observers in time of war could collect military information. Civilian clerks were to organize material coming into the committee, and MID was to take no initiative whatsoever in gathering information. Henceforth, there would be no purely intelligence work. The Military Information Division was consolidated with the War College Section of the general staff, and its commissioned personnel scattered among various committees of the War College. Records of MID were merged with those of the War College. For all practical purposes, MID had ceased to exist when the Mexican revolution broke out in late 1910.[9]

Since the Mexican war, sixty-five years earlier, the United States and Mexico had remained at peace. For the most part, the long border between the two countries that stretched through the arid Southwest was undefined by either nation. Small garrisons of American soldiers dotted the rough terrain, but these isolated outposts more frequently saw clashes with Indians who were determined to protect their homelands from encroaching Americans than with Mexicans. Although the border area was a violent one, with frequent gun battles between law enforcement officials and various dissident individuals, these conflicts seldom involved the United States army. For the most part, Mexican nationals crossed the border with little restraint, following kin north and recrossing the border again when they wished. For those Mexicans wishing to become citizens, there was a relatively easy naturalization process. By 1910, many thousands of Mexicans had changed their citizenship; others had settled permanently without becoming citizens. Most of the Hispanics in the Southwest, who remained a majority of the population, were native-born, Spanish-speaking Americans.

The American-born population from other parts of the United States, usually referred to as "Anglos" by the Spanish-speaking population, increased rapidly during the late nineteenth century. Most of these early immigrants came for two reasons—to recover from diseases such as tuberculosis that were endemic in the colder, damper climates, or to invest in agriculture, trade, or extractive industries. During the first decade of the twentieth century, groups of these aggressive settlers received federal funds to develop irrigation and hydroelectric power. Mammoth dams began to rise above the rivers of the Southwest. The Mexican government, which seemed to be thriving under the dictatorship of Porfirio Díaz, had neglected its northern border areas. Díaz, who launched his revolution from Brownsville, Texas, in 1875, should have known the danger from revolutionaries who used Texas as a base of operations. Most domestic threats to the Díaz regime came from northern Mexico. During 1908, for example, Magonistas attempted to capture Ciudad Juárez de Chihuahua, just opposite El Paso, Texas. Armies were often recruited from, and retreated to, the northern border lands to replenish supplies of men and arms. The border trade in arms flourished through these years, the border becoming a convenient protective zone for both revolutionaries and refugees. Thousands of refugees entered the United States through Juárez. War came to the border communities through the attacks of various groups of armed men competing for power. A picture postcard taken in Juárez after one of these attacks shows the municipal library riddled with bullet holes, buildings destroyed, and bodies lying unburied in the streets.[10]

By 1905 Díaz had a full-fledged revolution on his hands. The Partido Liberal Mejicano (PLM) set up a government in exile in the United States. Like its earlier Cuban counterpart, the Mexican PLM directed revolutionary activities and became involved in trials for gun running and neutrality violations. These activities gradually drew the United States into a network of surveillance that included collaboration with the agents of Díaz. The pattern was similar to that of the Cuban revolution, but the common border allowed more Mexicans, Mexican-Americans, and American agents to be involved. The surveillance networks were complex on both sides: they included *revoltosos,* private detectives, and government officials. At first the Mexican government depended primarily on private detectives, but it also used military intelligence and information gathered by Mexican consuls from American officials stationed along the border. The border was soon awash with plot and counterplot, spies and counterspies. Business boomed for private detective agencies.[11]

Open conflict in Mexico began late in 1910 when Francisco Madero, a political opponent arrested by Díaz, fled to San Antonio and called for a mass uprising. In the north and west of Mexico, seventeen thousand insurgents answered his call. By February 1911 it was evident that Díaz could not crush the rebellion. On 6 March Taft mobilized twenty thousand troops on the Mexican border.

Mobilization touched off a fear of Japanese agents. The *New York Sun* printed rumors of Japanese being in Mexico and of a secret treaty between Japan and Mexico. As usual, the Taft administration tried to dampen rumors of Japanese spies. An article in *World's Word* summed up the attitude of the administration as having no fear of Japan, no knowledge of Japanese plots, and no suspicion that any such plots existed. The general staff might tighten its sword belt whenever it learned of a stranger with a camera, the article noted, but Taft and his secretary of state were "undisturbed by dreams of burning cities and ports ravaged by hordes of barbarians descending out of the East." Taft continued to negotiate a trade treaty with Japan. It was signed on 4 April 1911.[12]

The scare lingered on. In April the *New York Sun* announced that Ambassador Henry Lane Wilson had received a copy of a secret treaty between Japan and Mexico. Wilson had not seen the treaty, and a reporter soon admitted that a German officer had given him the story. A clipping of the visit of the grand admiral of the Japanese who was visiting Mexico and his comments found its way quickly to the State Department. Mexico was alive with factional intrigues, but Taft refused to allow the War Department to become involved. He withdrew most of the troops from the border, and Mexico was hardly mentioned in the election of 1912.[13]

Taft dealt with the border problem in ways calculated to minimize army involvement. He decided to hold maneuvers in southern Texas to effect a show of strength, but he also subsidized the Texas Rangers, apparently in an effort to have them enforce neutrality laws. As with the Cuban insurgents, the enforcement of neutrality laws against Mexican revolutionaries proved difficult, drawing the War and the Justice departments into quarrels over jurisdiction. Some American generals felt it to be their duty to stamp out the Mexican revolution. The Justice Department insisted the army had no business becoming involved and that its own role was limited to arresting and prosecuting violators of the neutrality laws. With the help of Mexican secret service agents, the Justice Department did successfully provide evidence to convict a group of thirty-seven followers of Gen. Bernardo Reyes in Brownsville in January 1912 for conspiracy to violate neutrality laws. Although most of the men were found guilty, they received fines instead of sentences, and those who could not pay served light sentences under conditions so lax that even the Bureau of Investigation agents complained.[14]

The Taft administration collected little intelligence on Mexico. In 1907, Capt. William S. Scott was assigned special duty at Fort Sam Houston to watch the "Mexican immigrants" and spent two months collecting information along the border. The next year, MID sent an officer in disguise on a secret mission into Mexico. This was hardly enough for the War Department to elaborate war plans for Mexico should the revolution lead to armed intervention. Caught off guard by the revolution in Mexico, Hunter Liggett, new chief of the War College Division, sent a request for information on Mexico to the chief intelligence officer of the navy, T. M. Potts. Potts replied that he did not have any information on Mexico in his files because there was no naval attaché in Mexico and because Mexican ports were rarely visited by vessels of the navy. Potts subsequently asked the secretary of the navy to send an officer to Mexico to collect information. In 1912 Liggett also approved the use of money from incidental expenses of the quartermaster's department for the collection of information, the same process that had been used during the Spanish-American War, the Philippine War, and the Cuban intervention of 1906.[15]

The Army War College did formulate a plan for the widespread surveillance of the Japanese in 1912. The suggestion was based on reports from a hodgepodge of sources that the Japanese were obtaining information on bridges, tunnels, and the rolling stock of the railroad leading to the Pacific coast; that Japanese in Colorado, Montana, and other places were said to be making plans to blow up tunnels and bridges in the event of trouble between the United States and Japan; and that Japanese agents were making maps and plans of all U.S. railroads and fortifications. The Army War College wanted letters sent to the heads of the railroads asking for the number of Japanese employed and that reliable American employees, such as section supervisors, station agents, and track walkers report on the actions of any Japanese under their observation, whether employees or visitors. This 1912 plan was never implemented through railroad companies, probably because the administration recognized that the reports were inextricably intertwined with the desires of westerners to restrict Japanese immigration. Nor did the Military Information Committee take an active part in gathering intelligence for the formulation of war plans for Mexico worked out that spring. Printed maps and travel books formed the intelligence upon which plans were formulated.[16]

Congress did pass its first national defense secrets act, the legislation that Van Deman had initiated two years earlier. The bill applied to both aliens and citizens, in the United States and the Philippines. That bill was the single internal security legacy of the 1910 Mexican revolution and Japanese spy scare. The United States weathered the first years of the Mexican revolution without intervening militarily and without expanding MID either at home or abroad.[17]

The election of Woodrow Wilson in 1912 offered a time for reevaluation of the policies of expansion since 1898. The Democrats seemed to be the party of peace because antimilitarists were a strong wing of the party. The reform platform of the Democrats attracted the support of many Socialists. For some, 1912 seemed the triumph of years of agitation against war and colonialism. There was antagonism toward the general staff system as a whole, which, opponents argued, gave the military too strong a hand in the executive. Proponents of decentralization within the War Department—especially bureau heads—joined forces to oppose increases in the general staff and managed to get a cut in the number of general staff officers.[18]

With the emphasis on decentralization, it seemed unlikely that MID would be resurrected soon. Chief of Staff Wood made one attempt to reinstitute MID before Wilson took office. In January 1913 Wood wrote to Chief of the War College Brig. Gen. William Crozier complaining about poor intelligence or, as it was still being called, information. Lack of organization and coordination of work, of continuity, of officer training to carry work forward uninterruptedly, of cooperation with other departments, of regular exchange with the Navy Department, and of liaison with the State Department in closing information gaps all existed, according to Wood. Better relations were needed between the Manila office, the Embassy in Japan, and the legation in Peking.[19]

Wood's complaint brought no response from General Crozier. Chief of Staff Wood had spent much of his first three years in that office fighting with bureau heads, and he had exhausted his colleagues and subordinates. During the next year, reports from the Philippine MID about Japanese officers asking questions failed to rouse any interest. One of the adjutant general's assistants replied that these were questions frequently asked by the Japanese for a number of years, unquestionably to gather military information, but that no action was to be taken. A year later, when Rear Adm. Bradley A. Fiske received a letter about a rumor that the Japanese were getting information on the fortifications on Hawaii, he did not respond. A copy of this unconfirmed report was simply filed.[20]

Late in October 1913 the situation in Mexico became tense once again, and Wilson sounded out Congress on the possibility of armed intervention. Devising a new diplomacy based on morality rather than precedent, Wilson forswore annexation but threatened force, and during November war between Mexico and the United States seemed imminent. In his annual message to Congress, Wilson promised to protect American and other foreign life and property in Mexico. Without congressional approval, Wilson ordered the navy to take Veracruz after a dispute about the arrest of several sailors. Congress approved Wilson's action a few days later and provided for raising volunteers if needed.

Congress responded by making the first increase in the contingencies MID fund since 1903, from ten thousand dollars to eleven thousand dollars. Wood had already asked all units operating along the Mexican border to instruct officers to collect information from refugees and from other sources. Early in 1914, the chief of the War College assigned an officer to compile military information on Mexico. In June, the chief of the War College requested that four officers be assigned to help in compiling the military information being forwarded on Mexico. In this case, knowledge of history rather than contemporary intelligence may have slowed the administration in its intervention in Mexico. Based on records from the Philippine insurrection, Capt. John R. M. Taylor estimated that an intervention would last three months but that pacification would take three years. Wilson withdrew American troops from Veracruz late in November 1914. Unable to force a solution of the domestic quarrels of the Mexicans, Wilson watched from the sidelines. Wilson seemed determined also to keep the United States on the sidelines after European nations went to war in August 1914.[21]

The outbreak of a major war in Europe brought expanded internal security plans in all of the western nations. Because World War I coincided with an international socialist movement, European nations feared domestic opposition to the war. Rather than signaling revolution or resistance to the military, war in Europe led to an overwhelming response of patriotic nationalism. Still, countries spent considerable money on espionage, counterespionage, and loyalty programs. Governments rushed to use military surveillance and military trials to guard against subversion. In the first weeks of war, the Austrian Reichsrat put into force the War Services Act, which transferred such offenses as treason, sedition, and sabotage from civil courts to military jurisdiction. Britain had the Defense of the Realm Act, which allowed both the alien and subject accused of espionage anywhere in the British empire to be tried under military law and allowed military intelligence to control counterespionage. In France, the civilian government handled counterespionage but in 1916 interned alien women and children under the Ministry of the Interior, and alien males under the Ministry of War.[22]

The discovery of spies seemed to have justified the drastic action taken by governments. The British offered proof of the need for military control by the occasional executions of spies. In the early months of the war, the English tried Carl Hans Lody by court-martial, convicted, and shot him for espionage. In 1915, the Germans executed the British nurse Edith Cavell for helping allied prisoners to escape from German prison camps.[23]

The European spy scare spread to the United States as nations damned each other for their espionage attempts and employed private detectives to counter political activities of dissident émigrés. At first, the United States government did not join in the spy scares. The War Department came under the benign influence of Hugh L. Scott when he replaced Wood as chief of staff in 1914. Military Attaché Bentley Mott later described General Scott as the last of the old-style chiefs of staff—honest, conscientious, subordinate to his civilian superiors, and suspicious of his army subordinates. Scott, a somewhat deaf and grandfatherly man, was ill at ease in Washington and bored by office routine. Although committed to a strong general staff and to conscription, Scott was cautious about reform that would change army traditions radically. Tasker H. Bliss, also near retirement age and of the old school of generals who had great concern for public attitudes toward the military, became assistant chief of staff. Peyton C. March, who later replaced Scott as chief of staff, wrote of these two ranking staff officers that "neither of them had a certain ruthlessness which disregards accustomed methods and individual likings in striking out on new and untrodden paths." Such attitudes were to come into direct conflict with the desires of younger officers, such as Van Deman, for the development of army intelligence.[24]

Scott did not expand his formal intelligence capabilities, but he did remain alert to possible trouble with Japan. In the spring of 1915, when a Japanese battle cruiser was reported maneuvering at Turtle Bay, army information agents assured the State Department that the maneuvers were nothing new. Japanese warships had used Turtle Bay for months. Nevertheless, on 8 May the War Department sent telegrams to commanding generals in the eastern, western, Hawaiian, and Philippine departments asking them to take necessary precautions to prevent any incidents resulting from the presence of unauthorized persons in fortifications under their commands. The War Department referred all reports on suspicious Japanese, who were often reported sketching or taking photographs near forts, to the newly formed civilian Bureau of Investigation of the Department of Justice. Without systematic foreign intelligence, however, Scott found it difficult to evaluate Japanese activities. Late in September 1915, newspapers announced that a Russian-Japanese alliance would protect Japan's flank and give her a free hand to settle differences with the United States in the Pacific and that, because they feared a Japanese invasion of India, Great Britain would not stand by the United States in any conflict with Japan. Such reports forced Scott to rely on agents outside the government for information, just as the War Department had done before the Spanish-American War.[25]

Reporting had to be done by outside people, Scott wrote in September 1915, because "as soon as we try to talk about preparedness people say we are doing it because we have an axe of our own to grind." He sought the approval of Secretary of War Lindley M. Garrison before inviting one informant to the Army War College. Garrison warned him to keep the meeting quiet, lest he be thought "to get up a Japanese war scare." Scott asked this informant to send more newspaper clippings and the names of "such other people as I can reach quietly without laying myself liable to the reputation of being a jingo." Whatever network was worked out, if any, was kept so secret that it is not mentioned in War Department records. Reports continued to arrive about suspected activities of Japanese troops on the West Coast. One man from Los Angeles even suggested that Japanese immigrants be reconcentrated inland, but his and other letters were filed away in the adjutant general's office or quietly referred to the Bureau of Investigation for its reports.[26]

The army was not involved in the squabbles that developed over internal security among the Justice, State, and Treasury departments during 1915 and 1916. Attorney General Thomas Watt Gregory, a southerner and old friend of President Wilson, expanded his force of investigative agents slowly as reports of espionage gradually reached the cabinet and created a conflict on how to handle them. Secretary of State Bryan asked Treasury Department Secret Service operatives to investigate foreign diplomats in 1915. Spectacular newspaper exposés followed. The willingness of Secretary of the Treasury William Gibbs McAdoo to use reports on suspected spies for partisan purposes led him to expand Secret Service surveillance, which brought him into conflict with Attorney General Gregory. This conflict, in turn, led the State Department to appoint counselor Frank Polk to coordinate investigations, to avoid duplication of effort, and to make specific assignments where conflict occurred. Reports of conspiracy between German agents and Mexicans went to the State Department where they influenced the new secretary of state, Robert Lansing, to push for a stronger anti-German administration policy.[27]

Rising support for preparedness within his administration drove President Wilson stubbornly to resist military preparedness. In February 1916, Secretary of War Garrison resigned in conflict over Wilson's reluctance to support increases in the size of the military, and Wilson appointed Newton D. Baker, a young reform lawyer from Cleveland, Ohio, as his new secretary of war. Baker, a West Virginian by birth, had studied under Wilson at Johns Hopkins, and Wilson had complete trust in Baker. Although Baker was a physically small man, officers soon came to respect his quick mind and acceptance of responsibility, but they chaffed under his firm control. Wilson seldom interfered with the way Baker ran the War Department, and Baker stayed at his post until 1921. Baker depended mainly on his highest ranking staff officers for military advice and expected absolute loyalty. He ran a scrupulously honest department, keeping a tight rein on the tendencies of the army to expand.

Increasingly war with Mexico loomed as a greater possibility than conflict in Asia or Europe. Unrest along the border simmered on through 1915 and into 1916. The adjutant general gave Frederick Funston, commanding general of the Southern Department, nine hundred dollars during 1915 for "secret service" work in Mexico, and in the fall Funston began to put pressure on the War Department to allow him to organize a well-paid "secret service" to investigate "disloyal Mexicans" and to get hold of "Mexican ringleaders." Secretary of War Garrison vetoed the plan, referring Funston's recommendations to Attorney General Gregory, who replied that he would have the head of the Bureau of Investigation in San Antonio confer with Funston. In the Philippines, the army watched Filipinos, but Garrison kept the military out of domestic civilian surveillance. At the end of 1915 there were no civilians under military surveillance at home and no central MID.[28]

Then, after a five-year absence, Van Deman returned to the Army War College in Washington. Appalled at the lack of military intelligence, Van Deman prepared a memorandum for the chief of the War College Division, M. M. Macomb, reviewing the history of the division and listing the things that the army should be doing to gather military intelligence. Van Deman's memorandum presented a strong argument for a full general staff intelligence capability.

The arguments were not new, but now Van Deman was able to place them in the context of the conflict along the Mexican border, including the possibility that the United States might go to war with Mexico. Van Deman began by pointing out that no group was then studying military information or forming plans for its collection. He was the only officer who had intelligence training, and other officers assigned to military intelligence were being forced to do current general staff work. The Quartermaster Corps was collecting information on the railroads for use in case of war because no military intelligence group was doing it and yet, Van Deman pointed out, "We have none of the material which will be necessary immediately upon the outbreak of war and no plans for its preparation. . . . We are not prepared for military operations even in our own country and we are doing nothing to remedy the conditions." Van Deman urged that a Military Information Section be reestablished as a separate unit of the War Department, with its own personnel, records, and files to handle all matters connected with military information work; and that each unit of the army have an intelligence office with trained military intelligence officers. He hinted that the United States needed spies to supplement the work of military attachés and that secrecy was necessary to obtain needed information, since many people would supply information only if the source was kept confidential and since many things could not be committed to writing at all. He also recommended that military intelligence officers be assigned directly to the chief of staff.[29]

In the border town of Columbus, New Mexico, events were taking place that would ensure that Scott listened to Van Deman. Col. Herbert J. Slocum, commander of the Thirteenth Cavalry at Columbus, began to receive reports early in 1916 that Pancho Villa, one of the dissident Mexican generals, intended to raid American towns along the border. Slocum received reports from two Mexicans who claimed they had blundered into a band of Villistas fifteen miles below the border. Other reports said that Villa and his men were variously eight, forty, and sixty-five miles south of Columbus. Slocum and Maj. Elmer Lindsley, head of the cavalry detachment stationed fourteen miles west of Columbus, went down to the barbed-wire fence that separated the United States and Mexico and crossed into the small village of Palomas to ask the Mexican troops about Villa. When the Mexican commander appeared hostile, Slocum and Lindsley retreated. Unable to verify any of the reports about Villa, Slocum hired a Mexican for twenty dollars, had the Thirteenth Cavalry provide him with a rifle and binoculars, and sent him south of the border. The man reported that Villa's band seemed to be going away from the border.[30]

Instead Villa was heading toward the border. Villa and his troops attacked at Columbus on 9 March 1916, catching the Americans completely off guard. Within a week Gen. John Pershing was leading six thousand troops onto Mexican soil to scatter Villistas and end the threat of raids.

The Columbus attack turned Van Deman's arguments from conjecture to reality. By 18 March the head of the War College himself wrote a strong memorandum to Chief of Staff Scott urging the collection of military information for General Pershing's expeditionary force, emphasizing that there was no proper organization to coordinate and handle the details of this important duty. The War College Division had received no information when Veracruz was occupied by the army in 1914, Macomb reminded Scott, and such a thing should not happen in Mexico. The War Department should secure, coordinate, and distribute information for the use of troops. The work of military intelligence officers should be coordinated by a central agency. There should be an intelligence office in each military department, in each garrison, post or station, and with every independent body of troops in the field.[31]

Scott vetoed the plan. According to him, the plan would take too many officers, and the clerical work would be out of proportion to the benefits. He did, however, recommend that an intelligence office be set up in each department. Orders sent out on 25 April established an intelligence office in each department of the army and ordered that information be forwarded directly to the War College. The army now had a system similar to the one that Van Deman had established in the Philippines sixteen years before.[32]

Macomb continued to press for the reorganization of a central military information bureau. After two years as chief of the War College, Macomb was now convinced of the defects of the system. He wrote to Scott that MID must be a distinct organization, with permanent personnel, charged exclusively with military information work. He recommended a special course on military intelligence gathering at the Army War College as well as liaison with the State, Navy, and Treasury departments.[33]

As conflict with Mexico threatened, reports from consular agents in Mexico City turned concern to panic in the War Department. Wilson called up National Guard units in Arizona, New Mexico, and Texas to patrol the border. On 21 June, after the Mexican government had warned Americans to withdraw northward, Mexican troops fired upon an American scouting unit on Mexican soil, killing twelve Americans and capturing twenty-three. Early the following morning, the Western Union telegraph operator at Dallas received a code telegram to relay from Mexico City to Tokyo discussing Mexican interest in aid from Japan. The operator notified General Funston at 2:20 A.M., Funston notified the War Department. Hurried conferences took place in Washington while Funston delayed transmission of the message. At 11:26 A.M., after Funston had telegraphed to ask what to do, Secretary of War Baker ordered that the telegram be sent.[34]

The Army War College was not involved in the telegram decision. In fact, when Macomb heard about the telegram, he wrote angrily to Scott to ask that a copy of it be obtained from the attorney general. There were reports of Japanese activities in connection with Mexican affairs, Macomb wrote, and the War Department needed more information. Some reports were merely rumors, he admitted, but because of strained relations with the Mexican government, which already had arms and ammunition from Japan, it might be attempting to get more. Macomb also asked Baker to borrow from the Justice Department a copy of a Japanese directory published in San Francisco that had the names and addresses of all the Japanese residing in California, Colorado, Idaho, and Utah. Macomb had already asked for two Japanese linguists for the War College. Baker asked Gregory to forward the directory and met with Secretary of State Lansing to discuss the Mexico City telegram. Wilson mobilized the entire National Guard and federalized it.[35]

With the European war spreading spy alarms and the possibility of a war with Mexico looming, the Wilson administration decided to ask Congress for additional power to deal with internal security. The Army War College wanted a bill for censorship, but Attorney General Gregory thought it wiser not to include this provision in a batch of bills he introduced to tighten up internal security. There would be too many objections, Gregory wrote to the adjutant general, and it would only complicate matters. Gregory did ask Congress to pass a stricter bill preventing the disclosure of national defense secrets and to legitimize the collection of information by the Bureau of Investigation of the Justice Department, which investigated violations of federal law. Bureau agents could then be free to conduct intelligence gathering on foreign diplomats and other foreigners in the United States for the State Department. Congress gave Gregory what he wanted on 3 June 1916, in the National Defense Act.[36]

Because the National Defense Act did not include military censorship, Macomb urged Scott to go ahead and draw up his own plans for censorship. Officers of the army and navy were scheduled to meet with the representatives of press associations and managers of leading newspapers to draft regulations for communications. Macomb, however, wanted the president to direct censorship, if necessary by martial law, and to suppress arbitrarily the publication of material that might "prove detrimental to national defense or useful to a possible enemy." Macomb counseled that such drastic intent should be masked by omitting the words *censorship* and *censor,* words likely to "create adverse popular impression." Unless steps were taken to restrict the supply of information to daily papers, Macomb warned, the Mexicans in the United States would freely furnish information on troops to friends in Mexico. On 5 July the judge advocate general submitted legislation on censorship, the Joint Army and Navy Board approved it, and Baker sent letters supporting it to the Committee on the Judiciary.[37]

Wilson chose to engage in diplomatic negotiations for the withdrawal of Pershing's troops. The need for a central intelligence agency and special censorship legislation disappeared quickly. Still Macomb continued to be greatly alarmed by the possible activities of Japanese and Mexican aliens. He ordered an officer to go to Fort Sam Houston to collect information on the cooperation of Japanese and Mexicans in obtaining arms and ammunition. Funston's chief of staff at Fort Sam Houston attempted to calm Macomb's fears. He responded that there were few Japanese activities in

Mexico and it was not necessary to send an intelligence officer: "If he were here there would be nothing for him to do."[38]

Indeed, there was little for the army to do. Nevertheless, in September 1916 Scott arranged with the auditor of the War Department for a special "secret service" fund of eighteen hundred dollars for Funston. Reports were soon flooding in and, inevitably, began leaking from the War Department. Baker immediately shut the lid on information from Mexico. He was already investigating reports that army agents were part of a plan to assassinate General Villa that involved General Pershing. Van Deman deftly covered up the plan, and Baker wrote confidently to the attorney general in February that his officers knew nothing of it.[39]

Except for reports on Germans from Mexico—submarines in the Gulf and espionage agents—there seems to have been little concern by the War College about the Germans either in the United States or abroad in 1914-16. The British refused to allow their information on Germany to be circulated within the United States army. When an American military attaché suggested that the United States send to the British copies of reports from military attachés in Berlin on the organization and equipping of the German army, the acting chief of the War College, C. W. Kennedy, indignantly dismissed the exchange as a "manifest breach of good faith" and reprimanded the attaché for even entertaining the proposal.[40]

Despite his opposition to European intelligence gathering, Kennedy enthusiastically took up a proposal for a military secret service in Panama, which the United States had occupied to build the canal and where the army was planning fortifications. Undoubtedly, Van Deman was the chief architect of this surveillance plan for Panama. In forwarding the plan to Scott, Kennedy argued that no civilian secret service could meet the requirements of this purely military situation. A force of civilians should be trained, but they must be directed by a military man. A raid from within was possible at any time, and no existing service was competent to discover the conspiracy. Foreign-born enlisted personnel stationed in Panama were a menace that only a secret service could ferret out. Constant surveillance in the cities of Panama and Colón, in the Canal Zone, and in the military garrison was necessary. Special facilities for investigations in Central and South America and the West Indies should also be set up. Civilians among the employees of the Canal Zone could handle some of the work, but a Japanese specialist and two local agents should be planted to report regularly. Kennedy recommended a budget of $16,400 for the first year.[41]

Kennedy suggested that this surveillance program not be made public knowledge or even known to the army generally. If, he wrote, the preliminary work of securing an appropriation from Congress and organizing the force of operatives was properly handled, it would be possible to establish the program "without its existence being generally known." The Quartermaster Corps had an allotment for 1917 of $18,000 for interpreters, guides, and spies, and for 1918 an estimated $20,000, which would not be enough to establish the Canal Zone office. Kennedy suggested that a fund of $11,000—an amount still allotted to the military information section, part of which was being used to pay clerks in the islands—be increased to $36,000 to establish the office secretly. He suggested that Secretary of War Baker go before the congressional appropriations committees in person and in closed session explain in detail the use of the money. He suggested that Van Deman, who was most familiar with the "necessities of the case," accompany Baker to explain to members of Congress the need for a suitable secret service in the Canal Zone.[42]

By late 1916, the War Department had already increased its reports to Attorney General Gregory about German activities in Mexico. Reports from army intelligence in El Paso were alarming. They reported German capital financing a Villista movement in Mexico to capture oil fields in Tampico. Funston was convinced that Germans were transferring their activity to Mexico. In fact, Germany did step up its espionage and sabotage activities in Mexico, apparently in an effort to divert the United States from involvement in Europe.[43]

Instead, such activities simply made Americans less willing to stay out of the European war. The reports from Mexico helped harden Wilson into a posture of no compromise with Germany. These reports also assured that Wilson would take seriously the famous Zimmermann telegram— sent by German foreign secretary Arthur Zimmermann to the German minister in Mexico, intercepted by the British, and forwarded to Wilson. This telegram, in which the German foreign minister asked for an alliance with Mexico and Japan in case of war with the United States, seemed to confirm the possibility that the United States would have to fight Mexico and Japan as well as Germany. Wilson held the telegram at first, but when Congress refused to support armed neutrality he released the telegram to the press on 1 March 1917. Publication of the telegram linked the fear of Japanese, Mexicans, and Germans together and drove the administration and the American people toward war. By 21 March the entire cabinet was convinced that German agents and submarine warfare were menaces to national security. They voted for war. That same day, the War Department notified commanding generals in all departments to "sternly repress acts committed with seditious intent." Wilson approved the action a week later, but urged Baker to warn army commanders to distinguish carefully between "ordinary offenses against law and against public order" and "acts committed under the provocation of the present excitement and with seditious or disloyal intent."[44]

As the United States moved toward war, the army began to review its military information gathering process again. Material on the war had been forwarded from attachés in Europe and from military observers operating with combat forces. Congress had increased the yearly appropriation to fifteen thousand dollars, but material simply piled up in the War College. Finally, at the end of 1916, Acting Division Chief Joseph E. Kuhn reorganized the division and assigned personnel to study military intelligence reports from abroad. A month later, Kuhn complained to Scott that material collected on the European front had not been circulated among officers and that the War College Division was in a helpless condition, lacking organization and personnel to do the job.[45]

Scott refused to budge. Much of the material was confidential, he replied, and it was too expensive to disseminate nonconfidential material. Baker did ask that some of the material be furnished to army officers, and Kuhn finally recommended that information on trench warfare and the training of troops be printed, distributed, and disseminated through service journals. The adjutant general, however, vetoed this plan to use journals as illegal. By March the army had done nothing to prepare itself with intelligence on a war toward which the administration was moving rapidly. Congress was still unwilling to expand the internal security role of the federal government. The Senate passed a number of laws to tighten internal security, but the House refused to pass any legislation on censorship. Opponents of the administration, including Theodore Roosevelt, expressed concern that a "spy" bill would forbid criticism of the government. Still the army moved toward a broader mission on the home front. During March Kuhn finally arranged with Scott to have National Guard officers trained in counterintelligence in Washington. These men were then to return to hundreds of cities and towns in the United States to provide the nucleus of a domestic intelligence network.[46]

The Bureau of Investigation was also taking up arms against the internal enemy. The chief of the Bureau of Investigation, A. Bruce Bielaski, encouraged a Chicago advertising executive to unite businessmen into a volunteer counterespionage network to defend the home front. Organized with the industrial, financial, and business sectors of major cities, this volunteer group took the name American Protective League and enthusiastically began to look for domestic enemies. Members swore secretly to report disloyalty, industrial disturbances, and other matters likely to "injure or embarrass" the government. As civilian volunteers and National Guard counterintelligence groups rushed to arms, both federal and state agencies moved to prevent the sabotage of public power plants, bridges, and railroads. The nation seemed to be swept into a giant surge of fear over espionage.[47]

These fears permeated the administration during the last days of peace. Wilson, Gregory, and Baker, the three men responsible for internal security, were cautious, but others were carried along by the spy alarms. Secretary of State Lansing warned that Mexico was teeming with spies. Secretary of the Treasury McAdoo urged that knowledge of German activities be used to "arouse and stir the people." And Gregory's assistant attorney general, Charles Warren, urged that alien enemies be summarily arrested. When Baker opposed the arrest or internment of alien enemies who had committed no crimes, Warren wrote excitedly to Gregory that surely Baker did not understand the situation, for there were many dangerous leaders and plotters in New York and elsewhere who had committed no crimes but who were very dangerous if left at large. Finally even the cautious Gregory seemed ready to believe that trouble was being planned by German citizens.[48]

When Wilson spoke to Congress on 2 April, he justified the war in part by citing German threats to internal security through espionage and sabotage. He spoke of spies, the course of intrigue, disturbing the peace, dislocating industries, and of the intercepted note of the German foreign secretary to Mexico City. He made it appear that war had already begun at home.

Even when Congress responded with a declaration of war, the older generals did not cease their cautious ways. General Kennedy, the chief of the War College, suggested that army intelligence should be "strictly confined to military supervision" and that the army should cooperate with but not interfere or mix with work that could be done by the civil government. He recommended that an information section be reestablished in the War College to handle secret service work, but that it be confined to military matters. Scott and Baker authorized that an officer be put in charge of intelligence work at once.[49]

Van Deman now launched a major campaign to establish a full-fledged military intelligence division with broad powers. He forwarded to Kuhn a report of the London military attaché about the importance the

British army attached to the organization of military intelligence. He argued that allied governments would object to receiving United States troops unless "efficient" means had been taken to eliminate possible German and Austrian spies from their ranks. Kuhn endorsed the report. "Nothing can be done affirmatively until diplomatic exchanges have taken place," Baker scrawled across the report in reply. Baker did approve the forwarding of confidential reports from American attachés in Germany to the French. The navy had already established the Office of Naval Intelligence as a separate agency within the Office of Naval Operations, and both Kuhn and Van Deman chaffed at the restraint in the War Department.[50]

Kuhn was soon back urging Chief of Staff Scott to establish a separate army intelligence agency. The chief of the British imperial general staff, Sir William Robertson, offered to send select officers to the United States to help set up military intelligence. The head of the British counterespionage and censorship bureau, Gen. G. K. Cockerill, suggested that six or seven officers be established in the intelligence branch to deal with the press, cables, mails, secret service, and counterespionage. Military attachés assured Kuhn that an intelligence system would be absolutely necessary if the United States sent an army to the continent, that much espionage was going on, and that the British were said to be spending $15 million a month all over the world and $3 million a month in Belgium alone. Scott did not reply.[51]

When Kuhn's messages brought no response, Van Deman went in person to see Scott. He pleaded the poor condition of United States intelligence; the necessity of exchanging information with France and Britain; the importance of having information on an enemy organization and an efficient service for discovering and eliminating spies and saboteurs within the United States; and the need for an organization to establish and maintain a central register of individuals to control and supervise espionage and counterespionage. Van Deman had two or three interviews before an exasperated Scott ordered him to cease his efforts to establish the organization and not to approach Secretary of War Baker on the subject. "I think this would be intolerable to our people," Scott wrote angrily to Kuhn of Van Deman's proposed intelligence operation.[52]

Van Deman did not continue attempts to change the policies of the chief of staff. Instead, he lobbied behind Scott's back through the Washington chief of police and through a novelist friend (probably Gertrude Atherton) to get an audience with Baker. Such tactics brought results.

Baker allowed Van Deman to spend a half hour explaining the need for intelligence, then ordered Scott to approve the Army War College request to organize secret service work.[53]

By 5 May the order was official. Van Deman became chief, with authority immediately to hire civilian assistants; correspond directly with departments, agencies, and individuals within the War Department; and begin secret service work. His job was to collect, collate, and distribute military information; to supervise military attachés abroad; to supervise intelligence officers and offices at posts and stations and within commands in the field; and to consider policy questions regarding army intelligence for the general staff. He also was to supervise and control any system of espionage and counterespionage established by the chief of staff or secretary of war; to cooperate with the allied military intelligence; and to prepare instruction in military intelligence work for the use of forces in the field.[54]

Van Deman's responsibilities seemed vast. He received no funds, however, and only two assistants, one active and one retired officer. Moreover, Baker and Scott had not yet given approval to proceed with espionage and counterespionage, which they expected to control directly. They waited for guidelines from Kuhn. On 13 May Kuhn sent Scott a memorandum spelling out exactly what Van Deman thought should be included in counterespionage of enemy agents: prevention of the collection and transmission of military information; of sabotage activities of property, especially munitions plants and transportation facilities; and of the causing of strikes and spreading peace propaganda. Military agents under military control would conduct certain types of investigative work; civilian agents under civilian control would conduct others. Reports from all agents would be gathered under a central office in army intelligence with a central registry to enter and collate information. Since this information was "exclusively military," it should be under the general staff, as it was in Britain and France.[55]

Scott remained unconvinced. When Baker ordered Scott to accompany Elihu Root on a mission to Russia and General Bliss became acting chief of staff, he too opposed the plan. Finally, Kuhn said he would use army intelligence within the War College as a nucleus, allowing the other duties to evolve through experience, and consult with other agencies to work out cooperation. Baker asked the comptroller for a five hundred thousand dollar allotment for intelligence.[56]

Other members of the administration shared the impatience of Van Deman with the lack of a central intelligence agency. Secretary of the

Treasury McAdoo urged Wilson to establish an agency independent of existing groups, housed either in the State Department or in the Treasury Department. McAdoo clearly saw the political potential in such a central intelligence agency. Given his prewar manipulation of the spy scare, it is not surprising that Attorney General Gregory, Secretary of State Lansing, and Postmaster General Albert Sidney Burleson objected to McAdoo's plan. Gregory vehemently complained about McAdoo's Secret Service agents intruding on his domain to investigate aliens. New machinery might be necessary later, he wrote, but the Justice Department was doing an adequate job. Wilson agreed with Gregory about the danger of too much machinery. Like the high-ranking generals, he wished to move slowly on intelligence.[57]

There were several other abortive attempts to create a central intelligence agency. Secret Service Chief Flynn and William Pinkerton both suggested counterespionage agencies. McAdoo pursued the idea into July, warning Wilson and Baker that the German spy system was operating efficiently. Publicity kept the public fearful of spies but merely led Wilson to ask for some system of cooperation.[58]

Van Deman and Kuhn continued to push General Bliss to expand military intelligence. Memorandums to Bliss kept coming, reviewing past recommendations, and repeating the suggestion that espionage be placed under the general staff and MID coordinate counterespionage. Kuhn emphasized that the enemy had a very complete and efficient espionage service over the entire country, in every walk of life, in ranks of the military service, in arsenals, offices, and munition plants, and that army intelligence should have the job of discovering spies. The chief could consult with departments and work out formal plans for coordination. Since the United States was now at war, Kuhn argued, military matters must be handled by the War Department, especially the discovery and elimination of enemy agents. "Espionage is repugnant to the ideas of our people and rightly so," Kuhn concluded, but he went on, "We have certain conditions confronting us which must be met." The War Department was "compelled" to employ counterespionage methods to fulfill its responsibilities to the people to protect the lives of soldiers and replace unofficial civilian organizations for "spy hunting." Untrained spy catchers would suspect all Germans, cause needless embarrassment to a large number of loyal, harmless American citizens, and seriously hamper the controlled and directed efforts of agencies charged with discovering spies.[59]

The arguments finally worked. Two days later, on 17 June 1917, the War Department officially assigned the War College the job of espionage and counterespionage. By 7 July a call had gone out to commanders of all departments to recommend 160 men, preferably young college professors and instructors, to train as military intelligence officers. (Military Information was now referred to as Military Intelligence.) By that time, the entire National Guard had been called into federal service; states were hurriedly forming Home Guards to replace National Guard units; and commanding generals had been ordered to deal directly with local officials and businesses in suppressing sedition and safeguarding "public interests."[60]

War had changed the reluctance of civilian and military leaders to institutionalize military intelligence. In the interplay of constraint and expansion, the Mexican crisis and then involvement in the European war moved the United States government to establish its first systematic army internal security apparatus. Van Deman had been working for such an agency for almost two decades. Van Deman had his mandate. He had now only to implement it.

CHAPTER SEVEN

Watching the Workers

During World War I, federal officials put in place a radically new internal security system to safeguard industrial production. They called the system plant protection. For the first time in American history, the government systematically watched vast numbers of workers. These were not workers suspected of espionage or sabotage, or even of the more vague charge of disloyalty. Instead they were ordinary workers who happened to be working for companies that had government contracts. During World War I the federal government may have signed as many as thirty-seven thousand contracts with private companies. The policy of the War Department was to maintain a surveillance system composed of volunteers in the companies that signed these contracts. The job of the volunteers was to spy on their fellow workers as they produced the war material so critical in this new industrial war.

The army had given relatively little attention to Germany as an enemy before the United States entered the war in April 1917. Concern about the Germans in Mexico drew the attention of MID to the border, but it had largely avoided the squabbles over who should chase Germans during peacetime. The War Department policy remained one of no peacetime surveillance in the United States with ad hoc exceptions for Japanese and Mexicans. The entry into war, however, was the signal for MID to expand its surveillance throughout the United States. The use of troops in the

West, where worker-employer conflict was still open and crude, led the army into its first extensive internal security experience with American civilians. The immediate causes were the activities of the Industrial Workers of the World (iww).

In the years preceding World War I, iww became the leader of the militant workers' movement in the United States. Brash, aggressive, daring, willing to denounce racism, and to admit women, iww was known more for its activism than for its anarcho-syndicalist theories. The iww had sponsored free-speech fights in the West, organized strikes in the East among immigrant workers, and drawn to its ranks some of the most dedicated organizers in American labor history. It spread quickly among the unskilled, the unorganized, and the migratory workers of the South and West, as well as among the immigrant workers of the East. In 1912, iww members divided into eastern and western factions contesting for control—disciplined and sympathetic to state socialism in the East, individualistic and anarchistic in the West. By 1914, leaders had emerged who concentrated on organizing farm laborers and harvest hands in the Midwest. By 1917 lumber, mining, and agriculture had become the main industries from which iww recruited workers. These industries had traditionally depended on marginal surplus laborers and now had to compete for workers as war production began to boost employment and wages. An agricultural workers' organization formed within iww soon boasted a membership of one hundred thousand.[1]

The iww was also making inroads among longshoremen and Philadelphia dockers. On its way to becoming a mass movement, iww was bargaining and making agreements with employers while forming political alliances with socialists, foreign-language federations, and feminists. Although iww did not take a formal antiwar stand, it continued to organize and refused to allow employers to make unchallenged profits. Locals called strikes in the copper mines and timber lands of Arizona, Montana, and Washington.

Even before the United States joined the European war, rightists were calling the iww "treasonous." Private detectives in the pay of corporations had infiltrated iww, with as many as four agents in some locals, all unknown to each other. These men were often among the most violent provocateurs and sometimes the first arrested. Fear of iww had taken root among a large number of men who linked their fortunes to corporate capitalism. James A. B. Scherer, president of the private college that later became the California Institute of Technology, summed up the emerging sentiment for counterinsurgency in May 1917. Members of iww, he wrote, were missionaries of class warfare who wanted social revolution and "should be exterminated as we would exterminate a nest of vermin—swiftly, secretly, and completely, since otherwise it will more and more infest the body politic and ultimately reach the very heart of government." Scherer wanted the army to patrol the Pacific states to prevent insurrection. Western National Guard units, the military backup force that had buttressed corporate control, were scheduled to depart for the East and then overseas duty in early August. One hundred twenty-five thousand combat-ready troops, Col. Brice P. Disque warned, would be needed to keep order west of the Rockies.[2]

The army had been particularly vulnerable to the hysteria of businesspeople in the West during the Philippine war. One of the important exceptions to the general policy of restraint in involvement with posses and detectives after 1878 had occurred at the Coeur d'Alene mines in Idaho. The army went into Coeur d'Alene three times in the 1890s, and each time state and local officials used the army in ways that violated the intent of the Posse Comitatus Act. The most blatant example was in 1899, after policies regarding the law had seemingly been established in the army. In that year, Brig. Gen. Henry C. Merriam assisted in more than one thousand arrests, held prisoners under military guard for long periods of time, and allowed his name to be used on state orders outlawing a miners' union.[3]

In most of the previous interventions, presidents had carefully considered their constitutional powers and issued proclamations to disperse when sending in troops to maintain order. The proclamation itself symbolized the extraordinary role of the army in these disturbances. In 1894, the president had used troops to enforce federal injunctions. Troops were used as a posse comitatus during some of the strikes and sometimes had made arrests, but federal injunctions or proclamations gave constitutionality to these actions. The 1899 Coeur d'Alene intervention violated almost all of the constraints built up during the preceding decades. President McKinley issued no proclamation, and General Merriam reported to the attorney general that there was no sign of resistance and that officials had decided a proclamation was not necessary. Because the National Guard was still on duty in the Philippines, the president allowed the governor to use the regular army on a scale much vaster than in any previous disturbance. Soldiers engaged in house-to-house searches, guarded prisoners, and apparently joined in investigations. The activities evoked broad public criticism of the executive's use of the army.

Congress once more responded to public criticism of the army's role in law enforcement. Although the Republicans kept the investigation in the House Committee on Military Affairs, which they comfortably dominated, the War Department was clearly under attack. Officials maintained that although they had warned Merriam not to take orders from civil peace officers, not to arrest or to guard during disturbances, they had not issued explicit orders. Merriam had ignored orders not to act as a posse comitatus. The majority committee report condemned the miners as a mob and "a dangerous cancer," arguing that the president could delegate authority over the army to whomever he wished despite army regulations. The minority report called the conduct of the president and military forces "reprehensible, violative of the liberty of the citizen, and totally unwarranted by the laws and the Constitution of the United States."[4]

Federal intervention in peacetime strikes in Nevada in 1903 was carefully monitored by President Roosevelt and did not result in congressional criticism of the executive's military policy. Intervention in labor disputes through mediation seemed to gain support. Such national calm was only superficial, as labor-management conflict continued in many parts of the country. For the time being the federal government seemed above the bitter class warfare that swelled and subsided in response to economic conditions.[5]

Although there was strong evidence of growing class consciousness among officers and an increasing tendency to consider the interests of management identical to the national interest, there was still little interference by army officers in domestic affairs. Domestic conflict remained primarily the concern of the states and, until World War I, officers had relatively little to do with these conflicts.

The anarchist scare of 1901–03 shifted the interest of government from the labor movement to left-wing political activists. Anti-Chinese legislation of the late nineteenth century, particularly the Geary Law of 1890 that ordered Chinese immigrants to carry identity cards and led to ruthless federal raids to ensure compliance, had already compromised America's place as an asylum. The new anarchist laws, however, legislated against political views rather than race and affected primarily European immigrants rather than Asian immigrants. In 1908, Congress also excluded material from the mails that tended to incite arson, murder, or assassination. The exclusion in the 1870s of birth control and abortion material as obscene had preceded this governmental intervention into areas traditionally protected by the First Amendment, but now direct action against political creeds replaced action against supposed immorality.[6]

These slight shifts only confirmed what most Americans believed before World War I. The federal government would remain relatively isolated from the military and civilian repression that sometimes occurred at the state and local level, and it would expand its control over society without engaging in repression. Most military officers were aware of that sentiment. In 1903, when the adjutant general's office prepared its first history of federal aid in domestic disturbances, it contained only a mild defense of army intervention. After noting that the army had been called out almost every year since the birth of the nation, the author concluded: "It is a favorite argument of opponents of a military system since the beginning of history, that the existence of organized troops is, in itself, a temptation to use them. In the face of our compilation, one can not but wonder what would have been the course of our history without them." The reasoning was not complex, but the appearance of the book with its brief defense of the army was symbolic. Called upon to defend the army's activities in domestic disturbances, the professional officers were still reticent about the army's role. Professional soldiers had successfully weathered an era in which there was not much use for their services, maintaining their prestige by minimizing controversy, particularly their involvement in internal security.[7]

An important test of civilian acceptance of army involvement in internal security occurred in 1914 in Colorado. In the spring of 1914, when violence occurred in the coal fields of southern Colorado, labor leaders appealed to President Woodrow Wilson to intervene. Mother Jones, the fiery old labor organizer, had been held by the state militia for nine weeks and imprisoned later for almost a month, but the Justice Department refused to intervene, saying it was a state matter. In April, the Colorado National Guard fired on a workers' tent colony at Ludlow. Bullets and a subsequent fire left a score of women and children dead. Again the workers asked Wilson to intervene, sending a delegation that included one of the mothers who had lost three children in the blaze. Congress held hearings on the conflict, but the companies involved ignored Secretary of Labor William B. Wilson, a former coal miner and labor union member who was attempting to help negotiations. Union leaders warned that the workers were arming for protection and would retaliate if the federal government did not intervene.

Women's groups in Colorado exerted strong pressure on the governor to request federal troops. State guardsmen were reluctant to return to the mine areas because of the unfavorable publicity resulting from the "Ludlow massacre" and because of the news that the militant workers were arming. The Colorado governor, yielding to these pressures and concerned about the expense of National Guard duty at the mines, called on Wilson. On 28 April Wilson ordered federal troops into the Colorado mine fields where many remained for eight months.

The army occupation began with overwhelming public support. The workers surrendered their guns to the army and appeared satisfied. Mother Jones praised President Wilson. While the period of occupation was relatively free of incident—troops acted well, and there was apparently no military surveillance of workers—Wilson could not get the companies to negotiate. By December the miners had capitulated and recognized defeat. In January 1915 the troops were withdrawn.[8]

The 1914 intervention proved to the corporations that the presence of the army did not mean their defeat but that it could contribute to their triumph over the workers. Public opinion accepted intervention by the federal government much better than by the National Guard. The state found that it saved money by using federal troops and avoided the political consequences of using the National Guard in labor disputes. Intervention showed striking workers that the presence of the army would not necessarily benefit them. The significance of the Colorado intervention would become evident only after the United States entered the European war. When the War Department established MID and authorized army officers to repress acts "committed with seditious intent" and to guard "public utilities," the army began to respond to the calls of businesses for regular army troops to keep peace on the home front.

In mid-July 1917, IWW called a strike in the western lumber areas. State authorities believed that IWW was also calling strikes in Minnesota's Mesabi range, in the wheat fields of South Dakota, and in Arizona copper mines. South Dakota Home Guards and volunteers drove IWW laborers from wheat fields. United States attorneys in Minnesota ended strike talk by making wholesale arrests and prosecuting for failure to register for the draft. In western Arizona, the Citizens' Protective League and Workmen's Loyalty League rounded up more than sixty suspected IWW members and sent them across the California border in a boxcar. In eastern Arizona, a Bisbee mob headed by the sheriff of Cochise county rounded up almost twelve hundred workers and supporters, then deported them to New Mexico in boxcars. In Gallup, New Mexico, the county sheriff deputized armed guards of the Gallup American Coal Company and deported another thirty men to Belen, New Mexico.[9]

The Arizona–New Mexico deportations brought the army into the dispute. Wilson ordered federal troops to care for the Arizona refugees,

Attorney General Gregory alerted U.S. attorneys that the IWW was dangerous, and the chief of the Bureau of Investigation ordered a country-wide investigation. While the Justice Department investigated, the army responded to calls from owners of Washington spruce timberlands to prevent a lumber strike there, and from mine owners at Butte, Montana, and Globe, Arizona, to prevent miners from striking. In Montana, troops raided IWW headquarters and held leaders and members in jail for several weeks without charges. In Washington, troops broke up camp meetings, searched freights for migrant workers, arrested organizers, and jailed dozens of IWW members. The army turned over persons legally detainable to civilian authorities for legal action, but those held illegally were simply given to the sheriffs with orders to hold them until officers in command ordered their release. In other cities, commanding generals began to respond to calls by mayors for federal troops. Never had so many federal bayonets been in the streets of so many towns. The IWW retaliated by calling a strike for 20 August to force the release of "class war" prisoners held legally and illegally.[10]

The action of the military in the West combined with increasing pressure from governors in the Midwest led Attorney General Gregory to support widespread investigations of IWW members as a prelude to prosecution. In Chicago, Bureau of Investigation agents opened a secret office where volunteers assisted in the nationwide investigation. Reports from private and company detectives, local police, and sheriffs were forwarded to the secret office along with agents' reports. Meanwhile, in Montana, copper company thugs lynched IWW organizer Frank Little while vigilantes and Home Guards in Oklahoma arrested hundreds of protesting farmers and Socialists. By 10 August the county jails in the southeastern part of Oklahoma were jammed and the state prison was being filled. The United States attorney there talked about asking for the death penalty, and newspapers called for prisoners to mount a "federal scaffold." Almost three hundred men were charged with draft resistance in this so-called Green Corn Rebellion, and eight IWW leaders were charged with conspiracy. On 19 August troops shut down the Spokane headquarters of IWW, prohibited assembly in the streets, and detained all activists and leaders. In Arizona copper towns, the army dispersed crowds, prevented meetings and gatherings, guarded mine and mill property, and patrolled the community.[11]

Large-scale military intervention in strikes merely increased the clamor for federal action elsewhere. It seemed the predictions of Colonel Disque about needing 125,000 combat-ready troops to keep order west of the Rockies were coming true just days before the first draftees were to report to southern cantonments and National Guardsmen were already on their way east. Because open strikes were being suppressed, iww adopted the slowdown as a tactic on 1 September. Men stayed on the job and used more covert methods. To employers, undercover agents now seemed even more necessary in the shops. Employers began to accuse all dissident workers of being iww members.

Secretary of War Baker recognized that the continued use of the military in labor disputes could both deplete the army and lead to the disaffection of other workers. He recognized the need for an alternative. Massachusetts reformer Felix Frankfurter thought that if iww leaders could be identified, the government could mediate the grievances of more moderate groups, isolate iww members, and render them impotent. Frankfurter obtained the endorsement of Justice Louis Brandeis and other reformers before presenting his plan to Baker on 4 September and suggested that Sidney Hillman be appointed special investigator. Frankfurter and Walter Lippmann volunteered to help MID in a campaign for more intelligence funds. Baker asked for, and Congress soon appropriated, $1 million for intelligence for the coming year.[12]

The Justice Department also put increasing trust in the investigation of dissident workers. The first fruits of those investigations were massive raids on iww offices. On 5 September the Bureau of Investigation and civilian volunteers raided twenty iww offices and iww headquarters in Chicago. Justice Department agents confiscated tons of literature and arrested hundreds of suspected iwws to prevent what newspapers called "a nationwide plot." The myth of a general strike was being used by the right as they painted a vista of burning wheat and corn fields, disorganized mining ventures, and disrupted home-front efforts. German spies also figured in the conspiracy, according to the vigilant *New York Times,* which affirmed that the iww raids had been a good beginning. The *New York Times* editorialized: "The country must protect itself against its enemies at home." The press generally supported the raids, though a few newspapers, like the *Detroit Free Press,* cautioned against overriding constitutional safeguards and resorting to extralegal methods. The *New Republic* counseled discrimination in raiding techniques but endorsed putting down the "reckless and disloyal" fomenting of strikes with a "strong hand." Wilson wrote to Max Eastman on 18 September that "a line must be drawn" about what should be considered legitimate and illegitimate opposition to the war, "and we are trying, it may be clumsily but genuinely, to draw it without fear or prejudice." The IWW raids crushed the dissident labor organization. Indictment of 166 IWW members followed in Chicago for violation of the Espionage Act.[13]

The administration did not use troops as prominently in labor disputes in 1918. Instead of employing troops, the army developed a vast plant protection system. There is little record of discussion of the Posse Comitatus Act, but certainly that must have played a role in the decision to rely less on troops. The Pinkerton law of 1893 also restrained Baker from hiring private detectives. Thus, he began to expand his own force of undercover agents.

The plant protection system functioned this way. A government plant protection agent conducted fire and safety inspections of each plant. After conducting an open inspection, he secretly secured from a company executive the name of a plant official to act as head of an "Interior Secret Service Organization." The plant official provided him with a list of the company's most trusted employees to act as captains. The agent called these workers together in the evening, appealing to them as patriotic citizens and as laboring men to lend their support. He asked these workers to supply a list of additional workers they felt they could control and who were loyal to them. The agent then called together these men—future lieutenants—and lectured them, as well as asking for lists of workers to enlist as privates. To inspire personal identification with "doing good for the government," the agent might issue small identification cards on which were printed the member's number, the name of the plant, and the pledge of allegiance to the American flag. If workers left employment in the plant, the agent might refer them to voluntary surveillance organizations within which they could continue to send in reports wherever they worked.[14]

In large corporations, agents developed a quasi-military system. At the bottom, 250 privates watched their fellow workers, then reported to twenty-five lieutenants, who reported to five captains. The captains then sent "captain's weekly reports" to the War Department's plant protection agents and to company officials. Privates could also send reports directly to the federal agents if they wished. Naturally, such a volunteer structure was not possible for all companies. An estimated 70 percent of all contracts went to companies in Massachusetts where, especially in large plants, the system was easily adapted. But in vastly different work sites—lumbering in the spruce forests of the Northwest and picking in the castor fields of the South—the Plant Protection Section (PPS) simply urged its agents to put some type of internal security mechanism in place. The goal of the War Department was to make thousands of workplaces secure from any possible attack on the home front.[15]

The plant protection policy was an abrupt departure from past American experience and ideology. Previous surveillance systems were relatively small because of a limited federal government and public distrust of espionage systems. However, this was a new international "industrial war." It came at a time when workers and capitalists seemed to have embarked on their own industrial war, one that many workers and businesspeople already saw as a potential class war. Long before the United States joined World War I and the rhetoric of patriotism swept thousands of Americans into a fervent war effort, the fear of industrial war at home had provoked efforts to reform the social and political system to ameliorate the conditions of workers. International war promised to further dissipate the danger of class conflict, but the conditions that gave rise to opposing interests did not disappear. War raised some fears while it stilled others.

The original impetus for plant protection came not from government officials anxious to expand their bureaucratic control, but instead from businesspeople who demanded that the federal government protect their industrial plants. Companies had a far older tradition of industrial surveillance than did the federal government. By the late nineteenth century, large corporations were emphasizing the surveillance of workers as a way to avoid strikes in the first place and eliminate opportunities for unions to gain strength when a strike conflict did develop. Surveillance, often combined with an ideology of company loyalty, became a major way of countering the activities of union organizers and of checking labor disputes before they began. In the early twentieth century, the establishment of in-house surveillance departments to supplement hired detectives became common among railroads and larger corporations such as the Ford Motor Company. The government plant protection policy of 1917–19 drew on the experience of corporate surveillance practices already begun but also spread the idea of surveillance to a far wider range of companies.[16]

As the United States prepared for war with Germany in early 1917, businesses clamored for government protection of their plants. Some owners feared that foreign sabotage might occur upon a declaration of war with Germany. Most suspected that labor groups would take the opportunity to press for greater control over working conditions. Pressure came from all parts of the country for the War Department to provide armed guards and for the Justice Department to provide surveillance. The army moved into some areas to act as guards but Secretary of War Baker refused to respond to requests from worried industrialists once the crisis of the first war days had passed. Attorney General Gregory was also reluctant to allow the Justice Department to become involved in any system that used armed marshals or employed large numbers of federal undercover agents in industry.[17]

In the first few months of the war, therefore, the Justice Department sanctioned the expansion of the private volunteer group of businessmen who offered to form a secret undercover network to watch for spies and saboteurs within plants. Eventually this group became known as the American Protective League (APL) and worked with both the Justice and War departments. The APL developed a quasi-military organization to operate secretly within industries. It reported to the government and to owners on workers suspected of espionage or sabotage. The APL was financed entirely through volunteer work and through donations by corporations and businesspeople.[18]

The War Department asked Edmund Leigh, the head of the Maryland APL, to set up an industrial espionage system through the Signal Corps in July 1917. During the summer of 1917, Leigh established networks in plants having contracts with the Ordnance, Signal, and Gas Defense departments. Paid for from congressional appropriations to the Signal Corps for war contracts, the money spent for this domestic surveillance was never accounted for separately. Five months later, officials asked Leigh to head the Plant Protection Section as a separate organization within MID. In July 1918, MID absorbed PPS into its own structure. By that time, agents were already infiltrating labor unions and reporting on strike situations so that strikes could be prevented. The surveillance of workers allowed the government to dispense with military guards at almost all defense plants. Instead, companies organized small forces of civilian security guards and PPS took the major responsibility for maintaining surveillance within the plants. The goal was to decrease costs and to undercut any public opposition that might result from the open use of military force to control civilian workers.[19]

In establishing PPS with Leigh as its head, the government did not intend to be controlled by corporate interests. The Plant Protection Section was a compromise to avoid extending federal control to all plants or paying companies for plant espionage. Although PPS operated in every kind of plant, from textile companies in Lowell, Massachusetts, to castor bean fields in Florida, it did not do everything the companies wished. Despite frequent requests, officials refused to go into plants that did not have government contracts. The War Department also refused to pay companies to hire their own detectives and bill the government, as some companies with war contracts demanded. Several large corporations manufacturing engines and airplanes wanted to hire their own detectives to "hold down labor troubles and seek out sabotage among the enemy aliens," then include the cost in their cost-plus contracts. In the case of companies like Standard Aircraft of New Jersey, which employed the William J. Burns detective agency, these costs ran as high as thirty-four hundred dollars during some months. Leigh, the head of PPS, objected to companies hiring their own detectives under contract costs and insisted they rely on his operatives, offering in support of his position the example of one plant where a PPS investigation showed that a detective agency had ordered its own agents to stir up unrest.

Nevertheless, the PPS practice of hiring detectives on "furlough" from their companies brought antilabor detectives into the system. A number of private detectives from railroads joined. Four New York City detectives, three from the "bomb squad," managed the important divisions in New York and Boston. A former railroad agent from Georgia headed the Los Angeles branch through most of the war, and he brought with him one of his former agents who had infiltrated the local Carman's Union in Atlanta and became its president. In theory, the War Department insisted that because of the 1893 directive prohibiting the employment of private detectives, these men must not remain in the pay of private agencies. In practice, both police detectives and private detectives were given leaves or furloughs to work with the War Department during the war and then returned to their former jobs. They brought to their temporary government jobs not only old attitudes and experience but also tactics, ties, and sometimes files, developed over long, bitter years of conflict between labor and capital.[20]

Leigh allowed each agent to form his own company network. An agent could create a separate recruiting mechanism, use APL, or, in areas where there was no APL, use other local "patriotic" groups. Leigh warned agents to be sure not to invest the volunteers with government powers, but it was difficult to establish an organization with the responsibility to conduct surveillance and yet forbid its informants from assuming some "color of government authority." In spite of this basic confusion, perhaps even because of it, the first volunteer network grew rapidly within the workplace and outside of it. As the number of plants increased, Leigh established separate divisions to supervise them.

The division chief about whom we know most is F. B. Stansbury who headed first the Portland office and then the Los Angeles office. Stansbury had a penchant for writing long letters to Leigh, thus leaving a fairly detailed account of his attitudes. Leigh trusted Stansbury because he always followed Leigh's orders and was willing to separate his actions as a PPS chief from his beliefs about what should be done to labor dissidents.[21]

Stansbury had considerable experience studying the left-wing labor movement in the United States. He boasted to Leigh that before the war he had adopted the practice of visiting IWW and Socialist headquarters and checking up on their reading habits so that he could describe their beliefs and attitudes. He had concluded that Jack London's *Iron Heel* was the main source of radical ideology. Published in 1907, but set five hundred years in the future during a utopian, socialistic era, the book purported to be compiled from the recovered diary of a revolutionist who had helped the proletariat overthrow the capitalists during the period from 1912 to 1932. From this "study" of radical ideology, Stansbury concluded that all socialists were IWWs and Bolsheviks.[22]

His fear of socialism led Stansbury to argue that the army should play a greater role in controlling the activities of these radicals. He criticized army officers when they refused to act against radicals without a declaration of martial law. That restraint should be overruled, Stansbury advised Leigh. Soldiers should round up all IWWs in the Northwest and give them the "alley treatment," because they were native-born troublemakers. The alley treatment, as described by Stansbury, was a method "used by night city coppers who try their cases themselves up a dark alley when the case is bad but where no charge covers or where the evidence is not sufficient to justify their losing sleep in presenting the case in court in the morning." A "good mauling" administered by intelligence men and their civilian aides would put an end to the activities of IWW. "We had got to kill Prussianism with Prussianism at home as well as abroad. . . . These fellows fighting the Government here are no better than those on the fire-step in the opposite trench across the way," Stansbury wrote. Such vigilante rhetoric did not disturb Leigh, who later replaced his Los Angeles chief with Stansbury and extended his duties to cover San Francisco.[23]

As division chief, Stansbury had two tasks. The first, to inspect plants and provide for such things as improved safety and fire procedures, was done fairly systematically and was apparently welcomed by plant owners, fire underwriters, and workers generally. The second, to establish secret surveillance networks, was known only to company officials, not to most workers. Particularly during 1917, when Stansbury was establishing his first office in Portland, there was confusion about additional functions of

PPS. Some of this confusion continued throughout the entire period of the war. Stansbury was either instructed to become involved in general intelligence work or at least not cautioned against it.

Not until early 1918 did letters begin to appear in PPS papers that explicitly cautioned Stansbury not to become involved in general intelligence activities. One exchange between Leigh and Stansbury is particularly revealing. Leigh wrote to Stansbury on 7 February 1918: "Our work is strictly plant protection and we cannot employ men for General Intelligence or to operate directly against the I.W.W. as an outside matter." Stansbury replied on 22 February 1918 that all the various memorandums and letters he had received previously had led him to just the opposite conclusion, that "we might work on anything which we came across if it helped the progress of the war." Nevertheless, Stansbury immediately abandoned his plans for general intelligence in the Northwest. He also carefully instructed his agent in Hoquiam, Washington, on the scope of their activities, but even this letter affirmed that the agent could keep in touch with IWW if members violated federal or state law. Agents could take no action but could make brief reports to their local offices of any information brought to their attention so it could be forwarded to the Washington office for appropriate action. A letter dated 27 April 1918 from Van Deman affirmed that PPS was not allowed to go into general intelligence work, was only to handle counterespionage matters within the plant itself, and was to follow such leads as were connected with the plant or personnel. Agents were not to go into espionage work of any kind outside of plants.[24]

After being forbidden to engage in general intelligence activities, Stansbury shifted his efforts to increasing the activities of the military intelligence agents in the Northwest. He played an important role in having the military intelligence extend surveillance to five hundred logging camps through the Loyal Legion of Loggers and Lumbermen (commonly known as the 4L), a government-sponsored, army-operated union. The army had planned to allow the workers of each local to elect their own secretaries, but Stansbury convinced the officers to appoint soldiers instead and to use them for the surveillance of the sixty-two thousand union members. Stansbury laid out the plan, showed how it could be implemented, and pushed until MID established the program. While MID was expanding its military surveillance independently of PPS, it might never have established the 4L surveillance program before the end of the war without Stansbury's aggressive action.[25]

While PPS agents often singled out IWW, Socialists, and enemy alien workers for special surveillance, many others workers risked PPS investigations as well. At the Ford company in Detroit, PPS agents were convinced that they had a case that the Justice Department was remiss in not prosecuting. Subsequent correspondence showed that a suspect had admitted under interrogation that he had damaged wing struts in the factory, but denied that he had done it with any intent to hinder the war effort. There was no federal case involved. Still, the divisional office continued to complain that the Justice Department was not doing its job efficiently.[26]

Agents also became involved in a large number of loyalty investigations regarding workers. Units of the APL conducted most of the routine loyalty checks for new employees, but PPS agents investigated a wide variety of accusations against workers already on the job. In one case, a PPS agent recommended that both a worker and her sister be discharged because the woman was "a most rabid Socialist" and not desirable. In another case, a worker resigned because, although he was not political and had not engaged in any activity that could in any way be construed as disloyal, he was embarrassed by the investigation of his private life and was afraid that personal activities that could jeopardize his job might become known. In numerous investigations of this sort, agents continually extended their jurisdiction over workers' activities both on and off the job.[27]

By far the most important aspect of these investigations was the increasing involvement of PPS agents in labor unions and labor disputes. The agents' activities ranged widely. Undercover agents used labor officials to recruit workers for in-plant espionage organizations. They also used detectives earlier planted in labor unions by private industry to recruit informants or to move suspected workers into line. There is little evidence in PPS documents that organized labor questioned or objected to the network being woven about it. While further research may show distrust or opposition by the rank and file, moderate labor leaders appear to have trusted the Wilson war administration.[28]

The controversy over the use of identification cards for workers in industrial defense plants illustrates the attitude of most union leaders. When PPS announced its plan to have workers carry identification cards with their photographs, union representatives complained to Secretary of War Baker. Stanley King, Baker's private secretary, met with the men and assured them that identification was strictly a war measure. The pictures would be destroyed immediately after the war. The representatives withdrew their opposition.[29]

Most locals acquiesced to the identification plan. Apparently only

Samuel Levitt, Socialist and agent of the militant Machinists' union in Bridgeport, Connecticut, was able to oppose the plan successfully. In other areas union leaders publicly championed it. In San Francisco, for example, P. H. McCarthy, president of the State Building Trades Council and vice president of the American Federation of Labor (AFL), even arranged a supporting editorial in *Organized Labor.* The article was captioned, "A Perfect Plan of Identification." It explained how the War Department by this method ensured the safety of the institution in which the worker was an employee and prevented him from becoming the unsuspecting victim of a propagandist who tried to do the work of the enemy. According to the article and to the publicized plan of PPS, three photographs were to be used, one to be forwarded to the War Department in Washington, one to be retained by the PPS agent in the district, and a third to be given to the worker.[30]

That the identification program worked in this controlled way is unlikely. The very agent who arranged for the *Organized Labor* editorial wrote to Leigh earlier that in his district he arranged for five, rather than three copies, of each worker's photograph. As promised, one picture went in to the local office files, a second to Washington, and a third to the worker. The two additional pictures went to the plant where one photograph was placed on the worker's job application form and another on his job performance card. How many other agents made similar arrangements is not known, but this particular agent seems to have received no rebuke, although he was one of the agents later replaced for general incompetence. Many plant managers, even where companies did not have pictures for their own files, felt that the identification cards had a strong psychological effect upon employees in restraining shop floor activities not directly related to production. True to his word, Leigh had the photographs in Washington destroyed in February 1919. What happened to the other copies is not evident from the records.[31]

Most of the investigative work remained unknown to union officials and to rank-and-file members. Agents infiltrated labor unions where they made regular, detailed reports on meetings, organizing, strike strategies, and the activities of leaders. Agents sometimes assumed leadership or took the initiative in causing dissension in the unions or submitted recommendations that employees be fired for union activities or for radicalism. Early in the war, agents infiltrated the machinists' locals in the Northeast, militant and under Socialist leadership, and reported members' activities regularly during the war. Other agents reported on unorganized workers in the plant. One female operative reported regularly on the women in her plant in the belief that these reports would give the government information on the miserable conditions the women had to endure. But she also reported all sorts of personal activities, including a clandestine affair between one supervisor and a woman employee.[32]

Such activities seem not to have troubled Leigh. Some of them occurred in 1917, before MID tightened up discipline, but others occurred during 1918. The PPS agents made arrangements with the post office to check suspects' mail, they searched suspects' apartments, collected information from banks, obtained copies of telegrams, installed Dictaphones, and investigated lawyers retained by suspects. New York state enrolled agents as assistant directors of the state military census to facilitate, as one agent reported, men "going up to a victim and gathering information," who could then "be locked up if he lies." Agents eavesdropped on bar conversations and attempted to get prosecutions for disloyal remarks made after the suspect had been drinking. They made reports on "disorderly women" and "second story hotels" (brothels). They arrested bootleggers in hotels. The Dayton agent attempted to push through a municipal ordinance requiring all proprietors of hotels, rooming houses, and boarding houses to register guests, roomers, or boarders with the police department and took a census of all people, enemy alien or otherwise, residing within one-half mile of a government plant.[33]

Leigh occasionally complained to agents about wandering off on tangents not relevant to their mission or making reports so carelessly that the cases did not seem relevant. Sometimes the activities were more serious, as when one agent threatened to arrest a labor editor for editorials that did not seem patriotic enough, used information gathered on his personal life to force a retraction, and then planned to get a further retraction that was more humble. A report from the Dayton office in June 1918 that PPS agents were giving street talks to educate workers about the dangers of venereal disease provoked a penciled note on the letter: "Do we want our agents making soap box talks on venereal disease?" A letter to Dayton soon expressed alarm at the "startling departure from the sober conduct of the run of work generally done by this office," and ordered a halt to such talks. Men's morals and sanitation were not the concern of PPS.[34]

Most activities probably took place with the knowledge of other federal officials. In all areas PPS formed only one segment of the vast surveillance system developed by the executive through the Justice Department, War Department, Treasury Department, and numerous other bureaus and agencies within the Wilson war administration. At the local level, PPS district heads met regularly, usually on an informal basis, sometimes at lunch, with the regional heads of the Bureau of Investigation, Military Intelligence Division, Office of Naval Intelligence, and Secret Service to discuss local conditions. Often the APL chief, and sometimes police chiefs, joined in the coordinating sessions.[35]

Civilian federal officials did not always sanction PPS activities. Overlapping jurisdictions, poaching, and conflicts often occurred. One case in the Midwest may not have been typical in all respects but it was illustrative of the type of difficulty that developed when PPS became overzealous in its activities. The special agent of the Bureau of Investigation in Dayton wrote to his chief, A. Bruce Bielaski, complaining that while the Justice Department had been attempting to have aliens suspected of disloyalty transferred to different departments in plants where they could do no harm yet be kept under surveillance, PPS was having them discharged.[36]

Nor could cooperation always be obtained with the commanding officers of military districts and arsenals. At Rock Island Arsenal in Iowa, the colonel in charge told the Davenport PPS agent that, "he did not care to have anyone in the Arsenal spying on him or his men and sending in reports upon conditions found in the Arsenal without first consulting him." In Boston, the PPS head did not meet with Gen. William Crozier until late in October 1918, at which time the general asked him flatly just what was the object of PPS.[37]

Stansbury, like Leigh's other division chiefs, recruited many of his agents from within the plants. These were the men who for fifty to one hundred dollars a month reported on their fellow workers. Agents of the PPS used two methods of recruiting informants. Usually, they asked company officials to recommend employees considered to be loyal. These workers were most often supervisors or those who had considerable freedom in moving about the plant. In one Bridgeport company, for example, informants consisted of a supervisor in the tool department and one in the salvage department. One list of undercover agents at the Nitro plant in West Virginia (government-owned but managed by the Hercules Powder Company) named interior agents as a teamster, a labor supervisor, a clerk in the commissary store, a material checker, and a laborer. The Plant Protection Section also recruited workers and then asked them to seek work within a specific company. This method bypassed the company management entirely and allowed a great deal of flexibility in jobs. These workers were machinists, carpenters, and even unskilled laborers.[38]

Beside these paid informants, there arose a pyramid of unpaid informants recruited on the basis of loyalty to the company. Indoctrinated through special sessions that emphasized the importance of their surveillance for the war effort, these informants pledged secrecy through a signed oath and were told only the name of the person in the hierarchy above them to whom they were to report.

The aggressiveness with which agents developed these "Interior Secret Service Organizations" and placed paid agents in plants varied. When the agents did not report considerable activity, the Washington office sometimes prodded them into action. In November 1917 Leigh wrote to the Detroit branch to criticize the agent for only suggesting interior secret service systems to the companies and not initiating them himself. Leigh urged the agent to establish "a first-class system of espionage" at the time he made fire inspections, to appoint captains and lieutenants at each plant, and to stress the fact that PPS was "a patriotic organization in the service of the Government." As late as August 1918 Leigh wrote to Albert Thomas, an agent in charge of the Boston office, to reprimand him for not having more undercover agents in his district. Chicago, Detroit, and Philadelphia now all had very successful networks of undercover agents, and Boston should increase its number, Leigh ordered.[39]

During the spring of 1918 a wave of disillusionment with the war spread through plants. Inflation had climbed almost 58 percent during the war while workers' wages held steady. Unions responded to worker disillusionment by sending organizers to help the workers in their demands for increased wages and collective bargaining rights. Time and again PPS reports indicate that union organizers were investigated as soon as they arrived in town. By April 1918, agents in Baltimore, Maryland, were reporting on union leaders who organized strikes and were making general investigations of the activities of these leaders in other parts of the country. In May 1918, Van Deman asked PPS to gather reports on all impending strike troubles. A Detroit agent responded with long reports on organized labor activities, including meetings of the machinists' local and their plans for organizing the shipyards. The next month Leigh wrote to army officers cautioning them to differentiate between "professional labor agitators" and "honest labor leaders."[40]

That was hard to do as PPS agents became drawn into the mounting conflict between workers and employers. The head of the Chicago PPS office, for example, had responded to calls from the Manufacturers' Association in Antigo, Wisconsin, for an investigation of labor agitation that might result in trouble and the obstruction of production in the future. Convinced of the neutrality of federal agents, the secretary of the International Timber Workers local allowed agents to examine union books unattended. The agents copied all the names of members, planning to use them in case any future labor trouble occurred in Antigo. The MID sent out a special request in July to the Boston division head to forward information where strikes seemed possible so that steps could be taken to reconcile differences between employers and employees. Reports were to ascertain if the strike was the result of pro-German activities or economic conditions and the number and nationality of workers involved. The agent responded by compiling long lists of alleged "labor agitators," whether or not they were union members.[41]

Reports from agents varied as to conditions, but together they seemed to indicate the probability of conflict peaking at the end of the war. Two letters in the PPS files, both of August 1918, one from an agent and another from an employer, illustrate the escalating fears of both labor and capital.

The first letter reported a mass meeting in East Hammond, Indiana, where various unions were soliciting membership. Union organizers emphasized higher wages rather than on-the-job comforts, arguing that only higher wages would allow them to have better conditions at home. One organizer referred to the coming "Industrial War," which would occur after the world conflict was over, and warned workers to organize into labor unions to protect themselves because the "big fellows" were planning behind closed doors what they would do to the workers after the war.[42]

The second letter, from the president of the Portable Elevator Manufacturing Company in Chicago, reported the first strike of car employees in fifteen years. He felt that AFL, through its "agitators," was making every effort to unionize Bloomington before the AFL state convention in October. Although PPS refused to investigate this complaint because the factory had no war contract, it is reflective of the increasing edginess of employers and the important role unions were assuming.[43]

Thus, it is not surprising that in the militant strike activity of the armistice period, PPS continued its role in reporting. In late November Leigh asked for reports on "Bolsheviks." Agents made hurried trips to strike sites to report on radical labor organizers and to advise city officials on taking proper precautions so that war material and machinery would not be destroyed. While there was some cutting back, for the most part PPS legitimized its continuation by arguing that government-owned products were still being produced or were still on plant premises. The head of the Philadelphia division, who had an undercover agent on an eighteen-hundred-a-year salary in IWW, wrote to Leigh on 20 November 1918 that he was retaining the agent to devote full time to IWW, Socialists, and general labor troubles in his district. In February, with only a brief caution to remember that he was a government official, Leigh gave this agent approval to visit larger cities for the express purpose of getting in touch directly with chambers of commerce, boards of trade, financial people, and manufacturers to secure information from them about Bolshevik and radical activities. Yet that official role was surely aimed at perpetuating peacetime control over workers, for the agent wrote: "If there has been no combative associations formed in these different centers in this district, I am of the opinion that my call, if handled in the right manner, will possibly implant the thought in the minds of these gentlemen that an association of this nature is not only possible, but necessary."[44]

The end of the war had signaled the resumption of the domestic industrial war in the eyes of many workers and businesspeople. What role PPS would play in this industrial war was still to be determined. As Leigh put it, his thirty-eight district offices were in "full bloom" by the end of 1918. The offices, he wrote to Capt. Robert Howlett, were "capable of producing the consensus of opinion as to labor, Bolshevism, I.W.W., eight hour day, and such things as that." The files were becoming particularly valuable, he wrote; it was a pity that work would have to end. As late as 9 December Leigh authorized his Minneapolis office to employ an undercover agent to secure data regarding IWW activities. Machinists' union leaders in Bridgeport remained under constant surveillance through December.[45]

Agents' reports in January affirmed that not only were more unions planning strikes but also that radicals were moving into positions of leadership in many other locals. An agent in Detroit, W. E. Rittenhouse, reported in alarm to Leigh on 31 January 1919 that at a meeting at the Machinists' union headquarters there, "Pitchfork" Henderson had not confined himself to speaking about trade unionism and organization in the field but had dealt with economic aspects and called for the organization of workers in politics as well. The entire meeting, Rittenhouse concluded, "breathed of socialism and Bolsheviki, rather than the old-time trade unionism." Furthermore, the audience was very enthusiastic. Handbills distributed to the workers at the meeting contained a message from Eugene Debs, the Socialist labor leader convicted for violation of the Espionage Act. They read: "I am with and for the radicals. The hour has struck for action. Long-winded resolutions and humble petitions to corporation tools in public office and corrupt politicians are worse than useless."[46]

The activity of PPS between November and February was particularly important for MID because immediately after the armistice Secretary of

War Baker ordered MID to cut back. Some agents of PPS continued to operate through March, however, allowing MID officers to make contacts with their APL volunteers and to secure pledges of continuing assistance after their jobs had been officially phased out. The PPS did come to an end in the spring of 1919, after it had already collected much material for the Washington MID on labor conditions, labor leaders, and the political attitudes and organizations of many workers. It had also made the necessary local contacts to ensure that businessmen would privately continue the work PPS had performed during the war.[47]

How much did PPS affect the labor movement? Until the 1960s, the traditional history of federal labor policy during World War I portrayed the Wilson administration as sympathetic to organized labor. Subsequent studies by William Preston, James Weinstein, and others challenged that view. Their research revealed harsh government policies toward left-wing labor. These scholars focused on a dissident minority, however, rather than on exploring the methods by which the government attempted to control the mainstream labor movement during the war. Although labor historians now saw World War I and the years just preceding and following it as crucial ones for labor organization, the role of the federal government and of new internal security techniques employed by both government and private industry were minor themes in their analyses. Records of the Plant Protection Section were not open to these scholars, for the National Archives kept them closed until 1975, longer than any other administrative records of the Wilson war administration.[48]

Scholars rightly saw the war and immediate postwar period as the peak of intense organizing by labor that declined after the postwar repression. Because of increased strike activity during this period, it could be argued that PPS had little overall effect in decreasing the thrust of worker unionization. Without PPS, however, strikes during and after the war might have been far larger and extended through the most crucial plants in the country. Such organizing might have caused the government serious troubles in maintaining its war program and, in fact, controlling the economy. Had widespread open conflict between labor and capital developed during the war, the liberal and reform element that was still dominant in the Wilson administration might have lost control to the right or the left. By controlling the more militant thrust of labor, PPS allowed the administration to avoid direct confrontation with either labor or capital.

Eighteen months, the length of time the United States was actively at war with Germany, is not a long time. Still intense crises of short duration can provide examples and experiences that have a far more lasting effect than long peaceful periods.

The postwar period is more difficult to assess in terms of the influence of PPS. There is no doubt that company surveillance increased immensely during the 1920s and that the war experience provided both models and experience for companies and for undercover agents. Agents working for the government scattered back to private industry after the armistice, bringing with them a much enlarged concept of control through surveillance. Perhaps the only way to evaluate the influence is to ask what did industry have to gain from the wartime experience of PPS organization, its methods, and its agents, and to contrast that with what workers, unions, and radicals had to gain. Postwar conflict existed not only between labor and capital but also between radicals and moderates within the labor movement. When that conflict had ended, not only was capital in firm control but also moderates rather than radicals dominated the organized labor movement. With the militant labor movement defeated and dispersed, the entire union movement declined. The war ushered in not only the triumph of the corporate structure but also a partnership with politicians that ensured there would be little challenge from labor during the 1920s, a partnership not contested by labor until the Depression years. In the meantime, surveillance by corporations flourished. With the militant strike movement of 1919–20 crushed, companies could maintain the disorganization of labor without government assistance. More importantly, PPS simply reflected the fact that in the crisis of war the split between the military and civilians had grown deep, so deep that the military now considered ordinary citizens as a dangerous enemy to be watched.

At War: The Disloyal,
the Pro-German,
the Malcontent

Van Deman had convinced Secretary of War Baker that the country needed intelligence and counterintelligence. Baker agreed. He assumed Van Deman meant military intelligence and guarding against German spies and saboteurs. Van Deman had much more ambitious plans. He saw not just the war front but also the home front as in need of protection. He wanted an MID system much like that in the Philippines to guard against opposition to government policies. What began as a system to protect the government from enemy agents became a vast surveillance system to watch civilians who violated no law but who objected to wartime policies or to the war itself. Agents considered such dissenters from government policy to be disloyal, pro-German, and generally malcontent. They became the enemy at home.

In July of 1917, Van Deman formulated a plan to train 160 lieutenants for duty as intelligence officers with overseas units. Such a plan seemed reasonable; intelligence was necessary for the front line troops. Major General Pershing, who headed the American Expeditionary Forces in Europe, had no need for such a large group of officer spies and counterspies, however. He asked for only fifty officers. After the fifty men left for France in October, the chief of staff authorized that 250 men (officers and enlisted) be assigned to the home front. Eventually, the War Department approved 750 men for overseas duty and 500 for the home front. This group of home front and war front agents became the Corps of Intelligence Police or CIP.[1]

Van Deman wanted to call this group a secret service, but Secretary of the Treasury McAdoo objected that only his agents could use that term. The British had already replaced *information gathering* and *espionage* with the term *intelligence,* so Van Deman adopted it as well. The Corps of Intelligence Police was not actually a corps in the technical military sense. Officers were detailed for intelligence work but commissioned in existing army units. Van Deman had to beg for his men from sections that had unfilled allotments of officers. In other words, this was a temporary force, with a temporary assignment. War was still the occasion for temporary, not permanent, *career* officer spies.[2]

Van Deman expanded his operation rapidly at the beginning of the war. He began by soliciting information from private detective companies, such as Burns and Pinkerton, and by hiring civilian detectives. By June 1917 these detectives were being used regularly in the Western Department and in Boston, Charleston, Chicago, New York, Pittsburgh, San Antonio, and Washington. As the volume of work increased, Van Deman also encouraged his agents to use volunteers as well as paid detectives. He even allowed one West Coast intelligence officer to begin enrolling civilians in a formal Volunteer Intelligence Corps.[3]

Most importantly, Van Deman began negotiations with the head of the American Protective League (APL) to have its members work directly with army intelligence on an increasing number of investigations involving civilians. Van Deman promised a commission for one APL director who would establish a Washington APL office and act as liaison with MID. Charles Daniel Frey, a Chicago advertising executive and the youngest of the three national APL directors, became this liaison officer. In response to Van Deman's aggressive expansion, the Justice Department moved to maintain major control over APL by recognizing it as an official "auxiliary." Attorney General Gregory separated APL administratively from the Bureau of Investigation and did not allow it to move into the Justice Department building, but he approved Washington headquarters for APL with Victor Elting, a lawyer and director of APL, at the helm. The Justice Department ordered its volunteers not to make arrests, gave them no Bureau of Investigation commissions or badges but allowed them to carry identification cards. Thus equipped, APL volunteers began to receive requests from the War Department for investigations of civilians. The APL field force, now approaching one hundred thousand members, had as its primary task for the military the investigation of civilians going overseas and candidates for officer's commissions.[4]

The APL also developed an espionage system within plants producing war matériel. This system was composed of old and trusted employees who acted voluntarily as secret agents but who did not know one another. The Military Intelligence Division paid a second group of almost four hundred trained and experienced agents to work undercover and report to officers at MID offices in industrial cities. Eventually, this became the Plant Protection Section discussed in chapter 7.[5]

The chief of the War College approved expanded use of military agents partly because the civilian detectives that Van Deman was already recruiting were charging more than the four dollars a day the army wished to pay. Enlisted men could perform the task cheaper. As far as officers were concerned, as one MID chief said, they wanted to have agencies under their control conduct investigations, not "unsympathetic civilian bureaus."[6]

The expansion of MID at the bottom reflected an expansion at the top. In October, Van Deman ordered all camps, posts, and stations in each department to establish military intelligence offices and every division of the National Guard to have counterespionage officers to work undercover. The following month, Van Deman began to open new branches of MID in industrial cities where he already had agents working and to assign additional military intelligence and CIP sergeants to the troubled Western, Central, and Southern departments of the army. Officers, enlisted men, civilian employees, and volunteers jointly staffed MID offices and conducted investigations.[7]

Early in the war, MID opened its Washington field office at 310 E Street, NW, under the cover name "Personnel Improvement Bureau." The MID brought in three New York City police detectives, dressed them in civilian clothes, and kept their presence secret. Eventually, this office employed eighty-five persons, some MID, some CIP, and some civilians (including a group of Boston socialites and an architect), all under the control of the former New York police officer, Henry A. Taylor. Except for the police detectives, who had done some investigative work, all were untrained. James E. Henry, Sr., a Harvard graduate, arrived at the Washington office in May 1918 and worked as a civilian agent for six weeks before his induction as a sergeant. Henry read over piles of applications for civilian employment in government offices, trying to spot poor security risks. The only job of importance he could remember was one guarding several truck loads of documents that President Wilson was sending to France.[8]

The New York office, organized in May 1917, also drew heavily on New York detectives for its staff. Van Deman put in charge Nicholas Biddle, a deputy police commissioner, who brought in over twenty-three members of the police bomb squad. This office eventually had twenty-five officers, fifty-two CIP agents, fifty-one civilian inspectors, and thirty-six clerical personnel. Bomb squad members drew the New York branch deeply into criminal cases, which it claimed was needed to protect against sabotage. The CIP agents made some five hundred arrests. This was the group, for example, that arrested Agnes Smedley and Asian Indian revolutionaries, interrogated anarchists who ran an "underground press," and generally hounded left-wing radicals. The New York office obtained an amazing number of convictions, but few were cases relating to espionage or sabotage.[9]

Van Deman also developed a counterintelligence unit in the Ordnance Department to eliminate undesirable employees for "disloyalty, pro-Germanism, or more malicious motives," and to investigate commissioned officers. This group began with one officer and one special agent from MID. Eventually it had 180 operatives, a budget of $250,000, and networks of officers, enlisted men, and civilian personnel. The Signal Corps, which had traditionally dominated combat intelligence, was not completely banished during World War I. At least through September 1917, Secretary of War Baker used officers of the Signal Corps to investigate the radical lumberworkers in the Northwest. Some code and cipher work continued to be done under the direction of the Signal Corps, especially at the Riverbank Laboratories in Geneva, Illinois, where the plant was put at the disposal of the government with a commissioned reserve Signal Corps officer as its head. But Van Deman blocked the development of a counterespionage section in the Signal Corps.[10]

By November, Van Deman had ambitious plans for further Washington expansion as well. He estimated that MID would require 150 officers and 400 clerks, more personnel than the entire War College Division. He renewed demands for the establishment of MID as a separate division under the chief of staff with quarters in a permanent building. To rationalize and at the same time defend expansion, he described the increase as "a rather modest estimate" in view of the "facility" with which enemies had established a vast espionage system in the United States. Van Deman was irritated at the attitudes of army commanders. Sometimes commanders sent men for intelligence training who were not regular army officers; other times they sent men they simply wanted out of the war. Van Deman suggested that divisional commanders be sent to France to observe the intelligence service with Pershing. There seemed to be a lack of appreciation of the "vital importance of the functions of intelligence in this war" and of the need for competent soldiers specially trained for intelligence duties, wrote Van Deman in urging WCD to send a letter on the importance of intelligence to all divisional commanders. He argued that modern warfare necessitated systematic organization, that all the efficiency and perfection in combat and staff functions could not compensate for deficiency in military intelligence. The army high command did not accept Van Deman's version of the indispensability of military intelligence. It did, however, send a bulletin urging that officers be selected for high professional ability and experience, and reminding commanders that MID was not an information bureau but dealt almost exclusively with information on the enemy.[11]

The War College Division opposed a separate MID under the chief of staff. The college operations committee argued that the files were intermingled and must remain together. The MID record clerk was quick to point out in response that records of espionage were already separate, that only military attaché records were intermingled with purely general staff records, and that a new section for these could be started. Despite Van Deman's separatist movement, WCD continued to hold on to its growing offspring, arguing that the increase in counterespionage that had been responsible for the burgeoning was only a temporary wartime increase. With the end of the war, MID would return to its previous inactive role.[12]

Opposition simply made Van Deman more anxious to prove his bureau's worth and drove him into further expansion. Early in 1918, APL officials proposed that a separate APL division be created in MID. With recognition by the Justice Department and quasi-official status, APL was now absorbing "patriotic" organizations around the country and enrolling a vast home front army throughout all states. Almost two hundred thousand members in fourteen hundred cities and towns were available to work with the War Department. In January the army commissioned APL Director Frey as an officer and invited other APL directors to attend daily MID conferences at the War College. Frey met officers of MID and was impressed with their camaraderie and receptiveness to ideas. He suggested APL engage in counterpropaganda as well as investigation. Van Deman insisted all plans be cleared with the chief of the Bureau of Investigation, A. Bruce Bielaski, but was enthusiastic about the idea. Frey began working on plans for a unit in the War Department. [13]

Van Deman encouraged other volunteers as well. Allan Pinkerton, a descendant of the famous Civil War detective and head of the Eastern branch of the Pinkerton Detective Agency, received a commission as major to use his force to help guard waterfronts, to keep alien enemies from barred zones, control crews of ships docked at piers, inspect watchmen, and watch for intruders in liaison with police. Van Deman also had insurance agents turning in reports regularly. In fact, he asked George Creel, the head of the Committee on Public Information, to keep all mention of the fact that they were turning information over to the government secret lest the practice be stopped. The manager of Squibb and Sons in New York had an organization of twenty-five men to report on pro-German activities. The Traveler's Protective Association used its large group of members who traveled constantly to report to MID on critics of the government and on disloyalty among foreigners, blacks, and Mexicans who they felt were being stirred up by pacifists. The Traveler's organization collected information, but only a select twenty conducted special investigations. These members operated in areas where APL was not yet organized. [14]

Volunteers also staffed new offices in Philadelphia where they worked with the Pennsylvania state constabulary. During December Van Deman took steps to plan with the constabulary the spreading of a counter-espionage system throughout the Pennsylvania coal fields where one employer had complained that two fires had held back production and that most laborers were foreigners and union members. Van Deman suggested that the son of the coal owner, a general manager of many of the mines, come to Washington to plan an organization. The volunteer concept opened new vistas for MID officers. [15]

Secretary of War Baker had other things to be concerned about and for the most part left MID to its own devices. The whole army training system was breaking down, and there was increased pressure to reorganize and increase efficiency. The chief-of-staff system had not fared any better in war than in peace. Scott was out of the country much of the time during his tenure, and Baker depended on bureau heads for advice. When Scott retired at the end of September, Baker sought Pershing's advice and appointed Tasker H. Bliss, another officer near retirement. During the less than three months Bliss was chief of staff, he was totally overwhelmed by the job and was unable to make decisions. The third wartime chief of staff, Gen. John Biddle, who took over on 10 December, also lasted about three months. During this year of weak and indecisive chiefs of staff, MID had been able to carve out its empire, though not to achieve the position Van Deman had wished under the chief of staff. A restless Congress held hearings in December and suggested a war cabinet. Baker subsequently set up a war council consisting of himself, the assistant secretary of war, and five ranking officers. In March 1918, nearly a year after the war began, Baker reorganized the general staff and appointed as its chief Peyton C. March, a younger general who had been in France with Pershing. Baker also approved the move that Van Deman had advocated, to shift MID to the executive division of the general staff and move it to a new building.[16]

Even before the administrative change, MID was in transition to a vaster counterespionage network. A six months' study of German espionage had confirmed that Germany did not have a complete, long-matured, or well-developed spy system in the United States. The MID simply concluded that the Germans must have employed traveling agents and therefore that it must develop an even vaster communication network through city police, railroad employees, post office, traveling salespeople, private detective agencies, large corporations, and volunteer groups. This network could then discover the financing of the Germans. Meanwhile, a strict system of control instituted at Key West and New Orleans could detain anyone attempting to leave the country while under investigation. A network of Washington socialites would cover the diplomatic corps, especially Germans and Austrians who had remained behind, but also diplomats from neutral countries and Russia. Other investigators would watch the owners and employees of German-American newspapers. Even musicians would be investigated since to be successful they needed German recommendations and thus, the reasoning went, would be subject to German influence. Pro-German Lutherans, German shipping lines, the sailors' union, associations that helped sailors, and German insurance companies and banks, should all be watched.[17]

The MID was developing a life of its own. It was setting its own broad limits according to its urge to control the environment through investigation. To be sure, Van Deman planned to defend the country with his thriving bureaucracy. Behind his drive seemed to be the fear that the people of the United States could not be trusted and therefore should be controlled. In February 1918 Van Deman gave each intelligence office in the field explicit orders to perfect a counterespionage system among all the civilians in their areas.[18]

The push to expand the surveillance of civilians coincided with external pressure on the government to establish a central intelligence agency. Chief William Flynn of the Secret Service began the drive in 1918 with a publicity campaign designed to compel the consolidation of intelligence forces. Flynn called in reporters and announced that he was resigning because he could not get the cooperation of the Justice Department. Secretary of the Treasury McAdoo followed up Flynn's resignation with another complaint to Gregory about APL, insisting that the Secret Service be allowed to investigate violations of wartime legislation and that a central intelligence bureau be established. Justice Brandeis lent his support to such centralization; so too did Theodore Roosevelt, who opened his doors to Flynn. After Flynn assured Roosevelt that the government needed a unified bureau because German agents were destroying property and jeopardizing lives, Roosevelt wrote a public letter to Sen. George Chamberlain, Democratic chairman of the Committee on Military Affairs, calling for a centralized intelligence bureau. The American Defense Society (a volunteer society formed with the support of Roosevelt and wealthy eastern Republicans, and already negotiating with MID to merge with APL) chose this time to announce that the War Department had already put to death fourteen enemy spies. Acting Chief of Staff Crozier denied it, but the announcement seemed to confirm the rumors of spies crawling over the United States.[19]

The congressional threat to take over and direct a centralized internal security operation encouraged Van Deman to take the initiative for total coordination of the entire home front war. He launched a counterthrust at the Secret Service with a proposal for weekly coordinating meetings. The Justice Department supported him, blocked the efforts of the Treasury Department to expand its investigative power, and established a clearinghouse. The new clearinghouse arranged for reports from the Justice, Navy, and War departments to be compared and investigations assigned to army intelligence. On 15 March 1918 Van Deman presided over the triumphant removal of MID from WCD to its new building at Fifteenth and M streets. He was now master in his own house and a dominant figure in internal security.[20]

In mid-March the Soviets signed a peace treaty with the Germans, and Germany turned to attack with renewed energy in the West. April became a month of fears. Would the Japanese use the war to expand in Siberia? Would American Indians stage uprisings in Utah and Nevada? Would Mexicans launch attacks along the border? In March, when the French condemned the adventurer Paul Bolo to be executed as a spy,

"Boloism" became the talk in America. One newspaper claimed that an American "secret service" agent, not allowed to operate at home, was responsible for five executions in England. He was purportedly supporting the Secret Service plan for a central intelligence agency in the Treasury Department. Spy hysteria washed over the country. A common complaint was that if the War Department had shot no spies, then it should begin forthwith. Translated into the urge to do something, the spy phobia led to support for the War Department to take over all trials of spies, as well as investigations.[21]

The War Department had very restricted jurisdiction over spies. Under article 82 of the Articles of War, persons definitely suspected of espionage who were within the military forces or under the jurisdiction of the War Department were subject to trial by general court-martial or military commission and upon conviction could be executed. An Espionage Act passed in June 1917 provided that other suspects came under the jurisdiction of the Justice Department. Under this act, trespassers within prohibited areas could be legally ejected but could not be arrested or punished. At the end of July 1917 the chief of the War College suggested an amendment to provide for the summary arrest and punishment of those trespassers, but his recommendation was not acted upon. Now many senators were lending their support to expanded war zones around defense plants where the military would have jurisdiction.[22]

Ironically, this expansion of jurisdiction found its strongest supporter in Charles Warren, a constitutional lawyer employed by the Justice Department. After the initial conflict with other departments, Attorney General Gregory put John Lord O'Brian in charge of all war work. A lawyer with an impressive understanding of constitutional law, O'Brian had gained Gregory's trust with his restrained internal security policies. Gregory placed Charles Warren, the constitutional lawyer who had previously handled war work but who had a more expansive concept of internal security, under O'Brian. Warren had consistently argued for harsher penalties. In the *Yale Law Journal*, for example, he advocated that like citizens, aliens should be punishable under the treason statute and liable to the death sentence. When Gregory had asked Warren about expanding Justice Department jurisdiction of sabotage, Warren had replied curtly that the whole matter should be handled by the War Department. "One man shot, after court-martial," he wrote to Gregory, "is worth a hundred arrests by this Department."[23]

Gregory was willing to compromise, to split jurisdiction in cases where munitions or supplies for the army and navy were produced or where ships conveying munitions and troops were injured or blown up. He opposed any additional laws regarding disloyalty, however, because O'Brian regarded the Espionage Act as adequate. Gregory argued that, once established around shipbuilding plants, zones would allow the military to define offenses in those areas and to try to punish civilians as well as military personnel. He argued that the Plant Protection Section had already established guards and patrols around war plants; that the regular criminal courts and judicial machinery were equal to the emergency; and that extension of military tribunals or of military procedure would be "inexpedient and of doubtful constitutionality." He also argued that such expansion would disrupt business organizations and cause "great uneasiness and apprehension" among unskilled shipyard workers.[24]

Gregory's arguments convinced Wilson to oppose the new drive for military tribunals. Wilson wrote that it would be "a very serious mistake to put our own citizens under court-martial because it would give the impression of weakness of ordinary tribunals." To quiet the demand for military control, Wilson and Gregory supported a bill to amend the Espionage Act to give greater latitude in prosecuting persons accused of "disloyalty"; to allow the courts to impose harsher punishment for violations; and a new Sabotage Act to prevent the destruction of war matériel. These bills passed the House but in the Senate ran into opposition from senators who used the rhetoric of patriotism and vengeance to advocate prompt trials and quick hangings. "Spies must be shot" became a common preelection Republican campaign theme. When a German-American Socialist was lynched in Illinois, conservative Republican senators, including Henry Cabot Lodge, raised the specter of a defenseless America in need of court-martials and shootings.[25]

Warren allied himself with this group of partisan patriots. Himself a friend of Lodge's and a conservative Republican, Warren sent a brief to the Senate critics arguing that the military should have jurisdiction over all spies, as well as a model bill revising the 82d Article of War to allow this change. Warren's brief explained how the article had originated in the Continental Congress of 1776; how it had been revised several times during the nineteenth century to include civilians who had traditionally traveled with armies as teamsters or servants; and how Congress had extended the act to include civilians leaving the country with the military in 1917. Judge Adv. Gen. Enoch Crowder had advocated that the entire country be declared a war zone on the theory that modern means of communication and transportation made it necessary. "In time of war," Crowder declared, "spies are within the jurisdiction of military tribunals."

Warren mustered all the historical precedent he could find to support Crowder's proposition—including William III's execution of a French spy in 1795—and emphasized the importance of industrial property in modern warfare. Democrat George Chamberlain, chair of the Senate Committee on Military Affairs, introduced the Warren bill in the Senate and scheduled hearings. He told reporters that the Justice Department could not handle the situation and that military authorities should be given the chance.[26]

Baker, who had left on a secret trip to Europe just before General March took over as chief of staff, returned two days before Chamberlain opened his hearings. No doubt his return dampened the enthusiasm of the proexecution crowd. At the hearings, Norman H. White, a civilian who held a roving commission for army intelligence in New York, testified that the Justice Department had left spies and disloyal aliens at large in New York. Van Deman followed White, refusing to criticize the Justice Department but admitting that he felt military courts could do the job more quickly and efficiently than could civilian courts. Judge John McGee of Minnesota followed Van Deman with an exhortation to organize firing squads everywhere and make up for lost time.[27]

In the Justice Department, Gregory continued to alternate pleas for passage of the amendment to the Espionage Act with assurances that his department was already doing an adequate job. O'Brian urged both Gregory and Wilson to make public statements denouncing the hunt for nonexistent spies and the outrages being perpetrated against people under the guise of patriotism. Gregory and Wilson publicly took this position on 21 April, saying that the bill was not an administration bill, it was unconstitutional, and inconsistent with the spirit and practices of America. Warren resigned in protest, Chamberlain withdrew the bill, and Congress passed a Sedition Act to operate only in wartime. The line had been drawn. Courts were to remain civilian.[28]

Congress said nothing about army intelligence and placed no restrictions on the role of the military in internal security. The new chief of staff, General March, interpreted this as support for further expansion. Older staff officers were concerned about the resentment of line officers to intelligence and reluctant to force them to accept a bureau that they did not trust. The new chief of staff, with his cold-blooded drive for efficiency and disregard for advice from civilians, ignored these concerns. Baker, who later described March as "arrogant, harsh, dictatorial, and opinionated," needed such efficiency and did not interfere. The way was now open to forge ahead on the home front as well as on the war front. Congress appropriated $2 million for military intelligence activities for 1918–19.[29]

The MID now had a huge, sprawling network of army agents, paid civilians, and unpaid volunteers. The APL continued to form the bulk of the field force of MID, but Van Deman encouraged other volunteer groups to proliferate. By 1918, with Van Deman's approval, the Western Department had a Volunteer Intelligence Corps with over a thousand members. In the Midwest, APL agents competed with a similar secret volunteer group. Van Deman recruited volunteers from among retired army officers, private detectives, lawyers, and businesspeople in the Midwest. He asked the American Bar Association to furnish him with the names of attorneys in five hundred cities and towns in fifteen states of the Midwest. He urged the intelligence office in the Southern Department to put the entire city of Atlanta under surveillance. These moves he made secretly. "For the present we must be careful how we handle civilians," read a June bulletin from MID to its officers.[30]

Over at the Justice Department, the civilians were getting suspicious. By mid-June, O'Brian had news of MID activities in the Midwest, Atlanta, and on the Pacific coast. In a memorandum, he warned Gregory that army intelligence had definitely decided to supplant the investigative services of the Department of Justice throughout the country. Gregory was so alarmed he wrote to Baker asking that the Midwest volunteer plan be abandoned and that the Volunteer Intelligence Corps be demobilized. "Rest assured," Baker replied, "that the entire policy of the Military Intelligence Branch will be one based not only upon an understanding of the proper spheres of the two departments, but also upon a sincere desire for cooperation." Baker kept his word. The rosters of the volunteers in the West were turned over to APL, and APL remained the primary civilian group operating for the War Department.[31]

Baker began to discipline MID. He removed its aggressive leader by ordering Van Deman to Europe to make a general investigation of intelligence methods being used by the allies and by General Pershing. He then appointed Lt. Col. Marlborough Churchill, an artillery officer with no experience in intelligence, as head of MID. Later in the year, MID sought the approval of the Justice Department before expanding to collect information from the Texas State Department of Agriculture on morale and loyalty. When the Justice Department said no to MID's working with Texas officials, MID acquiesced.[32]

With Van Deman gone, however, MID found a new champion for its expanded role in internal security in General Crowder. Now in charge of the draft and working with APL in locating deserters and slackers, Crowder issued a twenty-six-page opinion defining the crime of treason and authorizing the "detention" of all persons engaged in the destruction of life or property or in the delay or obstruction of the war effort. Crowder defined treason so broadly that all strikes and all organizing for them appeared treasonable. Persons so detained were to be turned over to civil authorities, but regulations governing investigation and arrest amounted to martial law.[33]

Baker tried to control the military through reform. In August, he reorganized the general staff; raised army intelligence to one of the four main general staff divisions; gave Churchill the rank of brigadier general; and made him directly responsible to the chief of staff. Churchill divided MID into a Positive Branch, which collected information on military, political, economic, and social conditions; and a Negative Branch, which investigated and suppressed sabotage and espionage. He established the MI4 section of the Negative Branch with responsibility for civilian investigations. For the first time the army had an effective organization for gathering intelligence. The original negative purpose of MID at home— uncovering espionage and sabotage—was still uppermost in the minds of its officers and volunteers, however. One MID pamphlet prepared for APL operatives stated the view clearly. Abroad there were only a few spies, but at home, thousands of enemy aliens could damage the war effort.[34]

At home, of course, also meant Hawaii, the Philippine islands, Panama, and Puerto Rico. Surveillance had originated in these overseas colonies and remained more pervasive there than in the United States. While these overseas outposts guarded noncitizen civilians as part of their regular activities, surveillance in these areas shows most clearly what MID could do when unhampered by citizen control and how its focus moved from alien enemy to dissenter. In Hawaii there were only three hundred German enemy aliens, but the Hawaiian Department kept the entire population of three hundred thousand under surveillance. In Puerto Rico, the intelligence officer for the district simply took over the insular police force of eight hundred men. In the Panama Canal Zone, the intelligence officer organized a civilian secret service and police force composed of Americans and Panamanians, and paid the police force of Panama and Colón "retainers" for information. The officer employed Asian Indians, Chinese, Greeks, and Japanese as undercover agents for special investigations and formed a special counterespionage organization among employees in the Canal Zone.[35]

In the Philippines, where there were only four hundred Germans, surveillance was extended to all Filipinos and Japanese. Before the war one American and four Philippine operatives made civilian investigations. By September 1918, sixty-one operatives were engaged in ferreting out disloyalty among the native population. Increased Japanese immigration, which brought their number to twenty thousand, alarmed American intelligence officers who had assumed that these Japanese laborers needed only a few Japanese officers to be mobilized into a force larger than the entire U.S. army of occupation. These fears even led MID officers to arrange for a private company of American and Philippine capitalists to purchase a section of the coast that Japanese immigrants were negotiating to buy.[36]

The American public received no news of these overseas developments and little of those on the mainland. Few citizens even knew that MID existed, and those who did assumed it operated primarily against the German enemy abroad. Although civilian APL investigators worked directly for the War Department on thousands of investigations, they carried Justice Department identification. The MID had federal officials omit all mention of military intelligence from news releases. It was the most secret of all the so-called secret services of the federal government. Thousands of APL volunteers remained undercover in industries, keeping their regular jobs, but receiving pay for reporting on their fellow workers to the War Department.

In spite of promises to the Justice Department to keep the men in line, the Washington office never exercised complete control over its field offices. In fact, there seems to have been little concern over the activities of these men unless they ran into opposition from the Justice Department. Director Churchill considered himself mainly a public relations man for MID, running interference against the civilians within the War Department and administration as a whole, while his team—the same men Van Deman had welded into an intensely loyal, ambitious cadre—hunted out those suspected of opposing the war and considered "disloyal."

Once convinced that surveillance would free soldiers for battle, the War Department allowed MID to expand with little control. The unit of MID in Washington tended to pass on this lack of concern to the field offices. Part of the problem was a heritage from the old army tradition. Commanding officers wanted to appoint their own intelligence officers, often untrained, unqualified, and out of touch with the regular intelligence offices. Where the Washington MID established city offices, the result was often the same, for some volunteers refused to work closely with these offices, while the offices themselves were often maintained by volunteers with a will of their own. Despite the complaints of the Justice Department, the Southeastern Department intelligence office retained a number of voluntary informants, and members of the plainclothes Corps of Intelligence Police investigated civilians. In addition to using sixty-one CIP sergeants, these field offices employed civilian informants, APL investigators, Texas Loyalty Rangers, sheriffs, and chiefs of police.[37]

In the Southern Department there was little conflict with civilian departments because the chief military intelligence officer was a former official in the Justice Department. The Bureau of Investigation sent him copies of all reports from the department; the lack of conflict led to lack of criticism of methods. The main labor problem was that of ripening harvests abandoned by alien Mexican laborers who feared they would be drafted. Intelligence officers there helped prepare proclamations in Spanish and English to counter the exodus and kept in touch with chambers of commerce, local councils of defense, clergy, all important employers of Mexican labor, and the English and Spanish press. Officers even helped organize mass meetings where educated Mexicans explained to their compatriots that rumors about the draft were without foundation.[38]

In the Southwest, the officers adopted more aggressive tactics. The army remained on guard in Arizona to maintain order in the mining towns. There the new governor had promised workers he would have troopers removed and the Home Guard disbanded, and in February 1918 the governor kept his promise by ordering the Home Guards to turn in their weapons. The Home Guards refused to disband until ordered to do so by the War Department, however, and the Loyal League demanded that the army send more infantry. Laborers insisted that the Loyal League was nothing else but the old Merchants and Manufacturers Association, a weapon of "big business" to fight the unions before the war, now grandstanding to "patriotic people." The situation was really serious, reported one Bureau of Investigation agent, since citizens tended to brand anyone belonging to a union as an IWW member, thus encouraging union members to become IWWs. Another Bureau of Investigation agent reported that IWW members were not only against U.S. laws but also religion and fecundity, a reference to their support for birth control. The Loyalty League, meanwhile, promised the intelligence officers to report on all words and deeds of a revolutionary character. Before long, weekly reports from the intelligence office to Washington on "Socialists, Anarchists, IWW, and suspected Bolsheviks" led the War Department to insist that the Rifle Club of Arizona—which had guns and a charter from the

War Department—be disbanded because the club reportedly had Socialist officers. By August, Churchill was soliciting suggestions on how MID
could suppress IWW. The MID made a complete investigation of the Arizona governor and IWW, and by September the force of the unions had
been broken by a combination of surveillance and federal prosecution.[39]

In the Western Department, surveillance was even more widespread.
In July 1917, MID had two offices, two operatives, and four clerks. By
December 1917 it had fifty-five men in the Corps of Intelligence Police at
fifteen offices in cities in eight western states. By the summer of 1918 it
had offices at thirty posts, five camps, and two stations, plus counterespionage organizations throughout the civilian population. The Volunteer Intelligence Corps was replaced with APL, which then expanded and
merged with local patriotic groups such as the Minute Men, which had
already created an antilabor surveillance network throughout the state of
Washington.[40]

In the West, MID agents and operatives carried special identification
cards and badges to be used when information could not be secured otherwise, and most were deputized to make arrests as deputy sheriffs or
special police officers. Occasionally, they were accredited as representatives of the telephone company, gas and electric companies, newspaper
publishers, and other commercial concerns to enable them, as the chief
intelligence officer for that area said later, "to enter offices or residences
of suspects gracefully, and thereby obtain data."[41]

Arrangements were also made with postal authorities to inspect and
intercept mail. In October 1917 Wilson, by an executive order, had established a censorship board; in February 1918, postal censorship sub-
stations were set up throughout the Western Department. At the end of
March the army asked for a more extensive censorship of the mails because border censorship had revealed "draft evasion, disloyalty, desertion, and indiscretions." In April, the censorship of soldiers on their way
to Europe began. Post office officials supplied clerical help for censorship
in Seattle and in Calexico, San Diego, and San Francisco, California. In
San Francisco alone during the summer of 1918 the military examined
one hundred thousand pieces of mail each week. Surveillance included
not only private mail, periodicals, and books but extended to movie scen-
arios that MID reviewed on request.[42]

In Portland, Oregon, MID officers established perhaps the largest
counterespionage system. There the army organized one hundred thousand workers into the Loyal Legion of Loggers and Lumbermen as an
alternative to IWW unions and to quiet the disaffection of men in crucial

spruce production areas. Officers put four hundred logging camps under surveillance.[43]

Although the army maintained some concern for workers' conditions in Oregon, in Butte, Montana, intelligence officers and the local APL came under the influence of the anti-union Anaconda Copper Company. Intelligence officers and APL members joined in vigorously opposing the reappointment of a United States attorney who refused to prosecute labor organizers and a United States judge who refused to sentence workers. When complaints to Washington brought no action, MID arrested IWW organizers, had them jailed, seized their Northwest membership lists, and distributed the lists to cities that had ordinances prohibiting membership in IWW. By the fall of 1918, MID activities had played a large part in encouraging the restless miners to strike. After workers did strike, MID agents and APL cohorts raided union headquarters, confiscated records, jailed organizers without charges, and used draft evasion as an excuse to round up union members. When the judge issued a writ of habeas corpus to free one man, the APL chief kidnapped the man and deposited him at the nearest army camp. The MID soon had its way. The United States attorney was removed and the federal judge transferred.[44]

The MID was also proud of its role in countering what it termed "hostile propaganda and misguided leadership." Under the heading of misguided leadership came leaders of the sixty thousand persons of the Mexican-American community in Los Angeles and pacifist groups such as the Portola Institute and the People's Council of America. The army investigated antiwar clergy and religious groups, such as the Theosophists. When army agents considered enemy aliens dangerous, even if they had violated no laws, MID kept them under surveillance, occasionally searched personal effects, watched their mail, and sometimes summoned them for a personal interview to explain suspicious actions. Investigators mingled undercover in the San Francisco Chinese community and sent reports on Chinese suspected of draft evasion.[45]

By September 1918, the Western Department intelligence headquarters at San Francisco was housed in eight large rooms of the Flood building. The Office of Naval Intelligence and the Bureau of Investigation had offices adjoining MID rooms. The files of all three agencies were housed in a common filing room; the offices were open night and day. Frequent conferences of the heads of the investigation agencies and their operatives often resulted in pooling evidence for many successful prosecutions of IWW members in the West.[46]

All this had been created from the original desire to gather intelligence and guard against German spies. The army did catch one German spy. On 1 February 1918 in Nogales, Arizona, the army arrested German naval Lt. Lothar Witzke as he entered the United States. One of Witzke's accomplices had informed army intelligence of a plot to cause strikes and violence along the border. The War Department won a jurisdictional battle with the Justice Department over Witzke, who was then court-martialed, convicted, and sentenced to execution. Wilson later pardoned Witzke, and he was released and returned to Germany in 1923.[47]

By the fall of 1918 MID had moved from counterespionage to counterdissent, from a small force endorsed by the secretary of war to find German agents, to a force for keeping the population in support of the war policies of the administration. It had grown from a small group under the control of the chief of the War College to a separate division under the chief of staff with its own brigadier general as chief, a thousand civilians tending the growing files, and hundreds of army officers overseeing the vast operation. In the field it had offices throughout the army and in major industrial cities. It had the Corps of Intelligence Police working undercover and hundreds of thousands of volunteers investigating everything from fraud to applications for commissions, as well as countering propaganda and working on morale.

Army intelligence had became a vast force at home for the first time in history. Brought into being by fear of German espionage and sabotage, it flourished by expanding to secure the home front against homegrown dissidents and critics of the administration. Van Deman had taken his counterinsurgency system from the Philippines and the Mexican border and fashioned it to fit the American home front. Once established, there were demands that it remain.

CHAPTER NINE

War Plans White

The concept of a continuing war with an internal enemy composed of civilians who could no longer be trusted, even in peacetime, came from World War I and the Bolshevik revolution. It led to the development of War Plans White, contingency plans for a war at home. White stood for American civilians who might cause civil disturbances and possibly overthrow the government. Officers of the Military Intelligence Division usually identified these potential domestic enemies as radicals, Bolsheviks, or internationalists who renounced nationalism. In practice, these radicals might be IWW members, socialists, communists, anarchists, pacifists, or reformers wishing political change. They might even be people who defended the right of Americans to seek political change. They were civilians who wanted more political change than those who controlled the government were willing to consider. Or so MID thought.

In the fall of 1917, the Bolsheviks seized power in Russia and pledged themselves to take a war-weary, revolution-torn Russian people out of the war. During early 1918, as the beleaguered Bolsheviks negotiated peace alone with the Germans, against the wishes of the allied governments, they tried to build support by appealing to allied populations over their governments to stop the war. When no help came, the Russians signed an unfavorable peace with Germany on 3 March 1918.

Wilson did not at first reject the possibility of working with the Bolsheviks, but his message to the Russian people on 11 March 1918 made it clear that he was willing to offer support only if the Russians remained in the war. Since the Bolsheviks had already agreed to peace, leaders interpreted Wilson's message as an invitation to the Russian people to revolt against them. The Congress of Soviet Workers and Soldiers retaliated on 15 March by urging the laboring masses in all bourgeois countries to throw off the capitalistic yoke and establish a socialistic state of society. The United States soon offered to assist any power in Russia resisting the German invasion, and by May the United States ambassador had recommended intervention in the country, now engaged in a bloody civil war. Early in September, twelve thousand troops of the American Expeditionary Forces (AEF) landed in Siberia, though no state of war existed between the Bolsheviks and the allies. American forces in Russia were soon supporting the opponents of Bolshevik control.

The activities of AEF in Russia led to widespread criticism. Socialists, many of whom already opposed the war, now vehemently criticized Wilson's policy. Government officials who had previously feared that German propaganda might undermine Americans' support for war now feared "Bolshevik propaganda," a fear that soon generated a new war at home. By October 1918, MID had developed a plan to use returning American soldiers and certain citizen groups for "the stimulation of morale of the citizens of the United States." This plan called for the investigation of all citizen groups and their classification according to whether they were loyal, loyal-but-ill-advised, or disloyal. Through cooperation with loyal societies—Rotary clubs, state Councils of Defense, and the Four Minute Men Division of the Committee on Public Information—MID expected to discover and curb disloyal and ill-advised organizations. The MID estimated that approximately fourteen thousand disloyal societies existed in New York City alone.[1]

The MID was concerned that opposition to the government no longer seemed to be based merely on opposition to the war. Instead, opposition seemed increasingly based on the radical idea that workers should not only influence the government, as the more moderate labor unions had been allowed to do during the Wilson administration, but also that workers and soldiers should control the government as in the Russian soldiers' and workers' soviets. In Russia, such coalitions had taken the country out of war. In the United States, MID officers predicted that a similar withdrawal might occur. Already they believed the prewar radical labor movement to be coalescing with foreign ethnic groups sympathetic to the Russian revolution.[2]

Before such predictions could be confirmed, the European combatants declared an armistice on 11 November. When the armistice was signed, American MID officers were already in Europe expanding their war front intelligence operation to include information on the spreading unrest among the European civilian population. In Washington, MID color-coded these reports on charts that showed disturbances—revolutions, counterrevolutions, strikes, food riots, military mutinies, racial troubles, and epidemics. Reports went to the chief of staff each day; each Friday the summary included a special report on Trotsky and Lenin.[3]

Despite this growing interest in civilian conditions abroad, General Churchill, the director of the Washington MID, took the armistice to mean the end of civilian investigations at home. On 20 November Churchill notified MID officers that the emergency that required investigation among the civilian population no longer existed. He ordered officers to undertake no new investigations except for plant protection and to discover graft in War Department contracts, and to turn all unfinished cases over to the Department of Justice.[4]

The same day, however, the head of the Negative Branch of MID questioned the policy of completely disbanding the work of MID among civilians. Counterpropaganda was, he admitted, a political question. Probably the American public would resent participation by the military authorities in shaping public opinion or in countering alleged propaganda, and probably they would want peacetime problems to be studied by civilian rather than military authorities. He recommended the retention of a skeleton structure of MID, however, until peace conditions took shape and the sentiment of the people found expression. There was, he affirmed, much to be studied in the meantime. Mexican conditions, foreign elements in the United States, and groups "inimical to the existence of our form of Government" all needed watching. A second intelligence officer added his support for even broader peacetime work among suspects, secret societies, and political groups "inimical to the interests of this country and calculated to upset peace conditions." Whoever the officers had in mind, their activities were clearly political.[5]

The Justice Department also hesitated in disbanding its wartime APL volunteer auxiliary and urged members to continue vigilance. Provost Marshal Enoch Crowder asked members to continue to watch "radicals" and to make propaganda reports. Members of APL in Los Angeles, who were especially interested in reporting on "the Bolshevik spirit," offered their files as a master index for conservative politicians. Chicago socialists, intimidated during the war by government surveillance and prosecutions, reasserted support for a socialist soviet republic; endorsed the attempts of revolutionary Germans to establish a working-class government on the Russian model; demanded that American troops be withdrawn from Europe immediately; and called for the release of political prisoners and conscientious objectors in the United States. The APL and MID continued investigations of civilians in Chicago.[6]

When queried by Washington as to why he had not discontinued his work, the head of the Chicago MID office claimed he had not received the 20 November order. Other MID officers also pressed to continue radical investigations. On 6 December MID headquarters reversed their November directive and told the Chicago officer to continue undercover work with radical organizations. The volunteers in the Midwest intensified the surveillance of radical meetings and probed group financing.[7]

By early December civilians in the Wilson administration had gauged the sentiment of the people as a desire to return to peace. At the Justice Department, War Division head John Lord O'Brian began a review of wartime prosecutions and ordered some indictments dropped. Attorney General Gregory opposed amnesty—thus the trials of radicals continued—but he ordered a reduction of special agents to the prewar level and a disbanding of APL volunteers. Realizing that investigative reports could be used for political manipulation, he ordered APL units to deposit their files with the United States attorneys.[8]

The War Department began to dismantle its home front army as well. At the end of the war, MID had 282 officers, 29 noncommissioned officers, and almost 1,000 civilians at work. It had used $2 million for its work, a huge sum for its time, especially in comparison with the few thousand spent in previous wars. General Churchill recommended a gradual reduction of MID for 1920, a reduction of civilian employees to 150 and of CIP to 18. He recommended the retention of 200 intelligence officers for a field force. Such a force was not only vast compared with the total prewar absence of any intelligence operation but also when compared with the projected peacetime Bureau of Investigation.

Secretary of War Baker disagreed with these plans. All departments must contract and retrench, he told Churchill; MID could be no exception. Baker demanded a plan for sharp reduction. Churchill left soon for Europe to participate in the peace conference. His subordinates hurriedly asked officers from various sections of the army to send in letters of support for retaining as much of the MID organization as possible. They asked to retain seven staff officers. Baker insisted on further cuts.[9]

Officers also attempted to keep APL volunteers in the field. The Chicago MID asked APL to keep "Socialist-Bolshevik agitators" under close surveillance and to send in reports. In other areas, MID officers asked for rosters of volunteer APL veterans so that they could contact individuals directly to conduct investigations. The Justice Department soon heard of the movement and complained to Baker, and he again ordered his officers to abandon all investigations of civilians. Officers could receive information, the directive ordered, but they could institute no investigations of their own. On 1 February the Justice Department disbanded its APL volunteers.[10]

Army officers turned to Congress for support in maintaining an increased peacetime surveillance of civilians. Before the Senate Judiciary Committee, they insisted that only constant surveillance had kept the German-Americans from overt disloyalty and pleaded for eternal vigilance. In response, senators and congressional committees asked about the wartime activities of MID. Secretary of War Baker ordered that officers give no information to Congress. When the House held February hearings on appropriations, some members of Congress argued that there was no need to have any military intelligence at all after 1 July 1919. Others, of course, wanted MID to expand its investigations of civilians.[11]

Without a public record available to prove its need to continue, MID turned to the current activity of "radicals" as a reason to exist. Early in February, the chair of the MID History Committee, P. M. Buck, made a hurried trip to the field to inspect files for a contemplated MID history. On his return, he urged intelligence officers to keep in touch with the radical movement, especially IWW and Bolsheviks. He believed a general strike would soon be called and that in response the government would dispatch troops to move interstate commerce and the mails. Therefore, the War Department should have accurate information on the plans of radical labor agitators, cover "labor agitation meetings," and keep in touch with the designs of the leaders. He suggested that MID send to Baker a "discreet memorandum" requesting a reconsideration of the orders to abandon the gathering of information on radical movements. In subsequent instructions to departments writing their own histories, Buck requested a special section on the surveillance of radicals that had led to arrests, indictments, internments, or convictions. He hoped through historical data to point out how important MID was in keeping potentially dangerous persons quiet.[12]

Reports now began to flow into MID affirming the dangerous wartime activities of radicals and their continued menace. The Southern Department reported that the IWW movement was growing in Mexico; that Pancho Villa still had followers in northern Mexico; and that Arizona was a "veritable hotbed" of iww and other radical organizations. Wages would be reduced following the declaration of peace, wrote one agent, and serious labor troubles could be expected. There was a need to stop the distribution of literature by iww—their posters, pamphlets, and other cheap publications. Word came from Los Angeles that pacifist groups were attempting to revive propaganda to unite radical and pacifist groups to bring about universal peace and to prevent the formation of armies and navies. On 1 May, when socialist parades took place throughout the country, soldiers and radicals had clashed in the streets.[13]

Wrisley Brown, the officer who had been in charge of wartime counterespionage, developed a strong argument for the continuation of peacetime activities by MID. He emphasized the importance of counterespionage, investigations of individuals or organizations of "doubtful or plastic loyalty," of communications at borders and ports, of finances of enemy activity, of sedition, disloyalty, and treason. Ethnic groups and their affiliations with the peoples of their nationality in Europe had to be studied as well as radical labor groups, Bolsheviks, socialists, anarchists, iwws, and the Non-Partisan League. The MID should index dangerous leaders, monitor pacifist propaganda, keep foreign diplomats under surveillance, and make "discreet inquiries" about their activities. Brown reviewed the radical movement, concluded that it had no effective leadership or centralized plan, yet recommended that MID continue its investigations of ethnic groups, radical labor movements, and foreign organizations that attempted to shape American public opinion favorably to their policies and aspirations. He warned that the army should be especially well informed about ultraradicals who had repudiated the doctrine of nationalism—the foundation of genuine patriotism, according to Brown—in favor of an internationalism that made its devotees unwilling to fight the workers of any country.[14]

Brown produced an elaborate plan for MID surveillance of civilians. Because modern war required the mobilization of whole nations rather than armies, Brown argued, it was vitally important to military authorities to understand the psychology of its potential soldiery and the civilian population upon which the army relied to run wartime industries. The MID must, therefore, study radical ethnic and pacifist movements, their theory, personnel, extent, inclination to spread, probable affect on the military power of the country, and on the will of the country to engage in war. He recommended a clipping bureau, a library of propaganda, indexes of these organizations, and records of the past and present activities of individual leaders. In foreign countries, military attachés, who now numbered thirty-three and who had sixty-five officer-assistants, should conduct the peacetime investigations of important agents and "dangerous revolutionary agitators" so that they could be kept out of the United States or watched upon entry.[15]

While Brown produced his argument for continued peacetime surveillance, the new attorney general, A. Mitchell Palmer, was also moving toward the continued expansion of surveillance during peacetime. Bombings in Washington early in June—supposedly the work of anarchists—led Congress to give Attorney General Palmer half a million dollars to investigate political radicals.

Churchill went before the Committee on Military Affairs to request that MID also receive half a million dollars in appropriations. According to news accounts, Churchill talked about maps of New York and Brooklyn where radicals were located and data collected on radical movements to impress members of Congress with the need for continued work. He assured them that MID could keep track of the proletariat and parlor groups who were trying to form councils of soldiers and sailors like those in Russia. He was reported as saying that MID expected to continue to exercise surveillance over radicals. Newspaper reports brought complaints from Albert DeSilver, director of the Civil Liberties Union, an organization born during the war to defend dissenters from prosecution. DeSilver objected that espionage over citizens was contrary to democratic institutions and that whatever had been the excuse in wartime, that excuse no longer existed. The stage was now set for a major debate over the role of the military in peacetime. Baker sent DeSilver's protest to Churchill.[16]

News reports had been garbled, Churchill replied to Baker. All MID heads agreed that investigations were not their proper peacetime function and were only being continued in certain phases during the transition period. During the war, Churchill wrote, MID did have a free rein and recognized no limit other than the danger of bringing down public disapproval for its acts in its efforts to secure information. He offered the 20 November memorandum ordering MID out of investigations as proof of his peacetime policy. Appropriations were being asked only for positive intelligence all over the world. Investigations of graft and fraud would be pursued by MID at home, but not radical movements. Officers of MID would confine their activities to reading radical publications and attending public meetings.[17]

Churchill composed a letter for Baker to send to DeSilver denying that MID had ever investigated the political beliefs of citizens using espionage methods during the war. The MID had only cooperated with other civil authorities in investigating alleged violations of the Espionage Act, and these had been discontinued with the 20 November order. Civil authorities, authorized to make investigations, now forwarded information to MID on radical movements. No money in the appropriations would be used to investigate civilians except for fraud and graft in War Department contracts. Baker signed Churchill's letter and sent it on. Baker told Congress that MID was being demobilized as rapidly as possible and that half of the force would be discharged by 1 July. Thus reassured, Congress gave Churchill $400,000 to continue his work, 80 percent of his request.[18]

Despite continued funding, MID had to reduce drastically the number of civilians employed in Washington and in the field. The Chicago MID officer, for example, discharged nineteen of his twenty investigators at the end of June. Funding allowed intelligence officers to remain on duty, but they now used volunteer agents undercover to investigate strikes, labor unrest, radicals, and the foreign language press.[19]

Racial conflict soon gave MID additional support from Congress. On 19 July 1919, Washington had its first race riot, kindled by a fight between black and white veterans. Violence touched off four nights of rioting, leaving at least fifteen dead, and over a hundred wounded. President Wilson quickly called out federal troops. At the end of the fourth day, two thousand heavily armed soldiers, sailors, and marines joined seven hundred police and several hundred Home Defense guards in patrolling the streets while armed tanks were held in readiness to scatter crowds. A week later, a race riot ripped through Chicago.[20]

After holding special hearings to determine the cause of the riots, Congress concluded that "radicals" were the cause of racial unrest. The executive made plans to suppress another outbreak should it occur and to watch black communities. The Justice Department hired its first black undercover agent in Washington and ordered other Bureau of Investigation agents to gather information on black communities. The assistant director of the Bureau of Investigation also urged MID to extend surveillance to blacks. By the end of July, the Chicago MID had fourteen of its former twenty paid agents back investigating the riots as unpaid volunteers.[21]

In Washington, MID ordered two black officers about to be demobilized to make special reports on the "Negro situation." These reports confirmed that radical propaganda had made headway among blacks, but the officers emphasized, this was because of the real grievances of black veterans who had been segregated and discriminated against during the war. The National Association for the Advancement of Colored People (NAACP) was urging black people to insist on equality and to resort to force if necessary to establish their rights. Principles of self-determination and democracy publicized by the United States during the war had made Negroes more sensitive than ever to lynching and to Jim Crow regulations. They were disappointed and embittered because their expectations of the removal of discrimination in return for patriotic cooperation had not been realized. The black officers suggested that the claims of radical race leaders could be undercut by vigorous federal action to safeguard the interests of the black people and by the fair treatment of black soldiers by the War Department.[22]

From the field, other MID officers submitted terse reports. Blacks buying ammunition. Pullman porters running guns to eastern points. Blacks being refused permits to buy arms and ammunition. Labor radicals joining black organizations in protests. The National Equal Rights League supporting an amendment to the League of Nations treaty guaranteeing the rights of Negroes, calling for mass meetings on race defense all over the United States for 21 September. The *Crusader*, a black militant newspaper, answered the accusation of being Bolshevik defiantly: "If to fight for one's rights is to be Bolshevist, then we are Bolshevists and let them make the most of it."[23]

As whites faced the long-deferred outrage of blacks, violence increased. Lynchings and burnings of blacks occurred. Black soldiers were shot. There were open gunfights between blacks and whites in Arkansas. Race riots spread to Ohio. Looking for some cause other than the normal pattern of discrimination, newspapers reported that IWW pamphlets were circulating and that white socialist agitators had inflamed blacks. White lawyers defending blacks were accused of being socialists, their offices raided. Whites called the protests an uprising brought on by radical propaganda. When the National Urban League called a convention in Detroit on 15 October to explore the causes of unrest, the Chicago MID sent a confidential report to Washington on this "radical Negro organization."[24]

Strikes by white workers dotted the country too. In Boston, police walked out, and the governor called state guardsmen to police the city. Officers of MID forwarded rumors and reports of threatened strikes from other areas. In late September 1919, thousands of steelworkers in Gary, Indiana, called the first major steel strike since the ill-fated Homestead strike of 1892 and walked out in protest over low wages and long hours.

Wilson, who had started a tour of the country using the spectre of revolution to gain support for the League of Nations, collapsed in Pueblo,

Colorado. The nation seemed to be drifting toward chaos. On 29 September 1919, Secretary of War Baker, in a move that the judge advocate general later determined was "probably illegal," ordered commanders in areas affected with internal disorders to respond to requests of state legislatures or proper state executives without prior approval from the War Department or the president. In effect, Baker put the army in the hands of local officials as a posse comitatus. The orders remained in force for over a year, until 1 December 1920, when the judge advocate general recommended they be revoked.

In Washington, believing that domestic unrest was threatening to overwhelm civilian governments, MID immediately mobilized. It developed resurgent units in major cities and remobilized APL volunteers to shore up civil power. The Chicago MID officer predicted race riots at factories because "radicals" were inciting both black strike breakers and white strikers. His volunteers began gathering maps and laying out routes from Fort Sheridan, north of Chicago, to Gary, Indiana.[25]

General Wood soon left Fort Sheridan and marched into Gary with fifteen thousand troops. Wood put the city under what he called "modified martial law." Former APL volunteers reorganized as the American Patriotic League and a Gary citizens committee, composed mostly of superintendents and steel mill supervisors, compiled lists of alleged Reds and urged raids. The raids became a regular midnight-to-dawn ritual. Volunteers searched homes, hauled suspected radicals before MID officers for interrogation, and then had police jail them. Investigative groups blossomed all over town. The police chief had one, the sheriff had another, and an officer soon arrived from MID in Washington with a stenographer, a corps of agents, filing clerks, and wartime files. He organized a master card index of all radicals being investigated.[26]

Union officials complained to the secretary of labor. They objected that MID and Bureau of Investigation operatives were cooperating with steel company officials and their private detectives to intimidate workers and coerce them into returning to work. The Bureau of Investigation disclaimed responsibility and said only volunteers were working with the military. Baker went to General Churchill. Churchill defended his subordinates as usual, this time insisting that operatives work only in zones occupied by troops.[27]

During early 1919, with Attorney General Gregory and his assistant O'Brian still in the Justice Department, MID was cautious about using volunteers to continue collecting information on Americans. O'Brian stayed after Gregory had gone and influenced Justice Department attitudes through most of 1919. The Justice Department let MID know that it considered APL volunteers a necessary evil, needed in wartime to expand the Bureau of Investigation's limited forces, but amateurish—with reports based on rumor and hearsay—and their activities dangerous. Getting "too thick" with the old APL volunteers "in an unauthorized way," Churchill warned Chicago officer Maj. Thomas Crockett, would bring a clash with civil authorities. He wrote on 20 October 1919: "The Constitution of the United States was designed to make the military power subordinate to the civil power, except when martial law is declared. We cannot get around this situation, and no good citizen wants to. We, ourselves, must be the first to obey the law of the land."[28]

Yet within a week Churchill had changed his mind. He recommended to Gen. William G. Haan, director of the War Plans Division of the War Department, that a program be developed and officers trained to handle "radical rebel groups" attempting to overthrow the government.

What had changed Churchill's mind? One factor may have been a conference held at the Army War College on 22 October 1919. The reports prepared by intelligence committees at that conference give some idea of the attitudes of the time. Three committees were set up to report in October 1919: one to study the British Empire, a second to study the Japanese Empire, and a third to study the United States. The United States committee studied the tendency toward "socialism and Bolshevism."

The committee charged with studying the United States concluded that it was an Anglo-Saxon nation with native-born whites of native parentage as "the real ruling class." Russians and Austro-Hungarians were the most dangerous element, but any area with a large foreign element was in danger. The "Black Belt" of the South similarly was a "region of potential danger." Neither blacks nor immigrants, particularly those who spoke Yiddish or Polish, made good soldiers. Officers concluded that a class war was a distinct possibility within two or three years. Each community would have its revolutionists and loyalists, and there would be no sectional division as there had been in the Civil War. Therefore, all people and the entire infrastructure of the country were in danger. Plants, railroads, telephones, telegraphs, roads—all were liable to fall into the hands of the revolutionaries. While the officers believed that eastern and southeastern Europeans were the fomenters of revolution, or at least the most active, the most radical leaders seemed to be from the very class they had found to be the core of support for the government and its rulers. They explained this contradiction as follows: although these Americans constituted a minority of radicals, they had been able to assume leadership through education and language abilities. No race or nationality was immune to radicalism, and the "women of the radicals" were more likely than the "women of the conservatives" to be active participants in the disorders.[29]

Although this was only a general exercise, the War Plans Division already had under way specific Emergency War Plans White based on the same premises. Using an ad hoc field force of intelligence officers, recruiting officers, hired agents, and volunteers, MID began to issue "weekly situation reports" on domestic conditions and to furnish reports to the War Plans Division. The MID continued to collect information on individuals and groups. One MID officer warned Churchill the situation was "practically a state of war."[30]

Although much of the alarm resulted from the growing disturbances in the streets of America, it also fed upon reports of revolutions under way in Europe. Established governments disintegrated under the shattering effects of defeat. Dissident groups silenced by harsh internal security measures during the war made efforts to replace the old, discredited regimes with new ones. Dissidents asked returning soldiers to join them in creating new structures run by workers and soldiers. Although many of these were broad-based urban worker movements, they were often led by socialists and communists willing to take over and lead the new governments.

When these movements began to spread during the winter of 1919, United States intelligence officers in Europe immediately alerted Washington officers to the danger of unrest spreading to America. "There is no use telling you . . . [that] this movement," wrote Van Deman to Churchill, "means . . . a world-wide social and political revolution. In other words, the fulfillment of the dream of the Internationalist. . . . With this revolutionary business on there is no telling what may happen." Northern Italy was ready to blow up, Austria-Hungary had gone to pieces, Belgium was taken over, Holland was honeycombed with dissent, England and France dangerous. "It seems to me that the Intelligence Services of all of us should take this work over, in close liaison with the civil services of the various governments." Though hardly a "war activity," it was necessary to oppose anarchy with every means at their disposal. Van Deman ended with an ominous warning: "Things look most dangerous for the future."[31]

Thus the reports from within and without moved Churchill to act very differently than his letter of 20 October would indicate. On 27 October Churchill recommended to General Haan, director of the War Plans Division of the War Department, that a program be developed and officers trained to handle "radical rebel groups" attempting to overthrow the government. In the meantime, MID officers could use recruiting officers to report on organizations and activities, establish liaison with APL volunteers, and call on an intelligence reserve, to be set up in the Quartermaster Corps. With these many sources in the United States, Canada, and Mexico, MID could soon report on all of North America. The Military Intelligence Division could estimate the strategic situation should it be necessary to prepare plans for a general movement of federal government troops against a domestic enemy.[32]

During the winter of 1919, the War Plans Division developed War Plans White. General Haan was convinced by MID reports that a well-organized movement for the overthrow of the government did exist, that personnel available for an overthrow amounted to more than 600,000, and that nearly 1,500,000 could be mobilized in thirty days. Though not a military organization, the movement was under "marked control," its aim being to seize main transportation lines to keep food from industrial centers and thus force the public to seize the food supplies. An organized force would then step in, seize food depots and distribute food, thus gaining control of local government and the support of the people. This, said General Haan, was the same method the Reds used in Russia, Hungary, and the Ukraine in taking control. Class war would begin within two or three years.[33]

Such estimates were pure fantasy. It is true that there was racial and social unrest in the United States as elsewhere following World War I. In Europe there were well-developed political movements ready to overthrow the authoritarian governments of old elites that had taken citizens to slaughter rather than an easy six months' war, and there was a willingness to turn the guns of war on their own leaders.

In the United States, the Communist party had grown rapidly after the war. As distinct groups, white workers and blacks felt themselves deprived of the fruits of the war; there was strong sentiment to change social conditions. However, the civilian government was functioning everywhere in the United States. There were neither starving masses nor a revolutionary movement. There was no central control, no organized movement to take over the country. The Communist party, which boasted it had seventy-five thousand dues-paying members and 1 million sympathizers, was itself riddled with dissent. There were many internationalists in the United States, but few who wanted revolutionary internationalism. Most wanted changes at home and were concerned about organizing to obtain them. Still, party leaders boasted they could control the masses, and the

United States army was so removed from its own people that it identified with the authoritarian governments of Europe. The isolation of the army from the mass of American people was never as complete as it was during that winter of 1919.

The army was not alone in its delusions. Civilian authorities also changed during that winter of discontent. With O'Brian gone from the Justice Department, Attorney General Palmer put a young assistant, J. Edgar Hoover, in charge of a new Radical Division. Hoover recalled APL veterans to conduct raids on radicals in November 1919. The New York Lusk Committee also used APL veterans to round up two thousand people in seventy-one raids. Early in December, MID forwarded APL membership lists to MID officers throughout the country. The accompanying instructions told officers to use APL volunteers only as correspondents to report observations, not as investigators or military agents. Volunteers were to keep their intelligence collecting secret, for as one MID officer warned, radical agitators were disposed to misconstrue and criticize the collection of information by military authorities. Former volunteers soon received requests for maps, strategic information for troop movements, and reports on radicals and Bolshevik agents. They also were asked for reports on loyal organizations that might be counted upon to combat un-American activities and to aid in preserving law and order in case the military needed assistance. Nearly five hundred APL members replied within eight days of the first call.[34]

The units of APL survived in many forms. In the Midwest, an APL wartime stronghold with the greatest MID support, new units flourished. In Cleveland, APL became a Loyalty League. In Cincinnati, it became part of the Home Guards. In Jackson, Michigan, where city officials employed APL operatives to continue the surveillance of Americans suspected of un-American activities, raids followed on the Union of Russian Workers and on the Bulgarian local of the labor party. The local APL organizer wrote with pride from Jackson on 17 December: "I am able to say to you that these results recently accomplished are a continuation of the A.P.L. spirit in this country and that the officers of the League have been a factor in bringing this condition about."[35]

Illinois, the home of APL, remained the center of the most concerted efforts to resurrect it. Six state inspectors indicated their readiness to continue their wartime work. The Chicago APL reformed as the Patriotic American League and submitted reports to MID. By 30 December, the Chicago MID officer had received 116 reports. He asked for more reports, naming specific radical groups.[36]

Raiding went on through January 1920, with federal and local agencies joining in an orgy of arrests orchestrated by Hoover and the Justice Department's new General Intelligence Division (GID). In Boston alone, Hoover mobilized 300 to 500 Bureau of Investigation and APL men. Raids trimmed the Communist party to a hard core of 16,000 members but increased public opposition to continuance of this peacetime home front war. When complaints reached the Justice Department, Hoover took the names of his critics, checked his files for radical associations, then went to Churchill and searched MID files for similar material.[37]

The radical raids of early 1920 only confirmed Haan in his estimate of the seriousness of the situation. He warned the Army War College that a well-organized minority had gotten control of governments in Russia and Austria, and that in all countries a radical element sympathetic to their ideas existed. In the United States, the symptom of an attempt to gain control was the general strike, already twice attempted and the wave of the future. The general staff must be prepared, and the best way was for the Army War College to include methods of combating "an enemy lurking within the masses and who has a secret and more or less intangible organization, yet in a sense very perfectly organized." These little strikes were part of a larger situation, not a transitory affair but a permanent feature of American life. Because MID officers believed radical organizations were centralized, they also believed a similar countermovement was absolutely essential, an organization to arouse and direct public opinion and engage in direct action to get "red" elements arrested or deported.[38]

How could the army prepare when the public was protesting against military involvement in civil life and, in particular, about the use of APL veterans? During 1920, MID negotiated with several volunteer groups in an effort to work out a satisfactory arrangement.

One such group was the United Americans. The New York–based United Americans was committed to opposing radicalism wherever it existed and counteracting the "dangerous trend toward class consciousness." The United Americans soon expanded into the Midwest, in an attempt to convince midwesterners that the increasingly popular Non-Partisan League was "nothing more nor less than the same thing and both are the Socialists under another name." It is clear from correspondence in MID files that at least one MID officer saw the United Americans as a permanent postwar APL. Some Chicago intelligence officers apparently envisioned this group as a paramilitary backup for the military in case of insurrection. The head of the Central Department's MID, Col. Gordon

Johnston, suggested that the United Americans be asked to enlist railroad employees in case they were needed to operate the railroads in an emergency, and that in states such as Washington, former APL officials be used to create a federation of patriotic groups.[39]

Officers hovered around the resurgent patriotic groups. Surely, they believed, Churchill meant only that they must not "appear" to be active. An officer was present when representatives from thirteen midwestern states met to form the National Constitutional League in Denver to oppose directly the Non-Partisan League. The group was a midwestern federation with each state organization taking its own name, financed by business associations of the state. Their goal was to exchange information on the Non-Partisan League.[40]

In most of the country, MID finally settled on the American Legion as its main volunteer group. From its beginning in spring 1919, the American Legion had determined to function as an anti-Bolshevik force. By fall 1919, the question was whether the American Legion would become an openly paramilitary force. Officers of MID had growing evidence of local American Legion posts engaging in lawless activities in their efforts to curb groups considered to be radical. American Legion members organized raids in many cities, burned literature, confiscated membership lists, and had leaders arrested. Such actions took place in Illinois, Michigan, Ohio, and Wisconsin during mid-November. A report from a Chicago MID informant in November 1919 said he had been asked to join in "Ku Klux" work against radicals, destroying their stores and buildings. In Centralia, Washington, American Legion members and radicals had clashed openly on the streets in armed conflict. Four Legionnaires had died.[41]

The American Legion held its first national convention in late November 1919 in Minneapolis. Colonel Johnston was there as an official delegate from Kansas and on the Resolutions Committee. Johnston had another delegate introduce a resolution for him proposing that the American Legion arm and be available to take charge of civil disturbances. A sharp debate followed, as Johnston later reported to Churchill in an informal handwritten letter, but he found no support whatsoever. Members protested that they did not want to become a military group but only act as a backup of last resort, called on by officials after all other groups had failed. "Even the murder of fellow members at Centralia," wrote Johnston, "drew no definite expression of organized action though this resolution was also referred to us and debated." Johnston not only found little support for his plan but also considerable antagonism toward the regular army.[42]

Haan, director of the War Plans Division, had been present at the same Resolutions Committee with Johnston. He listened silently as the arms resolution was debated and when Churchill showed him Johnston's letter, replied that his resolution was "senseless" and a violation of the law. "That would take us back to the old Pinkerton days," Haan wrote. He felt the attitude of the Legionnaires toward the regular army had actually improved since the Armistice and that anti-army rhetoric had faded on the convention floor, where more than 90 percent of the delegates had voted for universal military training. "If the Regular Army isolates itself in the future as it has in the past, it will again be considered as an isolated sort of useless body, the country not knowing what it is doing, and consequently cannot understand why it is maintained," Haan warned. Haan's attitude was probably the reason why MID went no further than it did in the winter of 1919.[43]

Instead of a paramilitary group, the American Legion became an unarmed volunteer intelligence auxiliary, supplying MID with information. By January 1920, MID was asking for confidential reports from its officers on state American Legion activities. The MID estimated that American Legion posts contained a quarter of a million members in twenty-three states, ranging from Massachusetts with 120,000 men to Delaware with less than 3,000. These thousands of men were soon to be used for War Plans White, as groups the army could call upon to maintain law and order should the necessity exist. Churchill wanted officers to be careful to "not give the enemies of law and order an opportunity to say that the military service is linked to capitalism" and cautioned them again to avoid connecting their name with unofficial groups. [44]

It is not clear just how War Plans White would be used against a domestic revolutionary force, this "enemy hidden in the masses." Seldom did MID mention the tactics to be used against civilians. Churchill did note in the fall of 1919 that tanks were "an ideal weapon" for civil disturbances. Germans used tanks in suppressing urban riots during the winter of 1918–19. The German Landesjaeger Corps made no attempt to minimize the destruction of property or lives: they used airplanes equipped with machine-guns to attack people on roofs; armored cars; infantry with machine-guns and hand grenades; and artillery with trench mortars. Churchill noted the effectiveness of the methods of the Germans and recommended their adoption for War Plans White. [45]

The public knew nothing about these plans. The objects of various investigations did know that army officers were active in investigations and in various activities, ostensibly under the control of civilian authorities. The public was confused but did not stop criticism. Painfully aware of the power of the federal government to use information to curtail political organizing, groups protested the raids by the Justice and War departments and their volunteers. Even more critical for MID, however, were the complaints of high officers that MID was investigating the private relations and business of individuals. As complaints mounted in the spring of 1920, Secretary of War Baker called Churchill in to discuss the situation.[46]

Churchill was particularly sensitive to criticism at this time. The recently formed Joint Army and Navy Planning Committee had ordered an investigation of MID. The planning committee might, Churchill worried, eliminate MID completely. He rushed a memorandum to General Haan demanding a representative on the committee and asking that no changes be made in his division without his approval. Haan reassured Churchill of his support but stated that no change in the committee seemed possible. Churchill issued a strongly worded order to MID officers: "The political beliefs of officers and men, their moral conduct, their discipline and their attitude toward their superiors are none of our business." The MID was to stick to investigating graft and fraud, enemy activity, and disloyalty and sedition. It appeared that the surveillance of civilians would continue.[47]

Even officers within MID began to question the continuation of the political surveillance of civilians. An MID officer, Gardner Harding, who made a report in early 1920, found eighteen hundred separate civilian files and a strong procapital bias on the part of investigators who regarded workers as disloyal, subversive, and suspect—an attitude that resulted in a wartime spirit of "getting" prolabor organizers. Harding warned that the use of too many European methods—spying on individuals, the use of agents provocateurs, terrorism, arrest—might be the ruin of MID. He felt that MID field reports were not to be trusted, that the military should rely on the weekly summary of civilian activities that the Justice Department had begun, and that the peacetime function of MID should remain purely strategic. The State Department was forming its own foreign intelligence section, and Harding advised that the Justice Department should form a parallel domestic intelligence section to study radical thought and socialism. Information concerning the influence of dangerous groups could then be obtained from liaison with the Justice Department, state officials, and unofficial organizations.[48]

Late in March 1920, MID and the Bureau of Investigation attempted to develop such cooperation. The chief of the Negative Branch, W. W.

Hicks, met J. Edgar Hoover on 24 March, and over lunch the two men worked out a plan. The Bureau of Investigation would loan reports to MID for twenty-four hours, during which time the reports would be copied and then returned. Hoover agreed to conduct investigations on individual radicals for MID if Hicks had to reduce MID investigators in the field. Hoover complained that although radical and labor movements were worldwide, he was prohibited from having agents or informants outside the United States and the State Department refused to forward him reports. Hicks offered to get the foreign information for Hoover. Hicks was, however, ready to trim his collecting efforts. He believed the public accepted the necessity of gathering combat and military information but was opposed to the collection of information on politics. Thus he dropped such topics as bolshevism, anarchism, and feminism, continuing only the preparation of plans for a propaganda campaign in time of war.[49]

In late August 1920, Brig. Gen. Dennis E. Nolan, head of Pershing's intelligence operations in France, replaced Churchill as head of MID. He ordered a thorough review of MID and in October made his peacetime recommendations. Nolan asked that the Corps of Intelligence Police be continued to combat Mexican agents on the border and radical groups attempting to promote disaffection within the military. On 23 October 1920, CIP became a part of the War Department's peacetime army. The secretary of war approved 41 men for the nine corps areas; 10 for Hawaii, Panama, and the Philippines; and 31 for the United States. The men became a field force for MID officers attached to each corps area. A structure was now in place for peace as well as war.[50]

Thus intelligence gathering at home went on. The American Legion still reported to MID on the Non-Partisan League, IWW, and on socialists. Confidential orders issued in March 1921 to MID officers ordered the collection of material on radical activities, labor unrest, anti-American racial groups that promoted internationalism and class hatred, and subversive activities. Accompanying instructions stressed that intelligence officers were to collect literature and "converse" with well-informed people but were not to interrogate or to institute search and seizures. Nor were they to investigate crimes, political beliefs, or the morals of officers or their men. Still, MID expected officers to collect large quantities of material on all radical groups and prepare weekly situation surveys. At least one private, stationed at Fort McPherson, Georgia, interpreted this to mean that he could operate undercover and join IWW. When notified of the Georgia incident, the director of MID refused to intervene. Corps area MID officers were to use their own discretion in deciding how to operate. In lectures at the Army War College, MID officers warned that many people in the United States were dissatisfied with the government and social institutions and that although this was not dangerous, the government by repression and deportation was rightly keeping radicalism within safe bounds.[51]

The MID was still in the field when Congress declared World War I officially at an end in July 1921. The official end of the war once more opened debate on the future of the army. Would the army be most likely to again fight small wars in the American southwest as it had in the past, against native Americans or Mexicans? Or should the army prepare for another war like the one just ended in Europe against the armies of highly industrialized nations? The one big war, for which officers did feel they had to prepare, was with Japan. Although officers respected Japanese military strength, they had little enthusiasm for a Pacific war. A war with Japan would begin with early defeat in the Philippines, for the islands were militarily indefensible despite the costly war against the Filipinos.[52]

On 1 July General Pershing became the new chief of staff. The appointment of Pershing meant that the army would prepare for small wars in America's colonial empire or along the Mexican border. Pershing started his tenure by restoring the much-debated leather Sam Browne shoulder belt, an indication that he was looking to the past. He also reorganized the entire general staff. Adopting the system he had created in France with the American Expeditionary Forces, Pershing changed the name of MID to G-2 and ordered a review of its functions. The reviewing officer concluded that radical activities in the United States were insignificant and that much of the current work by MID was a waste. "In going through the Department," he concluded, "I get the impression that MID organization during the war must have concerned itself with some phases of governmental activity only remotely connected with any possible military application, and that the employment of this branch has not yet been trimmed down, nor its objectives limited to best serve the present needs of Military Intelligence." He suggested that the control of radical activities was the legitimate function of the Justice Department. The MID personnel could be employed elsewhere more profitably. That fall another review recommended trimming the Negative Branch of MID and limiting its objectives still further. In October 1921, the War Department rescinded War Plans White and replaced them with peacetime Emergency Plan White. In case of war, the plan called for complete military occupation and the control of corps areas. The domestic enemy remained the same, but in time of peace there would be no surveillance of civilians. "The suspicion of gum-shoe work is doing the Army much harm," Col. Stuart Heintzelman, the new head of G-2, warned. In March 1922, the War Department rescinded orders allowing direct investigations. The war within seemed at an end.[53]

Or so it seemed. The March 1922 directive was a clear order to discontinue involvement with civilians. The Washington G-2 ceased its reports and turned over all of its information to other offices. It put aside War Plans White and did not discuss or revise them. Washington G-2 also cautioned its officers not to use the American Legion to collect information.[54]

Despite the orders from Washington, Corps Area commanders continued to have MID officers and Legionnaires go right on collecting and investigating. That became evident in the fall of 1922. First Lt. W. D. Long, the intelligence officer at Vancouver Barracks in Washington, decided to send a letter to all Oregon county sheriffs telling them that the purpose of MID was to conduct "surveillance of all organizations or elements hostile or potentially hostile to the government of this country, or who seek to overthrow the government by violence." He then listed some examples: the IWW, Communist party, socialists, the Non-Partisan League, World War veterans, and the American Federation of Labor. Copies of the letter reached the press. The *Labor Herald* published the letter and denounced MID. Editorial comment spread through the country, followed by a deluge of letters of protest addressed to President Warren Harding and the new secretary of war, John D. Weeks.[55]

The uncovering of MID activities at this time was especially embarrassing to the secretary of war. He had just begun a public campaign to increase the number of troops available under the new National Defense Act of 1920. Although initially providing for a regular army of 280,000 men, a National Guard of 454,000, and a large army reserve, Congress had halved the number of men in the regular army and cut back both guard and reserve. Pacifist groups were demanding more cuts. Weeks was trying to convince the public to support a larger peacetime army and to counter opposition by peace groups. Weeks had particularly singled out the Women's International League for Peace and Freedom (WILPF) to criticize. When WILPF queried the secretary of war about his policies, Weeks replied that the increased military spending would not mean increased civilian surveillance in peacetime, thus a peacetime army would be no threat to civil liberty. Then Lieutenant Long's letter hit the news. The WILPF released a copy of Weeks's letter to the press with the query: "Will Labor submit to arming against itself and pay for intelligence offices to keep their organizations under surveillance?"[56]

Furious at the bumbling of MID, Secretary of War Weeks sent another, more strongly worded order, to commanders on 22 December. Weeks cautioned that information gathering for War Plans White was keeping alive the idea that intelligence officers were conducting investigations of civilians, that in the future only specially selected officers should make inquiries, and that "as a rule," they should obtain information from the press and civil authorities. Exceptions to use of the Corps of Intelligence Police had to have the specific approval of the War Department in each case.[57]

Now convinced that pacifists were a threat to the War Department, G-2 had arranged for the Chemical Warfare Service to act as a collecting agency in late 1922. Brig. Gen. Amos A. Fries, chief of the service, was particularly stung by the denunciations by pacifists of chemical warfare and began his own campaign. He circulated "spider web" charts linking the names of prominent women activists to supposed radical groups. His theory, both in these charts and in public and private denunciations of pacifists was that they were either Bolsheviks or were doing the work of Bolsheviks. The new head of MID's Negative Branch used Fries's accusations and reports as the basis for warnings that pacifist and antimilitary organizations varied from "violent red to light pink," but that the "activities of all women's societies and many church societies may be regarded with suspicion." During 1923 the Chemical Warfare Service completed and distributed a spider web chart that linked major national women's organizations as part of an international Bolshevik plot to disarm America. When women's groups protested, Weeks ordered the charts destroyed and claimed they were not a product of the War Department. In March 1923, the adjutant general's office issued another explicit order directing intelligence agents not to collect information in peacetime.[58]

The War Department certainly thought it now had G-2 under wraps. G-2 seemed to be an inactive peacetime agency. Still, it continued to study political groups in the United States because its job was to forecast civil disturbances and identify cities in which labor unrest and racial disturbances might require the use of federal troops. Army intelligence officers sent questionnaires to "reliable" citizens, frequently American Legion members, and obtained information through liaison with the Bureau of Investigation, local police, and state officials on groups they considered "subversive."

Officers made contacts cautiously to give the impression that G-2 was not active in peacetime. Through such passive surveillance, G-2 was able to collect information on pacifists and to counteract their work through organizations friendly to the military. A 1925 civil disturbance training manual advised G-2 to collect information on "ultraradicals" as far as permissible under the War Department policy, to get information from the Justice Department, and to "connect up with groups working along similar lines in adjoining areas." This same manual listed a 1920 estimate of the probable cause of disturbances as radical and semiradical organizations and their nonenrolled adherents. These, together with elements likely to join in the disturbances, totaled over 1 million people. "There is unmistakable evidence that these intentions [of the radicals] include the extermination of the so-called capitalistic class and the abolition of private property, nationalism, and religion." The manual reported the effectiveness of tanks against mobs. If weapons had to be used, neither blanks nor shooting over heads should be employed, the manual warned. The soldiers were to be warned, however, to attempt to preserve life and property, and to be taught that the potential enemy within—radical leaders—were personally ambitious only for wealth or power and did not have the welfare of the people at heart.[59]

Officers were not happy about the limitations in preparing for such expected riots. After Pershing retired as chief of staff, in September 1924, MID officers hoped to resume domestic intelligence gathering. In April 1925, Col. James H. Reeves, the head of G-2, wrote a long memorandum for the new chief of staff recommending that active collecting be resumed for Emergency Plan White. His superior, General Nolan, disapproved the plan and instructed Reeves to continue to get material from the Bureau of Investigation. As instructed, Reeves went to Hoover to ask him to furnish information on radicals for the secret Emergency Plan White. Hoover had become a reserve officer in MID in 1922 and director of the Bureau of Investigation in May 1924. Reeves asked that the material be exchanged in the field and not sent to Washington.[60]

Hoover replied that his bureau no longer investigated radicals routinely, only violations of the law. Attorney General Harlan F. Stone had ordered Hoover to discontinue all intelligence gathering on radicals a few days after naming him to head the bureau. Hoover continued to investigate some radicals during the decade between 1925 and 1935. The bureau investigated American Civil Liberties Union (ACLU) meetings, for example, but such investigations were done clandestinely and on an ad hoc basis. Collaboration did take place at the local level between individual Bureau of Investigation agents and G-2 officers. At the national level, however, there was no exchange. G-2 continued to ask for the power to resume active investigations, arguing that the Bureau of Investigation was not collecting such information and thus could not furnish material to G-2.[61]

Reeves did not give up. When the new secretary of war, Dwight F. Davis, entered the department in 1925, Reeves went to him to ask that he be allowed to collect intelligence to counter the growing movement against the Reserve Officers' Training Corps (ROTC) in the country. In 1923, progressive legislators in the state of Wisconsin had passed a law making ROTC voluntary at the University of Wisconsin. After the secretary of the interior ruled that such an act was legal—land grant colleges were required by law to offer military training but not require it—debates over compulsory ROTC spread to many campuses. The Committee on Militarism in Education, a coalition of prominent educators, pacifists, liberals, and socialists, united to eliminate compulsory military courses in colleges and federal subsidies for military training. Reeves wanted the War Department to use civilian contacts and publicity agencies secretly to counter the committee. Davis approved the plan in November 1925 and thereafter when agents reported growing anti-ROTC activity, Reeves told them to recruit officers and civilians to make speeches or write articles, and if these did not work to contact G-2 in Washington. "We have certain contacts with patriotic organizations which can be used when local agencies are unable to handle the problem," Reeves advised.[62]

Secretly calling on patriotic groups to denounce citizens attempting to influence military policy was one tactic used by the army. Organizing students was another. Officers of ROTC organized "student defense leagues" and encouraged them to publish pro-ROTC magazines. At Indiana University at Bloomington, the G-2 officer organized two thousand students. Other officers worked through friendly administrators and professors or used patriotic groups to counter student activists. At the University of California, Berkeley, the pro-ROTC organizing seems to have gone furthest. There the American Legion apparently organized student vigilantes to spy on and rough up student activists in the 1930s.[63]

These incidents aside, G-2 did maintain a low profile during the late 1920s and early 1930s. In Washington, G-2 occasionally requested permission to engage in more extensive intelligence gathering in the 1930s, but it received little support from either civilians or high army officers during the period. In the seventeen years from 1922 to 1939, seven officers, most of them colonels, directed G-2, and they had little interest in resurrecting CIP or expanding its operations within the United States. Strong opposition came from within the army: the commander of the Seventh Corps Area, Maj. Gen. Johnson Hagood, who conducted counterespionage in France for Pershing, wrote vehemently that the army should have nothing to do, directly or indirectly, with political opinions. "In my opinion," he wrote,

> in time of peace in America, radicalism, communism, and efforts to overturn the existing form of government are political questions with which the Army should in no way concern itself, either directly or indirectly. . . . I do not believe that the Army has the right, the knowledge or the facilities for determining what individuals or organizations in America stand for good government and what stand for bad government. . . . The Army cannot condemn individual citizens or groups of citizens because of their political views so long as they come within the provisions of the laws which the army itself is required to enforce. . . . The contrary confirms the sentiment 'Standing armies are a menace to free peoples.' Some branch of the government must undoubtedly look after these matters but not the Army.

Such sentiments that opposed peacetime surveillance by the army seemed firmly in place.[64]

G-2 did manage to continue gathering information in the field through various officers. Van Deman had urged MID to organize an MID reserve in 1919, and General Nolan attempted to implement such a plan but found no support among higher officers. Instead, MID enrolled its former officers in a special intelligence section of the Quartermaster Reserve Corps and contacted recruiters and officers on college duty. All these officers secretly forwarded information on radicals during the 1920s, and G-2 assigned reserve officer Capt. John J. Maurer to coordinate such information. The chief of staff turned down an MID request in December 1930 to engage in more general intelligence gathering. The new chief of staff, Douglas MacArthur, also disapproved a February 1931 request as "not advisable."[65]

Despite this general disapproval, MacArthur made an exception for G-2. He gave it permission to report on communists, socialists, and pacifists. Six months later, he gave temporary approval to Corps Area commanders to forward monthly reports on subversive activities in their areas. After a decade under wraps, G-2 was back in business openly.[66]

General MacArthur's willingness to allow G-2 to resume investigations was due to his personal experience. Like his father, MacArthur had served as commander in the Philippines where the army maintained an elaborate surveillance of civilians. When he returned to the United States, he was alarmed by the political activities of civilians who he thought were a menace to the United States government. He publicly condemned "radicalism, communism, bolshevism, and other enemies of free government." The fact that he was willing to have G-2 resume partial activities against certain civilians indicated a general concern rather than a specific incident. General MacArthur was bringing Emergency Plan White out of mothballs and preparing for civil disturbances.[67]

The first major domestic disturbance of the Depression was caused by World War I veterans. In May 1932, veterans began to arrive in Washington with demands that deferred benefits be given to them immediately because of hardship caused by the Depression. G-2 sent a secret memorandum to all Corps Area intelligence officers directing them to investigate and report regularly on these men who were being called "bonus marchers." Captain Maurer, the reserve intelligence officer, processed reports of army agents who began to work undercover among the veterans, along with American Legion units and other volunteers. G-2 prepared a daily memorandum for MacArthur, describing the current status of marchers already in Washington. Under revised Emergency Plan White for Washington, the few Communist party members in Washington were to be isolated and noncommunists given a chance to disperse. Following the plan, the Washington chief of police tried to segregate the Communists in Washington from the rest of the veterans whom he organized into the Bonus Expeditionary Force across the Potomac River in Anacostia Park. The chief of police estimated that, despite the claims of Communists to be leading the movement, not more than 45 actual Communists and 150 followers were with the marchers. To undercut an 8 June Communist parade, he had the Bonus Expeditionary Force hold its parade the day before. Communist plans fizzled.[68]

Two days later, however, the chief of G-2 sent a secret code message to all corps commanders asking about communistic leanings in bonus groups. Many replies indicated little concern with the communist "threat" but most dutifully reported what they knew about radical activities. The Eighth Corps Area Intelligence officer stationed at Fort Sam Houston reported that among California bonus marchers were dangerous Jewish communists financed by Metro-Goldwyn-Mayer and backed by Russia. The G-2 reports began to percolate through the entire administration, causing a sense of fear greatly out of proportion to the actual danger from the assembled veteran protesters. As a result, the Justice Department's plan to clear the area was rejected by President Herbert Hoover, who authorized the army to put Emergency Plan White into effect.

Once authorized to employ force, MacArthur refused to allow even President Hoover to intervene. MacArthur considered the military subordinate only until military operations began. Against the wishes of Hoover, MacArthur used force to scatter the veterans, whom he later termed "insurrectionists" animated by the essence of revolution. The administration refused to question the tactics of the army but came under much criticism for its use of the army at the next election. Criticism drove G-2 underground once more.[69]

Despite public criticism of the bonus march incident, G-2 kept on collecting information. On 25 May 1933, the adjutant general sent a secret letter to all corps areas to forward monthly reports on the domestic situation. This included radical activities within Civilian Conservation Corps camps, as well as general reports on subversive activities. Officers reported on the speeches of communist leaders, such as Earl Browder, as well as on pacifists. Reports contained detailed information on key leaders in strikes. The Bureau of Investigation furnished some information in the field, other reports came from the Bureau of Investigation in Washington through Hoover; immigration and naturalization officials provided others; and army officers gathered information themselves from informants. By November, the new head of G-2, Brig. Gen. Alfred T. Smith, was writing that CIP agents still stationed with Corps Area commanders should be supplemented because of the increase of radical activity.[70]

With the approval of Smith, G-2 continued the surveillance of radicals. In the Second Corps Area, which covered New York and New Jersey, G-2 organized a special intelligence reserve composed of Justice Department officials, the local constabulary, and the municipal police to conduct investigations. This officer used friends in the New York police who not only did anything asked of them, as one officer later reported, but "loved it."[71]

The army was not called upon to quell domestic conflict in most strikes during the early 1930s. State National Guard units usually battled with workers, but those conflicts nevertheless influenced the army. Strikes and conflict grew during 1934, especially on the West Coast. During the Maritime Strike and subsequent general strike, the army kept a low profile, but at a conference in Washington in early 1935, the commanding general of the Ninth Corps Area, Gen. Malin Craig, reported that G-2 had been very active during the strike. The system of getting information from other agencies on radicals was not good, he said, "so a good G-2 has to take his commission in his own hands at a corps area headquarters and get that information." General Craig did not believe the California radicals had any link to the Soviets, but he did believe they were descendants of the home-grown IWW. These home-grown radicals had infiltrated the Maritime Union and now controlled the union, he said. "My headquarters," Craig boasted, "knew more about their leaders and methods than did all the civil authorities."[72]

Craig's experience in the San Francisco general strike and his belief in the usefulness of intelligence probably led him to push for reinstitution of G-2 activities. Foreign events may have been a part of the concern Craig brought with him when he came east to Washington from the West Coast. The events in San Francisco had proved the need of such a civilian force. Rather than avoid investigations as regulations required, the army relied on a whole range of illegal and clandestine agents and informants along the West Coast.

Van Deman headed one of these illegal secret networks from his retirement home in San Diego. After serving in the Philippines and Texas, Van Deman ended his active duty in San Diego where he retired in 1929. By 1931, he was writing to the head of G-2 in Washington that he was keeping an eye on "radical activities" in the area. By 1933 he had formed his own clearinghouse of information from federal, city, and county officials and had put his files at the disposal of MID in Washington and the Ninth Corps Area intelligence officers in San Francisco. In 1935, Van Deman wrote to the head of G-2 in Washington that he had "rather extensive records covering both organizations and personnel throughout the country." Van Deman was now working ten hours a day in his little office at home on Curlew Street—clipping, indexing, and filing. He had informants reporting to him on the activities of suspicious strangers and on well-known radicals. He was in touch with such volunteer patriotic groups as the Better America Federation of Los Angeles and the American Defenders. He had his own agents operating within the top councils of the Communist party of California.[73]

When President Roosevelt appointed Craig to replace MacArthur as chief of staff in October 1935, he put a man sympathetic to G-2 in charge. In 1936 Craig encouraged G-2 to write new civil disturbance contingency plans for all Corps Areas. One of the most elaborate was the plan worked out in the Sixth Corps Area, which covered Illinois, Michigan, and Wisconsin, traditional areas of isolationism and antiradicalism. Plans there called for the collection and indexing of the names of several thousand groups of "communist subsidiaries," including the ACLU and pacifist student groups. War plans identified Communist party members as being 50 percent women and young—under thirty. Sources of information were the Justice, Treasury, and Labor departments and the post office, as well as local and state police. In addition, agents were told to contact private intelligence bureaus run by corporations, such as the United States Steel

Corporation and General Motors Corporation. These were sizable private intelligence bureaus. General Motors had paid almost $1 million to the Pinkerton Company between 1934 and 1936 to conduct labor espionage and to sabotage the organizing efforts of the United Automobile Workers.[74]

All these operations were conducted secretly. Emergency Plan White acknowledged that officers were to operate so as to "preclude the Army's interest from becoming public" as they identified and watched "potential disturbing groups." In other words, official army orders told officers not to conduct investigations, but secret Emergency Plan White called for watching civilian groups.[75]

As the Depression deepened, the Army War College returned to the question of internal stability. At conferences in 1936 and 1937, officers reviewed the situation once more. By this time, officers had a considerably more sophisticated understanding of domestic instability in Europe and in the United States as well. Officers saw the government policies as a compromise between two great and incompatible ideals—liberty and equality. They did not see radical politics as a threat; in fact, they saw a less radical influence than two years previously. They saw no cause for concern about revolution, for there was a strong flexible central government, a heterogeneous population that would militate against revolutionary trends, a forceful and well-respected president. Capital and labor had been in continual conflict since industrialization, but the government was seeking to remedy economic maladjustment and unemployment, and there seemed no class so oppressed as to seek revolution. A change in political leadership in 1932 seemed to make revolution unnecessary. In conference discussions, officers again complained that the Department of Justice was doing no counterespionage, ducking responsibility because there might be "political repercussions on the question of counterespionage in time of peace." A request came from Secretary of War George Dern in January 1936 for civilians to establish a counterespionage system and collect information so that in case of an emergency any persons intending to cripple the war effort could be taken into custody; it received no response. Officers considered communist propaganda insidious, and they recommended peacetime surveillance against subversive activities "without unnecessary offense to public sentiment."[76]

And so surveillance continued as it had during the earlier interwar period. It was contained, kept underground, by public sentiment that opposed army interference in civilian lives and politics during peacetime. Nevertheless, it was there. In those days, when the public thought that army intelligence had been discontinued, G-2 officers were making confidential reports on the American Federation of Labor and the Congress of Industrial Organizations and spot reports on communist activities. Thus G-2 was able to maintain its structure intact and to continue to maintain Emergency Plan White during the interwar years.

PART IV

Paths to the Present

CHAPTER TEN

World War II:
Expanding the
Boundaries

T he head of the Federal Bureau of Investigation, J. Edgar Hoover, always claimed that World War II internal security policies began in August 1936 when President Franklin D. Roosevelt called him to the White House to discuss foreign espionage. That conversation began a debate that lasted through the entire war. Which agency would have primary jurisdiction over enemy espionage, counterespionage, sabotage, and subversive activities? For the agencies themselves, the critical question was always, who would investigate. The efforts to establish separate spheres for investigations—to establish boundaries—extended throughout the war.

The 1936 White House meeting indicated that Roosevelt wanted his civilians rather than his military agents to increase their activities. Hoover recorded that Roosevelt was concerned about communism and fascism and that, at a meeting the following day, Roosevelt and the secretary of state approved a general survey by the Federal Bureau of Investigation. According to historian Athan Theoharis, Roosevelt was concerned primarily about Russian attempts to influence domestic affairs, particularly the upcoming election.[1]

On 5 September, in a secret order, Hoover instructed his agents to send to him all information they had on "subversive activities" of individuals and organizations, but to initiate no investigations except on specific authorization by the Federal Bureau of Investigation in Washington. The order did not define "subversive activities," but instead instructed agents to gather information on communists, fascists, groups advocating the "overthrow or replacement of the government of the United States" and any information relating to "subversive activities." This investigation, as Hoover described it to the attorney general, was thus an intelligence-gathering operation rather than a release of agents to investigate subversives. It meant, however, that Hoover was now preparing systematic reports on domestic groups.[2]

The activities of the FBI and the army during these critical years from 1936 to 1938 were concerned primarily with subversion rather than espionage. Certainly there were espionage activities, particularly industrial espionage, and some of it was conducted by former Communist party members. Rearmament during this period had increased the desire of all nations to know what types of armaments were being built by others. Where there were new military secrets, there would be those trying to discover them. A spy scare swept Germany, Japan was engulfed in "spy-phobia," and the Soviets warned of espionage. Meanwhile, each country expanded its capacity to spy.[3]

Spy stories began to fill American newspapers as the United States government joined the movement to rearm in self-defense and the Nazis took over Austria. By early 1938, fifth-column hysteria was growing. The term *fifth column* came from the Spanish Civil War where a general of the revolutionary right had claimed he had four columns marching on Madrid and a fifth column within the city. Fifth-column fears blended with espionage fears as the Office of Naval Intelligence (ONI) began leaking spy reports to the editors of popular magazines. No doubt these stories were part of an attempt to get support for increased appropriations for national defense. Americans were complacent about European affairs, but they could be depended upon to respond to domestic threats. The spy stories not only helped push appropriations through; they also triggered demands for more spy catching by the FBI.[4]

The FBI had been investigating a German spy ring for several years. Its progress was slow and its work incomplete when public outcry and the competition for funds forced it to take action. In February 1938, Hoover announced that he had smashed the German spy ring, and in June the Justice Department obtained indictments against eighteen Germans in New York for conspiracy to violate the Espionage Act. The indictments put the FBI back in the front line of internal security. Hoover asked Congress to increase his $6-million-dollar budget. Roosevelt announced that he favored larger appropriations for the FBI and for army and navy intelligence as part of the military expansion program. He also urged the coordination and unification of intelligence to combat espionage activities. The New York espionage trial ended on 29 November 1938, with the conviction of two of the Germans, a rebuke of the FBI by the judge for carelessness, and a request for cooperation among federal agencies.[5]

The House of Representatives had meanwhile set up its own investigating committee in May 1938. Conservative Republican Martin Dies's Subcommittee on Un-American Activities heard testimony that the German secret police had a special United States unit. In August, a former investigator for the *Chicago Times* testified before the Dies Committee that the Nazis had headquarters in New York City and posts in Chicago and other cities. He claimed that the Germans were secretly organizing through the German-American Bund, a group of German immigrants loyal to Germany who thought of themselves as amateur spies, and that he had joined the Bund and drilled with them that summer. The Dies Committee began to issue public warnings about spies.[6] When Hitler moved into Czechoslovakia in October 1938, the public demand to catch spies and the criticism of federal intelligence agencies increased.

Roosevelt again intervened. In mid-1939, he assigned Under Secretary of State George Messersmith, recently recalled as ambassador to Austria, the task of establishing a system of coordination. Messersmith found the heads of the intelligence agencies hostile to coordination. Only a personal call from Roosevelt to Hoover threatening summary firing if he refused to cooperate brought the FBI director to the coordinating meetings. On 26 June, Roosevelt informed cabinet officials that MID, ONI, and the FBI would handle all internal security investigations. Early in September Roosevelt explicitly assigned all investigative work among the civilian population to the FBI and asked local law enforcement officers to turn over all information to FBI agents. But he also insisted that representatives of G-2, the FBI, and ONI continue to meet with Messersmith. This they did, however reluctantly, from 12 December 1939 to 2 August 1940. When Messersmith left Washington in early 1940, the coordination was working smoothly.[7]

Soon after representatives of G-2, ONI, and the FBI worked out an agreement to divide internal security among them. This formal delimitation agreement, signed on 5 June 1940, gave the FBI control of most civilian investigations. It left G-2 with civilians in the Canal Zone, Panama, and the Philippines, and civilians employed on military reservations or under military control.

The spy fears of 1939 and early 1940 led to an upsurge of citizens determined to protect the country just as they had in World War I. The American Legion was still working with G-2, but once France fell to the Germans in the summer of 1940 and the delimitation agreement was signed, the Legion offered its services to the FBI. In June of 1940, the Legion contacted Attorney General Robert Jackson to offer the assistance of its eleven thousand posts to investigate subversive activities. When Jackson told the Legion to stay out of investigations and to work to reduce hysteria over subversion, they threatened to work directly with local and state police agencies to investigate espionage, sabotage, subversion, and un-American activities. Hoover went to Jackson with a plan to use Legionnaires to report on foreign nationality groups and to work as informants in plants. Eventually, the FBI contacted almost sixty thousand Legionnaires to be informants. The American Legion plant informant plan immediately brought conflict with MID.[8]

Plant protection was one of the major points of dispute between G-2 and the FBI. The delimitation agreement clearly gave the FBI jurisdiction over domestic investigations of civilians. Yet G-2 began to expand into defense plants soon after the June 1939 coordination began. When the United States formally entered the war in December 1941, Roosevelt issued the National Defense Industries Proclamation, which assigned responsibility for plant protection to the army and gave G-2 a further claim for expanding its work in plants.[9]

The army was not without legal guidelines in what it could do. The Pinkerton and the posse comitatus laws were still in effect. In addition, the National Labor Relations Act (NLRA) and the rulings of the National Labor Relations Board (NLRB) imposed limitations on what the government could do. Since its establishment in 1935, the NLRB consistently held that all company spying on unions violated workers' rights. Although federal courts refused to agree with NLRB that surveillance alone, without some specific resulting discrimination, was cause for restraint, the investigations of labor espionage by Sen. Robert M. La Follette, Jr., the NLRA (or Wagner Act), and subsequent rulings of the NLRB did much to protect labor from surveillance in the late 1930s.[10]

Thus when defense spending escalated in 1938 and the army and navy began giving new contracts, labor laws had to be considered in the development of internal security plans. Both the FBI and G-2 mentioned NLRA before the war as a definite concern in expanding plant protection networks. At first the intelligence agencies agreed that in privately owned plants the FBI should be responsible for internal security plant surveys involving civilians; recommending steps to be taken by plants to guard against espionage and sabotage (including the hiring of their own plant security investigators); and investigating all sabotage and espionage reports. By January 1940, the FBI was conducting 12 surveys a week. By mid-May it had completed 300 surveys, by February 1941, 550. The list of plants important to national defense grew to 1,379. Corps Area intelligence officers also began making plant surveys, but the FBI protested at the weekly coordinating meetings, and G-2 ordered these surveys stopped. When G-2 officers, in turn, told FBI representatives they should be attending to unions, FBI officials replied they could not spy on labor unions because it was contrary to the Wagner Act. The FBI promised to put agents undercover wherever the army wanted them, however, and G-2 began to give the FBI lists of plants. By February 1941, Hoover had evolved a system, with the help of the American Legion, to employ 10,000 undercover informants. He hoped to expand this to 120,000 in civilian plants. Both Hoover and Gen. Sherman Miles, head of G-2, knew that the informant system could "run up against difficulties with the labor laws," but they collaborated in evolving a plant informant system similar to that of APL and PPS of World War I. As one officer instructed, agents should avoid investigating union activities to the "greatest extent consistent with development of information concerning subversive activities." This system continued as the main surveillance structure in civilian plants during World War II.[11]

Despite the extensive FBI expansion, G-2 was able to carve out a relatively large place for itself in the internal security of plants as well. Even before the war, as the FBI rapidly expanded its plant surveillance, G-2 drew a distinction between plant surveys, which it conceded the FBI should do, and plant protection, which it claimed as the responsibility of the military and which would require some surveillance of civilians. The delimitation agreements gave G-2 jurisdiction over civilians employed on military reservations or under military control. The fall of France in the summer of 1940 and the spread of theories about the work of fifth columnists in that defeat rekindled fears within the intelligence community about subversion. Sherman Miles, who had served under Van Deman during World War I, asked him to return to Washington for conferences during 1940. Van Deman brought along his obsession with sabotage and subversion, as well as a model counter-fifth-column plan he had worked out for southern California. Before long Miles was convinced of the danger from within and ordered fifth-column plans for the entire country. "I have become almost a fanatic on morale and the possibilities of disintegration in the rear," he wrote on 1 February 1941. Miles drew a distinction between espionage and sabotage by individuals and that by groups, the leaders of which he thought should be identified under a fifth-column plan. These leaders were already included in Emergency Plan White whereby American Legion and local networks reported on potentially subversive leaders. Since Emergency Plan White was a peacetime plan, Miles decided they should be supplemented by special emergency fifth-column plans to go into effect in case the country declared war. G-2 advocated legislation in 1940 that would outlaw strikes, but officers later based their claim for internal security responsibilities on the executive order of 12 December 1941, which assigned plant protection to the army.[12]

The army also claimed internal security responsibilities under a directive of 1 July 1940 in which the adjutant general gave to the chiefs of supply, arms, and services the job of supervising contractor-owned plants to ensure that the Espionage Act was not violated. This plan, similar to one already established by the navy, mandated a system for obtaining information from the chiefs through district supervisors and plant inspectors within industrial plants. This information was then forwarded to Corps Area intelligence officers for analysis and distribution. The army did not place its intelligence personnel permanently in these plants, partly because agents might be identified and partly because labor might consider them to be labor spies.[13]

An example of how this system worked in practice can perhaps best be seen by the confusion that resulted over Edmund Burke. Burke, a member of the California Communist party, was employed by Northrop Aircraft in Hawthorne, California, to head its plant protection service in late 1940. Burke had earlier approached Lt. Col. Lowell H. Smith, western district supervisor for the Air Corps, looking for a job. After an investigation of Burke, Smith concluded that he was probably a Communist and refused to employ him. Smith, meanwhile, had established his own civilian investigating group and was reporting on plant security to the intelligence officer in the Ninth Corps Area, which was based in San Francisco. When Smith discovered that Burke had been employed by Northrop, he complained to the intelligence officer, who in turn told him to contact Colonel Van Deman in San Diego. Van Deman informed Smith that Burke had been hired by ONI and had the head of ONI write a letter to Smith assuring him that Burke was loyal. Smith persisted. He did not understand why ONI should have an agent in Northrop when it had no navy contacts. In a series of letters to Brigadier General Miles, Van Deman explained that Burke, along with other agents now among high-ranking officials of the California Communist party, had been working undercover for him for ten years, that both the FBI and ONI were furnishing the funds for Burke and his other undercover agents, and that Smith should not be allowed to interfere. Miles soothed Van Deman, kept Smith's group on the job, and allowed Burke to continue operating undercover.[14]

By May 1941, ONI and G-2, in a joint report pushed for expansion of the FBI to investigate slowdowns and strikes as subversive activities "more harmful to progress of the defense program than actual sabotage." Secretary of the Navy Frank Knox passed on the report that communists and subversives were "acting in the interest of foreign enemies" and that the FBI should have its investigative responsibility broadened to the "subversive control of labor."[15]

In World War II, the War Department favored a national service act as the best way to prevent strikes in defense industries. Such an act would have made all men and women between the ages of eighteen and sixty-five liable for national service; it would have produced a type of forced labor. Roosevelt supported the War Department in its demands for national service, but the bill was not enacted owing to the opposition of the American Federation of Labor and the Congress of Industrial Organizations (CIO) as well as by women's organizations, and because of the army failure to convince Congress that it should be responsible for all industrial labor.[16]

Instead of national service, Roosevelt and the War Department depended upon the seizure of plants to keep labor at work. Under the 1940 Selective Training and Service Act and the 1943 Smith-Connally War Labor Disputes Act, FDR ordered the army to seize a total of thirty-four plants between 1941 and 1945. These seizures became the means whereby the government controlled all production. The occupation by the army of thirteen leather plants in Peabody and Salem, Massachusetts, in November 1943 was the first specifically to avoid strikes outside defense factories. The army opposed this seizure of a plant producing nonessential civilian goods where workers had struck in violation of Labor Relations Board regulations, but the administration ordered the seizure anyway. Without using troops, officers merely occupied the plants as symbols of military force, and federal mediators were able to settle the strike dispute. The main questions of internal security became: whom to bar or dismiss from national defense industries; how to maintain the surveillance of those allowed employment; and, of course, how much responsibility the administration should give the military in answering these questions. The FBI did subsequently expand its investigations of subversion in labor, but the entrance of the United States into the war in December 1941 signaled an increase in the military surveillance of civilians.[17]

General Miles constantly expanded investigations. He gave the G-2 its mandate to investigate in June 1940, asked that the small peacetime Corps of Intelligence Police be increased from 15 to 42 immediately, and to 246 during the first half of 1941. Not only did Miles get his first allotment, the adjutant general approved an additional 188 men in December. Miles gave CIP its own chief, Maj. W. S. Holbrook, and authorized a training school. At the small headquarters, CIP staff began to work feverishly from morning to midnight and on weekends. Its mission, according to Holbrook, was to organize combat intelligence, but CIP soon began accepting cases from G-2 Domestic Intelligence Section. By February 1941, Holbrook had become chief of the Domestic Intelligence Section, had a case load of fifteen hundred investigations a month, and had twenty-eight CIP investigators.[18]

The rest of the growing corps was scattered, as it had been traditionally, in the nine Corps Area commands and among American territories. To these were added Iceland and a lengthening list of British territories: Antigua, the Bahamas, Jamaica, and Trinidad. The corps was secret. Its agents lived and worked undercover among the civilian population, wore civilian clothes, and rented offices in towns adjacent to army bases. Usually CIP agents established a front, such as a sales agency, although these subterfuges frequently failed to fool adjacent office staff. In Chicago, their neighboring office hung a sign "Merry Christmas Army."[19]

In Washington CIP was taking on a life of its own under Holbrook's drive to expand and centralize. The expansion resulted in continued territorial squabbles among army agencies as well. The chief of staff, George C. Marshall, tried to stem the expansion of G-2. In October 1941, over the objection of G-2, he transferred many G-2 functions to the provost marshal, including most of the civilian investigations and the collection of data for the counter fifth-column plan. In December 1941, he transferred ninety CIP agents. The War Department in Washington now essentially had two internal security branches, one military and one civilian. Miles still favored the expansion of CIP and managed to keep a sizable detachment of agents in the field. By November CIP had established twenty-two separate district offices. As soon as war was declared, MID asked to double CIP and to call up its reserves. The Washington G-2 had more than one hundred agents, and Corps Areas within the United States had more than five hundred. Holbrook changed the name from CIP to the

Counter Intelligence Corps (CIC), and Miles asked it to function partly in the open. As the CIC grew, it had almost half of its five thousand agents on the home front.[20]

The CIC operated undercover among various groups of civilian workers during the war. The field investigators of CIC ranged widely in investigating all types of suspected subversion, often exceeding the boundaries set up in the delimitation agreements. Agents of the CIC used volunteer informants in the collection of material on radical groups, an activity agents considered particularly important for overall preventive security programs. These transgressions, Victor Johansen wrote later, were overlooked by the FBI, partly because none of these investigations became important enough, in its estimation, to be worthy of contesting military encroachment, and partly because the investigations were being done "in the national interest."[21]

Ironically, CIC agents spent half of their time during 1942 and 1943 investigating who would join them in their sleuthing. As the group expanded to five thousand, agents devoted more and more time to these investigations. It began to take on some of the characteristics of an elite fraternity but one with a strong sense of mission. More than twenty-five thousand men applied to CIC, which chose five thousand. To conduct the necessary background investigations required interviewing many civilians. Most agents refused to identify themselves and interpreted the rules as requiring the use of identification cards only if necessary to obtain information.

As it turned out, then, CIC agents spent little time actually investigating foreign agents. The German espionage system was largely eliminated at the beginning of the war. There was little pro-German or pro-Nazi activity among the population. Subversion among Italians or Japanese was not a problem either on the mainland or in Hawaii. Rather, in addition to concerns with military personnel, CIC investigated other civilians who worked for, or who wanted to work for, the government. And they investigated persons suspected of political subversion, primarily leftists and disaffected groups, such as blacks, for which CIC enlisted a special group of black CIC agents.[22]

Although some CIC agents ranged widely in conducting investigations, other agents extended a countersubversive system to civilian workers under military control. The Counter Subversive system, known simply as the CS, was the major surveillance system of the Counter Intelligence Group (CIG) and was designed to place one informant among every thirty members of the military establishment—both civilian and military. All civilians in military plants and reservations were theoretically covered by this system, including all the groups designated as military "plants," such as the Red Cross and the Women's Auxiliary Army Corps WAAC's as well as what the War Department called "shadow plants," those owned by the War Department but operated by private corporations such as Consolidated, Douglas, and Lockheed. The CS system never operated efficiently because it was simply too unwieldy to control. In one month, for example, the Fourth Service Command (the Corps Areas were now renamed "service commands") recorded over 1 million persons covered by 52,000 operatives who filed 162,000 written reports. Even G-2 knew that padding was necessary to achieve these numbers. Operatives included the Corps of Engineers, both military personnel and contractors' personnel, and at least some longshoremen and stevedores. The CIG did try to keep CS out of regular civilian plants. When CIG officers discovered, for example, that one service command had established CS systems in a series of Texas plants, it ordered them disbanded. It also opposed incorporating guards at civilian plants into the structure, in part because of the fear that the system would be uncovered by labor.[23]

The CS system was a command function, that is, under G-2 officers at each service command. Theoretically, these officers were to report directly to Washington, but commanding generals resented the independence of G-2 officers and often ordered them to investigate matters other than subversion. The result was that G-2 was never sure of the scope of the CS system, although CIC claimed it had 250,000 secret informants.[24]

A separate program removed subversives from civilian defense plants. Like other subversive investigations, according to delimitation agreements, these should have been the primary responsibility of the FBI. The program, begun by the Plant Intelligence Branch of G-2, investigated both individual employees and management, including key personnel. In November 1942, complaints led to explicit orders from Secretary of War Stimson to G-2 to discontinue making subversive investigations, not to receive FBI reports regarding suspects, and to abolish the Plant Intelligence Branch. Stimson then transferred the other duties of the Plant Intelligence Branch to the Personnel Security Section of the provost marshal general's (PMG) Internal Security Division (ISD). The Evaluation Branch of CIG took over the plant clearance functions—that is, investigating management—of the Plant Intelligence Branch. The CIG processed as many as two hundred requests a week for the clearance of commercial facilities and key personnel.[25]

Within three months of the time Stimson abolished the Plant Intelligence Branch of G-2, officers resurrected it. They reinterpreted the secretary of war's directive to mean that investigations could be made up to the point where enough evidence was collected to support a derogatory charge, that the suspect could then be removed from a sensitive job, and the case turned over to the FBI for a final criminal investigation. By May 1943, the Personnel Security Section had reported 2,213 derogatory cases investigated and 610 employees removed. By the end of the war, over 2,000 workers had been removed. Orders were to exclude employees from sensitive jobs only, but in practice the employer usually fired the employee. The Personnel Security Section of the provost marshal general's office remained the primary administrator of the removal of subversives program. The War Department initiated the request for the removal; had the responsibility of informing the union as well as management of the removal; cleared aliens for reemployment after removal; cleared union representatives and NLRB representatives for admission to plants; analyzed questionnaires filled out by key employees suspected of subversion; and reported on all strikes and slowdowns in war plants.[26]

While removal of subversives involved investigations of several thousand workers, a far larger number of civilians came under military investigations through loyalty and character clearances. Some of these clearances were conducted before employment, but many workers were investigated after they had been employed for years. The army decided initially that all those working at what were designated as "plants" should be investigated for loyalty. About nine hundred sergeant investigators were trained by G-2 for this task. These army investigators operated in civilian clothes, originally conducting investigations themselves, operating under the Internal Security Division of the provost marshal general.[27]

In May 1942, ISD decided that it would be more efficient to contract out routine loyalty clearances, freeing the sergeant investigators for administrative duties and to conduct special loyalty investigations. To avoid the 1893 Pinkerton law prohibiting the employment of detectives, ISD sought out credit investigators it defined as not covered by the statute. Selecting five national agencies, the War Department agreed to pay a flat fee of three dollars for each loyalty investigation.[28]

The new system allowed for an increasing number of clearances. By November 1942, most of the sergeant investigators were off the streets and at work in plants going through personnel files to gather names of workers for clearances. By July 1943, 1,005 of these plant level operations were in effect, and contract investigators were making an estimated four routine reports for each special report made by a sergeant investigator.

That month, according to careful ISD calculations, a total of 160,966 civilian cases were processed and closed. By the end of 1943, over 1 million civilians had been given loyalty investigations. Almost 2 million would be investigated during the entire war.[29]

Quantity did not ensure quality in contract investigations. Many of the first reports emphasized credit or morals, or were vague. One agency had a tendency to report workers as "safe, sane, and dependable," leaving ISD in doubt as to whether this added up to loyalty. Although agencies had agreed to conduct investigations with its own personnel, some agencies subcontracted investigations for sixty-five to seventy-five each. Agencies also promised to investigate their own agents but, ISD found that many did not and had to make its own investigations. At least one agency began hustling cases, writing to various officers recommending the complete investigation of the loyalty of civilians under its command since the cost would be borne by the provost marshal general. The practice of loyalty investigating spread to civilian contractors who had previously conducted only limited investigations of a portion of their personnel. Agencies were charging the War Department almost twice as much as the normal charge for investigations for civilian industries. Originally, civilian plants were to pay for their own security, but some were now able to get local ISD officers to include their plants in the official list. In its eagerness to extend loyalty screening, ISD was paying for what civilians were supposed to do and paying twice as much for the work.[30]

Eventually the loyalty system began to disintegrate under its own weight. As the war progressed, line officers in the field reasserted control over staff officers in Washington, opposed excessive attention to the home front, and emphasized military activities at the front. The "national surge" had passed, fifth-column fears had disintegrated, and the War Department was left with an extensive domestic intelligence system that was expensive and that antagonized high-ranking officers who resented the interference of intelligence officers in their commands. The system had been inaugurated to guard against subversives at the army's rear—to make the military secure through preventive action. The result was to make the military even more insecure and, in particular, to demoralize officers. The assignment of primary responsibility specifically to G-2 presented a problem to the War Department. G-2 was unwilling to subordinate itself to the regular hierarchy. At times, G-2 officers claimed that they were to operate directly under the president, thus bypassing the usual chain of command through regional commanders, the chief of staff, and even the secretary of war.[31]

Plant protection gave much the longest controversy, but there were several other important controversies. Army intelligence did not cease to function domestically in other areas. G-2 continued to collect information for War Plans White. It reported on radical labor groups, communists, Nazi sympathizers, and "semiradical" groups concerned with civil liberties and pacifism—well-intentioned but impractical groups, as one corps area intelligence officer labeled them, that played into the hands of the more extreme and realistic radical elements. G-2 still believed that subversive elements would seize the food supply and that "semiradicals" could assist extremists by undermining adherence to the established order by propaganda in newspapers, periodicals, schools, and churches.[32]

At first G-2 did not challenge the supremacy of the FBI outside of the plants. The FBI had prewar plans to intern five thousand Communist party leaders in an emergency, but Hoover had given relatively little concern to Germans, Italians, or the Japanese. The FBI managed to round up three thousand of the enemy aliens that it considered most dangerous. Although the G-2 reaction in San Francisco was hysterical—they believed a Japanese army was poised for an attack in Baja, California, and that an attack on Los Angeles was imminent—the navy more than the army seems to have been responsible for the ensuing public spy scare. On 15 December 1941, the secretary of the navy announced that fifth-column treachery rather than the real cause—unpreparedness and incompetence—was responsible for the Pearl Harbor disaster. A few days later the commander of the Pacific Coast area recommended the removal of all enemy alien subjects to the interior.[33]

Martial law was not declared; the West Coast was declared only a "Theater of Operations." No one knew what that meant in terms of the military control of civilians. The FBI maintained it could handle coastal internal security, and the attorney general authorized vigorous searches of the houses of enemy aliens on the coast.

The military increased pressure for the additional civilian control of enemy aliens. By January, the Justice Department had agreed to register all enemy aliens, to conduct spot raids, and to establish restricted zones around crucial military and defense installations on the Pacific coast. Although no sabotage had yet occurred, this was already far past the line that Gregory and Wilson had drawn in April 1918. The theory of a fifth-column "control" now flourished. According to this theory, there had been no sabotage because the enemy was holding back. By the end of January, a report was circulating of an inquiry into conditions in Hawaii that falsely claimed that the attack was greatly abetted by Japanese spies.

The attorney general agreed to move seven thousand enemy aliens from the new military zones on the Pacific coast. No detention was to be involved, and no citizens were to be included.[34]

Each time the attorney general agreed to go farther in controlling enemy aliens, the War Department demanded more. By February, the Justice Department had agreed to a plan to remove the entire Japanese adult population of California and to put them under surveillance and protection in labor camps in California. The plan was to be worked out by civilians, both by those being removed and by state and federal officials.[35]

This plan expanded when the chief of the Aliens Division of the provost marshal general's office insisted there was still the danger of sabotage. On 11 February Roosevelt gave his approval for the War Department to do whatever necessary, even if it involved citizens of Japanese heritage as well as alien civilians. Military men who opposed evacuation did so mainly because it would take too many army personnel. Gen. Mark Clark, for example, advocated a greater role for the FBI and local police, frequent raids, and the internment of suspects. G-2 in Washington did not support the mass evacuation of the Japanese either. Like other decisions, Roosevelt's decision to evacuate apparently rested on domestic politics. The removal of Japanese would be popular and would silence critics who argued that he was not doing enough against the domestic enemy. Some officers now began pushing for the removal of other enemy aliens, such as Germans and Italians on the East coast. Leaks about these plans, and public opposition, made the War Department cancel them.[36]

The *Quirin* case provided another opportunity for the army to expand its role in internal security. The case involved eight men, two of them American citizens, who apparently planned to sabotage transportation and industrial facilities. The men entered the United States in June 1942. They did not get very far. After landing on Long Island and eluding an unarmed Coast Guardsman, one team leader immediately turned himself in to the FBI in Washington and asked for protection in return for disclosing sabotage plans. Within fifteen days all eight men were in custody. None of the men was in a military zone—on this both military and civilians agreed. The attorney general thought the men should be tried by court-martial, like Major André, because they had come through the lines out of uniform to engage in hostile acts. President Roosevelt agreed. He also issued a proclamation on 2 July, after their arrest, declaring that any individual who entered the United States under the direction of a foreign power with the intent of committing sabotage, espionage, hostile acts, or violations of the laws of war were subject to the laws of war and to military tribunals. All this was done on the advice of the attorney general. In fact, the president appointed Attorney General Francis Biddle to act as coprosecutor with the judge advocate. The attorney general then turned the men over to the military, and the army immediately tried the men under the Articles of War. The defense attorneys, two army officers appointed by the president, charged that the proceeding was unconstitutional. The Supreme Court agreed to receive writs of habeas corpus for the defendants.[37]

This Nazi saboteur case occurred before the first surge of internal security fears had passed. It came less than seven months after the attack on Pearl Harbor and only a few months after Roosevelt's order to intern the Japanese. In many ways, it marked the high tide of the military in internal security during World War II. Although major newspapers, such as the *New York Times* and the *Washington Post,* approved of the decision of the Supreme Court to intervene, there was a great deal of criticism of the courts for interfering with the military.

The Supreme Court hurriedly assembled in Washington and heard the arguments. The main defense argument was that civilian spying had to be committed on or near a military installation or a zone of actual military operations to be triable by a military court, otherwise it must be tried in a civil court. In response, Attorney General Biddle and the defense argued an expansive concept of total war, in which anything that affected war was to be considered within the military sphere. The president and his attorney general were now arguing exactly the opposite of the position that Wilson and Gregory had taken in 1918.

The Supreme Court upheld the president's authority. The military trial commenced immediately. The generals found all but the two men who had given information to the government guilty and ordered them executed. The only appeal was to the president who promptly upheld the sentence. The men were immediately executed in secret.

The Court's written decision followed the execution. The Supreme Court held that individual rights must not restrict the capacity of the country to wage total war. It upheld the right of the president to deny civilian trials. One of the men had been a citizen who would normally have been tried for treason. Yet the court felt it necessary to endorse the president. What this decision meant was that the president did not have to worry about the Supreme Court intervening. In fact, the Supreme Court seldom did intervene during the war except to protect several small groups of religious dissenters. Thus it is not surprising that the Court allowed the army to intern Japanese-American citizens. It was not, according to the court, its place to review the actions of the executive war-making powers.

The court seemed to indicate that it would defend the right of civilian authorities to expand the role of the military.

The FBI thus had to share its surveillance of civilians with the military. The Counter Intelligence Corps, manned by "civilian soldiers," included among its duties the investigation of espionage, loyalty, and sabotage; security education; plant protection; and surveillance for disaffection, sedition, and subversion. The CIC field manual urged agents to investigate these matters because they affected the military service and placed no restrictions on methods, instructing them to "resort to any means, methods, or stratagems necessary to accomplish the mission assigned." The collection of information on civilian groups became an important part of this preventive security program, which used voluntary informants and investigators to collect information. Preventive plans called for recruitment of the American Legion, Veterans of Foreign Wars, and other patriotic organizations to help watch the home front. Although plant protection was curtailed in 1943 and the president affirmed that the FBI had jurisdiction over internal security, the military retained an active role. In San Diego, Van Deman functioned during the entire war as a clearinghouse for West Coast investigations. By 1944, he had agents reporting on communist meetings, adult discussion classes at the First Unitarian Church, activities of aircraft labor unions, Democratic rallies at a local junior high school, and on private groups in private homes.[38]

How did unions respond? And how much did they know of the structure of surveillance? The CIO was the only labor group mentioned by G-2 as having grievances during the war. The AFL seldom complained about the treatment of workers. Probably the radicals in the labor unions were affected most as they were the ones considered the most likely to interfere with production by encouraging strikes. There is some evidence that the vast files on workers collected by the army were used during the anticommunist scare that followed the war. Certainly the practice of loyalty clearances, introduced by the government into defense plants, flourished under private investigators after World War II as it had after World War I.[39]

The public generally accepted the surveillance structure created during World War II. Many people assumed that individual rights would be infringed or suspended in time of crisis. Fed by the "national surge" at the beginning of the war, reinforced by the "red scare" at the end, this acceptance did not encourage the critical analysis of military activities during time of war. Within most of the intelligence agencies, those few critics who did complain were considered enemies to be outwitted. During

World War II, the United States army developed a large surveillance network aimed at watching various groups of American people. Workers in defense plants, radicals, and the foreign born were the subject of much of the surveillance. The secrecy surrounding these programs, the lack of a civilian control policy, and an uncritical acceptance of surveillance by both officials and public led to relatively little discussion of these programs. It was not the public but the CIC itself that brought most criticism and caused a single major reorganization in late 1943.

As CIC grew, its headquarters also grew. From a single room in the Munitions building, it expanded to fill a second room in early February 1942, then to more space in the Security Exchange Commission building, and finally to a separate building on K Street. When the War Department limited the number of officers under thirty-five that were assigned to Washington, D.C., to one-third of each section, CIC chose to abandon Washington entirely rather than limit its number of younger men. The CIC moved to a former women's dormitory at Goucher College in Baltimore in January 1943. Agents operated from these headquarters in Baltimore, as well as from the field intelligence offices, and special secret offices in large cities. For the most part, it remained a secret agency, its agents conducting investigations for MID until April 1943.

In April, CIC heard the first rumors that something had gone wrong. The deputy chief of staff first asked for the names of all agents operating in Washington. Then, Harvey H. Bundy, special assistant to Secretary of War Stimson, asked why CIC enlisted men were not being sent to officer's candidate school and commissioned. Finally, in July, Chief of Staff Marshall ordered the army inspector general to conduct a thorough investigation of CIC and of the PMG office to see if there was an overlapping of work. In November, the inspector general submitted a report highly critical of CIC, including its training, which the inspector general considered to be inadequate; investigations of military personnel, which he considered expansive and superficial; the secret offices, whose very existence he considered to be wrong; and the lack of supervision of agents. He recommended that all case reports be recalled, reviewed, and destroyed, unless conclusive evidence existed for a case. The direct use of service command intelligence officers by G-2, he felt, violated strict command channels. Moreover, CIC and PMG investigators duplicated each other. He recommended that agents be consolidated and come under the service command unit or tactical units in theaters of operation. In other words, CIC should operate under line officers in strictly military duties. Late in November 1944, the deputy chief of staff endorsed the report. Soon after, he closed down the Baltimore office, reassigned some CIC agents to G-2, and merged the rest with the provost marshal general's office. War Department Circular 324 brought CIC to an end on 14 December 1944, just two years after CIP had begun its meteoric rise. Each service command established a new Internal Security Branch, giving the term internal security its first institutional form. In Washington, CIC and PMG were consolidated. Directives carefully limited the purpose of the new agency to investigations of loyalty, espionage, sabotage, subversion, and the disaffection of military and civilian individuals within the military and to "certain civilians vital to war industries"; personnel security inspections of important war plants, and facilities; and the investigation of disturbances that would require the use of troops. "Under no circumstances will the Security Intelligence Corps be used for any other purposes," the directive warned.[40]

Clearly, the "other purposes" were what brought CIC down. Which ones? The official CIC history, written in the 1950s, presented one interpretation. According to the chief of CIC, General Holbrook, CIC's investigations of communist subversives had to be carefully carried on because of "the sympathetic attitude of the White House." Officials "high in the Roosevelt Administration," wanted to know about the Washington CIC agents, and their displeasure came from "certain powerful politicians" who wanted to stifle reports "personally embarrassing" to persons high in government. The instant approval of the derogatory report, continued the CIC history, "left little doubt that someone—possibly communists who still held key positions in government—was determined to halt CIC investigative activities in the United States."[41]

The "embarrassing" information involved the surveillance of Eleanor Roosevelt and her friend Joseph P. Lash, then an Air Force sergeant. Agents of CIC had included Mrs. Roosevelt in what had become the routine bugging of hotel rooms in Chicago. They later told FBI Director Hoover that Eleanor and Lash were having an affair and, instead of destroying the Lash file, turned it over to him. There is no evidence to support this claim, but Eleanor did find out about the wiretaps and protested to White House Aide Harry Hopkins and to General Marshall. Roosevelt ordered an end to such surveillance. Marshall shut down the offending agency; closed the Baltimore headquarters; sent CIC agents overseas or merged them with PMG; ordered home-front files destroyed; and instructed remaining CIC agents to report only, not to make any recommendations. Early in February, he abolished the position of CIC chief.[42]

The CIC accounts, both of the communist conspiracy theory and the elaboration of later accusations that Eleanor Roosevelt and Joseph Lash were having an affair, indicate that CIC had totally assimilated the earlier conspiracy theories that riddled the Philippine islands with fear of the Japanese. The downfall came, as it had in World War I, not because of communists, but because line officers did not want independent corps of investigators who could threaten commanders and endanger the army's military mission by meddling in civilian political affairs. The reorganization might not have happened so abruptly, the ax not fallen so swiftly, without the bungling of CIC agents, but decentralization and the chain of command was much more deeply embedded in the War Department than was the specialization of intelligence and its centralization.

Inevitably, intelligence agents, especially many poorly trained ones lacking supervision, eventually blundered into the military surveillance of civilians that would threaten its military mission. Like a myth, the experience needed to be repeated time after time. The military hero—self-defined as "aggressive, daring, determined, shrewd, resourceful, and self-reliant," with unquestionable loyalty to country and army—tempted the civilian gods, and was punished.

Yet it was civilians who tempted the hero to begin with, by challenging the hero to defend his country in danger. If civilians should change their minds and become convinced they did not need heroes, they must be infected or controlled by some evil force. This was the emergence of an old myth in cold war clothing. Meanwhile, the war was still on and CIC, now under the control of PMG, continued to fight the war against the Germans, although no German spies or saboteurs appeared on the home front after the war began. Like World War I, the absence of spies and the urge to catch them resulted in a far vaster surveillance system than need or prudence would have dictated. The urge to spy, in fact, undermined the possibility of effective security measures by confusing both citizens and officials, allowing far too many agents access to investigative tools and power, and leaving agencies highly vulnerable to criticism and to inter-agency squabbles. That legacy followed the army into the postwar period.

CHAPTER ELEVEN

War without End

The atom bombs that moved Japan to submission in August 1945 brought joyous relief to the American people. As usual, following wars, Americans demanded a reduction of the military. Elsewhere, the world was convulsed with military conflicts as nations used wartime armies to extend their political power. The Truman administration decided to participate in these foreign conflicts. As the Russian Communists established control in Eastern Europe and the Chinese Communists consolidated their control over mainland China, Truman countered with massive economic aid to Western Europe and Southeast Asia. During the next thirty years, at the rim of Chinese and Russian influence, the United States chose to intervene militarily while keeping an uneasy peace with the two countries. This uneasy peace became known as the cold war. The United States erected a new Central Intelligence Agency to spy abroad. At home, the cold war against communism raged as well, until a hot war in Asia—the Vietnam War—finally brought massive dissent by Americans over executive war policies and the massive army surveillance of dissenters.

The cold war at home linked the fear of communism with the fear of economic and social change. As the war in Europe ended and American victory over Japan seemed assured, African Americans, pacifists, and workers began to organize to obtain peacetime political changes. In July 1945, the American Communist party abandoned its "popular front" strategy, which had supported government policies during the war, and pledged its support of black equality, peaceful coexistence with world communism, and strikes. Many domestic political groups in America still welcomed the support of American Communist party members despite growing hostility between Communists and the United States government overseas. It seemed possible that once joined on domestic issues, blacks, Communists, pacifists, and workers might unite to reduce the postwar military and demand changes in domestic and foreign policies.

By early 1947, Secretary of the Navy James Forrestal was concerned that religious people with pacifist tendencies and the Communists were allying to interfere with American expenditures for arms. At a cabinet meeting on 7 February, Forrestal raised the subject of Communists playing an important role in generating public demand for disarmament and argued for vigorous and centralized counterpropaganda. He spoke to General Marshall of a coming wave of pacifism and of his concern that the talk of awesome new weaponry by military men might heighten that wave.[1]

Soon after, Hoover launched his crusade against "Red fascism." Hoover's campaign signaled a significant shift in internal security policies. Long an opponent of the American Communist party, Hoover had previously kept his opposition to the secret monitoring of members because of the party's status as a legal American political party and because of its support for World War II. Roosevelt wanted Communist support for his war policies and attempted to keep interference with Communist political activity to a minimum. Truman, on the other hand, was alarmed at the success of Communists in Eastern Europe and Asia in 1946 but faced a potentially powerful political coalition that preached peaceful coexistence abroad and social change at home. He also faced a group of intelligence agencies bloated by the war and scrapping over diminishing peacetime resources. In late 1945, Hoover had identified revived Communist propaganda activities as one of the greatest prospective dangers to internal security, but there was little response by the public or the Truman administration. After the announcement by the Canadian government in 1946 that it had smashed a Soviet spy ring and subsequent press reports—which suggested that the spy ring extended into the United States—Truman allowed the Justice Department to expand its surveillance of Communists. In the midst of these domestic political and foreign military threats and the swirling intelligence agency wars, Hoover moved to a position of power he had never occupied previously. He appeared before the House Un-American Activities Committee and denounced the Communist party as a fifth column that was organizing opposition to aid to Greece and Turkey. An article by him in the rightist magazine *American* elaborated the theme that the main threat to the United States was the introduction by Communists of subversive ideas into American life. He also made a bid to control all intelligence, domestic and foreign, on the basis that both varieties were inseparable and that FBI control of Western Hemisphere intelligence activities proved the effectiveness of such unity of effort. The attorney general supported Hoover's plan.[2]

Truman, angry at the scrapping by intelligence agencies, decided instead to establish an entirely separate foreign central intelligence group with no internal security functions and no power to investigate within the United States or its possessions, "except as provided by law and presidential directive." Truman's directive said nothing about the FBI's Western Hemisphere control, nor about who should conduct internal security, only that the new agency should stay out of the United States. Because of these gaps, Hoover designed a strategy to obtain a key position in intelligence policy. He infiltrated the new central intelligence group with his own Latin American agents. The military, however, also transferred many of its intelligence officers and dominated the new service. The wrangling over intelligence ended when Hoover's direct foreign activities were eliminated, but his place in the intelligence community was enhanced. Hoover now concentrated on the home front war against communism, identifying them as "Red fascists" in an effort to isolate them from other domestic political groups.[3]

The next two years saw a rising fear of communism throughout the country. As usual, these fears were in part due to foreign events, in part due to the frequent claims by high officials that the Communists would attack from within as well as without. When Congress established the Central Intelligence Agency in spring 1947, it committed itself to a permanent civilian overseas intelligence agency. At the same time, Congress explicitly named the FBI as the main agency for internal security intelligence and enforcement. Attorney General Clark soon launched a massive attack to neutralize political organizations that were impeding administration efforts to win support for its cold war foreign policy. He spoke of the emergency, of national survival, and of temporary restrictions on normal rights and privileges. The Truman administration purged itself of thousands of employees for suspected disloyalty. By late 1947, the attorney general's list of subversive organizations had moved the attack from employees of the government to political groups. These lists, although restrained at first, greatly expanded as the cold war moved out of the administration and into the country at large. At the end of 1947, the Justice Department had three hundred active cases for deportation of Communist aliens.[4]

To men in the Truman administration the postwar crisis was in fact a new war. The administration considered continued involvement in international affairs essential to protect American political and military interests. The American people and Congress were reluctant to support the necessary levels of expenditure. Thus in the fall of 1947, the administration preached patriotism and encouraged the American people to look for subversives to obtain passage of foreign aid appropriations.[5]

At the same time, the cold war was bringing the military into greater positions of power within the administration itself. When Forrestal became secretary of defense in the newly united military departments in 1947, he tightened security over military news. American correspondents who were critical of the military found their credentials revoked; others were denied credentials on the ground of having communist connections. Forrestal required all reporters to apply for accreditation to the armed forces and to pass a loyalty test. Criticism followed and his plan had to be abandoned. He then asked the press to agree to consult with an information board in the Department of Defense before publishing information that was designated as vital to national security. Criticism from the press resulted in the shelving of this plan. The Security Advisory Board planned to apply military censorship to the entire government. Again, implementation was not attempted because of criticism from the press.[6]

While high military officials were attempting to keep information from the public, some of those lower in the chain of command were beginning to leak information. The use of the media to influence public policy was relatively new and on the whole was not handled very successfully. Nonetheless, it was possible for officers to contribute to the growing peacetime concern over spies and subversives. Van Deman, who still had his files intact in San Diego, was receiving reports on the National Urban League, the Youth of All Nations, on labor unions, on scientists, and on movie stars. Information from military intelligence reports in his files found its way into the hands of politicians crusading on anticommunist platforms in California, to the California Un-American Activities Committee in Sacramento, and to select members of the House Committee on Un-American Activities in Washington. The Tokyo G-2, which had survived and flourished under General MacArthur during the war, leaked confidential records on investigations of Soviet espionage in Asia to right-wing publicists who used them in political campaigns against Democratic policies. Gen. Charles Willoughby, chief of G-2 Tokyo, launched his own investigation of American political groups to link them to an international communist conspiracy and to counter libel suits against MacArthur for the release of intelligence reports. He warned publicly of the dangers to American civilization lurking in subversive systems that hid behind free institutions and were protected by them.[7]

The leaks coincided with a new joint assault on subversion by the FBI and army intelligence. In April 1949, following a new agreement between the two agencies, Hoover asked G-2 to monitor activities of the inactive reserves; developments affecting plants engaged in armed forces contracts; facilities and utilities designated by the secretary of defense; and the strength and intentions of civilian groups classified as subversive and potentially dangerous. Subversion by civilians was, of course, the key area. The FBI apparently retained responsibility for investigating individual subversive activities but did not quarrel with the army's claim that it should gather domestic intelligence on labor and racial disputes, on Communist party members, and generally on the organization, strength, and probable courses of action of subversive elements in army service commands.[8]

The year 1949 brought a deepening fear on the home front as the Chinese Communists triumphed on the mainland and proclaimed their national government. Then the Russians exploded their first atom bomb. The Defense Department called for a quadrupled defense budget for the massive rearming of the United States and Western Europe.

The political premium on past subversive files went up in that winter of widening fear. In Congress, Californian Richard Nixon lent files from the House Committee on Un-American Activities to Sen. Joseph R. McCarthy to document allegations that Communists were working in the State Department. Senator McCarthy gathered a coalition of former FBI agents and conservative publishers to provide more documentation. Hoover called for an end to tolerance. The small number of Communists in the country were, he warned, in no way indicative of the magnitude of their danger. Anti-Communist crusades flashed through the country in a "surge" reminiscent of earlier wars when citizens rushed to find spies on the home front. Then North Korea attacked South Korea, and Truman ordered American troops to Korea to support the south. The war at home escalated. On 24 July 1950, Truman announced that the FBI would retain central authority in domestic security during the Korean emergency. Four days later the Justice Department announced that communists were using cleverly camouflaged movements, such as peace groups and civil rights organizations, to achieve their sinister purposes—to replace the "American way of life." In the months that followed, civil liberties came to represent a threat to national security, as Congress passed a new internal security law. This omnibus antisubversive bill provided for the registration of communist-action and communist-front groups, the emergency detention of persons believed likely to commit espionage and sabotage, and a tightening of laws against espionage and sedition.

By now there was very little public pacifist sentiment in the United States. Instead, denunciation of the military tended to run along partisan lines. Thus in September when General Marshall became secretary of defense, the Republicans attacked him because he had advocated no military involvement in China to support the nationalists. MacArthur, on the other hand, was defended by Republicans because he wanted to invade mainland China. When MacArthur appealed to Congress for support over the heads of his superiors—President Truman and the Joint Chiefs of Staff—Truman dismissed him. Truman did promise support for the nationalist Chinese on Formosa and oppose admission of mainland China into the United Nations. To get congressional support for MacArthur's dismissal, Truman paraded his own generals in support of his policy. The legacy of the MacArthur dismissal was military involvement in countries rimming China and a fear that to permit communist power to grow in Southeast Asia was to invite political disaster at the polls at home.[9]

The legacy at home was a mushrooming of secret files, volunteer investigators, and anticommunist intelligence units—both civilian and military. The arrest of Julius and Ethel Rosenberg by the FBI and their indictment in 1950 for conspiracy to violate the Espionage Act in wartime by giving American military secrets to the Russians characterized the activities that extended through every level of government.

Hoover exhorted the public to help the FBI by reporting on neighborhood subversives. Private intelligence organizations, such as one organized by the Veterans of Foreign Wars, obligingly investigated neighbors and indexed persons they suspected of disloyalty. The American Security Council collected information from private investigators and former FBI agents, assembled "subversive" files, and provided internal security reports to corporate subscribers. This private intelligence organization sponsored speaking tours by generals and admirals who warned of the dangers of communism within U.S. boundaries. Scores of smaller groups, such as the Christian Anti-Communist Crusade, vied with the American Security Council for military officers to ride their anticommunist circuits.

The Christian Anti-Communist Crusade named MacArthur's old intelligence chief, General Willoughby, as its "intelligence aide." The use of army intelligence records for political purposes and the campaigning of former intelligence officers did much to cultivate Americans' fear of subversion and to provide the basis for the growing power of the military at home.[10]

It also helped cloud the fact that all the previous investigations of civilians had not protected the secrets of the atom bomb. The transfer of secrets extended back to 1943, the height of wartime internal security activities. Most important, of course, was the scientist Klaus Fuchs. The British had routinely cleared Fuchs for work in Britain without discovering his espionage activities. When he transferred to Columbia University in New York City in 1943, he continued these activities. After arriving at Los Alamos in 1944, Fuchs discontinued passing information to the Russians but then resumed in February 1945. In June and September 1945, Fuchs gave very complete information on the atom bomb to a Russian courier. Neither the army (the CIC remained in Los Alamos after cutbacks elsewhere) nor the FBI ever detected Fuchs. In the summer of 1949, CIA cryptographers discovered his work and passed the information to the British, who arrested him. Fuchs subsequently identified others involved in espionage for the Soviets. The trail led to Harry Gold and then to Joel Barr and Julius Rosenberg.[11]

Neither the FBI nor the army detected the activities of Barr or Rosenberg. Both were employed as civilians for the Signal Corps. Both were dismissed when routine loyalty checks turned up evidence that they belonged to the Communist party. Joel Barr and Julius Rosenberg were dismissed from the Signal Corps laboratory at Fort Monmouth in 1942 and 1945, respectively. Both immediately went to work for civilian contractors working on secret projects. Barr worked at the Western Electric Company and at Sperry Gyroscope Company on secret and top secret projects during which time he apparently passed secrets. He was denied clearance in October 1947 and dismissed, but he left the country undetected and was never apprehended. Julius Rosenberg went to work for the Emerson Radio Company and worked on some of the same military contract programs he had once inspected in the Signal Corps. According to a recent and careful history of the case, Rosenberg probably gave some information to the Soviets about these projects. Julius and Ethel Rosenberg were executed by the American government amid charges of subversion and repression. They would not admit their guilt; the government would not admit the failure of its own internal security system.[12]

Perhaps the greatest failure was the inability of the army to discover the espionage of David Greenglass. Greenglass was a committed Communist who went into the army along with thousands of other committed Communists in 1943–44 when the party was at its peak and supporting the war effort. If the army was truly concerned about security, it should have been able to detect the sentiments of this young recruit before it sent him to Los Alamos. Greenglass, himself, in letters to his wife talked about his open attempts to convert fellow recruits. When he was pulled from his battalion as it went overseas, Greenglass was certain it was because he had been detected as a Communist. To his surprise, he was sent to work on the top-secret Manhattan Project, first to Oak Ridge and then to Los Alamos. While on leave from Los Alamos, Greenglass later testified, he gave plans for a high-explosive lens to Rosenberg and later, in June 1945, turned over more detailed information to Harry Gold in Albuquerque for five hundred dollars. All this occurred while Greenglass was employed in a facility that was reported to have the tightest security in the country.[13]

The Department of Defense developed no general policy or guidelines for army departments in civil defense and domestic emergencies during the Korean War. Yet during 1951, army intelligence set up a central records facility at Fort Holabird, Maryland, where it began to catalog domestic and worldwide investigations. The FBI sent copies of its reports to the center and in 1952, when Van Deman died, a large portion of his vast files—with information on 125,000 individuals—went there too. Army intelligence also received information from counterintelligence groups with the National Guard.[14]

Continued army involvement in internal security during the 1950s occurred because it had two separate but related missions. The first was the use by the president of troops in civil disturbances. The second was the peacetime collection of information on subversive groups. In 1954, a strategic capabilities plan restricted the use of intelligence personnel in monitoring civil disturbances until the president judged deployment of troops to be "imminent." A 1956 directive suggested that the Department of the Army had some continuous peacetime responsibility for collecting information on subversive groups. These two directives kept the army in the field. The extent of its activities depended on a wide range of factors as the Eisenhower administration responded to the first stages of the civil rights movement. Monitoring of civil disturbances escalated as opposition to integration mounted in the South.[15]

The first large employment of army agents occurred at Little Rock,

Arkansas, in 1957. The federal courts said black youths had a right to attend Central High School. The governor used the National Guard to block their entrance. Eisenhower did not want to use the army to integrate the high school, but neither did the attorney general want to use marshals. Threats against the black youth increased as officials debated what course to take to enforce federal law. The army, meanwhile, dispatched members of CIC to Little Rock to watch the school and report on local press coverage. When the army arrived on 24 September, Cmdg. Gen. Edwin A. Walker brought twenty-two more agents to establish an intelligence command. The G-2 used the CIC of the Fourth Army, intelligence staff officers from the Airborne Division, and FBI agents indiscriminately in the hectic days that followed. Counterintelligence personnel had charge of the nine black youths enrolled at Central High School and of monitoring the Ku Klux Klan and other potential troublemakers. Surveillance continued on the orders of the secretary of the army after the regular army troops had been replaced by federalized National Guards.[16]

Troops stayed in Little Rock from 24 September to 29 May 1958. Three thousand regular army and federalized National Guards kept the peace. Widespread criticism followed Eisenhower's use of troops. Understandably, it was most vocal in the South, but scholars and lawyers in the North, many of whom favored integration, also criticized the use of federal troops. Such criticism led to more careful planning for domestic disturbances by the Kennedy administration. In 1961, when whites rioted over biracial "Freedom Riders" in Montgomery, Alabama, the attorney general dispatched federal marshals to restore order. Still hoping to avoid the use of the army but expecting the worst after the governor of Alabama declared martial law, Kennedy prohibited investigations until the use of federal troops was judged "probable." The army had to have specific authority from the president as commander in chief to operate within the investigative jurisdiction of civil authorities.[17]

At first it seemed as though the army would not have that probable cause. President Kennedy did not call the army into Montgomery in 1961. Instead the FBI extended surveillance to groups involved in integration problems in the South. During early 1962, as black southerners fought to obtain their civil rights, violence escalated in the South, but the Justice Department under the Kennedy administration moved slowly lest white southern Democrats be alienated from the party. When the courts ordered the admission of James H. Meredith to the all-white University of Mississippi in September 1962, early administration plans called for the FBI and federal marshals to handle the crisis. Then on 13 September, Mississippi Gov. Ross Barnett invoked the doctrine of state interposition, urging jail for himself and other officials rather than submit to court orders.

Barnett's defiance brought army intelligence south once more. Twenty agents from the 111th Intelligence Corps group arrived at Oxford, Mississippi, on 18 September. They conducted covert investigations of civilians, apparently in violation of their directive that called for specific authorization from the president. During the next two weeks army intelligence agents probed student activities at the University of Mississippi, the plans of "extremist" groups, and the reaction of civilians to troop movements. They investigated "agitators" and compiled "black, white and gray lists." Agents proved so interested in probing civilian activities that they neglected their legitimate task of assembling tactical intelligence. As a result, adequate reconnaissance information was lacking on the evening of 30 September when an angry mob occupied the campus and threatened the United States marshal. Army and Mississippi National Guard units were called in to disperse crowds near the campus, and incoming troops had to conduct their own reconnaissance.[18]

During 1963, President John Kennedy ordered a secret report on the total number of government employees engaged in intelligence and their annual expenditures. One analyst of the intelligence establishment affirmed that an estimate of sixty thousand people and $2.5 billion was on the low side. Much of the intelligence was foreign, growing out of United States involvement in Vietnam, but there was a parallel expansion of domestic intelligence during the Kennedy administration. Its reliance on force abroad was accompanied by a growing reliance on force at home.[19]

After the Mississippi intervention, the army became even more active at home. Third-army headquarters at Fort McPherson, Georgia, expanded its black, white, and gray lists to include all political activists and racial extremists in its seven-state area of operations. In May 1963, Gen. Creighton V. Abrams developed a project to expand the army surveillance of civilians. Hard intelligence was indispensable in making the decisions necessary during civil rights operations, Abrams argued. Current informal and patchwork arrangements for the collection of intelligence without collation and evaluation was wholly inadequate. Under his project, agents would identify black and white personalities, analyze civil rights situations in which they became involved, and establish a civil rights intelligence center to operate on a continuing basis to keep abreast of the current situation throughout the United States. Abrams's superiors never approved his vast domestic intelligence project, but neither did they curtail surveillance. That October, the Continental Army Command developed a Civil Disturbance Early Warning System. This system left the surveillance of civilians in the hands of the FBI but specifically authorized the military to file spot reports "as required" on events that might develop before the deployment of troops. Army commanders were to collect civil disturbance information mainly through liaison with civilian authorities and through news media reports. They could, however, if they felt the situation warranted, order covert operations in coordination with the FBI. This plan removed surveillance from central control. Such decentralization had in the past led to serious invasions of the rights of civilians.[20]

Under President Lyndon Johnson, army intelligence increased its activities as the war in Vietnam broadened. By 1965, the Counterintelligence Analysis Division at the Pentagon had established a "North American" desk and assigned a Women's Army Corps captain to organize reference books and collect information on right-wing and racial groups in the United States. That same year a new intelligence command at Fort Holabird, Maryland, began coordinating the work of counterintelligence agents assigned to G-2 offices of the major stateside armies. The function of the intelligence command was not to collect intelligence but to protect the army from espionage, sabotage, and subversion. Its main job was to investigate persons being considered for security clearances and to conduct security inspections of military installations.[21]

The new Holabird Intelligence Command was meant to replace the other army surveillance system and take over the early warning system for civil disturbances. The intelligence command prepared daily civil disturbance situation reports; field intelligence agents began their first photographing and reporting on small groups of antiwar dissidents. Surveillance was still sporadic until the administration began bombing North Vietnam and increased the number of ground troops in South Vietnam. Young white activists were soon criticizing the war, and although the monitoring of right-wing and racial activists continued, opposition to the war soon became the major concern of the army.[22]

Rechanneling the country's efforts into a foreign war bred disillusionment among urban blacks as well. Riots ripped the ghettos at Watts in Los Angeles and other urban areas in the summer and fall of 1965. The army feared it might be fighting a home front war with dissident blacks, angry civil rights activists, and a resurgent left-wing movement that based its opposition to the government not only on the war but also on a wider critique of American institutions.[23]

The army found itself being drawn deeper into civilian protests. In

February 1966, the army secretly revised its civil contingency plans again. These plans, coded as "Steep-Hill," gave the Holabird Intelligence Command a far broader role in civilian surveillance and definitely relegated the FBI to a minor role in domestic intelligence. Agents could directly observe demonstrations and other political activities, as well as watch specific civilian groups. Subordinate commands could employ "appropriate resources" in intelligence collecting before any Steep-Hill operations. Activities might include liaison with federal and local agencies but were no longer limited to such liaison. The Continental Army surveillance system, meanwhile, continued in violation of regulations and without the knowledge of senior army commanders. The army now had two networks conducting civilian surveillance, one legal according to their directives, the other not.[24]

As the war in Vietnam escalated, so too did the war at home. Military intelligence agents were soon being trained in counterintelligence and being assigned to posts in the United States. Given a badge, a civilian car, and money to buy civilian clothes, they circulated through major cities investigating security clearances and inspecting military installations. During the Detroit riots in summer 1967, intelligence officers expanded their counterinsurgency techniques. When federal troops were called out, officers at the Fort Holabird Intelligence Command believed they needed counterinsurgency information on black communities similar to that collected on Vietnamese guerrilla organizations. The army's chief intelligence officer at that time, Maj. Gen. William P. Yarborough, a long-time counterintelligence and psychological warfare specialist, considered rioters "insurgents" manipulated by the Communist party. During the Detroit raids he told his staff: "Men, get out your counterinsurgency manuals. We have an insurgency on our hands."[25]

From that time on, surveillance increased. The Fort Holabird center became known as the Continental United States Intelligence (CONUS Intel). Yarborough set up a communications network known as "Operations IV," with a nationwide teletype network to feed it information. Large amounts of information came from FBI programs that had been established to disrupt and harass black militants and white supremacist organizations, and from antired squads within local police intelligence units. An increasing amount also came from military intelligence agents. Over one thousand plainclothes army agents operated out of three hundred posts spread across the United States to gather personal and political information on civilians.[26]

Civilians investigated by military agents included a growing number of college students. Most historians mark the 1964 free speech movement at Berkeley as the opening battle of the student movement of the 1960s. Student protest spread eastward from Berkeley and California state colleges to eastern campuses in a wave that by April 1969 engulfed even Harvard University. During 1968–69 state officials called police and guardsmen to 127 campuses to quell student dissent. By spring 1969, thousands of students had been arrested, hundreds had been injured, and five southern students had been killed. Despite student turmoil, only a remote possibility existed that federal troops might be called onto campus. Police had, by this time, developed sophisticated riot control equipment and tactics. National Guardsmen stood ready as a backup force. Why then did military intelligence agents become concerned about the campus revolt? Apparently, because students challenged the legitimacy of the war in Vietnam, the army's conduct of the war, the draft, war-related research on campus, and ROTC programs.[27]

The FBI had clear jurisdiction over any student surveillance considered necessary by the federal government. The main reason for army agents to be on campus was to conduct investigations for security clearances. Army agents visited large campuses almost daily to check with clerks and registrars on educational records. Agents gathered information from college officials, professors, and staffs, who cooperated with little thought of student privacy. As army agents became known to clerks and officials, they seldom questioned the legitimacy of these inquires. Agents did not have to prove they were conducting specific security clearances. New York University allowed a black agent to report on black studies courses. The University of Dayton furnished the results of psychological tests. The University of Notre Dame gave free access to student disciplinary files. At the University of Michigan, officials gave agents letters of recommendation, personal essays, the names and addresses of character references, and financial records. Agents were soon checking files of students who had not requested clearance but who were active in political protests.[28]

Popular spy stories gave young intelligence officers a feeling of importance as they probed the political activities of college students. Investigations on campus allowed them to participate in activities that seemed to be at the center of a vital dissent. Away from army discipline and danger, they found student life congenial and far less boring than security clearance investigations. They appeared more and more frequently on campus and infiltrated off-campus demonstrations, such as that in October 1967 at the Pentagon. By early 1968, CONUS Intel was distributing "compendiums" on possible fomenters of violence to commanding generals. Soon after, the army began computerizing its spot reports on civilians.[29]

Intelligence agents expanded their campus activities without the knowledge or approval of civilian Department of Defense officials. Agents tore down posters and peeled photographs off applications for admission. They posed as reporters for the media to cover protests and as students to infiltrate campus groups. A military intelligence captain infiltrated Students for a Democratic Society (SDS) chapters at the University of Denver and at the University of Colorado. A sergeant who replaced this captain attended the SDS National Council meeting at Boulder in October 1968 with at least four other army agents. In March 1969, this same sergeant threw a chair at S. I. Hayakawa during a speech at the University of Colorado. When police arrested the agent and five other students, the army arranged for his release and reassigned him elsewhere. Some ROTC students found it difficult to remain aloof from the growing controversies. An intelligence officer stationed at the national headquarters of the Pershing Rifles, an elite ROTC unit, ordered all regimental G-2s to forward information on the New Left Movement—including membership, expansion, and attitudes—because of the threat that he felt the New Left posed. After public protests, the commander of the Pershing Rifles ordered this request to be "disregarded and destroyed if possible." Surveillance continued.[30]

The worst fears of army intelligence officers were realized when, in June 1969, the SDS splintered and one faction, the Weathermen, began to encourage the systematic used of violence, targeting ROTC units on campus. Bombing and arson soon rocked campuses. Surveillance extended far beyond self-defense, however. Predicting fall 1969 disturbances, military intelligence agents gathered reports on SDS activities in colleges, on members of underground newspaper staffs, and lists of persons alleged to be active in the Progressive Labor party. At Fort Holabird, officers kept track of college disorders with red pins stuck into a large wall map.[31]

Army agents covered the fall 1969 moratorium in which more than 1 million Americans in more than five hundred cities and towns and on most college campuses protested. At Rock Island, Illinois, where two church-related colleges planned candlelight vigils, four agents carried candles in the procession. Two agents stood ready in cars to monitor reports of violence. A captain in Minneapolis ordered special agents there to monitor a parade from the College of St. Thomas to Macalester College and to report on speeches, including one by Minnesota Sen. Walter F. Mondale. That November, when town and gown came together to stage the largest antiwar demonstration in the nation's history and 250,000 people marched on Washington in a peaceful demonstration, army agents were out in force.[32]

Campus dissidents were only one group of Americans watched by the military during those hectic years. The assassination of Martin Luther King, Jr., in April 1968 was followed by riots in one hundred cities. The Joint Chiefs of Staff estimated that 270,000 troops should be ready to quell civil disorders. Subsequently, the FBI began a new program against New Left organizations. Army agents ranged ever more widely along the home front, enlarging their blacklists of "potential troublemakers." A directorate for Civil Disturbance Planning and Operations was set up in what came to be known as the "domestic war room," constructed under the Pentagon's mall parking lot and paid for from contingency funds. After Sen. Robert Kennedy was assassinated in June 1968, Congress passed a resolution allowing the army to protect national political candidates and incumbents. The way was now open for unrestrained civilian surveillance.[33]

At the July 1968 Republican nominating convention, the army was out in force. It sent several dozen agents, dog handlers, and bomb disposal specialists to protect candidates and delegates. The following month at the Chicago Democratic convention, military agents circulated undercover inside while other agents outside the convention hall posed as camera people to videotape demonstrators. An army intelligence agent later even infiltrated a dissenters' commune in Washington, D.C., where the "candidate" of the counterinaugural, Pigasus the Pig, was being kept. Agents knew how many protesters would show up at the counterinaugural and all their plans. Neither Republican nor Democratic officials, the secretary of defense, or the secretary of the army, knew of these activities.[34]

Surveillance flourished until Maj. Gen. Joseph A. McChristian took over as the army's chief intelligence officer in August 1968. McChristian had been head of military intelligence in Vietnam and, after replacing General Yarborough, had made a thorough review of domestic surveillance. He decided that watching civilians was taking time away from more important military intelligence tasks and suggested that it be cut back. Although the Pentagon denied his request and ordered domestic war intelligence to continue, Under Secretary of the Army David E. McGiffert and Army General Counsel Robert E. Jordan III looked more closely at domestic surveillance after learning of army intelligence reports on labor disputes, prison riots, and a request from the Justice Department for videotaped interviews for use in obtaining indictments of the "Chicago seven." On 5 February 1969, shortly before McGiffert left office, he ordered an end to covert operations because such activities would diffuse the labor force and were unnecessary. He stressed reconnaissance, early warning, and combat intelligence rather than reports on individuals and movements, and tried to restore the military intelligence liaison with civilian agencies, rather than carry on independent investigations. McGiffert asked Jordan to explore ways in which the Justice Department could take over the major responsibility for collecting civil disturbance intelligence and to draw up guidelines to limit covert activities among civilians.[35]

Negotiations with the Justice Department followed. Under the new agreement, the Justice Department took responsibility for supervising the collection of civil disturbance intelligence and became the collection center for information prior to dissemination to the White House, the attorney general, and the Defense Department. A specific plan for the collection of intelligence was left for the future, however. In the meantime Hoover kept FBI counterintelligence programs in force, and army agents stayed in the field watching civilians. On 1 April 1969 the Justice Department and army intelligence agreed to a plan whereby the Justice Department would supervise intelligence gathering. Army domestic surveillance did not stop, however. The army deferred implementing the new plan.[36]

Under President Richard Nixon, surveillance went on. Nixon's new civilian chiefs tried to tighten the central control of covert investigations and to curb the activities of agents, but they continued to allow army agents to infiltrate civilian political movements. Agents made 1,200 spot reports a month during 1969. Any pretense at restraint was abandoned in the October and November antiwar moratoriums during which army agents took to the streets to report on marches, rallies, and prayer vigils.[37]

Apparently civilian officials in the army department never knew the extent of military surveillance on campus or elsewhere. What had been done, they believed, had been done because civilian agencies had not provided the material intelligence officers wanted. The structure for surveillance remained in place. Computers kept immense data banks on civilian protesters and civilian political activity. An elaborate network exchanged information with other agencies, including the FBI, police, and campus security officers.[38]

Those who have looked most closely at this expansion of surveillance on campus find little sinister in it as far as the motives of the men involved are concerned. Rather they find boredom, curiosity, a lack of training in constitutional law and civil liberties, and a tendency by bureaucracies to expand. The expansion met the short-range needs of a bureaucracy without a policy, with no comprehensive analysis of the army's domestic intelligence needs or its role in civilian law enforcement. Neither Congress, nor the presidents, nor even high military authorities, established a program of civilian surveillance. Secretary of Defense Robert McNamara was aware of the army's civil disturbance plan, but apparently he knew little of the straying from tactical intelligence to political intelligence. The secretary of the army knew little of the network below him. Because agencies sanitized reports, that is, censored them to omit the source of the information, even the under secretary of the army, who received regular counterintelligence reports, believed that most of the material came from civilian sources.[39]

One of the main reasons why the army expanded its surveillance during the 1960s was that little public criticism of army surveillance existed. During the 1920s, pacifists had consistently kept the public aware of any attempt to expand the role of the army into surveillance. During the 1960s, antiwar protesters seldom attacked military surveillance. In part this silence occurred because protesters did not know which department agents represented. Most protesters knew little about either the civilian or military bureaucracies they battled in opposing war policies. Sometimes they lumped all agents together as government agents. Other times, dissident antiwar newspapers and magazines reported, without criticism, incidents in which army agents were clearly involved in civilian politics. Public controversy surfaced only when former army intelligence officers began to publicize their activities. In January 1970, Christopher Pyle, a former military intelligence officer, published an article entitled "CONUS Intelligence: The Army Watches Civilian Politics," in which he sketched the nature and scope of the army's domestic intelligence effort and made proposals to curb excesses. His review opened the first full-scale public debate on army intelligence in the more than seventy years of its existence.[40]

Christopher Pyle's article focused on the growing concern of many citizens over the capacity of the executive to spy on people who dissented from its foreign policies. In early November, President Nixon announced the troop withdrawal from Vietnam, the small Southeast Asian country where an undeclared war now engaged over 540,000 United States troops.

Nixon's bombing of Cambodia a few days after this announcement mobilized more than 250,000 civilians who assembled in Washington for a "March against Death." That November, newspapers also revealed the first news of the My Lai Massacre, where United States infantry gunned down 450 unarmed South Vietnamese civilians. Dissent against the Vietnam War had grown from a mere handful of timid protesters in 1965 to massive demonstrations across the country. The executive had used the army in Vietnam and on the home front in seeming disregard of growing political opposition. The Pyle article made it seem that the use of the army in civilian politics had allowed the executive to maintain its war policies abroad by using the army against political critics at home.

CHAPTER TWELVE

The Constitution, the Army, and Internal Security

T he 1970s became a political battleground where citizens, embittered over the executive conduct of the war, looked to the courts and to the legislature to contain the activities of President Nixon and his subordinates. Slowly rifts opened in Congress. Influential members of both parties concerned about the growing political alienation of hundreds of thousands of Americans gradually asserted their constitutional authority to check and balance executive power. Gradually, a new bipartisan coalition emerged in Congress dedicated to blocking the executive use of army surveillance. Federal courts acted more cautiously, but they too were asked by increasing numbers of citizens to stop army involvement in civilian politics.

Press coverage of the Pyle article in January 1970 began this decade of discontent over the executive's use of army surveillance. Civil libertarians, news commentators, and senior members of Congress began to demand an explanation. The army admitted it had one thousand agents and three hundred offices but claimed that covert operations had been prohibited "for some time." Nevertheless, on 3 February, Sen. Sam Ervin, Jr., chair of the Subcommittee on Constitutional Rights of the Senate Judiciary Committee, complained in Congress about the army surveillance of domestic politics and its computers and data banks. He called the computer system a violation of First Amendment rights and asked the secretary of the army for a report.[1]

Ervin, a conservative Democratic senator from North Carolina, led
the campaign against army surveillance. He had attended Harvard Law
School in the era of Zechariah Chafee, Felix Frankfurter, Roscoe Pound,
and other staunch defenders of civil liberties, and was genuinely concerned about the violation of First Amendment rights. Ervin had used
his committee to investigate issues relating to Indian rights, but he was
also known as a vocal opponent of the Equal Rights Amendment and did
not support civil rights legislation for blacks. During his years as chair of
the Subcommittee on Constitutional Rights, Ervin had assembled a cadre
of articulate and able staff members, trained in constitutional law and
committed to civil liberties. Ervin might have ignored the increasing demands that his committee take action, but his staff members collected a
large body of material showing army infringement of First Amendment
rights. Ervin was soon involved in two challenges to army surveillance,
one through the courts, the other through Congress. The army had met
a formidable opponent.[2]

In February 1970, the American Civil Liberties Union filed a class
action suit to try to stop the army from its surveillance of civilians. The
ACLU asked the courts to enjoin the army from the collection, distribution,
and storage of information on lawful political activities of persons unas-
sociated with the armed forces. The army replied to the ACLU suit that
surveillance was justified on the basis of its civil disturbance mission. In
April 1970, the suit was dismissed. The American Civil Liberties Union
appealed the case to the United States Court of Appeals in the District
of Columbia Circuit. There the judge reversed the decision of the lower
federal court and returned the case to the district court to determine a
number of questions: the nature of the army's domestic intelligence system; whether any part of the gathering system was unrelated or unnecessary to the army's legal mission; and whether any overbroad aspects of
the system might have inhibited the appellants or others in exercising their
constitutional rights. To avoid judicial inquiry into its practices, the Department of Defense then appealed the decision to the Supreme Court,
thus bringing about *Laird v. Tatum*.

Ervin, who had several times appeared before the Supreme Court,
agreed to argue the case as a friend of the court. Although Ervin was not
involved in the original litigation, several religious organizations, each
with social and political action groups under army surveillance, asked him
to argue the case. Frank Askin, a professor of law at Rutgers University
and head of the Central Committee for Conscientious Objectors, argued
the case on behalf of Arlo Tatum, in whose name ACLU brought the orig-

inal class action suit, and on behalf of all other political activists on whom the army had collected information. As was customary, the solicitor general presented the case for the government.

The ACLU wanted to use the case to publicize activities that might engender public support for further congressional action. According to several people who worked with Ervin's Subcommittee on Constitutional Rights, one purpose of the case was to discover other army surveillance activities that could be used to develop a legislative case for congressional action to curtail army surveillance. Lawrence Baskir, chief counsel and staff director of Ervin's subcommittee, later wrote that a constitutional decision was less important to the subcommittee than "the creation of a firm political tradition that such surveillance was against the public understanding of the constitutional role of the military."[3]

Christopher Pyle, the former army intelligence officer who had revealed the army surveillance systems, later wrote that the *Laird v. Tatum* case resulted from his own desire to know how political systems changed. He hoped to use a court case as part of a three-pronged effort to have surveillance curtailed—the other means being the press and Congress. The purpose of the original lawsuit was to get relevant documents from the army into the safekeeping of the courts so they could not be destroyed. Pyle hoped to get additional information into the record of the original case through the testimony of former intelligence officers, but the judge refused. In response, a number of former agents called a press conference to relate the information they had gathered. Thus, in addition to being a vehicle to obtain a legal decision on army surveillance, the Tatum appeal was a way to publicize the information that had already been gathered, to gather additional information, and to move Congress to act.[4]

While *Laird v. Tatum* made its way to the highest court of the land, executive officials tried to assure Ervin that it was curtailing the surveillance of civilians. Unconvinced, Ervin announced in July that he would hold hearings on federal data banks, computers, and the constitutional rights of American citizens. During that year, while protests mounted and surveillance continued, Ervin's staff and Pyle collected all the evidence they could. In the fall, Pyle worked with reporters to put information in a form that would rouse the public from its acceptance of military surveillance as normal. In November 1970, reporters disclosed army surveillance at the 1968 convention in Miami and Chicago. In December NBC-TV presented a documentary detailing overt and covert operations of army intelligence agents. Former military intelligence agents described how they had infiltrated the Poor People's Campaign, staked out Martin

Luther King's grave, and monitored the Chicago convention. Others leaked information that files existed on Sen. Adlai Stevenson III, Cong. Abner Mikva, and Circuit Court Judge Otto Kerner. There was fury in Congress. Ervin announced he would hold hearings in February 1971. For the first time in a year, the army began to take Ervin's warnings seriously.[5]

Following the February 1970 request by Ervin for a report, the army launched its first investigation into civilian surveillance. The secretary of the army admitted ignorance of the data banks and ordered the military to destroy identification lists in the field and computer banks. The secretary was hardly convinced of the need to eliminate surveillance, however, for he had the army make a final printout for the Justice Department, and in secret directives he urged intelligence officers to maintain their normal counterintelligence files and to retain noncomputerized data on civilians. President Nixon had just ordered the ground invasion of Cambodia, and massive protests followed with two hundred thousand students marching on Washington. Although there was no massive civil disobedience in Washington, the army still distrusted dissidents.[6]

The acting adjutant general, Col. Robert E. Lynch, did issue a letter on 9 June 1970 regulating covert operations and the collection of civil disturbance information. The order brought the activities of military agents under higher army authority, but it did not prohibit domestic surveillance. It instructed units to retain their surveillance capability.[7]

As Nixon made plans to extend surveillance, he was aware of the criticism of army agents. On 23 July 1970, he notified his four major intelligence-gathering agencies—the FBI, CIA, National Security Agency, and the Defense Intelligence Agency—that he had approved a new plan to gather information on antiwar demonstrators, campus rioters, radical bomb throwers, and black extremists. Called the "Huston plan," this new directive allowed illegal break-ins and telephone and mail surveillance of suspected subversives but not the use of undercover army agents, because the risks of exposure were greater than the probable value. Military counterintelligence agencies could provide evaluations of domestic intelligence estimates and assist in carrying out the other objectives of the report. When Hoover opposed the plan and Attorney General John Mitchell supported Hoover, Nixon rescinded it. Army investigations continued. A letter from the adjutant general's office specifically permitted the surveillance of all "agitation, propaganda, or organized effort directed toward army personnel; or conducted on an Army installation, the consequences of which threatens the capability for mission accomplishment by an Army element." The letter referred to coverage of "racial matters" and did not define who exactly could be investigated or what methods could be used.[8]

Every high civilian and military official denied any knowledge of the computerized records and surveillance of elected officials. Army General Counsel Jordan admitted that the army should not have entered the field, that gathering went beyond the army's authority, and that it was "dangerous to create too much capability in this field." On 15 December, the adjutant general issued the first specific regulations of counterintelligence activities concerning civilians not affiliated with the Department of Defense and defined subversion for the first time in terms that gave it an objective meaning. Subversion was defined as "attempts to subvert loyalty, discipline, or morale of Department of Defense military or civilian personnel by actively encouraging desertion, disobedience of lawful orders or regulations, or disruption of military activities." The directive gave explicit guidance on collection of information and forbade storing unwarranted information, specifically, biographical sketches of civilians. On 17 December, the White House released a statement by Nixon that opposed spying by the military, insisted it was not going on, and that it would not be done by his administration. Nixon said that Secretary of Defense Melvin Laird was examining the allegations. Six days later, Laird declared that he was taking direct control of military intelligence from the Joint Chiefs of Staff, a revolutionary shift in the flow and control of both foreign and domestic military intelligence.[9]

Nixon's reassurances failed to postpone Ervin's hearings. The hearings coincided with the bombing of Laos, an event that once again pushed domestic affairs off America's front pages. Late in February, while the Ervin hearings were still in progress, Secretary of Defense Laird issued a directive flatly prohibiting the surveillance of elected officials and curbing the routine surveillance of civilian politics. The directive succeeded in taking the steam out of the legislative movement to control administrative surveillance and left the executive in control of monitoring internal security. When questioned about the administration's political surveillance during the Ervin hearings, Assistant U.S. Attorney General William Rehnquist argued that "self-discipline on the part of the executive branch will provide an answer to virtually all the legitimate complaints of excesses of information gathering."[10]

Such assurances in the past had successfully allowed the executive to maintain control of internal security. Under normal circumstances, Nixon too might have been able to end protests there, but times were not normal. The controversy made Nixon wary of using regular agencies for special investigations. When in June 1971 the *New York Times* began to publish the secret Defense Department study of the Vietnam War—the so-called Pentagon Papers—he created the "plumbers," a group supervised by aides and charged with plugging leaks, which Nixon considered so grave as to require "extraordinary" actions. The plumbers were soon investigating the military for alleged spying on civilian officials. In September 1971, they also broke into the office of a psychiatrist in search of documents that might discredit his client, Daniel Ellsberg, who had leaked the Pentagon Papers—first to Congress and then to the press. Then the plumbers obtained funds to conduct old-fashioned "dirty tricks" against the Democrats. They broke in and bugged the Democratic headquarters at the Watergate Hotel but so carelessly that they were arrested. The Finance Committee of the Republican Committee to Re-Elect the President immediately began destroying papers related to political espionage plans.[11]

What seemed to be restraint was actually stone-walling, promising reform while delaying it. In fact, the shift of control of intelligence from the Joint Chiefs of Staff to the secretary of defense never took place. The army retained control over its intelligence gathering; the Defense Department merely established an Investigative Review Council for supervision. The Laird directive did not prevent the retargeting of military intelligence operatives against active antimilitary civilians, nor did it guard against monitoring in times of threatened mass violence. Moreover, it allowed the secretary of defense or his subordinates to direct covert surveillance and infiltration and allowed new computerized data banks on civilians.

Early in 1972, Ervin went before the Supreme Court to argue the *Laird v. Tatum* case. The case was a crucial event in Ervin's growing distrust of executive surveillance policies as well as a significant moment in the history of internal security. *Laird v. Tatum* brought together political activists, constitutional lawyers, Defense Department officials, and high-court justices to argue the legal questions involved in the public policy of using the army to watch civilians. During almost three-quarters of a century, the army had developed the practice of watching civilians. Now, for the first time, the Supreme Court reviewed that practice.[12]

The ACLU lawyers based the requests of their plaintiffs for injunctions upon a relatively new body of judicial decisions that defined the "chilling effect" of government activity. The chilling effect, according to this theory, kept citizens from exercising First Amendment rights because they feared government retaliation. Between 1965 and 1979, a series of decisions involving various political activities seemed to indicate that the Court might expand the chilling effect to cover military surveillance. Although these cases had all involved injury or a reasonable fear of injury—such as ordering draft boards to induct students involved in antiwar activities over students not openly active—attorneys argued that because the military had been involved the defendants had good cause to feel "chilled" in the exercise of their First Amendment rights. To support their arguments, attorneys collected a great mass of sociological data, later filed as a forty-page appendix in the Laird case, showing how individuals responded to intrusive government activity by curtailing activities that came under First Amendment protections. Attorneys hoped an appeal to sociological jurisprudence, a strategy that justices had accepted in issues relating to social welfare, might buttress the rather limited legal precedent for their argument.[13]

Ervin, as well as other constitutional authorities, thought that basing the case on the chilling effect was not a winning strategy. Instead, Ervin based his argument on broad constitutional grounds. He argued that the government had no compelling interest to justify a program that had such an impact on First Amendment rights. To fortify his argument and to emphasize the broad scope of army surveillance, Ervin had Lawrence Baskir file a long brief discussing additional surveillance activities uncovered by the subcommittee since the first suits had been filed.

Justice William Douglas, long an eloquent defender of civil liberties, strongly supported the broad constitutional argument presented by Ervin. Douglas argued that there was no law authorizing surveillance and no implied authority in the Constitution; that the court's decision limiting the attempts of the military to try civilians in *Ex parte* Milligan was relevant also to limiting surveillance; that recent laws limited court-martial jurisdiction over civilians; and that therefore the services could govern only themselves and not civilians. Ranging back in history to the Declaration of Independence and then forward to pronouncements of Justice Hugo Black and Chief Justice Earl Warren, the angry Douglas ended his opinion in a stern denunciation of army surveillance as "a cancer on the body politic," a disease "at war with the principles of the First Amendment," with a Constitution "designed to keep government off the backs of the people," and a Bill of Rights that aimed "to allow men to be free and independent and to assert their rights against government." Douglas saw military involvement in civilian activities as a clear violation of First Amendment rights and dangerous to the political rights of all Americans.[14]

The majority of the Supreme Court felt otherwise. Speaking for the majority, Justice Warren Burger rejected the constitutional arguments, stating that military surveillance was a legitimate part of national security activities and that it was not the business of the Supreme Court but of Congress to monitor executive practices like surveillance. Burger also rejected the application of the chilling effects doctrine, arguing that because defendants could not prove any damage resulting from army surveillance, the federal courts could not claim jurisdiction. Since the defendants had not lost their jobs or otherwise suffered "cognizable injury," the Court would reverse the decision of the lower court that First Amendment rights had been infringed.[15]

In his decision, Burger also alluded to a larger political issue involved in *Laird v. Tatum*. The respondents, said Burger, had wanted "a broadscale investigation, conducted by themselves as private parties armed with the subpoena power of a federal district court and the power of cross-examination to probe into the Army's intelligence-gathering activities, with the district court determining at the conclusion of that investigation the extent to which those activities may or may not be appropriate to the Army's mission." The Court could not play such a role, according to Burger. Congress could curtail governmental actions that did not result in injury; federal courts could not monitor the wisdom of executive actions.[16]

Laird v. Tatum did provide a way to publicize the constitutional issues surrounding executive surveillance practices. In the months following the Supreme Court decision, major law review journals discussed in detail the constitutional issues involved, thus alerting a wider legal audience to the questions of the executive use of national security as a basis for implied powers. The discussions in law school corridors and the reflections of constitutional lawyers no doubt contributed to the later support by the legal profession for congressional activities aimed at curtailing executive surveillance activities. Public discussion of *Laird v. Tatum* probably hurried the curtailment of army surveillance that was already under way within the Department of Defense. Negative public criticism also acted as a restraint on President Nixon's use of army agents when he expanded domestic surveillance shortly after. The case served a practical purpose; it fostered greater control by the army of its own structure and gave additional public support for congressional action. *Laird v. Tatum* did not provide judicial protection for individual rights, however. On the surface, the protection of civilian rights remained where it had for the last seventy years of army surveillance—with the army itself. The rules governing army surveillance were made by its civilian leaders in response to public criticism.[17]

To experts who had been following internal security cases, however, there was a significant change in tone by the Supreme Court. In contrast to the denunciation of the evil effects of army surveillance by Douglas, the majority court had made a strong defense of surveillance practice. *Laird v. Tatum* reversed a strong case in defense of First Amendment rights by the United States Court of Appeals of the District of Columbia, but the majority decision did reflect a marked change in the judicial attitude toward army surveillance. Just two years earlier, in *Union v. Westmoreland,* when appellants argued that their First Amendment rights had been chilled by army surveillance activities, the majority of the Court found for the defendant, Chief of Staff Gen. William C. Westmoreland. In that case, District Judge Austin did not even take army spying seriously. After a brief look at the history of spying, Austin reaffirmed that the administration could use "all the facilities" available to it to preserve the Constitution from domestic as well as foreign enemies and proclaimed the possibility of a chilling effect only for the "thin-skinned, which none of the witnesses appeared to be." He spoke jestingly of the ability of the army to do any harm to the plaintiffs. The chief beneficiary of military intelligence, he said, had been newspaper circulation; the chief menace, air pollution from burning newspapers used to collect information for dossiers. He found no violation of rights, only a waste of taxpayers' money. That was 1970. In 1971, a district court judge, in deciding the first *Tatum* case, confirmed the growing seriousness with which some judges viewed executive surveillance.[18]

Burger's comments in *Laird v. Tatum* were the most significant. Although Burger, like Austin, argued that the military seemed to have relied chiefly on newspapers, he acknowledged the "strong resistance of Americans to any military intrusion into civilian affairs" and a "traditional insistence on limitations on military operations in peacetime." He affirmed the willingness of the Supreme Court to review claims where "judicially cognizable injury" had resulted from military intrusion into the civilian sector. Although such a statement provided little comfort for the political activists represented by the ACLU, it did reflect a major change in attitude toward surveillance between 1970 and 1972.

The change in tone in *Laird v. Tatum* was an important clue to a judicial shift in attitudes about giving the executive a constitutional blank check to expand its power under the guise of national security. In a different legal context, courts might question the activities of the military more carefully. The fact that Senator Ervin thought the case important enough to argue in person was a message to the Court that he, and per-

haps other members of Congress, considered army surveillance dangerous not only because of army activities, but also because of the freedom
with which the executive had been allowed to operate in a vague area
designated as *national security*. The public had not indicated much concern in Ervin's first hearings on army surveillance, in part because the
hearing coincided with the invasion of Laos in January 1971. *Laird v.
Tatum* was just one element in the broadening congressional and judicial
concern with surveillance. A few days before the *Laird v. Tatum* decision,
five of the plumbers were arrested for installing surveillance equipment
in the Democratic National Committee headquarters in the Watergate
complex.

The Watergate controversy that followed heightened the general concern that the courts, as well as the public, had about the political uses of
surveillance. By early 1973, journalists linked the executive to low-level
political surveillance, and when Senator Ervin introduced a privacy bill
in August 1973, he found considerable support among Republican as well
as Democratic senators. During the summer of 1973, Ervin's special Watergate committee was able to do what his previous hearings had not—to
focus the attention of the American public on the activities of the administration and on political surveillance. The emphasis was on "dirty tricks,"
apparently unconnected with the other domestic intelligence agencies.
These were issues that the people could easily understand: a small extra-
constitutional force operating with old, clumsy, and ineffective gumshoe
techniques of breaking and entering, employing prostitutes, and kidnap-
ping. Watergate encouraged a closer look at the relation of the executive
to the constitutional rights of citizens; led numerous people to realize the
weakness of congressional probes alone; and encouraged a belief that unless hearings could be linked to institutional safeguards, such as legislation or court decisions, there could be no permanent reform. Meanwhile,
another event occurred that shifted the focus of legal issues surrounding
military surveillance from the chilling effects on First Amendment rights
to the broader issue of the role of the army in law enforcement and to the
almost forgotten 1878 Posse Comitatus Act. On the evening of 27 February 1973, a group of Native Americans occupied a trading post in the
village of Wounded Knee on the Pine Ridge Reservation in South Dakota. By 2 March the United States army had arrived.

The Wounded Knee takeover triggered the army contingency plan for
domestic disturbances. Emergency Plans White—now coded as Garden
Plot—brought the army into South Dakota to perform a variety of internal security functions. Three army colonels, disguised as civilians, and

reconnaissance planes, assisted. This was the peak of a new "red scare," this time American Indian rather than Bolshevik or communist. Several incidents in the West involving militant Indian groups, such as the American Indian Movement, left the federal government with a much exaggerated estimate of the military capabilities of these political groups. In response, the government allowed national park officials to take extreme security precautions to protect federal property. The takeover at Wounded Knee seemed to confirm their worst fears. At last, the revolution had, in fact, begun. With no consideration of the limits of the Posse Comitatus Act, the Justice Department used the army to conduct intelligence for civilian law enforcement around Wounded Knee. The full extent of the use of the military by civilians did not become known until a series of suits filed by participants were heard in federal courts in 1974–75. These cases, and several never filed, described the involvement of the army.

In these cases, the courts examined the issues carefully. The courts upheld the activities of the federal government, but they issued strong warnings about federal military activity. In two cases, involving Dennis Banks and Gregorio Jaramillo, the federal courts supported a strict interpretation of the Posse Comitatus Act to prohibit military execution of civil law unless expressly authorized by Congress or the Constitution.

The issue of the Posse Comitatus Act and military involvement was raised by defendants in a Virginia case decided in January 1974. In that case, the circuit judge had upheld an appeal of the United States, saying that it was "the first instance of which we are aware in which the illegal use of military personnel in this manner has been drawn into question" and affirming that the letter of the act had not been violated. He did warn, however, that "should repeated cases involving military enforcement of civilian laws demonstrate the need for the special sanction of a judicial deterrent," that he would do so. This case involved the use of marines as undercover agents for the Treasury Department, and the court decided that calling attention to the problem would solve it. Obviously, the problem could not go away because the army was an integral part of many internal security plans, such as Garden Plot.[19]

The Jaramillo case, decided in August of 1974, provided the first full discussion of the Wounded Knee situation. The question, as framed by the federal court, was how much military personnel had been used. Investigation of the role of the military officers showed they had actually had a moderating influence on the Department of Justice. Nevertheless, the court decided that, in fact, the military had been involved in the execution of the law and that therefore the defendants must be acquitted.

Congress had declared the army must not be used and it could not. "It does not matter whether the use is to good effect or bad effect or whether the advice taken is good advice or bad advice," the court concluded. Congress could have passed a law permitting the use of military persons, or the people could have amended the Constitution. They had done neither. The court even used the words of Chief Justice Warren Burger in the *Laird v. Tatum* case to support its restrictive view of military involvement in civilian affairs. The Dennis Banks case soon reaffirmed the strict interpretation by the courts of the army's involvement in internal security.[20]

A year later, in the Red Feather case, the defendants argued that the Posse Comitatus Act made all the government's acts illegal. The court found it difficult to support this contention, as did the appeals court that upheld the decision. Chief Judge Warren K. Urbam of the District Court of Nebraska distinguished between active illegal and passive legal law enforcement. The military could, as passive law enforcement, conduct aerial photography, train, or give advice. The military could not, without presidential authorization, be present or influence the decisions of civilian law enforcement officers, or service or maintain equipment on loan to them. Nor could they investigate, search, or arrest. The courts also turned down a final appeal by the army for a broader definition of the appropriate role of the army in internal security. The Supreme Court did not hold army surveillance unconstitutional in 1972, but other courts did. The Posse Comitatus Act, rather than the Fourteenth Amendment, provided for civilian protection.[21]

Congress followed up these decisions with more explicit criticism of the military surveillance of civilians. During 1975 both the House and Senate had established select committees to study intelligence activities. The Senate committee, known as the Church committee for its head Democrat Frank Church, was a bipartisan committee that included the powerful Republican Barry Goldwater. In the fall of 1975 the Church committee held public hearings that exposed abuses by the intelligence community; in April 1976 it published a final report that documented these abuses and called for stricter executive and congressional oversight. The House Select Committee on Intelligence recommended that the Defense Intelligence Agency, which now oversaw all military surveillance, be prohibited from any intelligence operations in the United States. In May 1977, Secretary of Defense Harold Brown ordered that military agencies keep their operations within the law and report any violations at once. Most officers seemed relieved to have a clear standard. The judge advocate of the Marine Corps argued for the strict interpretation of the

Posse Comitatus Act upheld by the district courts. He argued that the Department of Defense should use the stricter interpretation even in the absence of a court decision because of the historical evidence of its intent and use.[22]

Public interest in intelligence then declined. President Gerald Ford managed to keep the issue out of the 1976 election. President Jimmy Carter took over what one commentator has called "a badly battered" intelligence community. The fear of further public criticism and stricter congressional and executive control forced all intelligence communities to keep a low profile. The army was no different. The end of the Vietnam War brought quiet on the home front.[23]

The decade of the 1970s left a legacy. Legal and historical scholars had recognized the importance of the two-hundred-year-old controversy and had made clear the issues involved. The debate over the role of the military in internal security had never been more open, more vocal, with such a broad spectrum of civilians engaged in it. The debate considerably broadened participation by civilians in public policy decisions once set aside for only high officials, civilian or military, or for professional military and the civilians of federal agencies involved in law enforcement. Civilians in turn involved Congress and the courts in new discussions of constitutional limits. These discussions drew on the expertise, insights, and talents of civilians outside the small intelligence elite. These people could take a broad view of internal security and see the institutionalization of both intelligence and civil liberties and the contested terrain between members of both groups. It was a sign of a maturing policy and a maturing public as well.

The American Constitution never mentioned army surveillance of civilians. The practice developed during wars and military occupations, in the American South, the Philippine war, in Cuba, along the Mexican border, and during two world wars. Although public criticism curtailed active surveillance after World War I, surveillance structures remained in place and some MID officers continued to believe they had a duty to protect the government from subversion. The development of War Plans White embodied the concept that within the civilian body politic lurked a potential enemy that the army might have to fight at any time—during peace as well as war.

During those years between the two world wars, the military in many countries developed theories about the role of civilians in war. Military bureaucracies felt increasingly dependent on civilians; they also felt hostage to civilian willingness to support expensive, technological wars. During the 1920s, the concept became entrenched in military thought that enemy civilians, not their armies in the field, were the true enemy. It is not surprising, therefore, that civilians on the home front should also have become an increasing danger to the military. In total war, civilians and armed forces were a part of the same war machine. Such a view was particularly attractive to intelligence officers because it enhanced their view that the home front was the critical site where wars were won or lost. Such an attitude encouraged a fear of civilian subversion and inevitably, spawned plans to counter subversion. After World War II, the cold war allowed such attitudes to continue. Neither the military nor most civilians saw an end to "living as a people in arms."[24]

Federal judges were reluctant to intervene in the day-to-day activities of the military. Judges believed that policy making legitimately belonged to elected officials and to the military community. Thus, they usually refused to review military activities. Judges occasionally challenged the jurisdiction of the military during the nineteenth century, but in the first decades of the twentieth seldom adjudicated even jurisdictional issues. Neither First nor Fourteenth Amendment rights seemed to the courts to be relevant in determining the limits of military surveillance. Such an attitude, relatively unchanged until the 1960s, meant that the courts would have little impact in shaping the surveillance policies of the military.[25]

In the absence of court action, the development of a surveillance policy depended primarily on Congress and the executive. Before World War II, Congress enacted only three pieces of relevant legislation, the Posse Comitatus Act, the Pinkerton Act, and the National Labor Relations Act. Each was, potentially, an important piece of legislation in limiting the use of army surveillance of civilians, yet each failed to limit army surveillance.

The most limiting was the 1878 Posse Comitatus Act, passed by Congress to restrain the use of the army in the 1870s. This act prohibited the use of any part of the army as a posse comitatus to execute laws and had as its purpose keeping the military out of civil affairs. But it played little or no role in the development of surveillance policies during war. Policy makers did not apply it in the formulation of peacetime surveillance policies. No one had ever been prosecuted under the statute, and it was, it seems, not considered to be a limitation by either high officers or regional commanders. The Posse Comitatus Act was not a crucial element in court cases involving military investigations and surveillance until the 1970s.[26]

The 1893 Pinkerton law that prohibited the executive from employing Pinkertons or other private detectives was far more of an active concern to policy makers. During World War I, consciousness of this law led MID and the Bureau of Investigation to rely on volunteers rather than hired detectives or to absorb detectives directly into the bureaucratic structure itself. The MID cooperated with professional detectives and volunteers in World War I, using them in a way that sidestepped the law. In World War II, a concern with this law—combined with White House and FBI opposition to the use of volunteers—led to a technical distinction being drawn by the War Department between credit investigators, whom it defined as not covered by the prohibition, and criminal investigators or detectives, whom it considered to be covered by the statute. Like the other laws, policy makers also sidestepped the National Labor Relations Act and the rulings of the National Labor Relations Board. At least part of the secrecy of actual MID investigations was to avoid complaints that the War Department was violating these laws.[27]

Congressional oversight of surveillance could have compensated for the lack of legislation. Permanent committees, congressional hearings, and investigations encourage a tighter reign on army agents. Congress allowed the executive almost full control in the formulation of policy with no more than a few privileged members knowing what was going on. Since no overview of the intelligence establishments existed, agencies dealt with only friendly congressional committees who kept secrets well. The question of how much to reveal to the public was usually answered by "very little." There was no attempt to separate the principles governing operations from the details of organization as British intelligence authority John Bruce Lockhart has advocated.[28]

Everything became a detail to be kept secret. Details could be important in influencing the political climate in regard to military appropriations and public support. Over the years intelligence reports not accessible through regular legislative committee investigations were leaked to favored politicians. While committee hearings, such as those conducted in the 1970s by Senators Ervin and Church, made some documents describing operations available to the public, earlier committee hearings seldom considered it their duty to do so. Congress made little effort to reassure the public concerning clandestine military surveillance or to accept joint responsibility for the policies regarding it.[29]

That left executive oversight as the only way to control army surveillance, without congressional or judicial checks and balances. Before the 1960s, presidents generally were concerned about the expansion of military surveillance into civilian politics. During both world wars, presidents supported the civilian FBI as the primary agency to investigate civilians.

Because executives had no process for reviewing or controlling intelligence agencies, however, the public had little knowledge of overall policies concerning surveillance. With the exception of brief press releases and a few comments on wartime controversies, the executive did little to provide material that the public could use in analyzing surveillance practices. The presidents remained clear about civilian jurisdiction during both wars, but the complexity of the defense efforts and the vast expansion of the bureaucratic apparatus for defense production ensured that principles would break down in practice, that foreign and domestic spheres would become confused. Although the home front received considerable attention from MID, it did not receive commensurate attention from executive management through an evaluation of programs. What evaluation and reduction of surveillance occurred in World War II came mainly at the end of the second year of war, after surveillance had occurred, and for a combination of personal and bureaucratic reasons. Presidents gave the intelligence services few guidelines and little oversight. Wilson left his trusted cabinet officers Attorney General Gregory and Secretary of War Baker in charge during World War I. These men, in turn, delegated authority to the directors of their respective intelligence services and provided little oversight. John Lord O'Brian, in charge of war-related matters for the Justice Department, established a clearinghouse in MID and coordinated war intelligence activities during World War I. Bureau of Investigation directors and MID, however, operated relatively independently and sometimes competitively as MID occupied areas of domestic surveillance that the Bureau of Investigation left open, or poached on territory explicitly claimed by them. Roosevelt attempted to coordinate and control intelligence agencies, but they also competed and expanded.[30]

The competition and expansion of MID during both world wars stemmed in part from a bureaucratic impulse based on its insecure place in the military hierarchy. Although claiming independence, MID was ultimately subject to control by the civilian secretary of war and to a high command still not sympathetic to an elaborate intelligence network at home or abroad. Shunted back and forth between War Department bureaus and periodically reduced to a skeleton force, MID officers developed a type of loyalty to intelligence and to each other that in part compensated for institutional insecurity. Because the army did not value intelligence, officers could not train for careers in intelligence. Some directors did not even want the jobs. Rotating top officers kept any individual officer from building a permanent intelligence empire but fostered a type of group loyalty that led to insubordination. The insecure place in the military hierarchy, changes in leadership, and a fear of public criticism fostered great secrecy in intelligence activities within the War Department, making departmental oversight even more difficult. In addition, MID could not draw on the popular detective ideology, available to Hoover in carving out a place in the public affections for the FBI in the 1930s.

The MID attempted to resurrect and elevate the revolutionary army spy Nathan Hale and the Spanish-American War army intelligence officer Richard Rowan to the position of national heroes, but neither became as popular with the public as the detective hero. In peacetime, such military heroes seemed out of place; in wartime, they were subordinate in importance to the front line officers and soldiers. The lack of a public and departmental image thus seemed to affect the development of MID.[31]

The expansion of MID was also affected by the personality of the men who had headed it. Van Deman's intelligence career, which began during the Philippine war of the early twentieth century, seemed to engender an exaggerated fear of subversion. His fear of subversion at home later led him to establish a private surveillance network in California upon his retirement and to continue counterintelligence work that had been cut to the bone during the retrenchment of the 1920s. High MID officers were aware of and tacitly approved of his secret intelligence activities. Sherman Miles, head of G-2 in the late 1930s, came to share Van Deman's exaggerated fear of subversion.

These fears could become so real for Van Deman and Miles because of their isolation from the political realities of the civilian world. At the same time, they were isolated from the concrete realities of the front line. The anti-intelligence, pro-action attitudes of the line officers seemed to encourage this fear of subversion and commitment to prevention through surveillance. The possibility that organized labor would support a change in government seemed an ultimate threat. In the desire to isolate politically suspect civilians from defense work, MID engaged in activities that might otherwise have seemed unnecessary or unwise. The officers of MID came to see themselves not only as defenders of the government but also as defenders of a government that should not be changed by a shift in politics. This ideological persuasion, although certainly not shared by all intelligence officers, nonetheless pervaded the higher ranks to such an extent that it appeared at times to take precedence over a commitment to the democratic political process. Such an ideology made it more likely that intelligence officers would analyze the internal security needs of the country in terms of their own interests rather than of democratic change.

That ideology became institutionalized in the 1950s and resurfaced during the Vietnam War of the 1960s.[32]

The climate of politics or what Baskir, former chief counsel and staff director of Ervin's subcommittee, later called "our unwritten constitutional law" of keeping the military out of civilian politics, was the single most important element in the development of military surveillance policy. It was the underlying expectation of a majority of the public and of their elected officials that military intervention in civilian politics would be sharply limited.[33]

Nonetheless, although it seemed to be an accepted political principle that military intervention at home should be limited as much as possible, even during times of crisis, the lack of a specific law to translate this political principle into practice together with a newly developing political climate undermined the traditional opposition to a standing army. Powerful and vocal national groups in the early twentieth century functioned as a promilitary lobby. On the other hand, domestic espionage by the military—as it was called before surveillance became widespread in World War II—was not controlled by specific legislation. Some opposition existed, but it did not successfully deepen or focus the vague public uneasiness that existed over the expansion of military power. Fear of public pressure became a main constraint in formulating policies. Unfortunately, both MID and the FBI considered public opposition to federal investigative policies primarily as a mandate to keep surveillance activities clandestine, rather than to regulate them systematically. The intelligence community saw opponents of extensive surveillance as enemies to be outwitted rather than as fellow citizens to be seriously considered in policy formulation.

At least two events in the political climate reinforced this growing belief in the necessity of clandestine operations. At the beginning of World War II, the public seemed to undergo again what intelligence heads would later identify as a "national surge." This impulse to do something to help the war effort took the form of concerned citizens searching out subversion in their communities. The executive attempted to channel this national surge in ways that could be contained, but the citizen reaction encouraged expansion within the intelligence agencies.[34]

The growing militancy of labor leaders in the early decades of the twentieth century also tended to be seen, in the eyes of some MID officers, as disloyalty rather than as legitimate political activity in response to grievances and needs. The belief that foreign agents were responsible for these labor activities pervaded the thinking of MID officers. While the pos-

sible presence of German agents concerned officers to a great extent at
the beginning of World War I, from 1918 forward the Bolsheviks became
a prime enemy. The thread of concern with domestic subversion by Bolsheviks began in the Red scare of 1918; spanned the interwar years;
emerged in plans for the internment of five thousand Communist leaders
in the late 1930s and in the surveillance of the Communist party during
the war; and culminated in a second Red scare at the end of World War II.
The involvement of Communists in the labor movement, often as leaders
and organizers, inevitably led to the surveillance of the labor movement.
Thus the political climate, or Baskir's unwritten constitutional law, failed
as an adequate safeguard for political rights in time of crisis.

Not all high army officers subscribed to these ideas. Many high officials, civilian and military, gave relatively little thought to methods of
controlling the needs and fears of the intelligence community. In practice,
the competing claims of line officers and civilian agencies revealed the
impulse to expand boundaries. Public knowledge might have helped to
channel their energy constructively. Hollering by the public sometimes
kept military intelligence restrained, but that was not a very efficient
method of restraint. When the hollering stopped, it frequently meant that
civilians were engulfed by a surge of fear that made them even more likely
than the military to demand the swift hanging of suspected spies. Some
civilians felt the military was better trained, more loyal, efficient, or just
cheaper than civilians for the job of surveillance.

Civilians were notoriously impatient of restraint—legal and constitutional—as well as committed to it. Civilians who argued against intervention were usually not popular heroes. Joshua Hett Smith, Lambdin
Milligan, iwws, communists, or even antiwar protesters during the Vietnam War were not considered American patriots. Yet the dissenting tradition was a fundamental necessity for correct decision making. The
larger, more heterogeneous the society, the more the government needs
dissenting views to form successful policy. The military operates best
when honestly committed to honoring the civilian need to make political
decisions without military intervention, in war, in crises, and in peace.

A reduction of secrecy might have helped the public to participate in
the evaluation of surveillance policies. By maintaining secrecy over documents, a dual tradition developed. Within the agencies, official histories
evaluated policy and practice. Outside, there existed no public studies of
surveillance practices. Intelligence officers often failed to see how changes
occurred, to understand when secrets were no longer secret, or to judge
when actions were successes or failures. No appropriate material was

made available to the public so that there could be a shared tradition of evaluation. A partial release of information was usually for purposes of manipulating the public record.[35]

The cold war, and its accompanying Red scare at home, made it difficult for the public to penetrate the secrecy surrounding intelligence agencies. A slight thaw in restrictions on the use of documents in the early 1950s was followed by a tightening of restrictions that led to a complete prohibition on the use of many documents and to security clearances, reviews of notes, and attempts to review the manuscripts of scholars who wished to analyze internal security policies. Because J. Edgar Hoover insisted that the National Archives restrict any document originating from his office and having his signature on it—including requests for supplies—and because many FBI records were interlarded with MID documents, only a favored few gained access to documents. Since the agencies had not developed techniques for sanitation and found it difficult to discriminate between the types of material originally classified, the declassification process was delayed many years after World War II. The passage of the Freedom of Information Act resulted in an increased withdrawal of material from the National Archives as agencies moved to cover their bureaucratic tracks. Intelligence leaks became an opportunity to denounce demands to make public the record of past intelligence activities. The public discussion of policy became impossible. The term *national security* came to be used as an excuse to withhold documents on domestic policy, a practice that eventually led to leaks regarding military surveillance policies in the 1970s and to the confusion of civilians as to their legitimate right to know about the agencies' past.[36]

Secrecy, internal security advocates argue, is absolutely essential. That is true, but surely not of policy, only of tactics that involve specific individuals and plans. Policy, by definition, must be contested terrain, for what makes strong effective policy is the accommodation of arguments against it. To extend military control over civilian politics is to tamper with fundamental structural needs in a democracy, as well as with ideological principles. Civilians need to know enough detail about internal security policies to be able to criticize them and to dissent from them.

Policies are most successful when based on information supporting and dissenting from a proposed plan of action. Dissent is a crucial element, for without it policy is not based on the realities that will affect its implementation. Internal security policies are no exception.

Sources

Published sources are cited in the notes. The following is a list of manuscript collections used in research.

Library of Congress, Washington, D.C. (LC)

Newton D. Baker Papers
Tasker Bliss Papers
Carrie Chapman Catt Papers
H. C. Corbin Papers
William G. McAdoo Papers
Peyton C. March Papers
National American Woman Suffrage Association Papers
Theodore Roosevelt Papers
Hugh L. Scott Papers
William Howard Taft Papers
Joseph P. Tumulty Papers
Charles Warren Papers
Roger Welles Papers
Woodrow Wilson Papers

National Archives, Washington, D.C. (NA)

RG 45, Naval Intelligence Records
RG 59, State Department Records
RG 60, Justice Department Records
RG 65, American Protective League Records
RG 85, Immigration and Naturalization Records
RG 87, Secret Service Records
RG 94, Office of the Adjutant General Records
RG 107, Office of the Secretary of War Records
RG 110, Provost Marshal General's Bureau Records
RG 165, Military Intelligence Division Records
RG 319, Army Staff Records
RG 389, Provost Marshal General, Internal Security Division Records

Nebraska State Historical Society, Lincoln, Nebraska (NSHS)
George Meiklejohn Papers

Suitland National Records Center, Suitland, Maryland (SNRC)
Plant Protection Records
Secret Service Records
Military Intelligence Division Records

National War College, Carlisle Barracks, Pennsylvania (NWC)
Army Military Research Collection

University of California, Los Angeles, Special Collections (UCLA)
Charles Daniel Frey Papers

University of Delaware, Newark, Delaware (UD)
George Messersmith Papers

Bentley Historical Library, Michigan Historical Collections, University of Michigan, Ann Arbor, Michigan (BHL)
Harry Hill Bandholtz Papers

ABBREVIATIONS APPEARING IN THE NOTES

AHR	*American Historical Review*
BHL	Bentley Historical Library, Michigan Historical Collections, University of Michigan, Ann Arbor, Michigan
LC	Library of Congress, Washington, D.C.
MA	*Military Affairs*
NA	National Archives, Washington, D.C.
NSHS	Nebraska State Historical Society, Lincoln, Nebraska
NWC	National War College, Carlisle Barracks, Pennsylvania
PHR	*Pacific Historical Review*
SNRC	Suitland National Records Center, Suitland, Maryland
UCLA	University of California, Los Angeles, California
UD	University of Delaware, Newark, Delaware
WMQ	*William and Mary Quarterly*

Notes

CHAPTER ONE: The New Nation

1. Richard J. Koke, *Accomplice in Treason: Joshua Hett Smith and the Arnold Conspiracy* (n.p., New York Historical Society, 1973), 105–11; Joshua Hett Smith, *An Authentic Narrative of the Causes Which Led to the Death of Major André* (New York: New York Times and Arno Press, 1969 reprint of 1808 London edition), 49–52; and Robert McConnell Hatch, *Major John André: A Gallant in Spy's Clothing* (Boston: Houghton Mifflin, 1986), 241–45.

2. John Clement Fitzpatrick, *The Writings of George Washington,* 39 vols. (Washington, 1931–44), General Orders, 4 July 1779, vol. 15, 364.

3. Ibid., Washington to Maj. Gen. Israel Putnam, 20 February 1777, vol. 7, 174; Washington to Brig. Gen. George Clinton, 5 May 1775, vol. 8, 18.

4. For André, see ibid., General Orders, 1 October 1780, vol. 20, 109–10, and Washington to Gov. Thomas Jefferson, 10 October 1780, vol. 20, 150. Examples of others handled as British spies are in Washington to Maj. Gen. William Heath, 12 January 1777, vol. 6, 497; Washington to Brig. Gen. William Maxwell, 18 February 1777, vol. 7, 361; and Washington to Maj. Gen. Israel Putnam, 18 August 1777, vol. 9, 91.

5. Ibid., General Orders, 27 June 1776, vol. 5, 182. See also Washington to President of Congress, 28 June 1776, vol. 5, 193. Harold M. Hyman, *To Try Men's Souls: Loyalty Tests in American History* (Berkeley: University of California Press, 1959), 74–76.

6. John Shy, *A People Numerous and Armed: Reflections on the Military Struggle for American Independence* (New York: Oxford University Press, 1976), 191–92, 207.

7. Washington was operating within the Anglo-American tradition of

subordination to civil authorities. See Ira D. Gruber, "The Anglo-American Military Tradition and the War for American Independence," in *Against All Enemies: Interpretations of American Military History from Colonial Times to the Present,* ed. Kenneth J. Hagan and William R. Roberts (Westport, Conn.: Greenwood, 1986), 29; Fitzpatrick, *Writings of George Washington,* Robert Hanson Harrison to President of Congress, 14 October 1776, vol. 6, 204n., written for Washington; Washington to Gov. William Livingston, 16 April 1777, vol. 7, 414; Washington to Gen. Preudhome De Borre, 3 August 1777, vol. 9, 6–7.

8. Ibid., Washington to Philip Livingston, Elbridge Gerry, and George Clymer, 19 July 1777, vol. 8, 439, and Washington to Gov. William Livingston, 15 April 1778, vol. 11, 262; Washington to Brig. Gen. William Maxwell, 20 December 1778, vol. 13, 441; Washington to Gov. William Livingston, 21 December 1778, vol. 13, 447; Washington to Col. Oliver Spencer, 9 April 1779, vol. 14, 357–58.

9. Hyman, *To Try Men's Souls,* 81; Fitzpatrick, *Writings of George Washington,* Proclamation, Jan. 25, 1777, VII, 61–62, and Washington to President of Congress, 5 February 1777, vol. 7, 102; Washington to Maj. Gen. Israel Putnam, 22 February 1777, vol. 7, 188.

10. Ibid., Washington to Gov. William Livingston, 25 March 1778, vol. 11, 151; Shy, *A People Numerous,* 206.

11. Smith, *An Authentic Narrative,* 130–32.

12. Fitzpatrick, *Writings of George Washington,* Washington to Maj. Gen. Nathanael Green, 16 October 1780, vol. 20, 196; Washington to Gov. George Clinton, 29 October 1780, vol. 20, 262.

13. Shy, *A People Numerous,* 191–92, 210, and his "The Loyalist Problem in the Lower Hudson Valley: The British Perspective," in *The Loyalist Americans: A Focus on Greater New York,* ed. Robert A. East and Jacob Judd (Tarrytown, N.Y.: Sleepy Hollow Restorations, 1975), 3–10. For laws and cases against Tories, see *The American Tory,* ed. Morton Borden and Penn Borden (Englewood Cliffs, N.J.: Prentice-Hall, 1972), 84. Catherine S. Crary, ed., *The Price of Loyalty* (New York: McGraw-Hill, 1973), 224, found sixty-five executions of Tories but does not distinguish between military and civilian executions. Frederick Bernays Wiener, *Civilians under Military Justice: The British Practice since 1689, especially in North America* (Chicago: University of Chicago Press, 1967), 107, pointed out that civilians who accompanied armies came under military courts. The British tried 156 persons unconnected with the army during the Revolutionary War. Disaffection was most pronounced in the mid-Atlantic, particularly in New York, but the machinery for detecting overt acts of loyalism remained centralized and moderate there. See Robert McCluer Calhoon, *The Loyalists in Revolutionary America, 1760–1781* (New York: Harcourt Brace Jovanovich, 1973), 397–98.

14. John Todd White, "Standing Armies in Time of War: Republican Theory and Military Practice during the American Revolution" (Ph.D. Diss., George Washington University, 1978); Lawrence Delbert Cress, "The Standing Army, the Militia, and the New Republic: Changing Attitudes toward the Military in American Society" (Ph.D. Diss., University of Virginia, 1976).

15. Richard H. Kohn, *Eagle and Sword: The Federalists and the Creation of*

the Military Establishment in America, 1783–1802 (New York: Free Press, 1975), 44–47, 57. See also Bradley Chapin, *The American Law of Treason: Revolutionary and Early National Origins* (Seattle: University of Washington Press, 1964); and Lawrence Delbert Cress, "Republican Liberty and National Security: American Military Policy as an Ideological Problem, 1783 to 1789," *WMQ*, 3d ser., 38 (January 1981): 73–96.

16. For the act of 1792, see 1 *U.S. Statutes at Large* 264 (1792), and comments by Clarence I. Meeks III, "Illegal Law Enforcement: Aiding Civil Authorities in Violation of the Posse Comitatus Act," *Military Law Review* 70 (fall 1975): 83–136. See also Lawrence Delbert Cress, "Reassessing American Military Requirements, 1783–1807," in *Against All Enemies*, ed. Hagan and Roberts, 52–53.

17. Robert W. Coakley, "Federal Use of Militia and the National Guard in Civil Disturbances," in *Bayonets in the Streets*, ed. Robin Higham (Lawrence: University of Kansas Press, 1969), 19–20; Leland Baldwin, *Whiskey Rebels: The Story of a Frontier Uprising* (Pittsburgh: University of Pittsburgh, 1968 edition), 224–57; Kohn, *Eagle and Sword,* 172; John W. Curran, "Lincoln Conspiracy Trial and Military Jurisdiction over Civilians," *Notre Dame Lawyer* 9 (1933): 31–32. Robert W. Coakley, "American Military History: The Early Period, 1607–1815," in *A Guide to the Study and Use of Military History,* by John E. Jessup, Jr., and Robert W. Coakley (Washington: Center of Military History, United States Army, 1979), 168, points out that no satisfactory work on the militia or the Continental Army as a military institution exists.

18. Kohn, *Eagle and Sword,* 214–29.

19. Ibid., 260–67, Coakley, "Federal Use," 23; James Morton Smith, *Freedom's Fetters, The Alien and Sedition Laws and American Civil Liberties* (Ithaca, N.Y.: Cornell University Press, 1956), 163–66; Manning J. Dauer, *The Adams Federalists* (Baltimore: Johns Hopkins University Press, 1953), 206; see also Frank Maloy Anderson, "The Enforcement of the Alien and Sedition Laws," American Historical Association, *Annual Report* (1912), 119; Joseph Cox, *Champion of Southern Federalism: Robert Goodloe Harper of South Carolina* (Port Washington, N.Y.: Kennikat, 1972), 145; and Edward C. Carter II, "A 'Wild Irishman' under Every Federalist's Bed: Naturalization in Philadelphia, 1789–1806," *Pennsylvania Magazine of History and Biography* 94 (1970): 331–46.

20. Dauer, *Adams Federalists,* 159.

21. Frede Castberg, *Freedom of Speech in the West: A Comparative Study of Public Law in France, the United States and Germany* (New York: Oceana, 1961), 15; Peter Squire, *The Third Department: The Establishment and Practices of the Political Police in the Russia of Nicholas I* (Cambridge: University Press, 1968), 57, 66, 196, 208, 213.

22. Theodore J. Crackel, "Jefferson, Politics, and the Army: An Examination of the Military Peace Establishment Act of 1802," *Journal of The Early Republic* 2 (April 1982): 21–38; Russell F. Weigley, *History of the United States Army* (New York: Macmillan, 1967), 109–10; and Leonard W. Levy, *Jefferson and Civil Liberties: The Darker Side* (Cambridge: Harvard University Press, 1963), 72–89, 107–37.

23. Ibid., 133, 154; and William B. Skelton, "Officers and Politicians: The Origins of Army Politics in the United States before the Civil War," in *The Military in America: From the Colonial Era to the Present,* ed. Peter Karsten (New York: Free Press, 1980), 89–110.

24. According to one early antislavery view, the Seminole War began when the approximately five hundred Blacks living as "slaves" among the Seminoles opposed their deportation because they feared they would be returned to Southern slavery and that the Seminoles threatened the internal safety of the South because the Blacks lived among them in comparative freedom similar to tenant farmers. William Jay, *View of the Action of the Federal Government in Behalf of Slavery* (New York: American Anti-Slavery Society, 1969 reprint of 1839 edition), 151–65. Few books on Indian wars analyze federal military policy. Richard N. Ellis, *General Pope and the United States Indian Policy* (Albuquerque: University of New Mexico Press, 1970), offers a partial analysis. For a case where army officers opposed militia trials of Indian rebels for treason, see *San Diego Herald,* 17 January 1852, 2:1.

25. Counterinsurgency among the slaves is only now beginning to be explored and analyzed. Angela Davis, "Reflections on the Black Woman's Role in the Community of Slaves," *Black Scholar* (December 1971): 3–15, and Eugene Genovese, "The Legacy of Slavery and the Roots of Black Nationalism," in *Red and Black: Marxian Explorations in Southern and Afro-American History* (New York: Pantheon, 1972), 129–56, first raised questions about insurgency. Theodore Weld, *American Slavery as It Is* (1839), discussed the use of domestic espionage by white Southerners. For the army in the Nat Turner rebellion, see *Nat Turner,* ed. Eric Foner (Englewood Cliffs, N.J.: Prentice-Hall, 1971), 5, 9.

26. For antislavery, see Joan M. Jensen, *Loosening the Bonds: Mid-Atlantic Farm Women, 1750–1850* (New Haven: Yale University Press, 1986), 188–95.

27. W. V. Hensel, *The Christiana Riot and the Treason Trials of 1851* (Lancaster, Pa.: New Era, 1911), 40–45.

28. S. W. Campbell, *The Slave Catchers: Enforcement of the Fugitive Slave Law, 1850–1860* (Chapel Hill: University of North Carolina Press, 1970), 104–5; Carl B. Swisher, *The Taney Period, 1836–1864* (New York: Macmillan, 1974), 534–46, 572–89. The opinion of the attorney general is in 6 *Op. Atty. Gen.* (1854), 465.

29. Alice Nichols, *Bleeding Kansas* (New York: Oxford University Press, 1954), 132, 133; and William Addison Phillips, *Conquest of Kansas* (Boston: Phillips, Sampson, 1850).

30. Jules Abels, *Man on Fire: John Brown and the Cause of Liberty* (New York: Macmillan, 1971), 275–76; and Steven Hahn, "Class and State in Postemancipation Societies: Southern Planters in Comparative Perspective," *AHR* 95(1) (February 1990): 75–98.

31. Robert Ralph Davis, Jr., "Buchanian Espionage: A Report of Illegal Slave Trading in the South in 1859," *Journal of Southern History* 37 (1971): 271–72.

32. Jacques Barzun, "Meditations on the Literature of Spying," *American Scholar* 34 (spring 1968): 167–78; John P. McWilliams, Jr., *Political Justice in a Republic: James Fenimore Cooper's America* (Berkeley: University of California Press, 1972), 57.

33. B. A. and H. K. Henisch, "Major André," *Journal of General Education* 28 (1976–77): 237–44.

34. For Hale, see Dixon Wecter, *The Hero in America: A Chronicle of Hero Worship* (1941, Ann Arbor, University of Michigan Press, 1963 reprint), 87–89; Henry Phelps Johnston, *Nathan Hale: 1776* (New York: DeVinne, 1901, and Yale University Press, 1914 edition); and Morton Pennypacker, *General Washington's Spies on Long Island and in New York* (Brooklyn: Long Island Historical Society, 1939), 21–23. Charles Dudley Warner, *Fashions in Literature, and Other Literary and Social Essays and Addresses* (New York: Dodd, Mead, 1902), 139–56, refers to Hale as the "Martyr-Spy" and chronicles the renewed interest in his exploits during the 1880s.

CHAPTER TWO: Domestic Law Enforcement

1. Wilbur R. Miller, "Police Authority in London and New York City, 1830–1879," *Journal of Social History* 18 (1976): 4–15.

2. Sigmund A. Lavine, *Allan Pinkerton: America's First Private Eye* (New York: Dodd, Mead, 1963), 1–74.

3. Peter S. Michie, *General McClellan* (New York: Appleton, 1901), mentions earlier hiring of Pinkerton. Allan Pinkerton, *The Spy of the Rebellion* (New York: Carleton, 1884).

4. Lavine, *Allan Pinkerton,* 81–109.

5. Jacob Mogelever, *Death to Traitors: The Story of General Lafayette C. Baker, Lincoln's Forgotten Secret Service Chief* (New York: Doubleday, 1960), 34; and Lafayette C. Baker, *History of the United States Secret Service* (Philadelphia: Baker, 1867). Although a century separates these two books, both approach surveillance in the same way. For a criticism of this approach, see Curtis C. Davis, "Companions of Crisis: The Spy Memoir as a Social Document," *Civil War History* 10 (1964): 385, 391. I have relied primarily on Harold M. Hyman and Benjamin P. Thomas, *Stanton: The Life and Times of Lincoln's Secretary of War* (New York: Knopf, 1962), 148–49, 157–58, 280, 472, and Harold M. Hyman, *A More Perfect Union: The Impact of the Civil War and Reconstruction on the Constitution* (New York: Knopf, 1973).

6. Barbara Jean Fields, *Slavery and Freedom on the Middle Ground: Maryland during the Nineteenth Century* (New Haven: Yale University Press, 1978), 98–99.

7. Frank L. Klement, *The Limits of Dissent* (Lexington, University of Kentucky Press, 1970), 149–56, 180, 258, and *Dark Lanterns: Secret Political Societies, Conspiracies, and Treason Trials in the Civil War* (Baton Rouge: Louisiana State University Press, 1984), 137–38.

8. T. H. Williams, *McClellan, Sherman, and Grant* (New Brunswick, N.J.: Rutgers University Press, 1962), makes this point most strongly. Mark E. Neely, Jr., "The Lincoln Administration and Arbitrary Arrests: A Reconsideration," Abraham Lincoln Association, *Papers* 5 (1983): 7–24, shows that over 47 percent of civilian arrests occurred in the border states and the District of Columbia, and over 25 percent were confederates. Another, almost 9 percent were foreigners. The Lincoln administration arrested over 14,000 civilians, most of them

after the War Department took over internal security from the State Department in February 1862. See also Scott Owen Reed, "Military Arrests of Lawyers in Illinois during the Civil War," *Western Illinois Regional Studies* 6, no. 2 (1983): 5–22.

9. Stanley I. Kutler, *Judicial Power and Reconstruction Politics* (Chicago: University of Chicago Press, 1968).

10. Harold M. Hyman, *The Radical Republicans and Reconstruction, 1861–1879* (Indianapolis: Bobbs-Merrill, 1967), 305, and 13 *U.S. Statutes at Large* 13 (1871). Under this act, the president had the authority to use "the militia or the land and naval forces" to suppress "insurrection, domestic violence, or combinations."

11. James E. Sefton, *The United States Army and Reconstruction, 1865–1877* (Baton Rouge: Louisiana State University Press, 1967), 30, 87, 214–17.

12. I have relied heavily on Stephen Ambrose, *Upton and the Army* (Baton Rouge: Louisiana State University Press, 1964), 90–95, for his interpretation of European armies, and on Michael Howard, *The Franco-Prussian War: The German Invasion of France, 1870–1871* (New York: Macmillan, 1961), 208, 249–50 for guerrilla warfare.

13. Emory Upton, *The Armies of Asia and Europe* (New York: Appleton, 1978); and Ambrose, *Upton and the Army*, 105, 169n, 133–34.

14. Lloyd Lewis, *Sherman: Fighting Prophet* (New York: Harcourt, Brace, 1932), 623.

15. U.S. *Congressional Record,* 44th Cong., 3d sess., 2151–61, 2246–49, quotes from 2248–49. The interpretation of the Posse Comitatus Act that is the closest to the one presented here is that of Deanne C. Siemer and Andrew S. Effron, "Military Participation in the United States Law Enforcement Activities Overseas: The Extraterritorial Effect of the Posse Comitatus Act," *St. John's Law Review* 54 (fall 1979): 1–54. For earlier views that emphasize the Reconstruction aspects, see Clarence I. Meeks, "Illegal Law Enforcement: Aiding Civil Authorities in Violation of the Posse Comitatus Act," *Military Law Review* 60 (fall 1975): 83–136, and James P. O'Shaughnessy, "Posse Comitatus Act: Reconstruction Politics Reconsidered," *American Criminal Law Review* 13 (1976): 703–35.

16. Jerry M. Cooper, *The Army and Civil Disorder: Federal Military Intervention in Labor Disputes, 1877–1900* (Westport, Conn., Greenwood, 1980), xiv, 240–41. Cooper emphasizes the qualitative rather than the quantitative importance of regular army intervention in strikes. He gives no numbers but implies that Weigley's figure (*History of the United States Army,* 281) of three hundred strikes is far too many. Barton C. Hacker, "The United States Army as a National Police Force: The Federal Policing of Labor Disputes, 1877–1898," *Military Affairs* 33 (April 1969): 255–64, overemphasizes strikes, although they perhaps were, as he says, "the most conspicuous function of the Regular Army during the last quarter of the nineteenth century." Vincent Pinto, *Soldiers and Strikers: Counterinsurgency on the Labor Front, 1877–1970* (San Francisco: United Front Press, 1973), also emphasizes the importance of the army. William H. Riker, *Soldiers of the State: The Role of the National Guard in American Democracy* (Washington: Public Affairs, 1957), 51, says that 30 percent of the active duty

of the militia from 1877 to 1892 was in connection with strikes but that the time was longer and the number of troops larger than for other activities.

17. U.S. *Congressional Record,* 45th Cong., 1st sess., vol. 6, 328–29, 348–51, 510, 514.

18. U.S. *Congressional Record,* 45th Cong., 2d sess., vol. 7, 3580–81, 4185–87. See also articles cited in note 4 above, and Cooper, *Army and Civil Disorder,* who also erroneously identifies the act as a Reconstruction Act.

19. *Davis v. South Carolina,* 107 US (17 Otto) 597 (1882); Darrell L. Peck, "The Justices and the Generals: The Supreme Court and Judicial Review of Military Activities," *Military Law Review* 70 (1975): 1–81.

20. For opinions, see 16 *Op. Atty. Gen.* (1894), 72. For New Mexico, see Larry D. Ball, "Our Useful Army: The Impact of the Posse Comitatus Act on Law Enforcement in the Southwest," Paper delivered to the Western History Association, Rapid City, South Dakota, October 3, 1974, and "Militia Posses: The Territorial Militia in Civil Law Enforcement in New Mexico Territory, 1877–1883," *New Mexico Historical Review* 55 (1980): 47–69. Frederick T. Wilson, *Federal Aid in Domestic Disturbances, 1787–1903* (Sen. Doc. 209, 57th Cong., 2d sess., 1903), 207–9.

21. Cooper, *Army and Civil Disorder,* 83, 104–5.

22. Ibid., 85, 167.

23. James T. King, "A Better Way: General George Cook and the Ponca Indians," *Nebraska History* 50 (1969): 239–50; Thomas Henry Tibbles, *The Ponca Chiefs: An Account of the Trial of Standing Bear* (Lincoln: University of Nebraska, 1972), 94–111.

24. Cooper, *Army and Civil Disorder,* 104–6.

25. W. E. Woodward, *A New American History* (New York: Farrar & Rinehart, 1936), 647. See also James L. Abrahamson, *American Arms for a New Century: The Making of a Great Military Power* (New York: Free Press, 1981), 31, 34, 50; and Cooper, *Army and Civil Disorder,* 13, estimates that the National Guard was used at least 150 times between 1870 and 1900.

26. Most of the accounts of the Pinkertons are popularized. I have used Lavine, *Allan Pinkerton,* 205, 208, and James D. Horan, *The Pinkertons: The Detective Dynasty That Made History* (New York: Crown, 1967), 330–32; *New York Times,* 8 July 1892, 2:4; U.S. *Congressional Record,* 52d Cong., 1st sess., 429, 1223, 4223–25.

27. Horan, *Pinkertons,* 348. Horan does not follow the pre-Homestead controversy over the Pinkertons. The Pinkertons were not deputized at the time but had been promised deputation by the sheriff, U.S., *Congressional Record,* 52d Cong., 1st sess., 5760–5831.

28. J. Bernard Hogg, "Public Reaction to Pinkertonism and the Labor Question," *Pennsylvania History* 2 (1944): 196-200.

29. U.S., *Congressional Record,* 52d Cong., 1st sess., 7006 for Sherman's speech of 2 August 1892; 27 U.S. *Statutes at Large,* 368 (1892).

30. Richard Stiller, *Queen of Populists* (New York: Cowell, 1970), 160–66.

31. Cooper, *Army and Civil Disorder,* 110–13.

32. Robert M. Utley, *Frontier Regulars: The United States Army and the Indian, 1866–1891* (New York: Macmillan, 1973), 277; Nelson A. Miles, *Personal*

Recollections and Observations of General Nelson A. Miles (Chicago: Da Capo, 1969 reprint of 1896 edition), 226; and *Serving the Republic* (New York: Harper, 1911), 126–27. See also Weigley, *History of the United States Army*, 268–69; Ellis, *General Pope*, 192–98; Robert G. Athearn, *William Tecumseh Sherman and the Settlement of the West* (Norman: University of Oklahoma Press, 1956), 288; and Erwin Thompson, *Modoc War: Its Military History and Topography* (Sacramento: Argus Books, 1971), 120–22.

33. Cooper, *Army and Civil Disorder*, 150–51.

34. Ibid., 114–27, 156.

CHAPTER THREE: Andrew Rowan: An Officer and a Spy

1. Upton, *Armies of Asia and Europe*, 330.

2. War College Index for Canada, NA, RG 165. The original reports have been destroyed. The first was dated 14 January 1879, "Military resources and plan of invasion." For the 1870 diplomacy, see Doris W. Dashew, "The Story of an Illusion: The Plan to Trade the Alabama Claims for Canada," *Civil War History* 15 (December 1969): 332–48. Bruce W. Bidwell, "History of the Military Intelligence Division, Department of the Army General Staff" (typescript, 2 parts, 1959–61), part I, VI-1, an official history by the Defense Department, gives Sherman's General Orders 64, 25 August 1880, for military officers.

3. Clippings dated 1 October 1885 and 6 October 1885, in NA, RG 94, AWC file 639. W. T. Sherman to John Sherman, Sept. 6, 1887, in *The Sherman Letters: Correspondence between General Sherman and Senator Sherman from 1837 to 1891*, ed. Rachel Sherman Thorndike (New York: Da Capo, 1969 reprint of 1894 edition), 377, indicates that he was interested in annexing Ontario, Canada.

4. Memorandum from Adjutant General to D. M. Taylor, 12 August 1886, NA, RG 94, AGO, 1547 ACP 1874. Louis A. Peake, "Andrew Summers Rowan and the Message *From García*," *West Virginia History* 44 (3) (1983): 227–40, points out that Rowan had secured appointments to the Naval Academy in 1872 and 1874 but flunked out both times.

5. Elizabeth Bethel, "The Military Information Division: Origin of the Intelligence Division," *MA* 2 (spring 1947): 19–20.

6. The MID began surveying Mexico and Central America in 1890. Concerned about leaks, after March 1891 it issued only oral orders for officers. D. M. Taylor to Secretary of War, 23 March 1891, NA, RG 94, AGO, 1547 ACP 1874; Carl Reichmann, "Notes," NA, RG 94, AWC file 639; U.S., Secretary of War, *Annual Report* (1893), vol. 1, 124; and U.S., Secretary of War, *Annual Report* (1894), vol. 1, 167, 182; *New York Times*, Dec. 11, 1896, 7:1; Daniel B. Schirmer, *Republic or Empire: American Resistance to the Philippine War* (Cambridge, Mass.: Schenkman, 1972), 50.

7. Louis A. Pérez, Jr., *Cuba Between Empires, 1878–1902* (Pittsburgh: University of Pittsburgh Press, 1983), xviii.

8. Randolph S. Churchill, *Winston S. Churchill*, 5 vols. (Boston: Houghton Mifflin, 1966), vol. 1, 255–57; Winston Churchill, "The Revolt in Cuba," *Saturday Review* 81 (15 February 1896): 165.

9. García and the *Bermuda* incident from *New York Times,* 26 February 1896, 1:7; 29 February 1896, 2:6; 3 March 1896, 3:2; 8 March 1896, 2:1; and Horatio S. Rubens, *Liberty, The Story of Cuba* (1932, New York: AMS, 1970 reprint), 193–94.

10. Pérez, *Cuba between Empires,* 12.

11. Rubens, *Liberty,* 106–40; *New York Times,* 7 April 1895, 5:1; Gonzalo Quesada and Henry Davenport Northrop, *The War in Cuba: Being a Full Account of Her Great Struggle for Freedom* (n.p.: Liberty, 1896), 103.

12. *New York Times,* 31 August 1895, 5:4; 24 September 1895, 5:1; U.S., Secretary of the Treasury, *Annual Report* (1895), vol. 53, 818.

13. Philip Foner, *The Spanish-Cuban-American War,* 2 vols. (New York: Monthly Review, 1972), vol. 1, 182–84.

14. Ibid., 203; *New York Times,* 12 June 1896, 4:7; 23 June 1896, 5:1; 31 July 1896, 1:5.

15. *New York Times,* 4 March 1896, 5:4; 14 April 1896, 5:3; 2 December 1896, 5:1; 13 May 1896, 5:1; 12 June 1896, 4:7. Pérez, *Cuba Between Empires,* 71.

16. Frederick Funston, *Memories of Two Wars* (New York: Scribner, 1914), 5; Foner, *The Spanish-Cuban-American War,* vol. 1, 197.

17. Ibid., 194, 196. Lewis L. Gould, *The Spanish-American War and President McKinley* (Lawrence: University of Kansas, 1982); p. 25 also notes the change.

18. A. S. Rowan and Marathon Montrose Ramsey, *The Island of Cuba* (New York: Holt, 1896). Most of the other books and pamphlets published after 1896 were actively pro-Cuban and for independence. Foner, *The Spanish-Cuban-American War,* vol. 1, 182–84, 192; *New York Times,* 19 November 1895, 5:1; Funston, *Memories,* 62.

19. For the navy, see *New York Times,* 9 November 1897, 1:7; for the army, see Maj. A. L. Wagner to the Adjutant General, 29 June 1897, in Graham A. Cosmas, *An Army for Empire: The United States Army in the Spanish American War* (Columbia: University of Missouri Press, 1971), 76; Newton T. Colman, *The Search for General Miles* (New York: G. P. Putnam's, 1968), 165–67.

20. No study has been done of the spy literature of the late nineteenth century, although Davis, "Companions of Crisis," 385–408 recognized the spy as a folk hero and warned historians about using these works as military history documents. He did not explore how they could be used, however. Baker's *History of the United States Secret Service* was reprinted and pirated in many editions, one in Chicago by Waverly in 1889. Lavine, *Allan Pinkerton,* mentions detective novels, 184; Allan Pinkerton, *Strikers, Communists, Tramps and Detectives* (New York: Arno, 1969 reprint of 1878 edition) portrays strikers of 1877 as foreign communists; William H. Riker, *Soldiers of the State: The Role of the National Guard in American Democracy* (Washington: Public Affairs, 1957), 61–63, shows how the best-selling novel of 1895, *The Honorable Peter Sterling* by Paul Leiscester Ford, presented the politician's solution to strikes—break the strike but negotiate a settlement favorable to strikers to retain their votes while yielding to demands for suppression from capitalists. Ford's book was a best-seller when

books by Crane and Hubbard were on the best-seller list and also sold millions of copies.

21. Memorandum from Arthur A. Wagner, 28 December 1897, NA, RG 94, AGO, file 6831-1-6; Maj. Arthur Wagner to Adjutant General, 30 December 1897, NA, RG 94, AGO, 367 ACP 85.

22. *New York Times,* 30 December 1897, 5:4.

23. *New York Times,* 27 March 1898, 1:5; 3:5; 3 April 1898, 2:5; Ralph E. Weber, ed., *The Final Memoranda: Major General Ralph Van Deman, USA Ret., 1865–1952, Father of U.S. Military Intelligence* (Wilmington, Del., Scholarly Resources, 1988), 4.

24. *New York Times,* 5 April 1898, 5:3; 5 April 1898, 2:1; 7 April 1898, 4:4; 8 April 1896, 2:6.

25. "The Man Who Delivered That Message to García," Literary *Digest* 74 (2 September 1922): 50–53; Marion Wilcox, "Captain Whitney's Opportunity," *Harper Weekly* 42 (25 June 1898): 613; U.S. Secretary of War, *Annual Report* (1898), vol. 1, part 1, 18.

26. From Rowan's sworn statement of 17 May 1898 with H. C. Corbin, Adj. Gen. to Secretary of War, 23 May 1898, NA, RG 94, AGO 367, ACD 851. Rowan also told his family to write to him in Jamaica, and his seven-year-old daughter, in a letter later returned, had warned: "Look out that the Spaniards don't catch you." Andrew Rowan, "My Ride Across Cuba," *McClure's Magazine* 11 (August 1898): 379.

27. *New York Times,* 10 May 1898, 2:5; Foner, *The Spanish-Cuban-American War,* vol. 2, 341; "Message to García," 50.

28. Hugh Thomas, *Cuba: The Pursuit of Freedom* (New York: Harper & Row, 1971), 386. See Portell Hermino Vilá, *Historia de Cuba en sus relaciones con Los Ustados Unidos y España,* 4 vols. (Havana; Montero, 1938–41), vol. 3, 465.

29. U.S. Secretary of War, *Annual Report* (1898), vol. 1, part 1, mentions only Whitney's message to Gómez. Rowan says two other officers were sent to Cuba but did not reach the island. Official War Department documents do not mention a third officer being sent to Cuba. Efficiency Record of Henry H. Whitney, AGO 37811, NA, RG 94. Whitney's orders were also verbal, but apparently he did not write any later account. He mentioned his communication with Gómez in *Who's Who 1899–1900* and to reporter Wilcox, "Captain Whitney's Opportunity," 613, which appeared before Rowan became a hero. Miles, *Serving the Republic,* 276, mentions Rowan and Whitney as gathering information on Cuba and Puerto Rico. By 1911, Gómez was not being mentioned in most discussions of the war. For Whitney, see also Patrick Eugene McGinty, "Intelligence and the Spanish American War" (Ph.D. diss., Georgetown University, 1981), 326.

30. *New York Times,* 26 April 1898, 1:4; U.S. Secretary of War, *Annual Report* (1898), vol. 1, part 2, 892, 966.

31. Charles H. Brown, *The Correspondent's War: Journalists in the Spanish-American War* (New York: Scribner, 1967), 173–80.

32. Weber, *The Final Memoranda,* 5; *New York Times,* 27 April 1898, 1:5;

26 April 1898, 1:4; 29 April 1898, 2:7; U.S. Secretary of War, *Annual Report* (1898), vol. 1, part 1, 19.

33. *New York Times,* 14 May 1889, 1:1; 16 May 1889, 7:1, 1:6; 26 May 1898, 3:6.

34. Reference to Corbin in Redfield Proctor to Ainsworth, 28 May 1907, which explains the reason for Rowan's deposition of 17 May 1898, NA, RG 94, AGO, 367 ACP 85. The requests for Rowan and his tours of duty are in NA, RG 94, AGO, 267 ACP 85; Marion Wilcox, "Lieutenant-Colonel Rowan's Exploit: The American Delegate's Visit to García," *Harper's Weekly* 42 (2 July 1898): 643; *New York Times Magazine,* 3 July 1898, 12:1, 2–7.

35. "My Ride Across Cuba," 372–79.

36. The figure of 40 million was Hubbard's but was commonly accepted and frequently repeated; "Message to García," 50–53. Robert W. G. Vail, *"A Message to García:" A Bibliographical Puzzle* (New York: New York Public Library, 1930), gives publication information on the first edition. Alice P. Hackett, *Sixty Years of Best Sellers* (New York: Bowker, 1945), 104, gives a figure of 4 million copies and in a later (1956) edition, divides up the same total into 1 million hardbound Roycroft copies and 3 million Roycroft original paperbacks. She does not, however, make any attempt to assay industrial publications, magazine reprints, which were said to run to several hundred thousand, and foreign publications. There was an incredible number of editions in English alone. J. H. Tilden, "The Stuffed Club," in *The Fra: For Philistines and Roycrofters* (August 1915) discusses son. Hubbard's description of the event dated 1 December 1913 is reprinted in a 1926 edition of *A Message to García* by the Veterans of Foreign Wars. See also Bert Hubbard's memoirs in "I Recall," East Aurora *County Chronicle,* 20 February 1963, 3. For an overview of Hubbard, see Freeman Champney, *Art and Glory: The Story of Elbert Hubbard* (Kent, Ohio: Kent University Press, 1968).

37. See *Crane Letters,* 220, for objections to Rowan; Robert Glen Deamer, "Stephen Crane and the Western Myth," *Western American Literature* 7 (summer 1972): 111–23, for his belief that Westerners were "truer men."

38. Correspondence of January 1903 in NA, RG 94, AGO, 367 ACP 85; Arthur L. Wagner, *The Service of Security and Information* (Kansas City: Hudson-Kimberly, 1903), 180.

39. Capt. T. Bentley Mott, "The Organization and Function of a Bureau of Military Intelligence," Silver Medal Prize Essay, 1902, NA, RG 165.

40. Adj. Gen. to Sen. C. W. Watson, 28 June 1911; Henry Stimson to Wetmore, 30 October 1911; Senate Bill 2854; and Edward H. Griffith to Newton D. Baker, 11 May 1916, NA, RG 94, AGO 367 ACP 85. Griffith directed a large number of popular films from 1921 to 1946.

41. Correspondence relating to Rowan is in NA, RG 94, AGO 367 ACP 85.

CHAPTER FOUR: Spanish Spies and Cuban Insurgents

1. *New York Times,* 27 May 1898, 4:5; Foner, *Spanish-Cuban-American War,* vol. 2, 347.

2. Ibid., 341, 390–96; Thomas, *Cuba,* 403; David F. Healy, *The United*

States in Cuba, 1898–1902: Generals, Politicians, and the Search for Policy (Madison: University of Wisconsin Press, 1963), 33–34; and Quesada to Meiklejohn, 5 August 1898, box 36, and Magoon to Meiklejohn, 13 August 1898, box 32, Meiklejohn Papers, NSHS.

3. W. S. Scott to Assistant Secretary of War, 10 July 1898, file 115052, NA, RG 92. Various comments on ciphographs are in J. H. Burnam to Meiklejohn, 4 July 1898, and Meiklejohn to Burnam, 16 June 1898, box 4, Meiklejohn Papers, NSHS.

4. Secret Service, Records of the Office of the Secretary of War, Record Cards, 8201, 6943, 5745; Meiklejohn to Secretary of Treasury, 19 December 1898, General Correspondence, file 7276, NA, RG 107; Statement by Scott on expenditures, Scott to Assistant Secretary of War, 12 August 1898, box 46, Meiklejohn Papers, NSHS; J. C. Burrows, "The Need of National Legislation against Anarchism," *North American Review* 172 (December 1901): 734–40; Sidney Fine, "Anarchism and the Assassination of McKinley," *AHR* 60 (July 1955): 777–79.

5. Harrisburg, Pennsylvania *Telegraph,* 28 March 1898, clipping in box 1, Meiklejohn Papers, NSHS.

6. John W. Griggs, Attorney General to Boyd B. Jones, 17 May 1898, NA, RG 87.

7. Reports are in box 42, Meiklejohn Papers, NSHS.

8. *New York Times,* 29 April 1898, 1:6; 2:7.

9. *New York Times,* 15 June 1898, 2:2; 14 June 1898, 2:1; M. W. Twitchell to J. B. Moore, 17 May 1898 and 21 May 1898, box 43, Meiklejohn Papers, NSHS.

10. Don Wilkie, *American Secret Service Agent* (New York: Burt, 1934), 6, 12–14, written by his son who was fourteen at the time of the Spanish American War and who later became a Secret Service agent.

11. Letter from State Department about Downing, Wm. R. Day, 21 June 1898, NA, RG 87.

12. For Meiklejohn see various biographical materials in box 1, and Pershing to Meiklejohn, 27 March and 29 March, 1897, box 35, Meiklejohn Papers, NSHS.

13. *New York Times,* 15 May 1898, 2:5.

14. For arrests and counterespionage orders, see Meiklejohn to Gen. J. R. Brooke, Commanding 1st, 3d, 6th Army Corps, Chickamauga, Georgia, 26 May 1898, box 43; Meiklejohn to C. H. Paul, 31 May 1898, box 32, refusing commission in "secret service," Meiklejohn Papers, NSHS. For Pinkertons, see H. B. Plant to Thompson and Slater, 4 May 1898, RG 87; Assistant Secretary of War to Robert Pinkerton, 19 May 1898, box 35, and Lyman J. Gage to Meiklejohn, 28 May 1898, box 14, Meiklejohn Papers, NSHS.

15. For surveillance, see *New York Times,* 5 June 1898, 4:1. For Pinkerton, see Wilkie, *American Secret Service Agent,* 17–18; and *New York Times,* 10 June 1898, 2:6, 12 June 1898, 1:1, 28 August 1898, 6:3. Secretary of the Treasury, *Annual Report* (1898), 866, contains Wilkie's report on the Secret Service. For agents' tactics, see Martin Kastle to Wilkie, 30 June 1898; A. de la Torre, Jr., to R. S. Browne, 11 October 1898; Chas. La Salle to Wilkie, 16 October 1898; and Special Operative to Wilkie, 6 February 1899, NA, RG 87.

16. Meiklejohn to Frank, 9 June 1898; John E. Wilkie to Frank, 11 June 1898; Royal Frank to Adjutant General, 12 June 1898; Frank to Adjutant General, 15 June 1898, NA, RG 94. Meiklejohn to Commanding General, Department of the East, Governor's Island, 28 June 1898, box 13, Meiklejohn Papers, NSHS. Martin Kastle to John Wilkie, 13 June 1898, NA, RG 87.

17. Office of Adjutant General, NA, RG 94, file 110300. W. S. Scott to Assistant Secretary of War, 23 June 1898, and extract of letter from Wilkie to Joseph Priest, 9 June 1898, for Elmhirst, NA, RG 87. *New York Times,* 25 May 1898, 2:5; 26 May 1898, 2:3, for newspaper account of the arrests of two of the accused.

18. Chief of the Secret Service Division, *Annual Report,* 30 June 1899.

19. William Davis to Meiklejohn, 15 September 1898, box 12, Meiklejohn Papers, NSHS; *New York Times,* 20 October 1898, 5:3; and Porter's work described in Healy, *The United States and Cuba,* 43–44.

20. *New York Times,* 13 December 1898, 6:3; letter to José Vilalan, Havana for Reubens, no date, discusses conference for disbanding, box 38, Meiklejohn Papers, NSHS.

21. Foner, *Spanish-Cuban-American War,* vol. 2, 431, 437, 441, offered no evidence of serious disturbance, though he clearly felt Wood underestimated the opposition. Healy, *The United States in Cuba,* generally agrees, as does Allan Reed Millett, *The Politics of Intervention: The Military Occupation of Cuba, 1906–1909* (Ohio State University Press, 1968).

22. Robert Pinkerton, "Detective Surveillance of Anarchists," *North American* 173 (November 1901): 610–17.

23. Bell to Roosevelt, 30 August 1906; Funston to Bell, 28 August 1906; and Roosevelt to Bell, 1 September 1906, in Millett, *Politics of Intervention,* 66–67.

24. *New York Times,* 22 September 1906, 23 September 1906; Millett, *Politics of Intervention,* 99.

25. Ibid., 106, 130.

26. Ibid., 130–31, 138–39.

27. Ibid., 177, 182.

28. Ibid., 184–85.

29. Ibid., 254.

30. Captain J. W. Furlong, "Notes on Field Service in Cuba," 2 November 1907, file 4352, Army War College Document file 1903-19, NA, RG 165.

CHAPTER FIVE: Filipino Revolutionaries

1. Bandholtz to Van Deman, 21 August 1907, box 2, Bandholtz Papers, BHL.

2. For background on Bandholtz, see Michael Cullinane, "Quezon and Harry Bandholtz," *Bulletin of the American Historical Collection* (Manila), 9 (January–March 1981): 79–90, 99–100.

3. For the Spanish period, see Peter W. Stanley, *A Nation in the Making: The Philippines and the United States, 1899–1921* (Cambridge: Harvard University Press, 1974), 16–36.

4. For an overview of this hostility, see Joan M. Jensen, *Passage from India:*

Asian Indian Immigrants in North America (New Haven: Yale University Press, 1988), especially 42–56. Filipinos did not begin to arrive until the 1920s.

5. John A. Larkin, *The Pampangans: Colonial Society in a Philippine Province* (Berkeley: University of California Press, 1972), xii–xiii.

6. John Leddy Phelan, *The Hispanization of the Philippines: Spanish Aims and Filipino Responses, 1565–1700* (Madison: University of Wisconsin Press, 1959), 120–49; and Alfred W. McCoy and Ed. C. de Jesus, *Philippine Social History: Global Trade and Local Transformations* (Manila: Ateneo de Manila University Press, 1982), 11–12.

7. Jonathan Fast and Jim Richardson, *Roots of Dependency: Political and Economic Revolution in Nineteenth Century Philippines* (Quezon City: Foundation for Nationalist Studies, 1979), 56–64.

8. Ibid., 76–84.

9. On early Filipino-American relations, see David Lawrence Fritz, "The Philippine Question: American Military Policy in the Philippines, 1898–1905," (Ph.D. diss., University of Texas, Austin, 1977), 46–99, and McGinty, "Intelligence and the Spanish American War," 391–400. Gould, *The Spanish-American War and President McKinley,* 62–66, traces the development of McKinley's policy. For Dewey, see Brian McAllister Linn, *The U.S. Army and Counterinsurgency in the Philippine War, 1899–1902* (Chapel Hill: University of North Carolina Press, 1989), 6.

10. Ibid., 2–3.

11. Ibid., 2.

12. Ibid., 8; R. A. Alger, *The Spanish American War* (New York: Harper, 1901), 327; and Thomas Bentley Mott, *Twenty Years as Military Attaché* (New York: Oxford University Press, 1937), 56–57.

13. "The Fall of Manila," *Harper's Weekly* 42 (15 October 1898): 1007; *New York Times,* 1 October 1898, 5:1.

14. Schirmer, *Empire or Republic,* 72, 94–96; John M. Gates, *Schoolbooks or Krags: The United States Army in the Philippines, 1898–1902* (Westport, Conn., Greenwood, 1973), 20.

15. Linn, *The U.S. Army and Counterinsurgency,* 7.

16. Gates, *Schoolbooks,* 25; *New York Times,* 7 June 1898, 1:7; 20 October 1898, 1:2; 20 November 1898, 4:3; 17 November 1898, 1:5; 22 November 1898, 1:4.

17. Schirmer, *Republic,* 112–13, 125; Aguinaldo to Otis, 3 November 1898, 18 November 1898, Otis to Aguinaldo, 18 November 1898, box 73, Meiklejohn Papers, NSHS.

18. *New York Times,* 17 December 1898, 6:1, 6:7; 6 February 1899, 1:2; Schirmer, *Empire or Republic,* 126, 128; Mrs. P. F. Steem to Meiklejohn, 4 April 1899, box 45, Meiklejohn Papers, NSHS.

19. *New York Times,* 22 February 1899, 1:2, 1:3; 23 February 1899, 1:5; 24 February 1899, 1:3; "History of the Philippine Department," undated, says only that the Insurgent Records Office was established, NA, RG 165, MID 10560152. On the history of the documents, see John T. Farrell, "An Abandoned Approach to Philippine History: John R. M. Taylor and the Philippine Insurrection Records," *Catholic Historical Review* 39 (January 1954): 385–407; and William

Henry Scott, *Cracks in the Parchment Curtain and Other Essays in Philippine History* (Quezon City: New Day, 1982), 234–41.

20. Schirmer, *Republic or Empire,* 239, 174, 187; *New York Times,* 25 May 1899, 3:1; 27 May 1899, 4:5; F. E. Leupp, "Philippine Round Robin," *Harper's Weekly* 43 (29 July 1899): 753.

21. James O. West to Meiklejohn, 8 July 1899, box 58, Meiklejohn Papers, NSHS; and Fritz, "The Philippine Question," 202–5, 223.

22. W. S. Jenkins to Meiklejohn, 29 July 1899, 22 January 1900, 14 April 1900, box 21, Meiklejohn Papers, NSHS; Gates, *Schoolbooks,* 95–96.

23. *New York Times,* 7 February 1900, 1:2, 9 February 1900, 7:4, 2 May 1900, 5:4. For internal class conflict, see Fast and Richardson, *Roots of Dependency,* 93–97; and Stanley, *A Nation in the Making,* 52–55.

24. Dean C. Worcester, *The Philippines, Past and Present* (New York: Macmillan, 1921), 331; Henry Fowles Pringle, *The Life and Times of William Howard Taft,* 2 vols. (New York: Farrar & Rinehart, 1939), vol. 1, 167, 185; and Ralph Eldin Minger, *William Howard Taft and United States Foreign Policy: The Apprenticeship Years* (Urbana: University of Illinois Press, 1975), 28.

25. *New York Times,* 8 April 1900, 11:2; Schirmer, *Republic or Empire,* 219.

26. Taft to C. P. Taft, 12 June 1900, and Taft to Helen Taft, 18 July 1900, in Pringle, *Taft,* vol. 1, 170, 185–86. Philippine Commission to Secretary of War, 14 July 1900, Taft Papers, LC.

27. Taft to Root, 26 July 1900, Philippine Commission to Secretary of War, 11 August 1900, Taft Papers, LC.

28. Memorandum of interview between MacArthur and Gen. José Alejandrino, 28 July 1900, MacArthur Memorandum for Col. Wilder, 30 July 1900, José Ner to Military Governor, 8 August 1900, box 73, Meiklejohn Papers, NSHS.

29. Linn, *The U.S. Army and Counterinsurgency,* 42–45.

30. Taft to Root, 10 October 1900, Taft Papers, LC.

31. W. S. Jenkins to Meiklejohn, 23 May 1900, 30 June 1900, box 21, Meiklejohn Papers, NSHS.

32. Ibid., 330; and Howard Beale, *Theodore Roosevelt and The Rise of America to World Power* (Baltimore: Johns Hopkins University Press, 1956), 186.

33. E. J. Hainer to Meiklejohn, 12 September 1900 and W. A. Simpson, MID to Meiklejohn, 17 September 1900, box 73, Meiklejohn Papers, NSHS.

34. Frank Freidel, "Dissent in the Spanish-American War and the Philippine Insurrection," in Samuel Eliot Morison, Frederick Merk, and Frank Freidel, *Dissent in Three American Wars* (Cambridge: Harvard University Press, 1970), 92; Schirmer, *Republic or Empire,* 221; and Christopher Lasch, "The Anti-Imperialists, the Philippines, and the Inequality of Man," *Journal of Southern History* 24 (August 1958): 319–31.

35. Taft to Root, 14 November 1900, 30 November 1900, Taft Papers, LC.

36. Taft's complaints are in Taft to Root, 27 December, 9 January, 13 January, 18 January, 21 January 1901, Taft Papers, LC; Taft to C. P. Taft, 9 January 1901, Pringle, *Taft,* vol. 1, 198.

37. Weber, *The Final Memoranda,* 7–8.

38. Taft to Root, 14 October 1901, Taft Papers, LC. For Chaffee, see

Michael H. Hunt, "The Forgotten Occupation: Peking, 1900–1901," *PHR* 48 (1979): 501–29.

39. Taft to Root, 10 February 1901, 3 April 1901, 5 August 1901, 3 September 1901, 26 September 1901, Taft Papers, LC.

40. Linn, *The U.S. Army and Counterinsurgency,* 59, 154–55.

41. Taft to Root, 17 November 1901, Taft Papers, LC.

42. Reports of January, February 1902, Chaffee to Corbin, 10 January 1902, 22 March 1902, 30 April 1902, 9 June 1902, Container 1, Corbin Papers, LC.

43. Weber, *The Final Memoranda,* 8; "History of the Philippine Department, NA, RG 165, file 10560-15.

44. Taft to Root, 13 September 1902, 14 April 1903, 13 May 1903, 15 June 1903, Taft Papers, LC; Fritz, "The Philippine Question," 648; and John M. Gates, "War-Related Deaths in the Philippines, 1898–1902," *PHR* 53 (August 1984): 367–78. The debate still stirs historians. See D. H. Smith, "American Atrocities in the Philippines," *PHR* 55 (May 1986): 281–83; and Glenn Anthony May, "One Hundred and Fifty Thousand Missing Filipinos: A Demographic Crisis in Batangas, 1887–1903," in Glenn Anthony May, *A Past Recovered* (Quezon City: New Day, 1987), 66–97.

45. Carol Morris Petillo, *Douglas MacArthur: The Philippine Years* (Bloomington: Indiana University Press, 1981), 64–70, 76; and Fast and Richardson, *Roots of Dependency,* 103–4.

46. Harold Hanne, *The Story of the Philippine Constabulary* (Los Angeles: Globe, 1949), 14–21.

47. Discussion of the military history is in "A New Military Policy for the United States in the Philippines," 22 June 1911; George B. Davis, Adjutant General to Secretary of War Taft, 25 May 1908, box 2, Bandholtz Papers, BHL. See also Fritz, "The Philippine Question," 390, 526–40; and James Richard Woolard, "The Philippine Scouts: The Development of America's Colonial Army" (Ph.D. diss., Ohio State University, 1975), 2–10, 40.

48. Bandholtz to General Bell, 5 September 1907, Bandholtz to General Allen, 11 September 1907. For labor unrest and politics, see Bandholtz to Gen. Leonard Wood, 22 March 1909, Bandholtz to Col. Mark L. Hersey, 23 March 1909, Bandholtz to C. R. Edwards, Chief, Bureau of Insular Affairs, 17 May 1908. All in box 2, Bandholtz Papers, BHL.

49. Bandholtz to General Allen, 2 August 1911, box 2, Bandholtz Papers, BHL.

50. Bandholtz to Col. W. C. Rivers, 17 October 1911, Bandholtz to Manuel Quezon, 11 November 1911, box 2, Bandholtz Papers, BHL. For the politics of the time, see Peter W. Stanley, *The Philippines and the United States* (Cambridge: Harvard University Press, 1974), 161–75.

51. Richard D. Challener, *Admirals, Generals, and American Foreign Policy, 1898–1914* (Princeton, N.J.: Princeton University Press, 1973), 228–29; and Louis Morton, "Military and Naval Preparations for the Defense of the Philippines during the War Scare of 1907," *MA* 13 (summer 1949): 95–104.

52. Michael A. Barnhart, "Japanese Intelligence before the Second World War: 'Best Case' Analysis," in *Knowing One's Enemies: Intelligence Assessment*

before the Two World Wars, ed. Ernest R. May (Princeton: Princeton University Press, 1984), 424–55.

53. Minger, "Taft's Mission to Japan," 48; Beale, *Theodore Roosevelt,* 237; John Edward Wilz, "Did the United States Betray Korea in 1905?" *PHR* 54 (August 1985): 243–70.

54. Taft to Roosevelt, 10 March 1908, Taft Papers, Secretary of War Series, LC.

55. Taft to Dean Worcester, 26 December 1913, Taft Papers, LC.

56. Taft to Martin Egan, 24 November 1910, Pringle, *Life and Times of William Howard Taft,* vol. 2, 712.

57. Dickinson to Taft, 6 March 1911, Dickinson to Taft, 20 March 1911, Forbes to Taft, 8 April 1911, Presidential Series, Taft Papers, LC.

58. For the 1920s, see Van Deman to Nolan, 24 May 1921, MID 6530-134; Robert G. Kirkwood to Assistant Chief of Staff, G-2, Hawaiian Department, 1 November 1924, MID 10560-731110; and Walter E. Prosser, Assistant Chief of Staff, G-2, to Assistant Chief of Staff, 19 November 1924, MID 10560-73126, NA, RG 165.

CHAPTER SIX: The Mexican Border: Bringing Intelligence Home

1. Biographical information on Van Deman is in AGO 220221, NA, RG 94.

2. Weber, *The Final Memoranda,* 7–11.

3. Ibid., 12.

4. Robert Pinkerton, "Detective Surveillance of Anarchists," *North American* 73 (November 1901): 609–17; William Preston, Jr., *Aliens and Dissenters: Federal Suppression of Radicals, 1903–1933* (Cambridge: Harvard University Press, 1963), 31–33.

5. Roosevelt to George Robert Carter, 23 December 1903, Roosevelt to Taft, 7 March 1904, Elting E. Morison, ed., *Letters of Theodore Roosevelt,* 8 vols. (Cambridge, Harvard University Press, 1964), vol. 3, 676, vol. 4, 744.

6. Memorandum, Oct. 4, 1907, Second Division for Secretary, General Staff; and Memorandum, Nov. 1, 1907, Albert Todd for Secretary, General Staff, GS 488, NA, RG 165.

7. Timothy K. Nenninger, "The Army Enters the Twentieth Century, 1904–1917," in *Against All Enemies,* 224; Weber, *The Final Memoranda,* 15; Annual Report, Military Information Committee, 19 October 1908, GS 3110, NA, RG 165.

8. Van Deman to H. L. Morse, 6 March 1910, GS 488, NA, RG 165.

9. D. A. Frederick Memorandum for Chief of Staff, 15 September 1910, GS 488, NA, RG 165.

10. The 1911 postcard is in the Ann Zohn Collection, Rio Grande Historical Collections, New Mexico State University Library.

11. W. Dirk Raat, *Revoltosos: Mexico's Rebels in the United States, 1903–1923* (College Station: Texas A & M, 1981), especially 175–99; and Anne Pace, "Mexican Refugees in Arizona, 1910–1911," *Arizona and the West* 16 (1974): 5–18.

12. "The Japanese Bogey," *World's Work* 21 (11 March 1911):14076–77.

13. Lowell L. Blaisdell, *The Desert Revolution: Baja California, 1911* (Madison: University of Wisconsin Press, 1962).

14. Jurisdictional quarrels are in NA, RG 94, file 1716345. See especially, Memorandum from Chief of Staff for Attorney General, 6 March 1911, and J. E. Morrison, U.S. Attorney, Tucson, 31 March 1911. Charles H. Harris III and Louis R. Sadler, "The 1911 Reyes Conspiracy: The Texas Side," *Southwest Historical Quarterly* 83 (April 1980): 325–48; idem, "The Underside of the Mexican Revolution: El Paso, 1912," *The Americas: A Quarterly Review of Inter-American Cultural History* 39 (July 1982): 69–83.

15. Liggett Memorandum, 13 March 1911, GS 6359, NA, RG 165; Raat, *Revoltosos,* 131, 188.

16. Hunter Liggett, Chief, War College Division to W. W. Wotherspoon, 27 March 1911; T. M. Potts to Colonel Liggett, 14 February 1911; and Liggett Memorandum, Secretary, General Staff, 13 March 1911, GS 6359, NA, RG 165.

17. 36 *U.S. Statutes at Large* 1084.

18. Robert F. Stohlman, Jr., *The Powerless Position: The Commanding General of the Army of the United States, 1864–1903* (Manhattan, Kansas: Military Affairs/Aerospace Historian, 1975), 130–31. Taft had made an effort to control bureau chiefs in 1911 by threatening Ainsworth with a court martial, but the problem remained. See Nenninger, "The Army Enters the Twentieth Century," 225–26.

19. Wood Memorandum for Chief War College Division, 20 January 1913, GS 6359, NA, RG 165.

20. F. E. Harris to Chief of Staff, Philippine Dept., 26 April 1913, John Hay to Adjutant General, 3 May 1913, Copy of letter to Bradley A. Fiske, 29 June, 1914, GS 639, NA, RG 165.

21. Chief of War College Division, Memorandum for Chief of Staff, 20 June 1914, OAG 2178718, NA, RG 94. See also Barbara Tuchman, *The Zimmerman Telegram* (New York: Viking, 1958), 58, 61. Gates, *Schoolbooks,* 287, quotes Taylor's estimate. For the story of Taylor's history, see John M. Gates, "The Official Historian and the Well-Placed Critic: James A. LeRoy's Assessment of John R. M. Taylor's *The Philippine Insurrection Against the United States,*" *The Public Historian* 7 (summer 1985): 57–67.

22. Frank P. Chambers, *The War Behind the War, 1914–1918: A History of the Political and Civilian Fronts* (London: Faber and Faber, 1939), 182.

23. Charles Warren, "Spies and the Power of Congress to Subject Certain Classes of Civilians to Trial by Military Tribunal," *American Law Review* 53 (March-April 1919): 221.

24. William W. Wotherspoon was Chief of Staff briefly after Wood. Mott, *Twenty Years,* 201; March to Baker, 5 October 1932, in Coffman, *Hilt of the Sword,* 41; Derthick, *The National Guard,* 38.

25. Chief of Staff to Commanding Generals, 8 May 1915; and M. M. Macomb, Chief War College Division, Memorandum for Chief of Staff, 6 July 1915, GS 12502, NA, RG 165.

26. George Bronson Rea, September 1915 to Major General Hugh L. Scott

and Scott to Rea, 30 September 1915, GS 12502, NA, RG 165. Internment letter dated 7 October 1915, OAG 2332201, NA, RG 94.

27. Joan M. Jensen, *The Price of Vigilance* (Chicago: Rand McNally, 1968), 10–16.

28. Adjutant General to Commanding General, Southern Department, 9 February 1915, OAG 2212358, NA, RG 165; Funston to Adjutant General, 20 October 1915, Garrison to Attorney General, 21 October 1915, and H. L. Scott to Funston, 23 October 1915, GS 6359, NA, RG 165.

29. Van Deman, Memorandum for Chief, 2 March 1916, GS, NA, RG 165.

30. Herbert Malloy Mason, Jr., *The Great Pursuit* (New York: Random House, 1970), 5–6.

31. Macomb Memorandum for Chief of Staff, 18 March 1916; Memorandum for Adjutant General, not signed; and H. L. Scott Memorandum for Chief, 23 March 1916, GS 8393, NA, RG 165; Acting Chief of Staff to Secretary, War College Division, 29 May 1916, GS 9544, NA, RG 165, discusses translators.

32. Chief, War College Division to Chief of Staff, 28 July 1916, GS 9544, NA, RG 165.

33. Memorandum for Chief of Staff from Macomb, Chief, War College Division, 23 June 1916, GS 639, NA, RG 165.

34. Memorandum for Chief of Staff from Macomb, 23 June 1916; and Baker to Attorney General, 24 June 1916, GS 639, NA, RG 165.

35. Macomb Memorandum for Chief of Staff, 24 June 1916, Macomb to Chief of Staff, Southern Department, 26 June 1916, and M. H. Barnum to Chief War College Division, 2 July 1916, MID 9544, NA, RG 165.

36. Macomb Memorandum for Chief of Staff, 22 June 1916, Gregory to Adjutant General Office, 3 June 1916 in Macomb memorandum for Chief of Staff, 24 June 1916; William M. Ingraham, Acting Secretary of War to Attorney General, 16 June 1916, GS 639, NA, RG 165.

37. Macomb, Chief of War College Division Memorandum for Chief of Staff, 24 June 1916, and Joseph E. Kuhn, Chief, War College Division, Memorandum for Chief of Staff, 17 February 1917, MID 9544, NA, RG 165.

38. Department intelligence reports are in OAG 2487166 and 2491999, NA, RG 94.

39. Scott to Auditor, 22 September 1916, for funds; Lane to Baker, 26 October 1916, and Baker to Wilson, 8 November 1916, Baker Papers, box 1, LC. Charles H. Harris III and Louis R. Sadler, "Termination with Extreme Prejudice: The United States Versus Pancho Villa," in Charles H. Harris III and Louis R. Sadler, *The Border and the Revolution* (Las Cruces, N.M.: Center for Latin American Studies/Joint Border Research Institute, 1988), 7–23.

40. C. W. Kennedy, Acting Chief of the War College, Memorandum for Chief of Staff, 23 November 1916, MIG, NA, RG 165.

41. Kennedy Memorandum for Chief of Staff, 9 December 1916, AGO 2212358, NA, RG 94.

42. Bliss Memorandum for Chief of Staff, 13 December 1916; handwritten note by Baker on Bliss Memorandum of 13 December 1916, AGO 2212358, NA, RG 94.

43. Funston to Adjutant General, 28 December 1916, and 3 January 1917,

El Paso report, and Gregory to William M. Ingraham, AGO 2212358, NA, RG 94.

44. Adjutant General H. P. McCain to Commanding Generals, All Departments, 21 March 1917, Baker to Wilson and Wilson to Baker, 28 March 1917, quoted in Preston, *Aliens and Dissenters,* 105.

45. Kuhn Memorandum for Chief of Staff, 1 February 1917, 9 February 1917, WCD 9309, NA, RG 165; Adjutant General to Chief of Staff, March 13, 1917, GS 13136, NA, RG 165.

46. Kuhn Memorandum for Chief of Staff, 1 February 1917; Hugh L. Scott Memorandum for Adjutant General, 1 February 1917; Kuhn Memorandum for Chief of Staff, 9 February 1917, WCD 9309; and Adjutant General to Chief of Staff, 13 March 1917, GS 13136, NA, RG 165. The Navy sent its first spy to Latin America in March 1917, Welles to Chief, Bureau Navigation, 1 January 1920, Welles Papers, box 203, item 11, LC.

47. Jensen, *Price of Vigilance,* 17–31 for APL and troop movements.

48. Ibid., 29; Warren to Attorney General, 30 March 1917, file 9-4-94, NA, RG 60.

49. Memorandum for Chief, War College Division from Secretary, General Staff, 13 April 1917, and Kuhn Memorandum for Chief of Staff, 17 April 1917, WCD 639-147, NA, RG 165.

50. Memorandum for Chief, War College Division from Secretary, General Staff, 13 April 1917, WCD 639-147, NA, RG 165.

51. Kuhn Memorandum for Chief of Staff, 17 April 1917, WCD 639-147, NA, RG 165; and memorandum, 13 April 1917, WCD 8721-4, NA, RG 165.

52. Weber, *The Final Memoranda,* 21–22, discusses his interviews with Scott; note from T. H. B., 19 April 1917, and memorandum, 19 April 1917, WCD 639-143, NA, RG 165; Bell to Adjutant General, 21 April 1917, quoted in Preston, *Aliens and Dissenters,* 105.

53. Weber, *The Final Memoranda,* 22–23.

54. Kuhn changes in Manual of War College Division, effective 3 May 1917, and Kuhn to Chief of Staff, 11 May 1917, WCD 639-145, NA, RG 165.

55. Kuhn Memorandum for Chief of Staff, 13 May 1917, Secretary, General Staff, Memorandum for Chief, War College Division, 15 May 1917, and Kuhn Memorandum Chief of Staff, May 17, 1917, WCD 639-149/51, NA, RG 165.

56. Bliss Memorandum for Secretary of War, 21 May 1917, WCD 639-152, NA, RG 165.

57. Jensen, *Price of Vigilance,* 40–41.

58. Ibid., 54–56.

59. Kuhn Memorandum to Chief of Staff, 15 June 1917, WCD 9373, NA, RG 165.

60. H. P. McCain to all Department Commanders, 7 July 1917, WCD 9153-90, NA, RG 165. McCain to Commanding General, Western Department, 3 July 1917, AGO 370.6, quoted in Preston, *Aliens and Dissenters,* 105.

CHAPTER SEVEN: Watching the Workers

1. The best overviews of the IWW are Melvyn Dubofsky, *We Shall Be All: A History of the Industrial Workers of the World* (Chicago: Quadrangle Books,

1969); and Philip Taft, "The Federal Trials of the iww," *Labor History* 3 (winter 1962): 79–80.

2. Harold M. Hyman, *Soldiers and Spruce: Origins of the Loyal Legion of Loggers and Lumbermen* (Los Angeles: Institute of Industrial Relations, University of California, Los Angeles, no. 10, 1963), 45. For undercover detectives, see MID 10110-311/14, NA, RG 165.

3. Cooper, *Army and Civil Disorder,* 165–91.

4. Ibid., 220–21; and Wilson, *Federal Aid,* 246–52.

5. Cooper, *Army and Civil Disorder,* 223.

6. Robert Justin Goldstein, *Political Repression in Modern America: 1870 to the Present* (Cambridge: Schenkman, 1978), 68–69, 79. For the Chinese, see 27 *U.S. Statutes at Large* 25 (1892), and 28 *U.S. Statutes at Large* 7 (1893). The antipolygamy laws against the Mormons were also an example of federal intervention in the family.

7. Wilson, *Federal Aid,* 260.

8. Billie Barnes Jensen, "Woodrow Wilson's Intervention in the Coal Strike of 1914," *Labor History* 15 (1974): 63–77; *The Autobiography of Mother Jones* (Chicago: Kerr, 1972), 178–94.

9. Jensen, *Price of Vigilance,* 63–64.

10. Ibid., 71–72.

11. Hyman, *Soldiers of Spruce,* 75; Preston, *Aliens and Dissenters,* 106; and MID 10110-311/14 for Oklahoma City report on private detectives, NA, RG 165.

12. Herbert H. White to Van Deman, 10 August 1917, MID 10148-5, NA, RG 165.

13. Jensen, *Price of Vigilance,* 76–78.

14. Powell, *The Army Behind the Army,* 390, gives the figure of thirty-seven thousand plants. A number of five thousand, far too low, is given in Milham, "History of National Espionage Legislation." Memorandum for Colonel Van Deman, 10 December 1917, box 2, entry 109, SNRC, RG 165.

15. PPS to R. H. Van Deman, 14 December 1917, box 2, entry 109; and Churchill, MID, to W. J. McCarron, Philadelphia, 12 November 1918, box 8, entry 117, SNRC, RG 165; Memorandum for Chief of Staff, 2 June 1917, from Brig. Gen. Joseph E. Kuhn; and other letters in Glasser file, box 9, NA, RG 60.

16. Cooper, "The Army as Strikebreaker—The Railroad Strikes of 1877 and 1894," 192. See particularly the letter from Gen. Nelson Miles to Adjutant General, 18 July 1894, Adjutant General Correspondence, 1890–1917, NA, RG 94, microfilm M698.

17. Horan, *The Pinkertons;* and J. Bernard Hogg, "Public Reaction to Pinkertonism and the Labor Question," *Pennsylvania History* 11 (1944): 171–99. The International Association of Railway Special Agents and Police was organized in 1896, and in the first years of the twentieth century, detective agencies began working for large corporations in the West, among lumber and grain companies. For an especially revealing history of one agency, see L. W. Boyce, General Manager, Northern Information Bureau to Capt. Fitzhugh Burns, 27 September 1918, MID 10110–932, NA, RG 165. By 1916 Boyce was receiving a retainer of

from $25 to $50 a month from public utilities, flour mills, and a number of other companies to report on IWW activities.

18. Jensen, *Price of Vigilance,* is the history of this organization.

19. Memorandum for Col. R. H. Van Deman, 10 December 1917, box 2; Memorandum for Captain Beauregard from Capt. D. C. Elphinstone, box 1, entry 109, SNRC, NA, RG 165; Edmund Leigh to Auditor, Secretary of the Treasury, 2 October 1920, MID 10608-96, NA, RG 165; American Protective League Headquarters Report, 17 January 1918, Frey Papers, UCLA.

20. PPS to W. J. McCarron, Philadelphia, 28 December 1918; H. R. Carty, Philadelphia, to Edmund Leigh, 22 November 1917, box 8; and Commanding Officer Frank E. Smith, Signal Corps, Approvals Section, to Leigh, 1 June 1918, box 2, entry 117, SNRC, RG 165. Smith thought the "cost-plus" detectives were acceptable, and undoubtedly some contracts did include pay for detectives. Alexander Bing, *Wartime Strikes and Their Adjustment* (New York, 1971 reprint of 1921 edition) remains the main source for World War I labor disputes. U.S., *Congressional Record,* 23, part 5, 52d Cong., 1st sess. (12 May 1892), 4222–25; 28 *U.S. Statutes at Large,* part 1, 7 (1893).

21. C. W. Burke, Los Angeles, to Edmund Leigh, 26 December 1917 and 27 December 1917, box 4; Albert Thomas, Boston, to Edmund Leigh, 24 September 1918, box 1, entry 117; and F. B. Stansbury, Portland, to Edmund Leigh, 25 June 1918, Stansbury to Edmund Leigh, 19 February 1918, box 8, entry 117, SNRC, RG 165. I have been able to find no record of any books published by Stansbury.

22. C. W. Burke, Los Angeles, to Edmund Leigh, 19 December 1917, Burke to Leigh, 12 April 1918, box 4; J. F. Trazzare, Atlanta, to PPS, 25 August 1918, box 1; Memorandum for Mr. Leigh re Boston office, 29 January 1918, box 1; Chief Military Intelligence to Police Commissioner, New York City, 21 November 1917, box 2, entry 117, SNRC, RG 165.

23. F. B. Stansbury, Portland, to Edmund Leigh, 12 March 1918, box 8, entry 117, SNRC, RG 165.

24. Edmund Leigh to F. B. Stansbury, Portland, 7 February 1918; Stansbury to Leigh, 22 February 1918, Stansbury to H. D. McKinney, Hoquiam, Washington, 23 February 1918, box 8, entry 117, SNRC, RG 165.

25. F. B. Stansbury, Portland, to Edmund Leigh, 28 October 1917, box 8, SNRC, RG 165.

26. George Black, Detroit, to Edmund Leigh, 28 May 1918, box 2, entry 117, SNRC, RG 165.

27. Edmund Leigh to R. R. Richardson, 21 June 1918, box 2, entry 109; and Report of Agent Brady on Complaint of Charles Dresser, 4 November 1918, box 1, entry 108, SNRC, RG 165.

28. C. W. Burke to Edmund Leigh, 27 December 1917, box 4, entry 117, SNRC, RG 165; Emerson Hough, *The Web* (Chicago: Reilly and Lee, 1919), 239, 258, 277; Victor Elting to Col. R. H. Van Deman, 23 April 1918, Frey Papers, UCLA. George Black to Leigh, 6 June 1918, and Leigh to Black, 18 June 1918; J. F. Trazzare, Atlanta, to Leigh, 7 June 1918, and Leigh to George Black, 10 July 1918, box 1, entry 117, SNRC, RG 165. Discussion of L. P. Eubanks, the

railway detective, is in C. W. Burke to Leigh, 19 December 1917, box 4, entry 117, SNRC, RG 165.

29. Leigh Memorandum to Colonel Masteller, 4 February 1919, box 4, entry 117, SNRC, RG 165.

30. C. W. Burke to Leigh, 20 August 1918, and 12 April 1918, box 4, entry 117, SNRC, NA, RG 165.

31. Leigh Memorandum to Colonel Masteller, 4 February 1919, box 4, entry 117, SNRC, RG 165.

32. See female operatives reports in Richardson file, box 1, entry 109; J. A. Kilpatrack, Albany, to Chief, MID, 20 August 1918, box 1, entry 117; Undercover Agent's Report on Machinist Union, Bridgeport, Connecticut, 19 October 1918, box 2, entry 109; and F. B. Stansbury, Portland, to Leigh, 7 December 1918; Stansbury to Leigh, 2 April 1918; Stansbury to Leigh, 17 April 1918, box 8, entry 117, SNRC, RG 165. Edmund Leigh to Auditor, Secretary of the Treasury, 2 October 1920, MID 10608-96, NA, RG 165, gives estimate of more than seven thousand, too high for paid employees but too low for volunteers. The figure of five hundred is from Powell, *The Army Behind the Army,* 390.

33. W. L. Campbell, New York City, to Edmund Leigh, 4 October 1917; W. L. Campbell, Report of Cases, 26 October 1917; Campbell to Leigh, 3 October 1917, box 5; Paul I. Zimmerman, Fort Worth, Texas to PPS, 26 December 1917; Zimmerman and H. R. Carty to Leigh, 10 November 1917; Zimmerman to PPS, 31 December 1917; W. J. McCarron, Philadelphia to PPS, 15 January 1918, box 3; J. F. Murphy, New Haven, to Leigh, 25 June 1918, box 4; E. McSherry, Nashville, to Leigh, 19 August 1918, box 8, entry 117; and PPS to R. E. Kennedy, Baltimore, 8 February 1918, box 2, entry 117, SNRC, RG 165; Col. R. H. Van Deman to Carl Reichmann, 27 April 1918, MID 9684-91, NA, RG 165.

34. Leigh to Albert Thomas, Boston, 12 April 1918, box 1; L. P. Eubanks, Inspector, Los Angeles, to C. W. Burke, Los Angeles, 18 June 1918; Burke to Leigh, 20 June 1918, box 4; and Frank T. Larkin, Dayton, to Edmund Leigh, 6 June 1918, and Leigh to Larkin, 18 June 1918, box 3; and Edmund Leigh to Frank T. Larkin, Dayton, 30 October 1918, box 3, entry 117, SNRC, RG 165.

35. American Protective League, Headquarters, *American Protective League* (1918), 13, Frey Papers, UCLA.

36. F. B. Stansbury, Portland, to Edmund Leigh, 22 February 1918, box 8; Joseph D. Wooldridge, Dayton, to Edmund Leigh, 29 April 1918, and enclosed copy of letter from Special Agent Harold L. Scott to A. Bruce Bielaski, box 2, entry 117, SNRC, RG 165.

37. C. R. Edrington, Davenport, Iowa, to David S. Groh, Chicago, 16 August 1918; J. F. Murphy, Jr., Boston, to Edmund Leigh, 28 October 1918, box 1; C. W. Burke, Los Angeles, to Edmund Leigh, 12 April 1918, box 4, entry 117; and Mr. Churchill to All Agents, Plant Protection Section, 26 July 1918, box 1, entry 109, SNRC, RG 165.

38. J. F. Murphy, New Haven, Connecticut, to Leigh, 7 June 1918, box 4; and E. Chapman, Nitro, West Virginia, to Edmund Leigh, 5 August 1918, box 8, entry 117, SNRC, RG 165.

39. Edmund Leigh to Albert Thomas, Boston, 21 August 1918, box 1, entry 117, SNRC, RG 165.

40. R. E. Kennedy, Baltimore, to Edmund Leigh, 3 April 1918, box 2, entry 117; George Black, Detroit, to Leigh, 31 May 1918, box 1, entry 142; and Leigh to Major Frank E. Smith, 4 June 1918, box 2, entry 108; SNRC, RG 165.

41. C. W. Burke to Leigh, 12 April 1918, box 4, entry 117; David S. Groh, Chicago, to PPS, 20 July 1918, box 1, entry 142; Churchill to Albert Thomas, Boston, 17 July 1918; and Thomas to Leigh, 22 August 1918, box 1, entry 117, SNRC, RG 165.

42. David S. Groh, Chicago, to PPS, 2 August 1918, box 1, entry 142, SNRC, RG 165.

43. G. B. Read, President, Portable Elevator Manufacturing Company to PPS, Chicago, 20 August 1918, box 1, entry 142, SNRC, RG 165.

44. Memorandum for Major Kinkaid, 22 November 1918, box 1, entry 109; David S. Groh, Chicago, to MI3, 30 November 1918, box 2, entry 117; W. J. McCarron, Philadelphia, to Leigh, 20 November 1918 and 7 February 1919, box 8, entry 117; McCarron to Edmund Leigh, 7 February 1919; Leigh to Stansbury, San Francisco; and Stansbury to Leigh, 3 December 1918, box 8, entry 117, SNRC, RG 165.

45. Unsigned copy of letter to Capt. Robert Howlett, 5 December 1918, box 1, entry 108; and Edmund Leigh to F. A. K. Butterfield, Minnesota, 9 December 1918, box 7, entry 117, SNRC, RG 165.

46. W. E. Rittenhouse, Detroit, to Leigh, 31 January 1919, with enclosed report and handout. J. F. Murphy, Boston, to PPS, 25 January 1919, box 4, entry 117, SNRC, RG 165. Ethnic competition of Mexicans was being used as an organizing weapon in Detroit; see W. E. Rittenhouse, Detroit, to Leigh, 28 January 1919, box 1, entry 142; and Leigh Memorandum for Kinkaid, 21 December 1918, regarding surveillance of Silverglide, a friend of Levitt, who was under surveillance and would be reported if he became active. Wrisley Brown, MI4 Memorandum for Masteller, 24 October 1918, wanted to prosecute Levitt to curb his activities (box 1, entry 109, SNRC, RG 165).

47. D. W. Sowers, Chairman, Secret Service Committee of the Niagara Frontier Defense League to M. Churchill, 18 January 1919, informed: "You understand that so far as the enemy aliens, socialists and radical members go we are still keeping records pertaining to these phases of our work." This group worked with the Justice Department mainly during the war (MID 10608-96, NA, RG 165); P. J. Curry, New York City, to Leigh, 19 February 1919, still had two agents assigned to cover "Bolshevism" (Edmund Leigh, Memorandum to All Agents, 25 November 1918, with letter to Stansbury, 3 December 1918); Stansbury, San Francisco, to Leigh, 4 March 1919, inquired what he should do with files; there was no answer (box 8, entry 117); and J. F. Murphy Lawrence, report to Col. A. W. Williams on Textile Strike, 18 March 1919, box 1, entry 141, SNRC, RG 165.

48. Preston, *Aliens and Dissenters,* focuses on the IWW in the West; Clayton R. Kappes, "The Kansas Trail of the I.W.W., 1917–1919," *Labor History* 16 (summer 1975): 338–58, adds to the analysis of federal suppression of the IWW; James Weinstein, *Decline of Socialism in America, 1912–1925* (New York, 1967),

presents the argument for suppression of the Socialists. John S. Smith, "Organized Labor and Government in the Wilson Era: 1913–1921: Some Conclusions," *Labor History* 3 (1962): 265–86, presents a favorable view of the Wilson administration. David Montgomery, "The 'New Unionism' and the Transformation of Workers' Consciousness in America, 1909–1922"; and James R. Green, "Comments on the Montgomery Paper," *Journal of Social History* 7 (summer 1974): 509–35. Montgomery argues that workers rejected the IWW as unreliable, but Green points out the attacks of management were often more important. The crucial questions, however, are what form did these management attacks take and how did they interact with conflict inside the labor movement. See also Bryan Palmer, "Class, Conception, and Conflict: The Thrust for Efficiency, Managerial Views of Labor and the Working Class Rebellion, 1903–1922," *Review of Radical Political Economists* 7 (summer 1975): 31–49.

CHAPTER EIGHT: At War: The Disloyal, the Pro-German, the Malcontent

1. *History of the Counter Intelligence Corps in the United States Army, 1917–1950,* 30 vols. (Baltimore: United States Army Intelligence Center, 1959–1960), vol. 3, 5–8, 59.

2. Ibid., 5–8.

3. Ibid., 59.

4. Jensen, *Price of Vigilance,* 86–89; Van Deman to G. P. Pross, Manager, Wm. J. Burns International Detective Agency, 8 November 1917, RG 165, MID 10320-6.

5. Jensen, *Price of Vigilance,* 119–24.

6. Powell, *The Army Behind the Army,* 388–90.

7. Chief, MIS, to Nicholas Biddle, 22 October 1917, MID 10148-22; and P. D. Lochridge Memo for Chief of Staff, 1 September 1917, WCD 10039-64, NA, RG 165.

8. *History of the Counter Intelligence Corps,* vol. 3, 65–68.

9. Ibid., 69–71, 102.

10. Harry A. Taylor to Chief, MIS, 31 December 1917, MID 10320-18, 10320-25; Maurice Tennant to Acting Director, MID, MID 10560-152; Memo for Chief of Staff from Lochridge, Acting Chief, WCD, November 1917, WCD 8056-11, NA, RG 165; and Hyman, *Soldiers and Spruce,* 80.

11. John E. Stephens, Chairman, Recruitment and Organization Committee, Memo for Chief, WCD, 3 November 1917, WCD 10148-33; Bulletins and drafts, November 1917, WCD 10148-26, NA, RG 165.

12. H. A. Smith, General Staff of Chief WCD, no date, J. P. Green memo for Lochridge, 1 November 1917, WCD 1014823; Memo for Chief of Staff from Acting Chief WCD, 29 December 1917, WCD 10148-35; and Memo for Chief of Staff, 29 December 1917, WCD 10148-33, NA, RG 165.

13. Lochridge Memo for Chief of Staff, 20 December 1917, WCD 10039-209, NA, RG 165; APL Headquarters Report, 14 January 1918, Frey Papers, UCLA.

14. Correspondence in WCD 9683-41, NA, RG 165.

15. Van Deman to Supt. Penn. State Police, 8 December 1917, Memo to

Major Parsons from Mason Peters, MID 1032013, 10321-24, 103–16; Travelers series of letters in MID 10320-5, NA, RG 165.

16. Memo Harry A. Taylor to Van Deman, 8 February 1918, MID 10320-22, NA, RG 165. For the Chiefs of Staff, see Donald Smythe, *Pershing: General of the Armies* (Bloomington: Indiana University Press, 1986), 46, 89.

17. Edward M. Coffman, *The Hilt of the Sword: The Career of Peyton C. March* (Madison: University of Wisconsin Press, 1966), 49–50.

18. Leland Harrison to Van Deman, 13 February 1918, MID 10661-8; Memo for Captain Hunt, 16 January 1918, MID 10560-113; Van Deman to Biddle, 27 October 1917, MID 10321-6; H. T. Hunt for Van Deman, 30 January 1918, MID 10661-8; Mason Peters Memo for Major Parsons, 29 December 1917, MID 10560-1a, NA, RG 165.

19. Richard J. Barnet, *Intervention and Revolution: The United States in the Third World* (New York: World, 1968), 17, discusses the independence of the bureaucracy and other theories of counterinsurgency.

20. Jensen, *Price of Vigilance,* 103.

21. Ibid., 115–16; "Boloism in this Country," *Literary Digest* 56 (2 March 1918): 14–15.

22. Jensen, *Price of Vigilance,* 121.

23. Ibid., 106–7.

24. O'Brian to Gregory, 18 April 1918, file 189083, NA, RG 60.

25. Jensen, *Price of Vigilance,* 109.

26. Charles Warren, "Spies and the Power of Congress to Subject Certain Classes of Civilians to Trial by Military Tribunal," *American Law Review* 53 (March–April 1919): 195–228.

27. Jensen, *Price of Vigilance,* 120.

28. Ibid., 121.

29. Baker quote and description of March is in Smythe, *Pershing,* 91.

30. Jensen, *Price of Vigilance,* 124.

31. Ibid.

32. Ibid., 125–27; Churchill to Bielaski, 12 August 1918, Bielaski to Churchill, 21 August 1918, MID 10320-28, NA, RG 165.

33. Jensen, *Price of Vigilance,* 224.

34. Ibid., 225.

35. For Hawaii, see Edward Carpenter Report, 31 January 1919; and for Panama Canal, Clarence H. Grove, 1919 report: "History of Puerto Rico," all in MID 10560-152, NA, RG 165.

36. "History of Philippine Department," no date, MID 10560152, NA, RG 165.

37. "History of Southeastern Department," MID 10560-152, NA, RG 165.

38. "History of the Military Intelligence Division, Southern Department, Fort Sam Houston, Texas," 20 March 1919, MID 10560-152; and Memorandum from Edward J. Reilly to Wrisley Brown, undated, MID 9685-3851, NA, RG 165.

39. For Southwest, see Glasser file, box 9, NA, RG 60; Churchill to Intelligence Officer, 2 August 1918; and R. L. Barnes, Intelligence Officer to Chief, MID, 15 August 1918, MID 10110-12, NA, RG 165.

40. For Western Department, see Jensen, *Price of Vigilance,* 127–28; Glasser

file, box 6, NA, RG 60; and Report of Western Department, MID 10560-152, NA, RG 165.

41. Ibid.

42. Ibid. For censorship, see Chester R. Milham, "A History of National Espionage Legislation and Its Operation in the United States during the World War," Ph.D. diss., University of Southern California, 1938.

43. See Hyman, *Soldiers and Spruce.*

44. For Butte, see Glasser file, box 9, NA, RG 60.

45. Report of Western Department, MID 10560-152, NA, RG 165.

46. Ibid.

47. Charles H. Harris III and Ray Sadler, "The Witzke Affair: German Intrigue on the Mexican Border, 1917–1918," *MR* 59 (February 1979): 36–50.

CHAPTER NINE: War Plans White

1. Memorandum for Major Brown from J. S. Buhler, 18 October 1918, MID 10560-172, NA, RG 165.

2. Annual Report of MID, 1919, MID 10560-152, NA, RG 165.

3. Van Deman to Churchill, October 20, 1918, MID 10560-235; and Churchill to All Military Intelligence Officers, 20 November 1918, MID 10560-54, NA, RG 165.

4. Jensen, *Price of Vigilance,* 238, 241.

5. Gilbert Bettman, Memorandum on Functions of MI4 in Peace, 20 November 1918, MID 10560-221; and Maj. Robert L. Barnes, Memorandum for Major Brown, 20 November 1918, MID 10560-221, NA, RG 165.

6. For the Los Angeles and Chicago APL, see Jensen, *Price of Vigilance,* 239–40, 242.

7. Dunn to Intelligence Officer, Chicago, 7 December 1918, MID 9684-200 confirmed telephone call, NA, RG 165.

8. For Chicago MID, Ibid., 243–46.

9. Retrenchment discussed in John Dunn cable to Van Deman, 12 December 1918, MID 10560-166; John Dunn, Acting Director, MI, Memorandum for the Files, 12 December 1918, MID 10560-237; Dunn to Assistant and Chief Clerk, 4 December 1918, MID 10560-147; and "Proceedings of a Board of Officers," 28 December 1918, MID 10143-43, NA, RG 165.

10. Jensen, *Price of Vigilance,* 252.

11. General Staff, Memorandum for Dunn, 29 January 1919; and A. C. Campbell Memorandum 21, 30 January 1919, MID 10560-262; and E. S. Hartshorn Memorandum for Dunn, 4 February 1919, MID 10560-207, NA, RG 165.

12. P. M. Buck Memorandum for Colonel Dunn, 4 February 1919, MID 10560-152, NA, RG 165.

13. Report from departments are in MID 10560-152, NA, RG 165.

14. Wrisley Brown Memorandum for Churchill, 13 May 1919, MID 10560-221, NA, RG 165.

15. Ibid.

16. *New York Times,* 18 June 1919, discussed in Churchill memorandum for

Mr. Hayes, 8 July 1919, Albert DeSilver to Baker, June 28, 1919, and 11 July 1919, MID 10560-277, NA, RG 165.

17. Churchill to Hayes, 8 July 1919; and Churchill Memorandum for Chief of Staff, MID 10560-277, NA, RG 165.

18. Baker to DeSilver, 7 July 1919, MID 10560-277; and Baker to Isaac Siegel, 14 June 1919, MID 10560-265, NA, RG 165.

19. Annual Report of MID, 1919, MID 10560-272, NA, RG 165.

20. William Cohen, "Riots, Racism, and Hysteria," *Massachusetts Review* 13 (1972): 373–400.

21. Ibid.

22. Ibid.

23. John Hope Franklin, *From Slavery to Freedom: A History of Negro Americans* (New York: Knopf, 1967), 485.

24. T. B. Crockett, Intelligence Officer to Director, MID, 15 October 1919, NA, RG 165, MID 10218-374.

25. Glasser files, box 9, NA, RG 60; Jensen, *Price of Vigilance*, 278.

26. Ibid., 279.

27. Ibid., 280.

28. T. B. Crockett to Director, MID, 15 October 1919; and Churchill to T. B. Crockett, 20 October 1919, MID 10218-129/374, NA, RG 165.

29. Summary of the Estimate on the United States, part 3, Military Situation, and part 4, General Situation, Course at General Staff College, 1919–1920, Intelligence; and W. G. Haan Memorandum for the Commandant, General Staff College, April 1920, CB.

30. M. E. Locke to Churchill, 20 October 1919, MID 10560-305; Churchill in Memorandum to Chief of Staff, 20 October 1919, recommends that recruiting officers have authority to collect information, MID 10560-305, NA, RG 165.

31. Van Deman to Churchill, 13 November 1918, MID 249-43, NA, RG 165.

32. Churchill to Haan, 27 October 1919, cited in Preston, *Aliens and Dissenters*, 245. See also Memorandum from Adjutant General to Corps Area Commanders, ibid.

33. See W. G. Haan Memorandum for Colonel Embick, 10 April 1920, file 1–3; NWC and Haan Memorandum of 23 April 1920 in Preston, *Aliens and Dissenters*, 245; and "Emergency Plan White: General Policies and Instructions," AG 383, NA, RG 94.

34. Jensen, *Price of Vigilance*, 282–84.

35. John C. Graham to T. B. Crockett, 17 December 1919, MID 10110-KK-6, NA, RG 165.

36. Correspondence from former APL state superintendents describe postwar work, MID 10261-128, NA, RG 165.

37. Preston, *Aliens and Dissenters*, 220–22.

38. Haan Memorandum for Secretary, General Staff College, 13 April 1920; Haan Memorandum for General McAndrew, Commandant, General Staff College, NWC.

39. *New York Tribune*, 26 March 1920, described United Americans; Memorandum for G-2, Eighth Corps Area, 28 December 1920, and proposed pro-

gram of work with Special Report from Colonel Gordon Johnston, 14 January 1920, MID 10261-144, NA, RG 165.

40. Assistant Chief of Staff for Military Intelligence, Eighth Corps Area, Memorandum for Director, MI, 6 January 1921, MID 10261-144, NA, RG 165.

41. Clippings in MID 10261-144; and Chas. Furthmann Report, 21 November 1919, MID 10261-128, NA, RG 165.

42. Col. Gordon Johnston to Brig. Gen. Marlborough Churchill, 21 November 1919, MID 10261-128, NA, RG 165.

43. W. G. Haan Memorandum for General Churchill, 28 November 1919, MID 10261-128, NA, RG 165.

44. Lists are in MID 10261-71; Churchill to Colonel Gordon Johnston, 12 February 1920, MID 10261144, NA, RG 165.

45. M. Churchill to Brig. Gen. Samuel D. Rockenbach, 24 September 1919, MID 10110-1389; and M. Churchill Memorandum for the Director of the War Plans Division, 24 March 1920, MID 242-18, NA, RG 165.

46. Baker to Director, MID, 11 March 1920, MID 1056054, NA, RG 165.

47. Director, MID, Memorandum 40, 19 March 1920, MID 10560-54, NA, RG 165.

48. Gardner L. Harding, Memorandum for General Churchill, 13 March 1920; and W. H. Hicks Memorandum for Colonel McCain, 16 March 1920, MID 10560-705, NA, RG 165.

49. Memorandum for Director, MID, 19 March 1920, MID 10560-54; and Memorandum for Acting Director, MID, 24 April 1920, MID 10560-231, NA, RG 165.

50. *History of Counter Intelligence Corps,* vol. 4, 23, 26.

51. Ibid., 21–32; G-2 course 24, Army War College, 1921–22, Summary of Estimate on the United States, MID 284-13, NA, RG 165.

52. Russell F. Weigley, "The Interwar Army, 1919–1941," in *Against All Enemies,* ed. Hagan and Roberts, 257–59, 265–66.

53. John B. Barnes, Memorandum for Director, MID, 20 August 1921, MID 10560315; and Discussion of Justice Department-War Department Cooperation on Radical Matters, 4 October 1921, MID 9343-337; Colonel S. Heintzelman, Memorandum for Colonel Palmer, 4 May 1922, MID 1026171, NA, RG 165.

54. M. E. Locke, Executive Officer, G-2 to Assistant Chief of Staff, G-2, Ninth Corps Area, San Francisco, 29 March 1922, MID 9343-337; Adj. Gen. C. H. Danielson to Commanding General, Boston, 9 June 1922, Adj. Gen. H. H. Tebbetts to All Corps Area Commanders, 6 December 1922, MID 271-A-9, NA, RG 165.

55. *History of the Counter Intelligence Corps,* vol. 4, 36.

56. Joan M. Jensen, "All Pink Sisters: The War Department and the Feminist Movement in the 1920s," in *Decades of Discontent: The Women's Movement, 1920–1940,* ed. Lois Scharf and Joan M. Jensen (Westport, Conn.: Greenwood, 1983), 210.

57. Ibid., 210–13.

58. Adj. Gen. H. H. Pfeil to Reserve Military Intelligence Officers, 21 March 1923, MID 271-A-9, NA, RG 165. The 16 October 1922 Long letter was reprinted

in the March 1923 *Labor Herald* and more recently in Frank J. Donner, *The Age of Surveillance* (New York: Knopf, 1980), 291.

59. See, for example, Birch Helms, Blair & Company, to John W. Weeks, Secretary of War, 8 November 1922, and Col. S. Heintzelman, General Staff, Assistant Chief of Staff, G-2, Memorandum for Chief of Staff, 10 November 1922, MID 51-337. M. Churchill, Assistant Chief of Staff, G-2, Memorandum to Chief of Staff, Second Corps Area, Governors Island, 29 November 1922, MID 287-26, NA, RG 165; and U.S. Army, General Service Schools, "Confidential Supplement to Military Aid to the Civil Power," (Fort Leavenworth, Kansas, General Service Schools, 1925), file 158-12, NWC.

60. Col. J. H. Reeves, Director, MID, Memorandum for the Chief of Staff, 2 April 1925, MID 271-A-9; and Reeves to J. Edgar Hoover, 29 September 1925, MID 9343-337, NA, RG 165. See also Richard Gid Powers, *The Life of J. Edgar Hoover: Secrecy and Power* (New York: Free Press, 1987), 147–48, 161–62; and Athan G. Theoharis and John Stuart Cox, *The Boss: J. Edgar Hoover and the Great American Inquisition* (Philadelphia: Temple University Press, 1988), 92–94.

61. Victor J. Johansen, "The Role of the Army in the Civilian Arena, 1920–1970" (U.S. Army Intelligence Command Study, 1971, mimeographed), 6. FBI monitoring of ACLU is in *Spying on Americans: Political Surveillance from Hoover to the Huston Plan,* by Athan Theoharis, (Philadelphia: Temple University Press, 1978), 255, n. 8.

62. Jensen, "All Pink Sisters," 160.

63. Joan M. Jensen, "The Army and Domestic Surveillance on Campus," in *Soldiers and Civilians: The U.S. Army and the American People,* ed. Garry D. Ryan and Timothy K. Nenninger (Washington, D.C.: National Archives and Records Administration, 1987), 160–72.

64. Comments on reserve intelligence officers are in Churchill Memorandums for Chief of Staff, 20 October 1919, 16 December 1919, and various other memorandums to Corps Area commanders and recruiting officers, MID 10560-305, NA, RG 165. See also Confidential Memorandum for Officers, Intelligence Reserve, 4 June 1920, Frey Papers, UCLA. *History of the Counter Intelligence Corps,* vol. 4, 49.

65. Ibid., 44.

66. Col. Alfred T. Smith Memorandum for Chief of Staff, 19 February 1931, MID 271-A-9, NA, RG 165.

67. MacArthur battled pacifism publicly, first as commander of the Third Corps Area from 1925 to 1928 and again as Commander in Chief, Petillo, *Douglas MacArthur,* 138, 159–60.

68. Roger Daniels, *The Bonus Marchers: An Episode of the Great Depression* (Westport, Conn.: Greenwood, 1971), 111.

69. Ibid., 159–60.

70. Ibid., 161.

71. Various reports are in MID 10110-2663, NA, RG 165. Smith quote is from *History of the Counter Intelligence Corps,* vol. 4, 52.

72. Notes of discussion following the Conference of Committee 8, College

of War Course, 1st part, 16 February 1935, Internal Stability of Nations, NWC; Ibid.; Charles P. Larrowe, "The Great Maritime Strike of '34," part 1, *Labor History* 11 (1970): 403–51, and part 2, *Labor History* 12 (1971): 3–37; and James J. Hudson, "The Role of the California National Guard during the San Francisco General Strike of 1934," *MA* 46 (April 1982): 76–83.

73. Van Deman to General Miles, 30 November 1940, MID 2801-110; Van Deman to Col. Alfred T. Smith, 20 November 1933, MID 8930-A-252; Van Deman to Colonel Smith, 17 February 1933, MID 8930-A-252; Van Deman to Col. Charles Burnett, 24 September 1935, MID 1766-Z-583; and Van Deman to Lt. Col. Lewis H. Watkins, 18 April 1935, MID 10989-Z-345, NA, RG 165.

74. Sixth Corps Area, Emergency Plan White, December 1936, AG 386, NA, RG 94.

75. Emergency War Plan White, 15 November 1935, AG 387, NA, RG 94.

76. Course at the Army War College, 1935–36: Conduct of War, part 1, Analytical Studies, Internal Stability of Nations, 1 February 1936; and 1936–37: Conduct of War, part 1, Analytical Studies, Internal Stability of Nations, 23 February 1937, NWC. By 1935, riot training manuals had been much improved; they were more precise and were not overtly antiradical as they had been earlier. See "Training in Riot Duty" (1935), Confidential Training Circular, NWC.

CHAPTER TEN: World War II: Expanding the Boundaries

1. Theoharis, *Spying on Americans*, 67.

2. Ibid.

3. Industrial espionage was handled through AMTORG. See Ronald Radosh and Joyce Milton, *The Rosenberg File: A Search for the Truth* (New York: Vintage, 1984), 28.

4. Richard Rowan, *Secret Agents Against America* (New York: Doubleday, 1939), is an example of the types of books published. This one suggested the potential strength of spies at over one hundred thousand (p. 2).

5. Theoharis, *Spying*, 70–72.

6. Rowan, *Secret Agents*, 25.

7. Messersmith was present when Roosevelt made the call. George Messersmith Papers, unpublished memoirs, 2018, UD. Adolphe Berle represented the State Department at a few of the early 1940 meetings. Delimitation agreements discussed in "The FBI's Stretching of Presidential Directives, 1936–1953," by Athan G. Theoharis, *Political Science Quarterly* 91 (winter 1976–77): 649–72, and in weekly meetings reported in MID 9794-186A, NA, RG 165. Early claims for MID for plant jurisdiction are in the minutes of a 26 July 1940 meeting, MID 9794-186A, NA, RG 165. Conference between representatives of Treasury Department, G-2, of War Department, the Office of Naval Intelligence, and the Federal Bureau of Investigation, 4 August 1940, MID 9794-186A, NA, RG 165.

8. Athan Theoharis, "The FBI and the American Legion Contact Program," *Political Science Quarterly* 100 (1983): 271–86.

9. Expansion after June 1939 is discussed in "Report of Army Intelligence

Officer's Conference, New Orleans, 17–19 November 1943, box 3562, G-2 regional file, NA, RG 165.

10. National Labor Relations Board, *Annual reports, 1936–40*. Cases were *Bethlehem Steel Co.* v. *NLRB,* 120 F. 2d 641 (12 May 1941), *Press Co., Ind.* v. *NLRB,* 118 F. 2d 937 (2 June 1941), and *NLRB* v. *Collins & Aikman Corp.,* 146 F. 2d 454 (28 December 1944). Concern by agencies over the Wagner Act is found in the minutes of a 14 May 1940 meeting when Tamm of the FBI said, "to spy on labor unions is contrary to the Wagner labor act." Fear of criticism from "labor circles" was also expressed on 9 July 1940, MID 9794-186A, and in Sherman Miles memorandum of 1 February 1941, for Chief of Staff, MID 2657-C-314/1, NA, RG 165.

11. Plant surveys and informants are discussed at almost all meetings, MID 9794-186A, NA, RG 165; Sherman Miles Memorandum for the Chief of Staff, 1 February 1941, MID 2657-C-3141/1, NA, RG 165. See also Theoharis, "The FBI and the American Legion," 278.

12. MID and legislation on strikes discussed in meeting of 3 June 1940, MID 9794-186A, NA, RG 165; Maj. W. E. Crist Memorandum for Colonel Lester, 26 November 1940, MID 004, SNRC. Fifth Column Plans discussed in Miles Memorandum for Asst. Chief of Staff, G-3, 3 September 1940, MID 2706-ZZ-22/6, and Miles Memorandum of 23 July 1940 on Internal Defense, MID 9794-186A, NA, RG 165. Victor J. Johansen, "The Role of the Army in the Civilian Arena," (U.S. Army Intelligence Command Study, 1971, mimeographed), 7–8, says that MID conducted advance planning and then relied "mostly upon information from the FBI." The Miles quote is from Sherman Miles Memorandum for the Chief of Staff, 1 February 1941, MID 2657-C-314/1, NA, RG 165. For the obsession of Miles with subversion and his claim that it was the sole responsibility of G-2, see Roberta Wohlsetter, *Pearl Harbor: Warning and Decision* (Stanford: Stanford University Press, 1962), 281–90.

13. Operation of Chiefs of Supply, Arms and Services, in "Extract from letter of General Van Deman to General Miles," MID 2801-110/318; Lieutenant Colonel J. A. Lester Memorandum for General Miles, 10 December 1940, MID 2801-110/319; Lt. Col. Lowell H. Smith to Asst. Chief, Material Division, 24 October 1940, MID 2801-110/519; and Col. J. M. Churchill, Chief, CIB Memorandum for Asst. Chief of Staff, G-2, 25 May 1940, 15–16, MID 10560-792/16, NA, RG 165.

14. Correspondence on Edmund Burke is in Col. R. C. Candee Memorandum for Counter Intelligence Branch, G-2 Division, 9 November 1940; Maj. Thos. H. Chapman, Memorandum to Chief, Air Corps Information Division, 1 November 1940; Van Deman to Lt. Col. Lowell H. Smith, 19 October 1940; and Capt. Ellis M. Zacharias to Smith, 18 October 1940, MID 2801-110/307. Miles to Van Deman, 25 March 1941, MID 2801-110/341; and Van Deman to Maj. John H. Wilson, 18 March 1941, MID 101041679/21. Other top-ranking Communist party informants are mentioned in Van Deman to Miles, 10 March 1941, MID 2801-110/339, and Lt. Col. John H. Wilson to Asst. Chief of Staff, G-2, 26 October 1940, MID 2801110/276. All correspondence in NA, RG 165.

15. Joint ONI and MID report Brig. Gen. Sherman Miles and Captain A. G. Kork, Director of Naval Intelligence to Secretary of War and Secretary of Navy,

May 28, 1941 and Frank Knox to the President, May 29, 1941, MID 2736–22–56, NA, RG 165.

16. Byron Fairchild and Jonathan Grossman, *The War Department: The Army and Industrial Manpower* (Washington, D.C., 1959), 219–38 has the fullest discussion of War Department support for national service.

17. Ibid., 60–80, 206, 208, discussed seizures. The peak came from November 1, 1943 to July 31, 1945 when 25 were seized by the War Department, 10 against their wishes. "Government Seizure of Leather Plants," November 24, 1943, MID 004.07, SNRC, outlines strategy.

18. *History of the Counter Intelligence Corps,* vol. 4, 93, 95, 100, 103.

19. Ibid., vol. 4, 115–16.

20. Ibid., vol. 5, 142–43, 34, 140, 145.

21. Johansen, "Role of the Army," 9–10. Restriction in Circular 324, 14 December 1943, Chief of Staff G. C. Marshall, "Transfer of Counterintelligence Functions within the Zone of the Interior; Maj. Gen. J. A. Ulio to Commanding Generals, 19 February 1944, ISD, Investigation Programs, Loyalty Investigations; and Col. O. L. Nelson, Memorandum for the Commanding General, Army Service Forces, Asst. Chief of Staff, G-2, 25 November 1943, ISD Inv. Program, Intelligence Division (ASF), PMGO, NA, RG 389.

22. *History of the Counter Intelligence Corps,* vol. 7, 20–21, 27, 44, 63. The Japanese did not recruit local Japanese in Hawaii for espionage. See John J. Stephan, *Hawaii under the Rising Sun: Japan's Plan for Conquest after Pearl Harbor* (Honolulu: University of Hawaii Press, 1984), 83.

23. CS system described in Capt. P. H. Way, Jr., Memorandum for Colonel Doll, 1 October 1942; Lt. Col. Robert H. Harris to Director of Intelligence, First Service Command, 18 June 1943; Maj. W. D. Brunig to Lieutenant Schaeffer to Director of Intelligence, Second Service Command, 21 July 1943; Capt. Robert R. Munoz, Memorandum for CS file, 11 August 1943; William S. Codd, Plant Security, Memorandum to Chief, CS Section, 17 September 1943; Colonel A. W. Roffe to Asst. Chief of Staff, G-2, 26 November 1943; and Weekly Estimate of Subversive Situation, 2 October 1943, MID 383.4, SNRC.

24. *History of Counter Intelligence Corps,* vol. 7, 15. Restriction of CS system discussed in Col. A. W. Roffe to Asst. Chief of Staff, G-2, 26 November 1943, MID 383.4, SNRC. War Department Circular 324, 14 December 1943, ordered change. See also John D. Millett, *The Army Service Forces: The Organization and Role of the Army Services Forces* (Washington, D.C., 1954), 155–56.

25. Maj. B. M. Bates, Memorandum for Maj. Stewart W. Mark, 26 June 1944, MID 380.01, SNRC.

26. Removal of Subversives, War Department Circular, 5 February 1942, gave removal authority. Also discussed in Internal Security Conference, Army Service Forces, St. Louis, Mo., 120–23 April 1943, I-22, MID 380.01, and Fairchild and Grossman, *The War Department: The Army and Industrial Manpower,* 92. Duties of PSC in Internal Security Conference, Army Service Forces, St. Louis, Mo., 20–23 April 1943, I-16, MID 380.01, SNRC.

27. Organization and Activities of the PMG Sergeant Investigators, 1 December 1943, ISD Subversive Program, Conferences, PMGO, NA, RG 389.

28. Maj. William L. Fox Memorandum for Colonel Miller, 9 September

1943; Capt. W. B. Richardson, 20 May 1942; Col. J. T. H. O'Rear, Chief, Investigative Division to Corps Area PMG's, 23 May 1942; Col. W. F. Magill, Jr., Provost Marshal, Western Defense Command, 3 October 1942, ISD Investigative Program, Instructions to Commercial Agencies, PMGO, NA, RG 389.

29. Numbers of clearances in graph, "Loyalty Investigations by Month (Civilians)," ISD, Investigative Program, Loyalty Investigation to Military Personnel, PMGO, NA, RG 389.

30. Problems of credit company investigations are in ISD Investigative Program, Instructions to Commercial Agencies. See especially Col. Alton C. Miller to Hooper Holmes Bureau, Inc., 1 May 1943, Capt. Bennett M. Rich Memorandum for General Lerch, 26 February 1943; Col. R. C. Jacobs, Jr., Memorandum for the Provost Marshal General, 5 October 1942; Col. J. T. H. O'Rear, Director, Int. Div. Memorandum for Provost Marshal General, 16 February 1943, PMGO, NA, RG 389.

31. Reduction of clearances in Brig. Gen. Archer L. Lerch, Asst. to the Provost Marshal General, Memorandum for the Secretary of War, 23 February 1944; G. C. Marshall, "Elimination of Unnecessary Loyalty Investigations," 1944; Lerch to Director Control, ASF, 31 May 1944; and Wm. H. Kushnick, Director of Civilian Personnel and Training, Memorandum for the Deputy Chief of Staff, 10 October 1944, ISD Investigative Program, Loyalty Investigations, PMGO, NA, RG 389. Claims of the independence of MID under the president are in Capt. Robert R. Munoz, Memorandum for CS file, 11 May 1943, MID 383-4, SNRC.

32. The FBI had approved prewar investigations of Communists and "parlor pinks" by MID on 6 May 1940 and tolerated MID investigations of radical groups during the war. FBI plans for arrest of five thousand Communist leaders are mentioned in minutes of a 18 June 1940 meeting, MID 9794-186A, NA, RG 165. The FBI continued to investigate the Communist party during the war.

33. Roger Daniels, *Concentration Camps, U.S.A.: Japanese Americans and World War II* (New York: Holt, Rinehart and Winston, 1972), 34.

34. Ibid., 45.

35. Ibid., 60.

36. Ibid., 64.

37. Michael R. Belknap, "The Supreme Court Goes to War: The Meaning and Implications of the Nazi Saboteur Case," *Military Law Review* 89 (1980): 59–95.

38. Pentagon report on Van Deman files, 22 February 1971, in the files of the Senate Subcommittee on Constitutional Rights; *History of the Counter Intelligence Corps,* vol. 5, 7.

39. CIO complaints in James P. Mitchell, Director, Industrial Personnel Division Memorandum for the Under Secretary of War, 20 October 1943, ISD Investigative Program, Division History, PMGO, NA, RG 389.

40. *History of Counter Intelligence Corps,* vol. 5, 66–72.

41. Ibid., 549, 67–70.

42. Ian Sayer and Douglas Betting, *America's Secret Army: The Untold Story of the Counter Intelligence Corps* (New York: Franklin Watts, 1989), 42–47; *The Counter Intelligence Corps,* vol. 7, 18; and Theoharis and Cox, *The Boss,* 192–

93. The bugging was first made public in fall 1965. See "Ex-agent Says He Bugged Room of Mrs. Roosevelt," *New York Times,* 1 November 1965, 1;3, 27:1.

CHAPTER ELEVEN: War without End

1. Lyman B. Kirkpatrick, Jr., *The U.S. Intelligence Community: Foreign Policy and Domestic Activities* (New York: Hill & Wang, 1973), 24; and Richard M. Freeland, *The Truman Doctrine and the Origins of McCarthyism: Foreign Policy, Domestic Politics, and Internal Security, 1946–1948* (New York: Knopf, 1972), 140.

2. Ibid. For other activities, see Theoharis, *The Boss,* 215–324.

3. Ibid., 143, 208, 217. Hoover's role in the 1946–47 intelligence debate is in *Armies of Ignorance: The Rise of the American Intelligence Empire,* by William R. Corson (New York: Dial Press, 1977), 268–90.

4. Ibid., 210, 214.

5. Ibid., 221.

6. Joseph Keeley, *The China Lobby Man: The Story of Alfred Kohlberg* (New Rochelle, N.Y.: Arlington House, 1969), 196–205, discusses use. Charles A. Willoughby, *Shanghai Conspiracy* (New York: Dutton, 1951); and Corey Ford, *Donovan of O.S.S.* (Boston: Little, Brown, 1970), 303–4, 313; and F. W. Deakin and G. R. Storry, *The Case of Richard Sorge* (New York: Harper & Row, 1964), 338–39, discuss various leaks.

7. Johansen, "The Role of the Army," 10.

8. Athan Theoharis, *Seeds of Repression: Harry S. Truman and the Origins of McCarthyism* (Chicago: Quadrangle, 1971), 352–57; and Robert Griffith, *The Politics of Fear: Joseph R. McCarthy and the Senate* (Lexington: University of Kentucky Press, 1970), 139–43.

9. Freeland, *Truman Doctrine,* 352–57; and Griffith, *Politics of Fear,* 243–56.

10. Jensen, *Price of Vigilance,* 299–300. Tristram C. Coffin, *The Passion of the Hawks: Militarism in Modern America* (New York: Macmillan, 1964), also discusses volunteers on the right.

11. Radosh and Milton, *Rosenberg File,* 12, 450; and Norman Moss, *Klaus Fuchs: The Man Who Stole the Atom Bomb* (London: Grafton, 1989), 86–118. The British did not include specific charges of passing secrets in Los Alamos, ibid., 195.

12. Radosh and Milton, *Rosenberg File,* 54–55, 108.

13. Ibid., 65.

14. Johansen, "Role of the Army," 11.

15. Ibid., 12.

16. Ibid., 14.

17. Ibid., 16.

18. Paul J. Schieps, "The Role of the Army in the Oxford, Mississippi, Incident, 1962–1963," (Office of Chief of Military History, 1965, mimeographed); idem, "The Army and Civil Disturbances: Oxford and Detroit," in *Soldiers and Civilians,* Ryan and Nenninger, 179–94.

19. Stewart Alsop and Thomas Braden, *Sub Rosa: The OSS and American Espionage* (New York: Harcourt, Brace and World, 1964), 243.

20. Johansen, "Role of the Army," 20.

21. Christopher Pyle, *Military Surveillance of Civilian Politics, 1967–1970* (New York: Garland, 1986), 70.

22. U.S. Subcommittee on Constitutional Rights, Committee on the Judiciary, Senate, *Military Surveillance of Civilian Politics: A Report* (Washington, 1973), 34–39.

23. Ibid., 16–17.

24. Johansen, "Role of the Army," 25.

25. Ibid., vol. 2, 1686.

26. Pyle, *Military Surveillance,* 20.

27. Robert Justin Goldstein, *Political Repression in Modern America: 1870 to the Present* (Cambridge: Schenkman, 1978), 511–13, 520–21.

28. *New York Post,* 22 December 1970; "Intelligence/Counterintelligence," *The Daily Cardinal* (University of Wisconsin), 14 May 1970, 6–7; 15 May 1970, 6–7; 16 May 1970, 9; 18 May 1970, 4; 20 May 1970, 5; Pyle, *Military Surveillance,* 234–36; and U.S. Subcommittee on Constitutional Rights, Committee on the Judiciary, Senate, *Army Surveillance of Civilians: A Documentary Analysis* (Washington, 1972); U.S. Subcommittee on Constitutional Rights, Committee on the Judiciary, Senate, *Military Surveillance.*

29. James Bond was mentioned as one inspiration in *The Daily Cardinal* (University of Wisconsin), 14 May 1970; U.S. Subcommittee on Constitutional Rights, Committee on the Judiciary, Senate, *Hearings on Federal Data Banks,* vol. 1.

30. Memorandums were published by the Liberation News Service.

31. Pyle, *Military Surveillance,* 219–20.

32. Ibid., 241–56.

33. *New York Times,* 22 June 1971, 15.

34. U.S. Subcommittee on Constitutional Rights, Committee on the Judiciary, Senate, *Hearings on Federal Data Banks, Computers and the Bill of Rights,* 2 parts (Washington, 1971).

35. U.S. Subcommittee on Constitutional Rights, Committee on the Judiciary, Senate, *Military Surveillance of Civilian Politics,* 85.

36. Ibid., 86.

37. Ibid., 88.

38. Ibid., 17.

39. U.S. Subcommittee on Constitutional Rights, Committee on the Judiciary, Senate, *Hearings on Federal Data Banks,* vol. 1.

40. Christopher Pyle, "CONUS Intelligence: The Army Watches Civilian Politics," *Washington Monthly* 1 (1970): 4–16.

CHAPTER TWELVE: The Constitution, the Army,
and Internal Security

1. Christopher Pyle, "CONUS Revisited: The Army Covers Up," *Washington Monthly* 2 (1970): 49–58.

2. Ervin's autobiography is singularly uninformative on this period. Senator J. Ervin, Jr., *Preserving the Constitution* (Charlottesville, Va., Michie, 1984).

3. Baskir, "Reflections on the Senate Investigation," 640–41.

4. U.S. Subcommittee on Constitutional Rights, Committee on the Judiciary, Senate, *Hearings on Federal Data Banks,* vol. 1, 150.

5. Ibid., vol. 2, 156, 197–200, 218.

6. U.S. Subcommittee on Constitutional Rights, Committee on the Judiciary, Senate, *Military Surveillance of Civilian Politics,* 89.

7. Ibid., 90.

8. Theoharis, *Spying on Americans,* 13–39; *New York Times,* 7 June 1973, 36. The text of the Huston plan is in *The Intelligence Community: History, Organization, and Issues,* ed. Tyrus G. Fain (New York: Bowker, 1977), 817–66.

9. See U.S. Subcommittee on Constitutional Rights, Committee on the Judiciary, Senate, *Hearings on Military Surveillance,* testimony of army officials, and U.S. Subcommittee on Constitutional Rights, Committee on the Judiciary, Senate, *Hearings on Federal Data Banks,* vol. 2, 1728.

10. Ibid., vol. 1, 603.

11. Jack Anderson and George Clifford, *The Anderson Papers* (New York: Ballantine, 1974), 24–34.

12. Baskir, "Reflections on the Senate Investigation," 618–53.

13. Ibid., 641.

14. *Laird v. Tatum* 408 U.S. 1 (1972).

15. Ibid.

16. Ibid.

17. See, for example, "Recent Developments: *Laird v. Tatum* (U.S. 1972)," *Villanova Law Review* (February 1973): 479–91.

18. *Union et al. v. Westmoreland* 323 F. Supp. 73 (1971); *Tatum v. Laird* 444 F. 2d 947 (1971).

19. *United States v. Walton* 490 F. 2d 372 (1972).

20. *United States v. Jaramillo* 380 F. Supp. 1375 (1974); *United States v. Banks* 383 F. Supp. 368 (1974).

21. *United States v. Red Feather,* 392 F. Supp. 916 (1975); *United States v. Casper,* 541 F. 2d 1275 (1976); Meeks, "Illegal Law Enforcement," 83–136. In the 1970s, lower courts also limited police surveillance in a series of cases. See Paul G. Chevigny, "Politics and Law in the Control of Local Surveillance," *Cornell Law Review* 69 (1984): 735–84.

22. Meeks, "Illegal Law Enforcement," 83–136.

23. Corson, *Armies of Ignorance,* 443–49.

24. Ronald Schaffer, *Wings of Judgment: American Bombing in World War II* (New York: Oxford University Press, 1985), discusses this attitude in chapter 2. Arthur E. Sutherland, Jr., "Freedom and Internal Security," *Harvard Law Review* 64 (1951): 383–416.

25. Edward F. Sherman, "Legal Inadequacies and Doctrinal Restraints in Controlling the Military," *Indiana Law Journal* 49 (1974): 539–80; and "Honored in the Breech: Presidential Authority to Execute the Laws with Military Force," *Yale Law Journal* 83 (1973): 130–52.

26. Darrell L. Peck, "The Justices and the Generals: The Supreme Court and Judicial Review of Military Activities," *Military Law Review* 70 (fall 1975): 1–81; James P. O'Shaughnessy, "Posse Comitatus Act," 703–35; and Meeks, "Illegal Law Enforcement," 83–136.

27. 28 *U.S. Statutes at Large,* part 1, 7 (1893). For World War II reference, see Colonel J. V. Dillon, Deputy Provost Marshal General to Commanding General, Services of Supply, 12 June 1942, ISD Investigation Program, Instructions to Commercial Agencies, PMGO, NA, RG 389; and Radosh and Milton, *Rosenberg File,* 504–5, n. 56.

28. John Bruce Lockhart, "The Relationship between Secret Services and Government in a Modern State," RUSI, *Journal of the Royal United Services Institute for Defense Studies* (June 1974): 3.

29. Executive oversight has received much support from intelligence agencies as an alternative to congressional oversight. For recent discussions of executive policy, see *First Principles,* publications of the Center for National Security Studies.

30. For O'Brian's coordination, see Jensen, *Price of Vigilance,* 101–2. For World War II, see also Paul A. C. Koistinen, "Mobilizing the World War II Economy: Labor and the Industrial-Military Alliance," *PHR* 42 (1973): 443–78; Koistinen, "The 'Industrial-Military Complex' in Historical Perspective: World War I," *Business History Review* 41 (1967): 378–403.

31. On New Deal support of an enhanced public image of the FBI, see Kenneth O'Reilly, "A New Deal for the F.B.I.: The Roosevelt Administration, Crime Control, and National Security," *Journal of American History* 69 (1982): 438–68. On the public image of the FBI and MID, see Richard Gid Powers, "J. Edgar Hoover and the Detective Hero," *Journal of Popular Culture* 9 (fall 1975): 257–78. Among intellectuals this image was not necessarily successful. See St. Clair McKelway, "Reporter at Large: Some Fun With the F.B.I.," *The New Yorker* 17 (31 October 1941): 59–65, and the Cal Tech professor's preference for ONI or MID in Col. W. F. H. Godson to Sherman Miles, 31 July 1940, MID 10566-336/1, NA, RG 165. Hale has become the recent favorite of both the FBI and the CIA according to "Nathan Hale's Mission," *Studies in Intelligence,* 12-1 to 12-8, and "The Statue of Nathan Hale," *Studies in Intelligence,* 7-1 to 7-3. See also Van Deman to Col. Alfred T. Smith, 17 February 1933, MID 8930-A/252/6; Van Deman to Smith, 20 November 1931, MID 2774-320/1; Van Deman to Smith, 24 January 1933, MID 8930-A-252/7; and Van Deman to Col. Charles Burnett, 24 September 1935, MID 1766-Z-583/2, NA, RG 165.

32. Letters from Van Deman to his successor Brig. Gen. Marlborough Churchill, 9 June 1920, MID 6530-118/3, Van Deman to Col. Stanley H. Ford, 15 December 1928, MID 271-A-9/127; and Van Deman to Colonel Ford, 4 March 1929, MID 279-A-9/130, are particularly revealing, but the attitude pervades memorandums and inter-divisional correspondence. See also 9 July 1940 meeting, MID 9794-186A/12, and Miles, Memorandum on Internal Defense, stamped 31 July 1940, MID 9794-186A/12, NA, RG 165. Ideological statements are scattered throughout MID correspondence but particularly pronounced during the formulation of Emergency Plan White and Fifth Column Plans. See, for example, Emergency Plan White, 15 November 1935, AG 385B, Sixth Corps Area Emergency Plan—White, December 1938, AG 386, NA, RG 94.

33. Baskir, "Reflections on the Senate Investigations," 648.

34. The "national surge" is discussed in 2 August 1940 coordination minutes, MID 9794-186A, NA, RG 165. For World War I, see the early chapters of Jensen, *Price of Vigilance.*

35. See, for example, *The Evolution of American Military Intelligence* (prepared for use by the U.S. Army Intelligence Center and School, Fort Huachuca, Arizona, May 1973). The "memoranda" written by Ralph Van Deman were also circulated after 1950 as informal intelligence histories. Johansen's "Role of the Army in the Civilian Arena," is another inside history, although some published histories, such as Corson's *Armies of Ignorance,* have many characteristics of the in-house intelligence histories. Many historians have become intelligence agents; see Woodbridge Bingham, "Historical Training and Military Intelligence," *PHR* 15 (1946): 201–6.

36. Central Intelligence Agency, "Secrecy and Intelligence in a Free Society," *Studies in Intelligence* (n.p., n.d.), 21-1 to 21-8; Christopher Andrew, "Government and Secret Services: A Historical Perspective," *International Journal* 34 (spring 1979): 167–86. Sources for difficulties in obtaining documents include the author's personal experiences and discussions with National Archives personnel and with other historians. The leaks of the 1970s are discussed in Baskir, "Reflections on the Senate Investigation," 53.

Index

Abrams, Creighton V., 239
Adams, John, 14–15
African Americans. *See* Blacks
Aguinaldo, Emilio, 91–101 passim
Akerman, Amos, 29
Alejandrino, José, 97–98
Alger, Russell, 60, 65–66, 75
Alien Enemies Act (*1798*), 76
Allen, Henry T., 104
American Bar Association, 171
American Civil Liberties Union (ACLU), 184, 200, 205, 249–50, 253, 256
American Defenders, 205
American Defense Society, 167
American Expeditionary Forces (AEF), 160, 179, 197
American Federation of Labor (AFL), 152, 156, 198, 207, 217, 226
American Indian Movement, 258
American Legion: and MID, 193, 194, 196; surveillance activities of, 193, 196, 201, 203, 214, 215, 216, 226; and War Plans White, 194, 216; and G-2, 198, 199, 214; and FBI, 214, 215
American Patriotic League, 187
American Protective League (APL): formation of, 131–32; financing and functioning of, 147; and Justice Department, 147, 161, 164, 173, 180, 188, 191; and War Department, 147, 161, 165–66, 171, 173; and PPS, 148, 154, 158, 162; domestic surveillance by, 151, 161–62, 164–65, 171, 173, 175, 176, 180–81, 182, 190, 191, 192; and MID, 161, 162,

164, 171, 172, 174, 181–82, 187, 188, 190, 191, 192–93; and Van Deman, 161, 164–65; and Secret Service, 167; disbanded, 181, 182; superseded by other groups, 192–93
American Railway Union, 44
American Revolution, 7–12, 28
American Security Council, 235
Anaconda Copper Company, 176
Anarchists, 35, 138, 184; surveillance and repression of, 113–14, 140, 174, 178, 183, 196
André, John, 7, 8–9, 11, 22
Antigo, Wis., 155–56
Arizona, 76, 127, 138, 142–43, 174–75, 183
Arkansas, 186
Army of Cuban Pacification (ACP), 85
Army War College (AWC), 69, 120, 124, 162, 164; and War Plans White, 1, 192; and MID, 115–17, 127; shortcomings of intelligence work of, 121, 125, 131; and intelligence operations in Mexico, 126, 127; and World War I spy scare, 128, 129; and World War I internal security measures, 134, 135–36; conferences on intelligence held at, 188, 206
Arnold, Benedict, 7, 8, 9, 22
Articles of War, 8, 9, 13, 168, 169, 225
Askin, Frank, 249
Atherton, Gertrude, 133
Atkins, Edward, 56–57

311